THE OTHER SIDE OF THE FENCE

FENCE

LIFE ON BOTH SIDES OF THE COLOR LINE

CYNTHIA HUDGINS

Because Book
PUBLISHING

ISBN: 978-1-970121-19-3 (eBook)
ISBN: 978-1-970121-20-9 (Paperback)

Cover images courtesy of May Gibbon Brouhard
Cover Design by Michelle Williams

Printed in the United States of America.

First edition. January 27, 2023.

Because Books, Ltd.
PO Box 620514
Littleon, CO 80162
info@becausebooksltd.com

for my family

There is no greater agony than bearing an untold story inside you.

— MAYA ANGELOU

A NOTE FROM THE
AUTHOR'S DAUGHTER
CYNTHIA MAY GIBBON BROUHARD

I remember standing in the kitchen with my mom. She looked a little anxious when she said to me, "May, I have something I want to tell you."

I said, "What is it?"

Mom took a breath and said, "Your Great Grandparents were Black."

I smiled and said, "Neat!"

It was 1966, I was 14 years old. The Civil Rights movement was happening and Motown was playing on the radio. I really wasn't concerned. In fact, I relayed the information right away to my best friend Kelly.

Over the years Mom told me the stories of racism and bigotry she endured growing up in Coronado. I remember this story in particular.

One of the men who worked on the ferry that crossed over the bay from San Diego to Coronado island was always nasty to Mom because of her background. He had even told my Dad once that he and Mom could never have any children because they'd be black. One day after I was born, Mom was holding me on the ferry going home from an excursion to San Diego. I was all pink and white with a thatch of reddish blonde hair. This racist man said to Mom, "Where did you get that?"

Mom blurted out, "From the usual place!" She was flustered and embarrassed but she laughed about it years later.

I remember my grandpa Al very well. Mom used to have him over from Coronado to our house in San Diego every Sunday for dinner. He drove over in his big brown Cadillac and brought Binks, his dog. There were two dogs named Binks. The first Binks was a doberman mix then when that Binks passed, Grandpa got a smooth hair fox terrier he also named Binks.

Grandpa gave me the same two-finger thump on the head that he gave Mom while he chanted, "May-May, May-May." Then he'd reach in his pocket and pull out a rubber change holder with a slit up the middle, squeeze it open, and give me a quarter.

I remember the night after my grandpa passed away we had our visit from him.

The metal shelves that divided our living room and dining room started humming. At first we thought it was a vibration from an airplane going by. But the shelves kept vibrating. We started touching the shelves and the knick knacks that were on them but the vibrating sound continued.

For some reason I bent down to touch a set of nesting abalone shells my great grandpa Amos had collected. A jolt of electricity shot up my finger. I jumped back and exclaimed that I got a shock from the shells. Grandpa must have been using them as a focal point. My sister-in-law suggested that Mom talk to the vibration.

She asked, "Papa, is that you?"

The humming sound got louder. Then Mom apologized to Grandpa for being a little short tempered earlier that day and told him that she loved him. The humming grew louder. Then, it started to subside until it faded away completely.

We all sat quietly for a few minutes. Afterward, we all decided that it had to be Grandpa communicating from beyond. It was an amazing experience.

I never got to meet my grandma May as she passed away so young and before I was born. I missed being born on her birthday by nine minutes. In this book, Mom mentions paddling me on the behind and my retort of, "When I was the mommy and you were the little girl, I didn't do that to you!"

Later, when I went to visit Glasgow, Scotland and Cousin Jean took me to the house Grandma May grew up in, I got the strangest feeling of *déjà vu* ever.

I said, "I feel like I've been here before."

My mom put the fear of God in me about getting into cars with any men, even my friends' fathers, because of what happened to her when she was young.

My mom was a wonderful mother. I had no doubt that I was loved and wanted. We did crafts together, she sewed beautiful clothes for me and later for my Barbie Doll. She took me to lunch at Marsden's and taught me manners at a formal tea. She always dressed me up with lovely accessories for Sunday school, little white gloves, pretty hats, and lacy socks. She was intelligent, artsy, well read, and slightly Bohemian.

I loved her dearly.

I didn't know about her dark past or why it was that way until I was older. Reading her book after she finished it was enlightening... it made me mad for her, the things that happened to her at school, in Coronado, because of her ancestry and vicious gossip.

She was a wonderful lady and she loved to entertain in our home. She always served a fantastic New Year's Eve buffet for friends. That was Mom and Daddy's anniversary.

She is always in my heart and in the things I learned to do from her. Things I taught my own daughters, as well.

Cynthia May Gibbon Brouhard
Platteville, December 2022

A NOTE FROM THE AUTHOR'S GRANDDAUGHTER
CLAIRE L. FISHBACK

My grandmother was an amazing woman.

I wish I could say that definitively, but the truth is, I didn't know my grandma very well. My dad was in the military and we moved every three years. My grandma didn't travel. So, I rarely saw her.

Yet I can distinctly remember her voice and the way she called everyone dear to her 'honey.' I can hear it so clearly in my mind. Just the way she said it made you know she cared about you.

She used to send the *best* care packages to us. Wicker cases full of costume jewelry, little books she put together with beautiful Victorian cards cut up and pasted back together into little scenes. She would write in what the critters and people were saying, either to each other, or to us directly. I remember always wanting to play the organ sitting against the wall in her San Diego home. I don't remember if she ever played it for us, but I loved pressing the keys and pretending to play. So many switches and toggles on that thing! It was this fidget's personal playground (as long as she didn't catch me and shoo me away).

I loved all the cats at her house. Chrissy who scratched me the first time I met her (I'm an animal lover just like her, just like my

mom) when I approached her, gung-ho to give her all the love I
possibly could. Kermit was another kitty I remember dearly.

Typing these pages, "digitalizing them," as I said while working
on this project, I could *hear* her voice. I could almost *feel* her presence. I spoke to her, whispering, "Oh grandma, I'm so sorry these
things happened to you." I laughed out loud at her turns of phrase,
her earned histrionics, and exclaimed when she talked about Vera,
Nancy, and others. People I knew, though they were already old
ladies when I met them.

I met my grandma—who she really was—through typing these
pages. Like my mom says in her note, everything about her makes so
much sense after learning her history.

While typing, I got to walk alongside her like the ghost of
Christmas past while she experienced the traumas of her time, of
growing up looking white but raised by a Black woman. I got to
know her during the chapters of introspection, in which she pulls
out of the story and breaks the fourth wall in order to talk *about* the
story. I felt like she was telling me personally, a fellow author, about
her process. A process very similar to my own, I might add.

I'd been wanting to "digitalize" this book for probably more than
ten years when Kevin Ashley, Coronado Historian, reached out to my
uncle, who told him to talk to my mom, who put him in touch with
me, since I have the only copy of this *epic* manuscript. Even then, due
to the busyness of my own life, I put off starting this project for a few
months.

Like my grandma, I believe things are supposed to happen when
they happen. I'm a fatalist just as she was. I believe that there is a
reason for everything. That things come to you at the right time, at
the time you need them.

Right before I started typing this book, from the ragged and cat-
gnawed-on-pages held within a black three-ring binder, I'd come to
terms with my own inner demons and had started working through
them.

This book has helped me in more ways than I could ever share in this short space.

Though my struggles are far different than my grandma's, there are so many similarities in our personalities and how we respond to things. Typing this during that trying time made me feel less alone.

How I wish I could talk to her about our similar experiences and intricacies of personality that always remind me of the nature versus nurture phenomenon psychologists talk about. How we both can't sleep with the closet open, how we never dangle any limbs over the edge of the mattress. The way she daydreamed in the outfield matching how I did the same when I played team sports. Her love of tradition and being a traditionalist. Maybe I picked up some of this from my mom, or maybe, just maybe a small part of her spirit came to me after her passing. I'm sure it's a combination of both.

Claire L. Fishback
Morrison, December 2022

FOREWORD

BY KEVIN ASHLEY, LOCAL HISTORIAN

In 1903, African American Civil War veteran and former Buffalo Soldier Amos Hudgins, along with his wife Annie and son Algernon, moved from San Diego to the small island community of Coronado, California, located just a mile across the San Diego Bay. There they would join 23 other African Americans who had made their homes there, among a population of around one thousand residents.

That same year in 1903, the great sociologist, historian, and civil rights activist W.E.B. DuBois published his seminal work, *The Souls of Black Folk*. He began his book with a prophetic passage:

> *Herein lie buried many things which if read with patience may show the strange meaning of being black here at the dawning of the Twentieth Century. This meaning is not without interest to you, Gentle Reader; for the problem of the Twentieth Century is the problem of the Color Line.*

The patience Dubois requested of his readers to understand the lived experience of black Americans is also needed for readers of Cynthia Hudgins important and timely memoir, *The Other Side of the Fence*. The "fence" that she refers to in her title is in fact, Dubois's

"Color Line," and her memoir is a searing tale of her life on each side of that line and chronicles her lifelong struggle coming to terms with the trauma and guilt that she carried with her.

She began writing her book in 1981, at the age of sixty, and completed it in 1993. After struggling to find a publisher for the book, she found other ways to get her story out to the public. In April of 2000, she participated in a stunning oral history interview conducted by historian Barbara Palmer that was later published in August of 2001 in the San Diego Reader. It was my reading of that interview twenty years later in September of 2021 that inspired me to learn more about the Hudgins family. I took a chance and reached out to Cynthia's son Ted through a company email address. In a quick and kind reply he suggested I contact his sister May to know more about their mother. Once in contact with May, she soon told me of the existence of the unpublished memoir which lay in a box in a closet at the home of her daughter, author Claire Fishback. After some friendly and encouraging correspondence with Claire, she agreed to take on the heavy lifting of publishing the book. I am honored that Claire has asked me to write a historical note for the book.

Today Coronado is a prosperous and quaint resort town of around twenty thousand residents which enjoys the nickname "Mayberry by the Sea." It is also a patriotic military town that is known as "The Birthplace of Naval Aviation." The community has an active and engaged historical association and museum, and the elegant and historic 135-year-old Hotel del Coronado is the crown jewel and centerpiece of the city's historic identity. Near the Hotel Del you will find a monument to Tent City, the famous campground that existed alongside the hotel for nearly forty years from 1900-1938. The Tent City monument is covered in ceramic tiles embossed with nostalgic black and white photographs from the glory days of Tent City, while the walls of the massive Hotel Del Coronado are decorated with classic photos of glamourous VIP visitors and tourists sunning themselves by the pool. At the museum you might find old photos of locals going about everyday life in Coronado, feeding the worthy image of Mayberry. There is not a single photo in any of these public displays containing a single African American, which in my experience has perpetuated a false image of Coronado's early history as a purely white enclave.

To their great credit, the Coronado Historical Association has recently made great efforts to provide other narratives that highlight the important contributions of minority communities in Coronado's past, including a just concluded exhibition documenting the history of the Japanese American community here. The exhibition included painful stories and images of the forced removal of Japanese residents to internment camps during World War II while also celebrating positive contributions made by the Japanese community here.

For the past few years I have been researching the nearly forgotten history of African Americans in Coronado and have confirmed that African Americans were among the first residents of the city in 1887. There are seven families that I consider the pioneer African American families of Coronado, comprised of families who moved here between 1887 and 1920. This group includes the Marshall (1887), Thompson (1887), Banks (1887), Hunter (1890), Hudgins (1903), Ellis (1910) and Ludlow (1920) families. These pioneering families owned homes in Coronado, while some ran successful businesses in town. Several of these pioneers started out working for the Hotel del Coronado while others worked in private homes as gardeners, drivers, or cooks. They were all law-abiding, hard-working patriotic Americans; they sent their children to the local Coronado schools and later, when called upon, sent their children off to war in World War I and World War II.

Importantly, among the elders of these pioneering families was a shared history, where nearly all were at one time enslaved. Two of these pioneers, Edmund Marshall and Amos Hudgins, escaped slavery to join the Union Army and fight in the Civil War. After the war, African Americans would watch with disillusion as America's noble efforts at Reconstruction collapsed, only to be replaced with the racist system of Jim Crow. These brave Americans would all eventually leave the homes they knew in the Jim Crow South and increasingly racist Midwest for a chance at a new life in California.

While Cynthia's memoir is ultimately about her remarkable life, it is also an homage to her grandparents, Amos, and Annie Hudgins, who were her primary caregivers for the first thirteen years of her life in Coronado. Annie told Cynthia very little of her early life in Kentucky, only that she was born into slavery as the daughter of an Englishman and an enslaved woman. Annie told Cynthia even less about Amos's early life, only that she believed he was the son of a Cherokee mother. From photos and her vague memories of her Grandfather, Cynthia was sure that Amos had African ancestry as well.

Census records, military records and photos do confirm Amos Hudgins was a light skinned and 'hazel eyed' African American man and in those days was categorized as "mulatto." While mulatto was a general term used in that period for someone with mixed African and European ancestry, more racially specific terms were also used then, such as "quadroon" and "octoroon," meaning a person of one-fourth or one-eighth African ancestry. Amos, and Annie were both very likely to have had one-fourth African Ancestry. His Civil War military records confirm that he was enslaved at the time of his enlistment and was born in Livingston County, Missouri. He was illiterate prior to his marriage to Annie (she would later help teach him to read), which would explain why his first name in his military records was invariably listed as Amas, Ansas or Amos and his last name ranged from Hutchinson, Hutcherson, Huggins, Higgins, and Hudgins.

His mother Mahala Hudgins was born enslaved in Kentucky in 1821 and was described as "mulatto" in census records from 1870-1900. The two photos available of Mahala in her old age show that she did have some Native American features. There is no clarity on the identity of Amos's father, though Mahala would marry local African American blacksmith Jacob Brigman at the close of the Civil War, and Amos's younger siblings would take on the name Brigman. Evidence suggests that the man who owned Mahala was William Hudgins, a prominent businessman from Virginia and an early settler of Kentucky in the years of 1817-1835. Hudgins would later move his family, along with his slaves to Missouri in 1836. Amos was born in the town of Mooresville, Missouri in 1845 and would later move to the city of Richmond in the 1850s with his mother Mahala, his siblings, and other enslaved persons. According the 1860 census, William Hudgins owned and enslaved eleven African Americans in Richmond, Missouri in 1860.

Amos Hudgins, at age 18, would escape enslavement in late August of 1863. He did so amidst the chaotic aftermath of Confederate guerrilla leader William Quantrill's raid and massacre at Lawrence, Kansas just days earlier. As retribution, Union troops had set fire to farms and houses in the Missouri counties that bordered Kansas, denying Quantrill and his raiders a base to conduct future raids. During this complete disorder, the incredibly brave Amos would set out westward alone toward Kansas and his freedom. He would cross the Missouri River to Elwood, Kansas and enlist with the 2nd Kansas Colored Infantry Regiment of the Union Army.

The well-trained soldiers of the 2nd Kansas Colored Infantry would set out for Arkansas in March 1864 as part the Union Army's Camden Expedition, during which Amos's regiment would be forever remembered for their bravery at the Battle of Jenkins Ferry. In this battle the 2nd Kansas would avenge the brutal massacre and mutilation of 117 of their fellow soldiers of the 1st Kansas Colored regiment at Poison Springs, which had occurred just days earlier. Amos's regiment took heavy losses in that rain-soaked battle; however, they were credited with rushing to take up firing positions on the front line, and later with charging and capturing a key enemy artillery position, an action that turned the tide of the battle. That action likely saved the lives of hundreds of fellow troops who were trapped as they struggled to retreat across a swollen river on a hastily assembled pontoon bridge. Historians believe this was the first successful charge and capture of an enemy artillery position by Colored troops in the Civil War.

After the Civil War, Amos would be among the first group of African Americans to join the 10th Cavalry Regiment at Fort Leavenworth, a regiment later to be famously known as the "Buffalo Soldiers." He spent five years with the Buffalo Soldiers, participating in what was known as the "Indian Wars" and playing a large but forgotten role in opening of the West for American expansion. After completing his service in 1872, he would marry Annie Renfro in 1874 in Richmond, Missouri, a wedding attended by his mother Mahala, stepfather Jacob Brigman as well as sisters Victoria, Amanda, and Ollie.

Amos and Annie established their home in rapidly growing Topeka, Kansas, where Annie worked in a millinery store and Amos established himself as a popular barber. In 1876 Amos would be enticed to utilize his unique skills gained from his years as a Buffalo Soldier by taking on a role as a private "Buffalo" guide for Major Marcus Reno of the 7th Cavalry, who served directly under George Armstrong Custer. Amos was reportedly with Major Reno and his troops when they narrowly escaped the massacre of Custer and his men at Little Big Horn. Not surprisingly, Amos quickly settled back into town life in Topeka with Annie, where he would eventually own and run a barber shop while Annie also owned and operated a hairdressing salon next door. They remained in Topeka until 1887, when they made the decision to move West to settle near San Diego.

They would remain in San Diego for nearly 15 years, with Amos working much of that time as a barber. Algernon was born in 1891 and the family would build a home in San Diego in the emerging Logan Heights neighborhood. Amos's thirst for adventure returned in 1896, when he would leave San Diego and join nearly 100,000 prospectors in Canada in a quest for gold in the Yukon, an event known as the Klondike Gold Rush. Amos returned to San Diego with a few gold nuggets and continued his work as a barber while also doing occasional work with a team of horses he owned. It was not until 1903 that Amos and Annie would make the final move of their lives, to nearby Coronado.

When Amos and Annie Hudgins arrived in Coronado in 1903, they had been respected and valued members of their communities in both Topeka and San Diego. They were well versed on the "ways of polite society" as both former business owners and civic volunteers. Amos spent many years as a barber to the rich and powerful of San Diego and it was well known that he was a veteran of the Civil War as a local member of the Civil War veterans' group, Heintzelman Post #33. Cynthia was very active in her local Church and was also a respected community leader in San Diego, once acting as a co-host during the visit of a delegation of African Americans from Los Angeles. Once in Coronado, Annie occasionally cooked for the family of city founder Elisha Babcock as well as Reverend Spalding of the Episcopal Church. Despite the high character of Amos and Annie, it was their color that mattered. The Hudgins family faced extreme prejudice in Coronado over multiple generations for more than forty years.

A painful fact that was concealed from Cynthia for most of her life was that she had African American cousins in nearby Los Angeles. Amos's sister Amanda's daughter, Lora Jacobs, had moved from Missouri to Los Angeles in 1905 and married prominent African American businessman and civic leader C.C. Flint. Their daughter, Olivia Flint, remembered playing with Algie Hudgins when she was a child, and kept a photo of Algie on her dresser in Los Angeles for her entire life. She always reminded her grandson who lived in San Diego, Agin Shaheed, that he had relatives in San Diego named Hudgins. In 1999, when Agin was the Director of Race and Human Rights for San Diego Unified School District, he would attend an event honoring Amos Hudgins and other Civil War veterans at Mount Hope Cemetery in San Diego. It was there that he would meet Cynthia for the first time. Local newspaper accounts of that chance meeting would quote Cynthia as saying, "Well, I guess I am out of the closet now!" The two would remain close until Cynthia passed in 2015.

Cynthia Hudgins lived one life in two worlds. She spent years reckoning with her experiences and eventually found peace within herself. Her memoir of her lived experience is an important and timely contribution to the recorded history of the African American experience in California. As you begin, please heed the advice of W.E.B. DuBois and be patient, gentle reader, as "herein lie buried many things..."

Kevin Ashley
Coronado, December 2022

PREFACE

In the beginning was the phone call that started me on the path to self-understanding. At the end was the phone call that stopped me from taking my life, which was the first step toward a new beginning.

The time frames in this book may not be exact. I have lived my three score and ten plus. Memories dim as age takes over. Some of the names have been altered in instances where I believe the person may still be alive. This is my life story, and all the accounts are as true as I experienced and remember them.

I use the terms dark, colored, and Negro because they were in common usage when I was younger, as was the word nigger, which I despise as much as I do African American. How can people born in this country, (albeit their ancestors may have come from Africa... how many years ago?) consider themselves Africans? I believe we should be Americans first, above all else. There has been enough name-calling, making differentiations, without doing it to each other. Even Africans today do not accept Blacks as African, but call them American Negroes, which indeed is what they are.

After I grew up, there was a period of quietude for me that I enjoyed, except for occasional bouts with fear when someone did or said something that stirred up the old feelings and memories. Then, with much of my life behind me, on a cold and sunny January day it came... the phone call that changed me over a period of time to understanding and acceptance of how my own reactions had caused me so much trauma in my lifetime.

With the Equal Rights demonstrations and changes of the sixties, I began thinking perhaps I could write a book. After a phone call in my own sixties, I felt compelled to, but the words did not come easily. The pain, the tears, the memories, the frustration, and the anger as I remembered it all, and the way it came out in such a completely disorganized manner, was very hard to handle. Thoughts of suicide became very strong. I had to face the fact that I was prejudiced against people of color. I didn't want to be, but I was... and in the eyes of the white world, I am colored.

The infamous single drop of Black blood that makes one a nigger to some is in me somewhere, invisible to the naked eye, but there, nevertheless. Because of it, as a child, I was ostracized, called names, and physically abused by my peers... a pariah. I didn't know what I was, but I knew I didn't want to be a nigger and I didn't believe it either. Then, when I was eleven, I was told in so many words that no matter what I believed or didn't want to believe, it was true.

What a skeleton to have hiding in one's closet, to be exposed at an inopportune time, disrupting one's feelings of complacency. I should know.

PROLOGUE

I've been told I have a story to tell and have often felt that I should tell it.

When my old demon came back after forty years to haunt me, I was so upset and depressed that I came close to suicide... so close, it frightened me. Something happened that stopped me just in the nick of time. Maybe I'll tell about it later and maybe I won't, as it had meaning only to me and the person who called to deliver a message which had come from one who had passed on.

How cruel people can be to one another. Sometimes deliberately, sometimes in innocence, sometimes with thoughtless lack of consideration for the feelings of others. We all have crosses to bear. In these times, they are called challenges. No matter, it is still painful when a remark or some happening awakens the demon in its hiding place, the dark recess of the mind where we hide things so we can go on.

A lot of water has passed under the bridge in my life, but I am still not completely free of the unhappy memories and feelings of my childhood and early youth. They insert themselves into my consciousness on nights when I lie tossing and turning, unable to sleep.

My story will be written about someone writing an autobiography, not me, but someone I have known very well, an alter ego perhaps. I started this about ten years ago and put it aside after I had nearly torn myself apart doing it. Now, I think I can continue. Times have changed and are still changing, but I sometimes wonder if it's for the better. People still hate other people for things over which they have no control... their nationality, religion, the color of their skin, their sexual persuasion, whatever makes them different.

I'm an old lady now. Most of the people in this book are gone. My children are midway through their lives; my grandchildren and my great-grandchildren will live in a different world – I sincerely hope. Only time will tell.

Was I supposed to write this book? I don't know. My father told me many times as I was growing up, "When you write your book, Thum, begin the first paragraph with 'I was born of poor but drunken parents.'" It was a joke, of course.

We *were* poor. I grew up during the Great Depression. Papa made very good home brew during prohibition and there had been many happy parties at our house when a batch was ready. Later, a drink or two before dinner was the norm, but drunken in the alcoholic sense of it just wasn't true.

BOOK ONE

CHAPTER ONE

Cynthia hung up the phone. She was shaking and breathing with difficulty. Her throat was tight; her head swam. Her greatest fear had just come to pass. After over forty years, it had caught her with her guard down. She felt found out, helpless, exposed, angry, and terribly frightened. She took a deep breath and told herself, "They didn't say my name. They don't know it's me. They got this number from Papa's name in the phone book."

Her father had lived with them for two and a half years following a stroke that had left him partially paralyzed. After his death, Cynthia had kept his name in the phone book. She hoped that friends with whom they had lost contact over the years would look for the family name and find her, or old friends of her parents would call looking for them.

The young woman who called said that the San Diego Historical Society was doing an exhibit on the contribution of Black pioneers to the history of the area for the first Black History Month. She asked if Cynthia would lend them photographs or other family mementos for display. Cynthia heard her out, then with difficulty through the tightness in her throat, and the pounding of her heart, she said, "I don't know why you called me. I don't have anything. I'm not Black." She hung up the phone and sat down; she felt faint.

Cynthia wasn't Black. She hated the word Black and wondered why anyone brown, light or dark, would want to be called that. She had an olive complexion, hazel eyes, dark brown slightly wavy hair now going gray. There was nothing in her features to indicate she was of mixed parentage although she had once thought there was.

Coronado, California, the town she lived in, was very small. Born there, she had attended school from kindergarten through high school. Everyone knew everyone else. Many people made it their business to know everyone else's business as well. She heard stories when adults met. That one was a person to be respected, admired, a good worker, or very wealthy. This one was a drunk or ne'er-do-well, or beat his wife; that one was most likely illegitimate; another's wife was playing around with his best friend when he was out of town. There were no secrets that someone didn't know or whisper about. From partial conversations that were hushed if she walked into the room or heard when adults were not aware that she was nearby, she learned that some people were not worthy for reasons usually of their own making... a lack of moral responsibility, a love of drink, shiftlessness, or other weaknesses of character. Everyone's life in the small town was an open book to those who wished to make it so. They told all they knew, and things they didn't know but only imagined, to anyone who would listen. Gossip, it seemed to Cynthia when she was older, had been the flesh and blood of conversation. She had known as she was growing up that she was one of these subjects, but she hadn't known why.

She finally got herself under control and told her husband, Ted, about the call. He agreed with her that she wouldn't hear from them again and that would be the end of it. They were both wrong...

A few days later, the letter came. When Cynthia saw the return address her heart started to pound again, and she could hear the blood rushing in her ears. She walked around the house, thoughts flying willy-nilly as she fought to control them before she finally opened it. The words struck her like a blow in the face. They knew her married name and somehow had gotten the connection.

"What old gossiping busybody has felt compelled to tell what they know about me?" she wondered.

The request was the same. Would she lend them photographs or souvenirs for the exhibit? She began hyperventilating; her head started to throb. She had to do something, but what? She paced the house thinking, forcing herself to be calm. Finally, she decided the best approach was to be direct, to call the Society. She wanted to know who the tongue-wagger was who was still making her ancestry their business after all these years.

Cynthia had a thought with the death of her father that it was all over and behind her. Most of her parents' friends were dead. Some of the young people she had gone to school with had left the area; some had died or been killed in WWII. Few knew her married name. She had friends who didn't know. If she detected racial prejudice in their attitudes and remarks, she kept quiet about herself, but she told others sooner or later. She had made no real effort to pass as white, but she felt guilty about not being entirely open and honest with everyone.

She had not felt this trapped and helpless in years. "Who told them? What did they want? Why?" she asked herself. Was she never to be free of that specter that was always popping up when least expected throughout her life, catching her off guard and upsetting her?

She had intended to stay cool and calm, but when a young man answered the phone, she lost control. She became hysterical and started to cry. Words poured out in an uncontrollable flood. She told him they had no right to harass her in this way. She had spent years of her life trying to live down the shame of what she was. She didn't appreciate the actions of the person who had felt it necessary to hand out information about her ancestry that was none of their business. She asked him if he had any idea of what it was like to face discrimination and racial prejudice. She spoke of her children and the fear she had always carried with her of what their heritage might do to them or their lives.

The young man could do nothing but listen. When Cynthia ran down and he was able to speak, he said he knew how she felt, but there had been nothing to be ashamed of. Cynthia grew calmer. She said that she knew that, but she had been made to feel ashamed so what was the difference? When he said that he understood, he sounded as though he really did. So with embarrassed hesitancy, she asked him, "Are you... are you... Black?" It pained her to use that word. He answered that he was, but all his life he had suffered from reverse discrimination because he had been too white for Blacks to accept him. She knew of this, and she also knew that Blacks ostracized other Blacks who were fair enough to cross the Color Line and pass themselves off as whites. She was contrite. She apologized to him, becoming less angry.

The young man was the caretaker of a Victorian mansion that belonged to the Historical Society. He and a young woman, who was also employed there, were both of Negro origin. Because the coming February was the first Black History Month, they were organizing and exhibit of contributions to the city's history by Black pioneers, in spite of opposition from some of the members.

"There is no denying that Blacks have made contributions," he said. "And we feel that these contributions have been kept from public knowledge and acceptance long enough." He explained that no one person had told them about her family background. Her grandfather's name had come up in interviews they had been doing with long-time residents of the county. Someone had remembered that he had worked in, or owned, the first barber shop in the downtown area and had given them his name. They had gotten hers from her father's obituary.

She asked to be excused from any participation in the exhibit. He told her that although she might not be aware of it, there had been a good deal of interest in Black history in recent years that she might get other phone calls. A white student at the state college was doing his thesis on the contributions of Blacks to the settlement of the area; it was likely she might be hearing from him. As the inevitability of it sank in, Cynthia said, "Oh, my God! My poor mother! She thought it was over when my grandmother died. I never told her how it was for me."

As they spoke, Cynthia noted that the Society seemed to know as much about her grandparents as she did. There was so much she didn't know; perhaps they knew more.

The subject had never been discussed at home. She had not been asked any questions, nor had she asked any or told anyone of the petty, shaming things that had been said and done to her while she was growing up. Her father, Al, also known as Algie when he was young, had told her about the barbershop. He always called it "Pop's Shop," but in these days barbers often bought a chair in a shop owned by someone else. The shop's name had been different from her grandfather's, so she never knew for certain whose it had been. Maybe he had bought it and left the name the same. It was a possibility...

The shop had been a social center for the men who were the founding fathers of the city. They came in for haircuts, shaves, or shoeshines and stayed to talk. These were influential men, business-men, the owners of downtown property who had an interest in what was going to happen to their investments. Therefore, much of the planning for the city which was to be was made in her grandfather's shop. Her father had listened to their talk as a boy. He knew doctors, lawyers, judges, bankers, and businessmen. When the town was small, their families had been neighbors and the boys had grown up together. Fathers or their sons would stop and talk to him on the street. At the dinner table, he often mentioned the well-known names of those with whom he had spoken that day. As the city had grown, the families moved away into other areas, but the men still retained the friendships of their youth.

As Cynthia thought about it, she decided that, with her mother and father gone, there would be no one to hurt by exposure except herself, her husband Ted, and her children. Most of their friends already knew; those who didn't were not apt to go into the part of the city where the mansion was for a Black exhibit.

"I can handle it," she decided.

She collected what family photographs she had and some other things, just to see what she did have. There was not much. Her mother, May, had thrown away most of the family mementos when her husband's mother, Annie, had died. There once was a family album with a purple velvet cover, gilded edges, and a clasp. Cynthia had loved to look at it when she was a child. Her grandmother had told her who the stiffly posed Black people in Victorian dress were, but since she'd never met any of them, she didn't remember. Her mother had thrown the album away with everything else... her father's books and record collection, anything and everything that had belonged to the old lady except for some pieces of handiwork, a few family photos, a handful of letters, and a postcard scrapbook. She had probably thought that by doing this she was exorcising the family ghost, but she had not.

Cynthia asked her father years later, after her mother had died, why he had let her do it, as some of the furniture would be considered antique now, perhaps valuable. Al told her that May had done it while he was at work, and he didn't know until after it all was gone.

She decided that she would go down to the mansion to see what they knew that she didn't. She'd agree to lend them some things if they would promise not to use her married name. She called and made an appointment for the next day because she wanted to get it over with as soon as possible. It was agreed over the phone that no one but she would be involved, and they would use only her maiden name.

Cynthia told her Goddaughter, Nancy, about the letter and the phone calls. Nancy was interested; she had never been to the Society's mansion. She was aware of how upset her 'Aunt Cynthia' was and asked if she might go along for moral support and because she wanted to see the place. Cynthia gladly said, "Yes." She was certain Ted wouldn't want to take her; he'd never wanted her to talk about her ancestry with him. He'd become upset with her when she felt she had to bring something out of her past into the open or try to explain why she sometimes acted the way she did. He couldn't seem to understand this need in her or why she was so often quickly angered. He was a complete person with no need to rely on others for anything. He didn't feel that he needed any explanation or understanding on anyone else's part. He had been very angry and had spoken hotly of "invasion of privacy" when she showed him the letter and told him about the call to the Society. She found herself calming and reasoning with him, saying, "This is a matter of public record, Ted, *not* an invasion of privacy." He replied that he just didn't want her to be hurt, to her surprise.

Her hurts were all behind her, done in her early years long before she had ever even known Ted existed. She never quite understood his attitude, interpreting it to be embarrassment on his part, or not caring that she had a need to talk about their past. She had wanted help with the decision of whether or not she should tell the children about her ancestry, but he didn't answer. He had hurt her himself many times in the years of their marriage by acting as though no problem existed and by his attitude toward Blacks. It had not gone unnoticed by Cynthia that Ted often spoke of them as "stupid Blacks." Each time she heard this when they were younger, she would think, "Present company excepted, of course." But as they grew older and he sometimes became more vehement, especially in the sixties, she told herself that he honestly did not care about her ancestry and would make racist remarks without thought. She began to think that saying it without thought was inconsiderate and insensitive. Didn't he realize it hurt her? But as was her way, she kept it to herself, saying nothing. She was glad he didn't want to go along; she would have been more nervous than she already was.

· · ·

THE OLD VICTORIAN HOUSE, called the Villa Montezuma, was a horrid color. Reddish brown and maroon with yellow trim, it had been painted and kept up, a fine example of the period, with its stained glass, cupolas, gables, and gingerbread trim. Nancy found a place to park; they got out and went up the steps to the front door. When Cynthia rang the bell, the young man who opened the door looked more Negro than she'd expected. She was prepared to see someone who looked much like herself and her father from his description of his own appearance and his remarks about reverse discrimination. Cynthia was olive; he was lighter. His eyes were green, his hair curly with a reddish cast, but there was no mistaking him for Caucasian. He apparently was not so sure of her. He looked at Cynthia, then at Nancy, who was fair and blond, and back again. He noted that Cynthia was carrying a large envelope so asked carefully, looking at her, "Are you...?" Cynthia replied, "I am."

He held the door open and led them into the dining area of the house. Asking them to be seated, he left the room. Cynthia and Nancy sat looking around, admiring the stained-glass windows, the architectural features, and the Victorian furnishings. When he came back, he held an index card which he laid on the table in front of Cynthia and asked, "Does this name mean anything to you?" She saw the name Amos Hudgins on the card, looked up at him and said, "Yes, this is my grandfather."

Home again, Cynthia laughed a little ruefully to herself. Before she had learned the secret about herself from Nancy's mother, years before, she had thought that there was something wrong with her. Afterward, that somewhere in her appearance there was a clue to her background that everyone would see plainly but she couldn't. Everyone she came in contact with when growing up in Coronado had already known or soon found out, and they made it their business to tell everyone else who and what she was as well. After she learned the secret herself, she realized white people had not been able to tell until someone else told them, before they turned away from her. But she still thought that anyone who was colored or part colored could tell at a glance.

The young man had obviously not expected her to look the way she did. He was prepared to see someone like himself. He had been unsure of her identity and not committed himself until she had recognized the name on the card. It was a revelation to her that he hadn't known immediately.

He sat down at the table with them, and she began to show him what she had brought and to tell him what she knew of the family history, where her grandparents had lived, and what they had done to earn their living. The young woman who had called came in and was introduced. She was young and very pretty. Her hair was covered with a kerchief, as it was in subsequent meetings, so Cynthia couldn't tell what color it was or if it was curly or straight. She was fairer than he was with huge green eyes, but her features, like his, told of her origins. She sensed how nervous and apprehensive Cynthia was; she was very kind and understanding. It helped Cynthia a great deal to find that these young people didn't seem to hate or resent her. Gradually she relaxed, got herself under control, and was able to talk more calmly and get her thoughts into order. It was disappointing to her that they were unable to tell her more than she already knew about her grandparents.

They kept most of her things: a portrait of her grandfather, Amos; a snapshot of him in his Civil War Uniform; her grandparent's wedding picture; and several photos of her father as a small boy with Annie, his mother, and one or two of him as a young man. Al, with his dark hair and olive skin, could have been any dark-skinned nationality. As he grew older, the American Indian ancestry of his grandmother on his father's side had taken precedence in his features. The two didn't keep any photographs like these. Al apparently didn't look Black enough for their exhibit.

The young woman asked for handiwork and Cynthia agreed to lend some things to them. Annie had been a seamstress; there was a quilt-top, Cynthia's handmade christening dress, some crocheted things... not much.

The two in charge of the exhibit seemed to think that more Blacks had lived in Coronado than actually had. Cynthia knew of only three other colored families circa 1921 who had owned houses there. She later learned that there had been two or three others, at the most, but she had seen no children of color except the few Mexican and Japanese until a boy appeared in her first year of high school. The two families Cynthia knew who had been friends of Amos and Annie's were no darker than they were.

When Cynthia was older, she saw many Negro women waiting on the streetcar benches in the afternoon going home from working for white families. They were nurse maids, did housekeeping and cooking. A few lived in, with rooms provided for them by their employers, a maid's room or a room over the garage. Many coloreds, as they were called then, were employed by the hotel. There were two white clapboard buildings that were used as dormitories for the help, one for the men and one for the women. Many Filipinos were also employed by the hotel. Cynthia knew that many of the whites and some of the Filipinos stayed in the dormitories, but she did not remember seeing any Negroes going in or out of the buildings. She tried to make it clear that she didn't think the town had been populated with many colored families, that most of the ones who were working there had lived in the city and commuted daily. The young man in particular did not want to believe her, seeming to think that there had been more.

"Well," Cynthia thought, "I'm certain I'm right, but I was only a kid after all. Let him think what he wants to if it makes him happy." She didn't argue the point.

To her surprise, her family's exhibit was the largest in the room of the participating families' mementos. She felt proud as she looked around watching people leaning forward to look at the photos. Twice she went up to ask if anyone was familiar with the name Hudgins, but they shook their heads. Afterward, Nancy told her that watching, she had felt the old colored people hadn't suspected that Cynthia was asking about members of her own family but was only curious. They didn't stay long when Cynthia realized that no one there knew or remembered the Hudgins family, and she didn't want to hang around all day. She would have liked to meet someone who had remembered them as she'd always been proud of her grandparents but had never felt able to express it freely.

CHAPTER TWO

Coronado, where Cynthia was born, was connected to the mainland by a strand of sand with a two-lane concrete highway which, because it gleamed like silver in the moonlight, was called the Silver Strand. It enclosed a bay that the U.S. Navy kept filled with ships as far as the eye could see. The island, as it was called, was exclusive. The fine old Hotel Del Coronado was there and drew many wealthy people from the East in winter to stay, either in it or in the famous Tent city which was run by the hotel down on the beach. Others rented houses for the season and many Navy officers rented houses in Coronado during their tours of duty in the area, which included North Island Naval Air Station and the 11th Naval District of San Diego.

Cynthia's family had come to the county in 1887 because the area was open for homesteading by Negroes. Her grandfather, Amos, filed for a homestead in El Cajon Valley, but an injury to his leg, received in the Civil War, made it difficult for him to till the land. So they moved to San Diego where Cynthia's father, Al, was born. Amos did hauling for a time with a team of horses to earn a living, later going back to barbering which he had learned in the Army. These things had been the reason for the Historical Society's interest in her family. Cynthia learned, after the exhibit, that her grandfather had also been one of the three founders of Prince Hall Lodge No. 10 in San Diego in 1903, a Negro Masonic Fraternity.

AL, her father, had been a pioneer in early radio. He'd had a little radio shack in the back of the family home in Coronado. It was assumed by some of the old timers in radio with whom she had spoken after the exhibit that it was quite possibly the first one on the island. It was a matter of record that it had been one of the first sending and receiving stations in Southern California, but the Society had not been interested in her father. They were interested only in Amos and Annie, Al's parents.

When Cynthia decided to participate in the Society's exhibit, she knew that her mother would have been upset beyond belief, but her mother had been dead for thirty-four years. Whites who would attend an exhibit on Black contributions to the history of the community would be few. The mansion was in an old part of the city; the same area where Al was born. It had been a nice neighborhood then but had become a slum with an increasing crime rate. There were gang wars, arson fires, shootings, and knifings every week; people didn't go there unnecessarily. If someone who didn't know about her found out and was upset about it, she would not be any worse for their loss. It had happened before, more times than she could count, and she had survived. She had been very hurt when she was young when people she had thought were friends had turned their backs on her when someone told them about her. But she was older now. She was sure she could handle it, and it might not happen anyway.

"No sense in borrowing trouble," she thought. "Let the chips fall where they may. I'll pick up the pieces later." It was not going to be that easy, but she didn't know it then.

CHAPTER THREE

Cynthia felt a lift in her spirits after the exhibit. She had two or three phone calls from people who had seen the article about it in the paper and recognized her father's name. They were old friends curious about her reaction. One was from her preschool years, a sometime playmate who, in the course of conversation said there had been no prejudice in Coronado. Cynthia was surprised. Wryly smiling to herself, she replied, "Well, that depends which side of the fence you were on." There had been a silence on the other end of the line before the conversation continued. It had been confusing to her when this person, whom she had considered a friend of sorts, had turned against her after they'd started school, joining with others in the harassment she'd had to endure. They hadn't played together much after the first grade because of it. "I guess we see only what we want to see," she decided after they'd hung up, and thought, "She must not have noticed that her mother never let me come into their house when the other children went inside, but always sent me home."

She'd written to her children when the Society first called. Her son, Ted Jr., whom they called Tee Gee, had been concerned, but less so when he was told the family name would not be used. He had not taken it well when she had told him about his familial ancestry back in the fifties. Her daughter, May-May, eleven years younger, had been concerned only for her mom. She'd been told in the sixties, when change was in the air, and had immediately told her best friend, much to Cynthia's dismay.

The family secret had been made public! Cynthia had not been hurt by it and neither had her family. There was no need to feel shame any longer and she felt relieved. She showed a few close friends who hadn't seen them, the clipping from the paper, the souvenir book of the exhibit, and the photographs of her grandparents that she had never shown to anyone but her children's spouses, her friend Vera, and Vera's daughter, Nancy.

Her sense of well-being did not last long. The exhibit was over and probably forgotten by everyone except herself, but it had stirred up old memories and feelings. She found herself lying awake at night reviewing her life, trying to reconcile what she had been, what she had become, and how past events had affected her along the way. Things that had happened when she was young began to pop into her mind at random. She tried to rationalize how and why they had come about, why she'd reacted as she had at the time and been hurt by them. She hadn't had a happy life and as she had grown older, she'd found herself becoming bitter because it had not gone as she'd hoped and dreamed it would when she was very young and had been happy for such a short while. She began to see that in some instances, she had overreacted to things that had been said and done, keeping her feelings bottled up to the point where they had eroded her spirit, leaving it scarred.

Ted could not, or would not, understand why she had to pick at old wounds, reopening them. He thought she should lay it all to rest and let it be, but she'd found that it didn't work. Even friends who knew about her told racist jokes, unintentionally stirring up old feelings which reminded her of things she'd rather forget.

Sometimes, when Cynthia was very young, before she started

school and for a short while afterward, she would be overcome with such a joyous happy feeling that it was as if fireworks were going off inside her. She thought of it as her 'golden sparkly feeling.' She'd look at the blue sky above her, the clean white clouds, the green of the trees and of the grass, feel the warmth of the sun, and the earth beneath her bare feet, and inside of herself feel as though she could burst with the happiness of being alive and that something wonderful and magical was going to happen to her. There was an invisible doorway just above her, but she had no way to open it. Behind it was a place wondrous beyond description.

What happened to the feeling? When did it disappear, never to return? She couldn't remember, except it had been after she started school. It had been ecstasy and she wondered if others had felt it too, and did they still, or had they lost it as she had? Since the loss, she felt empty and unfulfilled, as if a promise had been broken.

She remembered what Papa had said about writing a book when she was younger.

"I could," she thought. "But it would be painful for me and boring to others."

Still, the idea began to grow. She knew people went to psychiatrists and paid to have them listen as they reviewed the memories of their lives to help put the past into perspective and go on unfettered by old guilt, mistakes, pain, and grievances. Perhaps if she wrote a book, it would be a catharsis for her. She began making notes as things came to mind.

CHAPTER FOUR

Cynthia bought typewriter paper, correction fluid, and a new ribbon for her ancient portable. She cleaned the machine, arranged her materials, and was ready to begin what would be one of the most traumatic experiences of her life— the exposure of her soul and its scars for others to see, probably not understand, think she was a fool, or worse, a cry-baby.

"Am I? They say the child we were is still inside us. Is mine still crying? I suppose so, otherwise, I wouldn't be doing this trying to find an answer. How to begin? At the beginning, of course, but where was that?"

Did it begin with the circumstances of her birth, or with the phone call that had been such a threat to her peace of mind and feelings of security? Others had told her that she was good with words and should write.

Vera, her dearest friend, had said after his death, "Write about Papa."

A psychic had told her she would live long enough to finish writing years before she had ever thought about it.

"Writing what?" she had wondered then.

So, "I was born of poor but drunken parents," she typed. "There Papa, that's for you. You always told me to begin my book that way. Did you know something I didn't know or were you joking? Did you know that I might someday really write a book?"

Her father had a gift for seeing into the future. He had said, back in the thirties, that unions would be the ruination of the country given enough time. Cynthia could see as she looked around in the nineties that there had been truth in what he'd said so long ago. Unions were killing the goose that laid the golden egg with their demands for more and more, driving their companies out of business, or out of this country into others where labor is cheaper, seeming to think that all the monies made by the companies they work for should be theirs, with none going to their employers or for the upkeep of the facilities and equipment. Al had seen the advent of WWII and been called a warmonger in his workplace.

As a young man, he and some of his friends were in the bar at the Hotel del Coronado when some Japanese naval officers came in. Al got into a conversation with one of them and asked how it was that he spoke such perfect English. He'd answered that he had attended college in the U.S. He'd been sent by his country to learn the language and as much about our country as he could because it was Japan's intention to take over the U.S. one day.

This was just after WWI, but Al believed what he'd been told and he remembered. In the thirties, when the U.S. was selling scrap metal by the ton to Japan very cheaply, he told his associates that what we were selling to the Japanese would be made into arms and ammunition to be used against us in the near future. No one wanted to hear it. Pearl Harbor had come as a shock to all Americans, but no surprise to Cynthia's father.

Al had been violently anti-American Civil Liberties Union (ACLU), hating the organization with a passion.

"They are going to have too much power," he said. "And too much control over peoples' lives." This certainly seems to be the case when the perpetrator of a crime had more rights than a law-abiding citizen and gets off or does minimal time in prison while the victim continues to live with the memories and the anguish or lies buried in a grave.

"I have a little of that gift myself," Cynthia thought. "I knew the first night I met Ted that he was going to ask me to marry him. I told Vera so, and I also said that I didn't ever want to get married or have children. I didn't want them to have to go through what I had when I was a child. I wanted to be an artist. Marriage would interfere with my plans for my life. I knew when I first met Ted's mother that someday she would be my responsibility, but when I told him, he said that I wouldn't be marrying his family, I'd be marrying him. What a fool I was. Of course, you marry into families; didn't I end up taking care of her at the end of her life? If you don't marry into families, then why is his elderly aunt living with us now?"

She'd had a premonition about her mother before she went to Guam to join Ted after WWII. Ten months later she flew home for her mother's funeral. So a gift for seeing into the future is no great thing. The future is best left alone to unfold as it will, leaving one free to think of other things until its time comes.

"I thought I had my mind all in order," she told herself as she began writing. In her brain, neatly labeled boxes were stacked in alphabetical and chronological order on high shelves in neat rows like the stacks in a library. It was not so. The messy manuscript, some pages typed, some in long hand, small scraps of paper with single words as reminders, began to grow. Whole sentences and paragraphs became a hodgepodge of uncoordinated episodes to be put into order.

"My God," she thought. "It's like Fibber McGee's closet in there!"

Things came to mind that she had completely forgotten. At the time apparently, she'd blotted them out. She realized her mind, which she had thought was so orderly, was no more so than her notes.

Memories long buried thrust themselves up, surprising her, bringing the hurt feelings, or the small pleasures they had given her when they happened. She remembered friends of her grandparents and parents long dead, forgotten probably, with no one left to remember them but herself. She recalled encounters, good and bad, with people in her own life whom she had not thought about in years.

"What am I doing? I'll never get this into any kind of order if I don't stop remembering all this stuff."

But still, it kept coming. Over sixty years of memories.

Sometimes at night, she couldn't sleep. A thought would come to mind, a sentence would grow, leading to another and soon become a paragraph or a whole page. She would have to get up and either write it down or make enough notes so she could bring it back the next day when she began to write again.

Her life had always been divided into parts she could never seem to reconcile. She had never felt either Black or white; she had gone back and forth between two houses, neither of which had felt like home. There was her time at school and her time out of school. She'd lived behind masks she put on for each situation or relationship, hiding her thoughts and feelings, never letting anyone know what went on inside her.

The two houses, her grandmother's and her mother's, were where she divided her time when she was not in school when she was young. She had casual summer acquaintances who didn't know about her because they came over from San Diego or other locales, whom she met at the beach when she was older. There were her schoolmates who did know and from whom she kept her distance.

These parts of her life were separate from each other. She often felt like she was two people in one body, living two lives in two worlds.

From her childhood and on, her life had been divided by an invisible fence, too high to climb with no way to go through. She lived first on one side and then the other. The separation was obvious only to the one on the wrong side. It was a covert glance, and overt stare, an overheard whisper, a snicker, someone pointing, someone staring with curiosity, or obvious disbelief because she didn't look like what she was.

The one on the wrong side of the fence is very aware of these subtle messages which go unnoticed by others.

Cynthia, while still very young, became self-conscious, constantly on guard, monitoring facial expressions, watching how she behaved, and what she said. She felt like she was on display and was careful not to draw attention to herself, pretending not to notice that she was being watched and talked about. She wondered why. Even after she learned the reason, this paranoia remained with her for the rest of her life.

Her need to do things just for herself, to be creative with art or music or words, had been pushed aside as she grew older, by her obedience and need to please, coupled with the strong sense of duty and commitment instilled in her by her father.

She had taken a hack writing course in her fifties. The instructor told her she had a neutral vocabulary, good for many markets.

"I must be a neutral person, too, at least on the outside," she told herself. "I've kept myself bottled up too long."

Most of her youth had been spent trying to keep a low profile, to not draw unwanted attention to herself, because of the consequences. Even to Vera, her only childhood friend, she hadn't opened up completely, and never to her grandmother or her parents. She'd tried with Ted, but to no avail, and had quit trying. There were things that had happened that only she knew about and had forgotten that she knew until she started writing.

"You also have a tendency," the writing instructor said, "to write run-on sentences, which you should try to keep under control."

"Oh well," thought Cynthia. "My mind runs on and on too, one thought triggering another. I can't change now I'm too old. This probably won't be a raging best seller anyway if it gets printed at all. So I'll just write the way I've always written. It's about me... It should be in my own words and my own style. Besides, I'm really doing it for myself. If some publisher wants it, it'll be a bonus."

As her typewritten pages and scraps of paper with notes began to fill a yellow file folder, she was alternately calm and upset. Sometimes she could write about an episode in her life with cool objectivity. Other times her heart would pound; her head would ache and she'd have trouble breathing, making mistakes nearly every word as she remembered how she had felt at the unfairness of it all and old angers arose and tears welled.

Perhaps she had been the cause of her own unhappiness. It has been said that one way or another, we are responsible for our own lives, that we are what we believe ourselves to be. She'd long since forgiven her parents for what she'd thought had been a lack of concern, never telling her or warning her about her background. She'd forgiven others for what she had considered their big-mouthed busy-bodiedness, making sure that no one made any mistakes about her.

They had lived within the prescribed rules of society as it had been then, undoubtedly never giving it a thought that what they were doing and saying was devastating to a child.

During a nervous breakdown after the death of her mother, she had learned that one can only help oneself. No matter how well-meaning friends are, they cannot help.

Nor can a doctor, a minister, or even one's own husband or father.

They listen with sympathy; they mouth platitudes about how one needs to quit thinking about one's self so much. One needs to get out more, or find something to do to keep busy. All well and good, but when one is falling apart, consumed with fear, fighting to function normally, it doesn't help.

From the doctor, it was, "Take a warm bath before you go to bed, drink a cup of hot milk, and try not to worry."

"I'm not worried," she would think as she left his office. "I'm terrified. I can't sleep at night. I'm afraid I'm going crazy and I'm going to end up in a looney bin, and no one can help me."

The first draft of the book was stilted and detached.

"I'm still trying to hide," she told herself as she read it over. "I don't want to face the fact that I'm part Black. I never did. Oh, what a hypocrite I am, and a racist too, obviously. Shame on me!"

The manuscript such as it was, sat for months while she considered whether to throw it out or go back to it. The prospect of all that revision was overwhelming. She'd gotten all the bad remembrances out and purged herself.

What was coming now was understanding of her parents and of herself and memories of good times. There had been good times, after all. She was surprised because for so many years all she remembered was the rotten stuff.

"It curdled me too," she told herself. "I learned more about the dark side of human nature than most adults while I was still a child. It made me bitter, distrustful, cynical, and suspicious."

CHAPTER FIVE

Annie told Cynthia that she was a slave until she was twelve years old. Her father was English, but she told Cynthia nothing of her mother. She had been one of twelve children, the only one still living. Had she been the youngest? Had the others met their deaths by means that she could not bear to tell the child? Had she been separated from them or her mother, which was not uncommon in slave days? She had come with Amos to California on doctors' orders, to die of asthma.

"And I outlived them all," she said proudly.

She was a mulatto, not dark, more like strong coffee with milk. She did not have Negro features and was petite and delicate. In her wedding picture, beside her six-foot husband, she looked like the tiny, pretty, young girl that she was.

She had done hairdressing, was a dressmaker, and a milliner. She didn't need a dress pattern; she could take a few measurements and cut a pattern out of newspaper that would be a perfect fit. She could make hair pieces, knit, crochet, and embroider.

Cynthia had a wooden box that her grandfather had made,

which Annie had lined with pleated red silk. It had poinsettias on the outside which appeared to have been burned into the wood, then stained, so Cynthia's grandmother had been an artist as well.

These things, Cynthia had read, weren't usually taught to slaves. Her grandmother had been fortunate for some reason to have been trained as a house servant and not a field laborer. Cynthia thought it was because of Grandma's white father. She'd read that this was a custom.

Had Grandma's mother been the woods-colt of her owner or one of his sons?

Could she have married a white overseer?

Any of these liaisons could have been a reason for special treatment. Annie had not been taught to read and write. This too was in accordance with the customs of the time.

"I taught myself," she told Cynthia proudly. "And I taught your grandpa too."

Grandma may have been a tiny little thing, but she surely had spirit. She could have been punished severely for learning to read and write.

Cynthia knew little about her grandfather, Amos. Grandma had told her nothing. What she did know came from her father, who spoke of his father with pride and affection. She learned little more when she sent for his Civil War and Cavalry records. She had once attempted to trace the genealogy of her grandparents but was unable to find anything; the records for their birth states and the time they had lived in Kansas had been destroyed by fire.

Furthermore, she had not been able to locate their names in the local census for the time they had lived in San Diego or Coronado, and she wondered about it since they had lived in the area for over fifty years.

Amos was born in Missouri in 1844, the son of a Cherokee Indian mother and a Negro/Cherokee or mulatto father. His mother's maiden name was Brigman, and it was possible one of her parents was at least part white.

There had to be more than a tad of Caucasian blood for Cynthia and her father to look the way they did. The portrait of Cynthia's Indian great-grandmother hung in Annie's house was a lady who was very light, but with Indian features.

Had Amos's parents walked the Trail of Tears?

It was possible since he'd been born only three years after that shameful episode in our history.

Did he have siblings?

Cynthia wished she knew.

Amos was over six feet tall. A tinted photograph of him was of a handsome man with grey eyes, dark wavy hair and light skin, but features that told of his Negro blood. It had survived May's purge and been tucked away on a closet shelf. Cynthia wondered why Mama had saved it when she had thrown away nearly everything else.

Four days after his eighteenth birthday, Amos signed up in to fight in the Civil War. Had he got to Kansas from Missouri, a slave state, alone or with others of whom some were runaway slaves? Or was he a free man because of his Indian roots? His company the 2nd Kansas Volunteered Colored Infantry, distinguished themselves in battles in Arkansas and when the war ended, were mustered out in Camden, Arkansas, and marched back to Leavenworth, Kansas, to be disbanded, cold, ragged, barefoot, and near death from starvation, surviving on the mules' feed and then the mules, according to a history of the 2nd Kansas.

In July of 1867, Amos signed up with the 10th Cavalry for the Indian Wars, serving until July of 1872. Did he stay in Kansas or return to Missouri? Did he meet Annie then?

They were married in Missouri in 1874. He was thirty, she was twenty. While he had been fighting the war for freedom from slavery, she had been a slave in Kentucky.

Cynthia had no idea of how, when, or where they met, only that they were married in the Methodist-Episcopal church in Ray County, Missouri and lived in Topeka, Kansas, before the move to California in 1887 because of her asthma, she'd said, but also because of the homestead offer.

How did they come? By wagon train with others, by themselves, or by train? Amos had a team and wagon when Al was a child. She knew this much from his childhood remembrances about his father.

Amos found himself unable to do the hard labor required to keep the homestead in the El Cajon Valley because an injury to his left knee from a Minie ball in the Civil War had left him with a gimpy leg, so they moved into the city of San Diego where Cynthia's father was born in 1891, and did hauling for a time with the team and wagon.

In 1897, the Spanish American War broke out and Amos signed up with the California Militia, ready to go off to fight for his country again, leaving a wife and a child behind, if necessary.

As she wrote about him, Cynthia thought to herself, "It would seem Grandpa was a bit more of an adventurer than he was a family man."

On his return, Amos settled down and took up barbering. Had he sold the team and wagon to finance the trip to Alaska, or was the money used for the shop or a chair in it?

In 1903, when Algie was twelve, the family moved to Coronado, later bought a lot and built the house Amos and Annie would live in for the rest of their lives. After a time, the standing began to bother his leg again, so he gave up barbering and in 1905 was in Arizona working for the San Diego and Arizona railroad.

Shortly after, a Mexican hurricane hit Coronado hard, washing out the beach and inundating the houses along Ocean Front Blvd. When Amos's crew came back from Arizona, they were set to work building a sea wall. It was while they were doing this that he received the injury that crippled him for the rest of his life.

Huge granite rocks were brought in by horse and wagon. A horse getting skittish in between the shafts dislodged a rock, which fell on Amos, seriously injuring him. The other men put him on a board, passed the hat, and carried him home. There was no workmen's compensation in those days; what had happened was too bad, but one had to make the most of it.

Amos made a poor recovery, used a cane for the rest of his life, and was in pain most of the time.

The railroad hired him back as a night watchman for their holdings down by the Coronado ferry landing, a job he held until his final illness. He died in 1925 of old age and digestive complications.

Cynthia's memories of her grandfather were few. Because he had been a war veteran he rode with the others in the Memorial and Armistice Day parades. She remembered seeing him when there were only three or four veterans in the car and Papa saying that soon all the old Civil War vets would be gone. Amos always wore his old G.A.R. Felt hat with the emblem and cord decoration. His hair was long and snow white.

Cynthia remembered the long white locks lying over his shoulders like the picture of Custer in history books. He had been with Custer's troops, but went with Reno on the flanking maneuver, thereby escaping the massacre at Little Big Horn. He had been a buffalo hunter and a scout in the Indian Wars. He once told Al, who told Cynthia, that they had lain hidden watching a herd of buffalo take a day and a night and part of another day to go by as they waited to kill stragglers for food.

Cynthia remembered saying her prayers at her grandparents' knees as they sat side-by-side in their rocking chairs in the kitchen of the little house, which served as a living room and dining room, too. The house, her father's former radio shack, had no heat, only a coal oil stove was used in the winter, and was never left on at night.

There was a hot water heater, but her grandmother didn't use it. For baths, she heated water in a kettle on the gas stove and brought in a galvanized tub. She spread newspapers on the floor and after filling the tub from the kettle, and cooling it, bathed Cynthia.

She would sit in her rocker as she did so, because of her rheumatism, she couldn't get down on her knees anymore. She took her own baths in the same tub because she said she was afraid of falling in the bathtub. Cynthia never saw Amos taking a bath in this manner, so he must fearlessly have used the tub, the brave soldier that he was. After Amos died, Grandma threw newspapers into it, and it was never used for anything else again.

One night Cynthia was awakened and taken out into the yard to watch a dirigible come across Coronado to dock at North Island. It was in the paper that it was coming; people had been talking expectantly about it all day. She wasn't sure until after she was grown which one it was, but when she read about it years later, it had been the Shenandoah.

It was October 24, 1924, when she was only three years old, but she still remembers Grandpa holding her, telling her to look up, as he pointed.

"Here it comes," voices called up and down the alley in the dark. Quietly it came into view, flying slowly and very low. It filled the sky overhead. It was so big Cynthia was frightened and hid her head against Amos's shoulder.

"Look! Look!" he said, so she did.

All the searchlights on the ships in the bay were turned on it, the beams shooting back and forth across the sky, flashing on the bottom and sides of the huge silver airship as it glided over. It was a sight to behold! People called back and forth to each other excitedly. Nothing like this had ever been seen before.

Regally, it moved out of sight. People called "good night" to their neighbors and went back inside their houses, their screen doors slamming behind them.

Later, when other airships came to Coronado, Cynthia saw the Macon and the Akron, but nothing ever compared to that first viewing with all the searchlights and the huge ship so low that it seemed one could reach up and touch it.

It was overwhelming. She never forgot it. That was the last memory she had of her grandfather alive. He died when she was four, in 1925.

One night, Cynthia was awakened by the sound of voices in the house. She heard Papa's voice and called out to him. Someone came in to check on her.

"Hush. Go back to sleep. Your grandfather is dying."

There was a lot of activity, strange voices and people coming and going. Finally, the lights were turned off and everyone was gone. It was quiet and she slept.

The next morning Grandpa wasn't there.

"Your grandpa has gone to heaven," she was told.

A day or two later she was taken to see him lying in a box looking almost like he was asleep. Her grandmother was crying, all the grown-ups seemed sad and talked in whispers. Music was playing softly and there was the scent of flowers, lots of flowers.

She and her family, Mama, Papa, and Grandma, were behind a thin curtain so she could see the flowers and a lot of people on the other side and hear them murmuring. Their minister was there. He talked for a while and then everyone got into cars and drove to a place with lots of green grass and trees and statues and marble stones stuck in the ground. The minister talked some more, then everyone left.

Cynthia kept expecting Grandpa to come back even though she had been told he would be gone forever. Sure enough, one night not long after, as she lay in the semi-darkness of the bedroom, he appeared, standing alongside her crib. He was back, just as she knew he would be, but he looked different.

He was standing up straight, not all bent over leaning on his cane. His G.A.R. hat and his long white hair were gone. He was bareheaded; his hair was short and dark. He opened his mouth to speak and suddenly she was terrified. She screamed for her grandmother, and he disappeared.

When Annie came hurrying in, Cynthia told her Grandpa had been there, but Grandma told her that she had been dreaming and to go back to sleep.

Cynthia hadn't been dreaming. She'd been awake and she knew

it. When she was older and thought about it, she was more certain than ever of what she'd seen. She had known Amos only as an old man, yet she knew this younger man was her grandpa.

That was her first psychic experience. There would be others in her lifetime whenever there was a death in her family.

CHAPTER SIX

S hortly after Amos's death, Cynthia was very ill. The Public Health Nurse came to the house. She took Cynthia's temperature, showed the thermometer to Annie, and Cynthia heard Grandma suck in her breath. Cynthia drifted in and out of consciousness, aware of her parents standing at the side of the bed talking in hushed voices, but she was too sick to open her eyes or move or speak. She never knew what it was, but it must have been serious because she was sick for so long and Mama and Papa came so often. Perhaps it was diphtheria, which was common in those days before a vaccine against it was found. She remembered Grandma saying that her throat was almost completely closed... one of diphtheria's symptoms. Christmas came and went and she neither knew nor cared.

When she was recovering, Mama and Papa brought her Christmas presents to Grandma's and watched her open them while she was still in bed. Santa had outdone himself! Had her parents been afraid she was going to die? Perhaps.

Diphtheria claimed many children.

There was a set of real China doll dishes, a little table and chair, a set of pots and pans, toy silverware, a beautiful doll with red hair and clothes, a wicker doll buggy, and a red tricycle!

As soon as she was well, she rode her new trike up the alley. The ice truck was there, and the iceman was away making a delivery.

In those days, people hung a sign in a back window if they needed ice. It was a cardboard square with a number in each corner indicating how many pounds were needed when it was hung with the desired amount at the top. The iceman hacked off a chunk, grabbed it with a huge pair of tongs, threw it over his leather-covered shoulder, carried it to the back porch, and put it in the icebox. No one locked their doors then. Iceboxes were kept on the back porch because if the tray did not get emptied as the ice melted, there would be water all over the floor. Some houses had a hole drilled in the floor under the drain to prevent this, but that could allow rodents to come inside.

When Cynthia was very small and they'd lived in the front house, she remembered hearing cries of dismay when someone started out the back door and stepped in a puddle.

In the little house, there was only a cooler. A cooler was a cupboard open on the bottom which let cool air in from under the house, screened to keep out bugs and mice.

Cynthia had seen the big kids run up to the back of the ice truck to grab broken pieces to suck on, but she was too short to reach the tailgate. Now, on the trike, she could. She rode up to the truck, stood on the pedals and was reaching when the iceman came back unnoticed by her. He didn't see her, either. The motor had been left running; he got in and backed up.

She felt herself falling; there was a crash.

She heard an exclamation. "Oh, my God!"

And everything went black with flashes of light.

Then she felt herself being lifted and carried back to Grandma's.

Annie, hearing the crash, had come to the gate to see what it was.

Cynthia's head was spinning; her eyes didn't want to focus. She was still seeing bright flashes of light.

When the man handed her to her grandma, she heard him say, "I didn't know she was behind me. I'm so sorry."

Grandma took her inside and put her back to bed. She was there for a while again, drifting in and out of consciousness... She never knew for how long.

When she was well, the first thing she wanted to do was ride her wonderful trike again. Grandma said she couldn't.

"Why can't I?"

"It's wrecked," Grandma told her.

"I want to see it anyway."

So Grandma took her to see the twisted ruin. She looked at it with dismay and started to cry.

"Will I get another one?"

"No," Grandma said.

And she didn't.

SHE GOT a bicycle when she was eleven. Her friend, Vera, had gotten a brand new one for her eleventh birthday. Her mother and her older sister and brother who were both working had all chipped in and bought it for her.

"Can I have a bicycle for my birthday like Vera's?" she asked Mama and Papa, not sure what they would say.

Mama looked at Papa, "We'll see," she said.

Cynthia knew this could mean yes or no; she also knew how hard times were. A new bike could cost more than ten dollars! She was sure she wouldn't get one. But a few weeks later, Al came home carrying a bus boy's frame that someone had given him. She was disappointed. She didn't want a boy's bike. Vera's was blue; Cynthia wanted a red one.

Al told her not to worry; he'd see if he could trade it at the bicycle shop for a girl's frame and he did. Then, pinching pennies by rolling his own cigarettes, not buying the ready-mades he treated himself to sometimes, by going without lunch, and with what Mama could squeeze from the house money, he bought the other parts piecemeal.

It took from Vera's birthday in October until Cynthia's in August for him to finish it. Al, who usually could do anything, found himself stymied on the spoking, but the man next door knew how to do it. Between them, they got it done with enough time left to paint it before her birthday.

Red and black it was, and it was beautiful. Not like Vera's, but the rusted chrome had been painted with aluminum paint and it looked really nice, almost like new. She knew she was lucky to have gotten it at all and it was all the more special because Papa had made it just for her.

Looking back, she could see from her own experience that what children need to let them know they are loved is not things, but for someone to be there, someone to listen, someone to care, someone to give them some time.

Time is the most valuable commodity in the world because none of us knows when what we have is going to run out. To use it for someone you love is the greatest gift anyone can give.

Cynthia was sure Papa loved her because he went without to get the parts for her bicycle and spent hours in the garage making it as nice as he could.

How lonely must be the child who comes home to an empty house whose parents are too busy or too tired to give them the gift of attention because they think they need more money for things instead of giving the child more of themselves, which costs nothing.

CHAPTER SEVEN

Al had been born late in life to Annie and Amos. They'd been married seventeen years, and she was thirty-seven years old. She told Cynthia, as the child played on the floor beside her White Rotary treadle sewing machine, that she'd given up hope of ever having a baby, thought she had a tumor, and was preparing to die. When the baby was born, he was so puny he wasn't expected to live.

"His head would have fit into a teacup. We wrapped him in a blanket and put him in a bureau drawer lined with heated flat irons wrapped in newspapers to keep him warm and sent for the minister to baptize him before we lost him," she said.

He was christened Amos Algernon, after his father and a character in a book she'd read, and he didn't die. He lived to be eighty-one years old!

Cynthia's grandma was still ironing with the same flat irons when the child was small, so Cynthia knew what they were. Heavy cast iron things which were heated on the gas burner, with a detachable coiled wire handle. It was a chore to iron with them. They were lifted off the stove and tested with a wet finger. If it sizzled, it was ready.

Women often burned themselves using them or scorched what they were working on. They got blisters on their palms from them too. When the first electric irons came on the market, they were very heavy. It was believed that weight was necessary to get wrinkles out. Women still got blisters on their palms which, in time, changed to calluses.

Cynthia herself had ironed with one of these early electric irons when she and Ted first married. They couldn't afford to send out their things to the laundry or to buy a washing machine, so she'd scrubbed on a washboard as Grandma had done, too.

The flat iron was good for other things, like holding down a pile of newspapers the way newsboys did so they wouldn't blow away (every newsstand or newsboy had at least one for that). After heating, they were wrapped in newspapers and then run over the bed sheets on a cold night to take off the chill before putting them at the foot of the bed to keep the feet warm. They were used for propping doors open, too.

There was no electricity in Grandma's house until around 1927. Cynthia came home from school and the handyman was stringing the wires, fastening them to the walls in plain sight with brads and installing the porcelain switches.

Now, as her memory took her back to the things Grandma had told her, she thought, "Papa must have been a preemie. But of course, they weren't called that then. In those days most of them probably died. It must have been awful for Grandma to birth the baby she had always wanted, and a boy, which husbands usually wanted, only to think she was going to lose him."

John Osborne, the minister who baptized Algie, as he was called when he was young, had been friends with the family for years. It was he who verified that Al had indeed been born when he said he had. Al's birth records had been destroyed in a fire at the church and they were needed for him to register for the draft many years later.

When the Japanese bombed Pearl Harbor, Al went to enlist the very next day, but he was too old. He was very disappointed but took consolation in the fact that his daughter's husband, a Marine, was fighting in the South Pacific.

The last time John Osborne was called upon was when Cynthia and Al asked him to preside at May's funeral. He was very old and was deeply touched by her loss at so early an age.

When he said, "I remember the first day I met this bonnie Scottish lassie," Al gave a moan and began to sob. Cynthia, seated beside him, reached for his hand and her own tears came.

Cynthia hadn't cried for her mother from the time she got the cablegram, not on the plane, in the thirty-three hours it had taken to fly from Guam to San Francisco, or in the time it took for her and Tee Gee to reach San Diego, nor in the days that followed before the funeral. She and Papa had both been in shock as they made the arrangements and set the date. They had spoken of little else but May, discovering that each knew things about her the other didn't.

Cynthia had loved her mother, but she hadn't shed a tear for her until Papa broke down at the service.

When they returned home that day, some friends dropped by for a short time. After they'd gone, she and Papa sat in the living room, he in the Papa chair and she in Mama's.

They sat for a time in silence, then she said, "Up until now it felt like Mama was still here, that she was upstairs at her dressing table or out in the kitchen, that she wasn't really gone, but now the house feels empty."

"I feel that way, too," Al said. "She was here until today, and now she isn't."

"Knowing Mama, she probably stayed around long enough to 'count the house,' and then she went wherever it was she was supposed to go next." Cynthia laughed a little as she said it, and after a moment, Papa laughed too.

That, apparently, was one thing they both knew about Al's May and Cynthia's Mama May.

CHAPTER EIGHT

Logan Heights in San Diego, now called Barrio Logan, where Al was born and lived until the move to Coronado, was nothing like it is today.

On the outskirts of the young city circa 1890, it was a rural area where families lived in harmony, kept chickens, cows, and horses, and grew vegetables. It was a racially mixed community of Mexicans, Indians, Negroes, and whites who were neighbors and did neighborly things. Milk was traded for eggs, and they shared the abundance of their gardens. They watched each other's children and, when there was an illness or a death in the family, they did whatever they could to help.

A Mexican lady, Mrs. Villagrana, taught Annie how to make tortillas. Her son and Algie were close friends... perhaps the same boy who later walked across a board on the unfinished Cabrillo Bridge when they were teenagers.

Annie had asked Mrs. Villagrana's mother why the missions in the area were in such a state of disrepair. There was a terrible earthquake that changed the course of the Colorado River, she remembered.

"The earth shook day and night for a week." She went on to say that when the Indians, who were helping to build the missions saw the priests, whom they looked to for protection, were as frightened as they were, they refused to do more work for them and left.

In the late 1800s, there was a financial panic. Al remembered that Amos, who was working in the barber shop a couple of doors east from the Golden Lion restaurant on a corner of Fourth Street, walked to the Cracker Factory on Market to buy broken crackers. He'd come home with a bag full, which cost no more than a nickel. Al had these crumbled in milk for breakfast or lunch, sometimes supper. This, bread and milk, or oatmeal and cornmeal mush were the cereals of the day. The first commercial cereals were in Cynthia's time. She remembers Kellogg's Corn Flakes, Nabisco Shredded Wheat biscuits, and later, Wheaties.

By the time Cynthia was born, milk was being delivered by horse and buggy from Arden's dairy farm in San Ysidro. She remembers hearing the clip-clop of the horse's hooves coming down the alley and the jingle of bottles in the metal carrying rack. Milk came in glass bottles with a tabbed cardboard cap then. It was pasteurized, but not homogenized and woe to the child who forgot and shook the bottle without first pouring off the cream at the top!

This was called top milk and was used for the adults' coffee or to put on desserts like Jell-O, bread, rice puddings, or fresh strawberries. Kids drank the reduced fat milk that was left. No one saw anything wrong with it and it was undoubtedly more healthy for their cholesterol levels than the homogenized milk they get today.

When Al was growing up in Logan Heights, he told Cynthia he could see the famous Hotel del Coronado, with some parts still under construction, and watched as it grew to completion. He also told her that he and a friend had walked across the Cabrillo Bridge while it was still being built. A plank had been left across the unfinished highest span and the two boys walked across it on a day when no work was being done.

"My God," Cynthia said. "You could have been killed. Did Grandma ever know about it?"

"I certainly never told her. She'd have had a conniption fit."

"I can just imagine," she said.

YOUNG AL WAS BEGINNING to have an interest in radio. After the move to Coronado, by setting pins at the bowling alley in Tent City and doing odd jobs, he bought materials and built his first Ham set. The family was living in a small house on the corner of F Street, the only house on the block, across the street from the old wooden schoolhouse.

When the move was made to the larger house at 845 B Avenue, a small shack in the back became the site of what was possibly the first radio sending and receiving station in Southern California. He was on the air illegally in 1905 because, at age fourteen, he was too young to be licensed. He later received the call letters 6IZ. This early experience stood him in good stead when WWI began, and he went off to fight. After he came back from his service, he taught radio to a Boy Scout troop and was president of the San Diego Radio Club. The station was dismantled after his marriage and the birth of Cynthia.

She couldn't understand why all this had not been of interest to the Historical Society. True, her father hadn't been a Black settler, but he was the son of a man who had been. This, along with his own exploits, it seemed to her, should have been worthy of mention.

Annie rented the little house on F street for a time to Glenn Curtis's mother and they became good friends, as did Glenn and Algie. Glenn, a pioneer aviator, was practicing taking off and landing his sea plane in the slough between North Island and San Diego. He wanted to teach Algie to fly and take him on as an assistant, feeling, at that time, Algie's radio experience would be useful in aviation.

Annie was horrified.

She told Mrs. Curtis that if she let Glenn take her Algie up in that contraption, she'd never speak to her again. Al was terribly disappointed, but what could he do? He was only a schoolboy.

Not too long afterward, Algie was offered a scholarship with the Ford Motor Car Company. Cynthia never knew exactly how this had come about, but he'd mentioned it and she'd heard the disappointment in his voice. His mother put her foot down again. He'd have had to go back east to the plant, and she was not about to let her precious boy that far out of her sight. First, there'd been the chance to go into aviation with Curtis, then the opportunity to learn automotive engineering, but his mother wasn't through with him yet. She would make a major change in his life one more time and this one after he was an adult.

When Amos was injured at the sea wall Al was in his first year at Russ High School in San Diego, called Grey Castle because of the huge granite rocks used in its construction. He'd had to drop out to look for work to help support the family. He got a job in the office of the San Diego and Arizona Railroad because his father had been hurt on the job working for them. It was not for long, however; soon he was asked to leave. Someone in charge didn't want him there. He didn't say in so many words, but evidently, they'd felt that a colored was okay for an outside job, but not in an office. Al had been bitter about it.

Over the years, as she grew up, Cynthia heard him mention the lost job occasionally and she thought she knew who it had been. There was a man he often mentioned seeing on the ferry. He'd speak, trying to be friendly, but Al couldn't stand him, referring to him as that son of a bitch, Mike Mills.

Many, many years later, after her father's funeral, as Cynthia looked through the guest book, she was surprised to see the name. Why had he come? Had the years mellowed him, so he realized that what he'd done had been a dirty thing to do to a young man who really needed a job to help his family?

She looked up his name in the phone book and called, curious to see what he might say. A nurse answered the phone. She told

Cynthia that he was very old. Attending the service had tired him and he was asleep.

She didn't call again, and not too long afterward, she saw his name in the obits. Whatever he may have done to feel guilty about was now between him and his Maker.

Young Algie got a better job anyway. He was taken on as an office boy for Union Title and Trust in downtown San Diego. He took an engineering course by mail, becoming a surveyor and a draftsman; in time he worked up to being a poster, recording deeds and titles in his beautiful script. He then became a title searcher. After working for the company for fifty years, he was considered the dean of title men in San Diego county at his retirement. He certainly knew the city and its environs well, having been born and raised in the area and watching it grow.

WHEN THE WAR FOR DEMOCRACY was declared, Al joined up the next day, taking a leave of absence from the company. His mother was devastated, but he was now twenty-five years old. He'd signed up with the California Naval Militia thinking he was joining the U.S. Navy, but there was no difference since he did his service aboard Navy ships. He left from the Santa Fe Depot on April 13, 1917, with a group of other young men from the area who were going to San Francisco for training.

His first billet was aboard the battleship California. The new men lined up on deck and anyone with radio experience was asked to step forward. Al was made a radio electrician on the spot, becoming Chief a shorter time later. It wasn't CPO then, but CE for Chief Electrician. He told Cynthia he thought he had been the first man to ever check out all the connections and wiring aboard a battleship. Perhaps he was the first CPO of color as well. Since he, like Cynthia, was white, had he kept his secret to himself like she often did?

He served for a short while on the USS Data and the USS Frederick. This is recorded in a log he kept for two-plus years of service.

He then served for a time aboard the collier Pueblo before being transferred to the USS Sioux, a mine carrier transporting mines across the Atlantic from Norfolk, Virginia, via Rio de Janeiro, to Scotland and France.

He told Cynthia that the first time they sailed into Glasgow, a Limey aboard a British vessel had hailed them.

"Ahoy there, you aboard the *Sy-oh-ux*."

It had been very funny, and in time became a Hudgins family joke because Al pronounced it that way from then on.

After he died, his old outfit had a final meeting, a mustering-out ceremony. The remaining men, whose numbers were dwindling, were getting too old and some too ill to attend the annual meetings. It would include a reinstatement ceremony for the California Naval Militia, which had been disbanded years before and would be a very special occasion, the old guard and the new coming together for the one's first and the other's last time.

Cynthia called to see if she could attend in Papa's name. They would be pleased to have her. She went with her daughter, May-May. It made them both feel very close to Papa.

That same day, Cynthia and May-May went to a pet store and came home with a new puppy. He was named Sioux in honor of Papa and that special day. Of course, it was pronounced their traditional way, so he ended up being a boy named Sioux, called Sye. Al would have loved it; he'd always had a great sense of humor.

During Al's time of service in the Navy, he'd had a close brush with death. In a way, it was not different from the way Amos had escaped the massacre at the Little Big Horn... a different location had been their salvation.

Earl Cotton, a very young radioman, came aboard the Sioux. She was underway in the Atlantic on her way to Europe in the area called the Bermuda Triangle. When Cotton woke up on this particular day with a premonition that he'd be killed on his watch he was very upset, asking the other men if one would trade with him. They were older than he was, and they teased him, kidding around about it, not unkindly, just having a little fun. But he was very serious, growing more desperate as the day wore on until finally, when he was begging with tears in his eyes, Al took pity on him.

"Alright, Cotton, I'll stand your God damned watch for you."

According to the personal log Al kept of his two and a half years in the Navy, they had been going through the fringes of a storm for a couple of days. The radio antenna had been broken and only just repaired. That night, as young Cotton stood the watch that should have been Al's, the storm hit head-on.

The entry Al made for that day reads:

AT 2:40 AM, DECEMBER 8, 1918, WE TOOK ASEA.

He told Cynthia he'd been in his hammock when the Sioux had gone completely under and he said to himself, "Oh, gosh, this is IT!"

After a breathless moment that had seemed like an eternity, the ship had given a shudder and come back up. All hands rushed to assess the damage. Al ran the length of the ship to the radio shack, to find it crushed and Cotton mortally injured.

The log goes on:

RADIO SHACK SMASHED, KILLED EARL D. COTTON, E2C[R]... HE DIED AT 5:59 AM. LIFEBOATS #2 AND #3 AND THE DINGHY DESTROYED, ALL ROOMS ON THE PORT SIDE FLOODED. DISPENSARY AND CPO MESS WRECKED. LATER, THE STEERING GEAR BROKE AND LEFT US WALLOWING IN THE TROUGH FOR 45 MINUTES. ALL HANDS GATHERED IN WARDROOM AND SPENT A LONG LONG NIGHT. I LOST ALL MY CLOTHES, LETTERS, AND TRINKETS. THE SEAS WERE ENORMOUS, DRIVEN BY A 90-MILE WIND AND US IN THE MID-ATLANTIC.

There was more. The next morning, he told Cynthia, he looked down the side of the ship along which he'd run the night before in the dark, in the middle of the storm, and he saw that the railing had been torn completely away when the ship went under. If he'd lost his balance, there'd have been nothing to keep him from being washed overboard. Cynthia always broke out in goose pimples at this part of the story.

They'd continued on across the Atlantic where Cotton was buried with full military honors on January 30, 1919, in the Navy Plot at Kerfautras Cemetery in Paris. Cotton had had a rendezvous with death, and in trying to sidestep it, he'd met it head-on.

Al wrote to Cotton's mother telling her how Cotton had been killed and how sorry he was. Every year after that until her death, she wrote him at Christmas. Every year, when the card and letter came, Al told the story again. It never failed to touch Cynthia deeply. She felt for the young sailor and his mother, and she wondered if Mrs. Cotton had ever gone to Paris to stand at the grave of her son.

"Twice," she thought. "First my grandfather and then my father. If they'd been killed, I wouldn't be here now." Sometimes she wondered why.

"I was nearly killed three times myself... when I was hit by the ice truck when I was four; when I made a jump for the ferry ramp like I'd seen the big kids do, and when I nearly drowned when I disobeyed Papa when I was nine or ten. For what reasons, I wonder, were we saved?"

THERE WAS MORE. Al told Cynthia, when she was reading a book about disappearances in the Triangle, that he'd been in radio contact with the operator aboard the Cyclops on the evening before she disappeared a few months later that year. Cyclops had been in sight behind them on the same course heading back to Norfolk. During the night, a sudden storm hit and the next morning when the weather cleared, Cyclops was nowhere to be seen. It was assumed aboard the Sioux that she'd been blown off course. It wasn't until sometime later that they received word that she'd completely disappeared.

Unfortunately, Al did not record this in his log, so it is not documented.

Cyclops has been written about in several books as one of the mysterious disappearances in the area. In one, Cynthia read that the weather had been fine, no storms anywhere, but Al had told her there was a storm and also that Cyclops had a heavy superstructure. If she'd taken the same sort of asea that Sioux had earlier, she'd have gone straight to the bottom with all hands on board.

"We were luckier than she was that we didn't disappear the same way," he said.

As Cynthia was writing this story, she realized that Sioux had been returning empty and therefore would have been more buoyant than the Cyclops, which was carrying a full load of manganese. She wondered if the log of the Sioux is still extant, moldering in some Navy archive with the story of the night in question recorded in it. It was unfortunate that Al hadn't mentioned it in his log. They'd been battling the same storm and didn't know she'd been lost, so there'd been no reason for him to make any comment on it.

CHAPTER NINE

For a year or two after Amos died, Annie and Cynthia went to the cemetery at Mount Hope nearly every week. One day they caught the streetcar as usual and the conductor told them that the line had been shortened. It no longer went to the cemetery gate; they must walk the rest of the way, a half mile or more. It was a very warm day, but the walk was downhill, so they managed.

The visit to the grave was as usual. Annie had brought enough flowers from her garden for the grave and one other. She set about throwing out the dead ones, sending Cynthia to put them in the trash can and filling the tin can they had set in a hole at the head of the grave with water for the fresh ones. There was no headstone at this time. Then they walked across the street and some railroad tracks and up a hill, from the G.A.R. Section to the colored section where they went to a triple headstone that said, "The Three Sisters."

One of them had been an old, old lady Grandma and Cynthia had gone to visit after Cynthia had started school. A day Cynthia never forgot.

The names on the stone were Casey, Pierce, and Morton. They had lived and died in the period between 1842 and 1927. One of them had been the mother of a lady named Rita O'Neil who sometimes came to visit Cynthia's grandma, bringing with her a daughter who was several years older than Cynthia.

Gina, the daughter, was a beautiful girl, quite fair. Her mother, Rita, was very proud of her, always bringing pictures of her with various white male friends or husbands, of whom there had been a few.

After Annie died, Rita continued to come for a time to visit Al and May, but finally stopped coming altogether and sent a wire with money for flowers for The Three Sisters' grave on Memorial Day. May's family was in Scotland. A telegram could mean a death. May would be afraid to open it and when she did, would get very angry because Rita had scared her half to death.

"Why can't she just send a letter with the money instead of wiring it? She always waits until the very last damned minute; doesn't she have sense enough to think ahead?"

Before May died, telegrams stopped coming, but the family continued to put flowers on the grave of the three. After May died, the custom continued until after Al had been gone for a year, and Cynthia told herself that if Papa was still here, he wouldn't be hanging around the graveyard... he'd always hated going out there, so she quit going too.

They had long since lost touch with Rita, so Cynthia never knew what had become of her. She wondered what Gina's life had been like, colored with the taint of her ancestry, like her own had been. Had that shadow come between Gina and her relationships as it often had with Cynthia's? Was that why her liaisons with men had never seemed to last very long? Had she had emotional problems too?

The ritual visits finished, and Cynthia and Grandma started back to the streetcar stop. It had grown very hot and halfway back, Annie in her long black dress and coat began to falter. Suddenly she collapsed. Cynthia was frightened.

"Grandma, Grandma, what's wrong?"

"I'll be all right. Just let me rest a minute."

Cynthia looked around frantically, but no one was nearby. They were still a long way from the end of the line and the first houses, three little cottages in a row.

"Shall I run for help, Grandma?"

"No, just let me catch my breath, then you can help me up."

With Cynthia's help, the old lady struggled to her feet, leaned heavily on the child and they started off again. It was very hard on Cynthia. Grandma was old and frail, but Cynthia was just a little girl, five, maybe six years old, and small for her age. She was scared, wondering how much longer she could manage by herself, when to her relief she saw a colored lady come out of one of the houses to sweep her porch. She looked up, saw them, dropped the broom, and came running. She took charge, helping Annie back to the house, up the steps, into a chair, and went inside to get a glass of water.

When the streetcar came, she helped Annie to the step, explained what had happened to the conductor and he took over, helping Annie to board, seating her, then going out to change the trolley, and coming back to reverse the seats for the return trip with Cynthia helping him.

After that day, Cynthia and her grandma never went to the cemetery alone again. May and Al took them to the graves on Memorial Day in the car.

When Cynthia was twelve, Grandma died. Now she and Grandpa were side by side in the G.A.R. Plot with the headstone between them. After putting flowers on their own, Mama, Papa, and Cynthia would get back into the car and go to the colored section of the grave of The Three Sisters.

Cynthia knew that her father had had a terrible time getting the headstone for his father's grave. Grandpa had died when she was four.

The government didn't send the stone, which was supposed to be free to Civil War veterans, until after Grandma had died. She remembered Papa writing letter after letter and sending photocopies of Amos's military records and the death certificate. Why had it taken so long? Was it because of the Depression or because he had been a Negro?

There had been a similar problem she'd heard Papa tell when Amos was still alive and had applied for a disability pension for his war injury. Al had to take over writing the letters and getting copies of the necessary papers. Again, after Amos died, there had been maddening bureaucratic complications in getting Annie's widow's pension. Was it just red tape or something else?

The family had to pay for the stone, when it finally came, to be delivered to the stone cutter for the dates of Amos's birth and death to be carved into the white marble and for it to be delivered to the grave site. This made May very angry, Cynthia remembered. Mama said the least the government could do for a veteran was to take care of the whole thing and not leave it up to the family, especially in these hard times.

After it was all done, they made a special trip to see it, surrounded by similar stones lined row on row on the side of a hill that was surmounted by an old cannon and a flagpole at Mount Hope Cemetery.

The family always attracted stares when they went to the grave of The Three Sisters. It was obvious that the colored people were wondering what white people were doing in their area. They paid no attention, going about the business of getting water, placing the flowers next to the stone, and leaving.

"That's done for this year," Mama would say as they drove off.

Usually, someone had been before them at both graves, leaving homegrown flowers. It had gone on for years, then stopped. They concluded that the person who'd cared enough to remember friends had probably died without them ever knowing who it had been.

In time, the family got a lot of mileage out of the family plot. It had been May's wish to be cremated and Al opted for that too, so as their times came, their ashes were also buried with Amos and Annie in the same grave. Was it just retribution that May, who had not gotten along with her husband's mother and who had done her best to put her out of her life, ended up sharing a grave with her for all eternity, or was it just one of those little ironies of life?

CHAPTER TEN

When the war ended, Al wanted to make the Navy his career, but his mother made her move again. She wrote letters to Naval authorities requesting that he be released immediately because he was needed at home. It was the major disappointment in his life. He told Cynthia's husband years later that he had been recommended for Warrant Officer, which would have been a real feather in his cap, perhaps leading to more advancements in the future.

However, his parents were old, his mother sixty-two, his father seventy-two and incapacitated; they needed him.

The title company had held his position open for him, so he went back to work for them. After thirty years of service, the company gave their loyal and respected employee a luncheon and an engraved Tavannes watch. At forty years of service, they gave him a handsome battery-operated clock and brought him up to date with Social Security, paying all the back deductions which had not been taken from his salary because the program wasn't in effect at the time he'd started with them.

May was very disappointed; she had hoped for a banquet. She

didn't understand what a wonderful thing the company had done for Al. Because she died so young, she never saw any of the benefits which, with his pension included, would have given them a decent income in their old age... a regret he spoke of often.

Al had met May on a liberty in Glasgow. He was walking down a street alone when he spotted a shipmate coming toward him with a Scottish lassie on each arm. They stopped to chat, and he was introduced. When they moved on, he stood watching them go and noticed that May had trim ankles.

"At the same instant," he told Cynthia, who thought it was very romantic. "A little bell rang in my head, and I heard a voice say, 'there goes the future Mrs. Hudgins'."

When he got back to the ship, he asked which of the two girls his friend was interested in, hoping it wasn't May. It was the other girl, so he asked for May's address, wrote to her, and she answered. They corresponded for two years, exchanging photographs and learning about each other. He wrote to and received letters from her father, Angus, as well, telling them about his ancestry, but since there was no racial prejudice in Great Britain then, they weren't concerned.

He asked her to marry him and wrote to Angus requesting her hand. Angus was agreeable; she accepted, and Al began saving the money for her to come to the U.S. He was making very good money for the time; real estate was booming in San Diego in the pre-twenties, so it didn't take long. He sent the money, arrangements were made for her passage, the date was set, and he contracted Travelers Aid in New York to meet her and see that she got safely to Kansas City, where they would be married. With legendary Scottish frugality, her father put her aboard the ship and sent a one-word cable.

"Sailed," it said. Signed Angus.

It must have been very difficult for Angus to let his youngest daughter leave to cross the ocean and a continent, uncertain if he'd ever see her again. They wrote to each other religiously, but May kept no letters from her father or sister, nor had she kept any of Al's letters.

May wrote to her sister when she learned she had cancer, but she told no one else. Cynthia's cousin, Jean, told her that when the letter came, her mother cried, but didn't tell her why. Well, it had been said that the Scots are taciturn, so May and her family certainly lived up to that reputation.

Poor May was deathly seasick the entire trip, never even getting out of her bunk. She arrived at Ellis Island and was met by the aide who took her to a hotel and the next day went with her on the train to Kansas City. Al met them and they went immediately to a church to be married, with the aide and a passerby called in from the street by the minister as witnesses.

May told her, after Cynthia was grown, that when she stepped off the ship, she was so scared that she would have turned around and gotten right back on it to go home, but she was still so sick she couldn't bear the thought, even if it had been possible.

Their wedding night was spent in a hotel, and they left by train the next day for California and her new home.

After May's death, a friend told Cynthia that on her mother's first time out alone on the street in Coronado she was accosted by strangers who wanted to know why a nice white girl like herself had married into that family of niggers. May was shocked. There may have been harassing phone calls, too, because after they'd moved into a place of their own, May refused to have a telephone in the house.

May was just twenty-one years old, alone in a strange country, undoubtedly homesick, married to a man she knew only through letters. She withdrew into herself, making only a handful of friends in her entire life in this country. Shortly after Cynthia was born, she went to work at a department store, leaving the baby with her mother-in-law and didn't take her back even when she quit work for years, until Annie's death, when Cynthia was twelve.

Cynthia asked her father about it after May's death because she'd always felt so left out of their lives. He told her that when May quit work, after Amos died, they'd asked for her, but Grandma had cried and begged to keep her because she would be left all alone. This may have been partly the reason, but as Cynthia remembered her life, she felt that this was not the whole truth. She'd sensed that her mother didn't really want her.

Cynthia had wanted, desperately needed, someone to love her, someone to hug her, someone to pat her, someone to say, "There, there. Everything's going to be all right."

No one ever hugged her, not Grandma, not Mama, not Papa, not Vera… they didn't hug each other until they were middle-aged… not even Ted. There was something inside her that wouldn't allow her to admit that she needed to be told and shown that she was loved.

After Cynthia married and Tee Gee was born, she and May began to be friends. Their relationship changed; they could talk as two women, not mother to daughter. But before they had a chance to open up and reconcile the past, May died. She was only forty-nine years old.

May had made a bargain and for good, bad, or indifferent, she had stayed with it. She and Al had stayed married until death had parted them. They'd been together twenty-eight years. Cynthia was twenty-seven when her mother died.

So when the call from the Historical Society came, Cynthia's first thought had been for her mother, who had tried to break the tie to her husband's family and apparently thought she'd been successful. Cynthia was thrown back into a sea of old feelings of being different, of shame, and fear for her own family's welfare… especially her son, Tee Gee.

WHEN CYNTHIA WAS A LITTLE GIRL, hanging around with Papa, there had been a steamer trunk with a rounded top in the garage. Papa's assignments from high school mechanical drawing class and the materials from his Civil Engineering course were in it, with a few other items she could no longer remember. It had disappeared when they moved into their second house, built after Grandma's death, when Cynthia came to live with her parents at long last.

"Whatever happened to that old trunk in the garage on "J" and your drawings?" Cynthia asked Papa when she came home from Guam, and they reminisced about May.

He told Cynthia that the trunk was May's and she'd gotten rid of it when they'd moved. She'd brought it with her from Scotland. When she'd opened it up in the hotel room, he'd been surprised to see it nearly empty.

"Didn't you wonder about it? Did you ask her?" Cynthia wanted to know more, but Al said he hadn't wanted to pry. So they wondered if that had been all she'd had or if she'd given her things away, to her sister perhaps, thinking she was coming to America to marry a rich man. Of course, he was, by their standards, but perhaps not as well off as she may have anticipated. Or maybe it had been all she'd had... a few changes of underwear, a couple of nightgowns, two or three shirtwaists, and skirts, barely covering the bottom of the trunk. Maybe she'd bought the trunk just so she'd look like other travelers. May had been proud and she'd always cared about what other people might think.

She had often talked about returning home to see her father, but first, there was the Depression, then came WWII. Angus died during the war. She had her sister, a niece slightly older than Cynthia, and a brother with a son still in Glasgow, but after Angus died, she never spoke of going home again. She and her father had written regularly, as did her sister, but May never shared the letters with Al or Cynthia.

May never spoke much about her family, except her mother, so Cynthia didn't feel she knew her mother's relatives. Her grandpa had sent her a teddy bear when she was very young, and for birthdays and Christmas, he sent books with pictures of children and animals. Later, story books which Cynthia had loved. May had thrown them all out when she cleared out her husband's mother's house.

Years later, after both the aunt she had never known and Papa had died, her cousin came to the States for a visit. She told Cynthia that she looked just like her mother and Cynthia told her in return that she resembled May, which was true. It was surprising to them both. For the first time, Cynthia felt a continuity with her mother's side of her family.

Her cousin also told her about Mama from her point of view. May had put up a front of being well-to-do in her letters to them, regularly sending money and gift packages. Cynthia knew that; she'd seen the boxes sitting on the dining room table as May gradually filled them for the next mailing. There have been things in them that Cynthia would have liked to have but May told her they weren't for her; they were for her family. Cynthia was jealous when she saw a photograph of Mama's niece standing with a much nicer doll buggy than hers, with her long hair fanned out over the fur collar of a coat. She'd wondered then if Mama liked her cousin better than she did her. She told Grandma about the fur collar, so Annie bought some wool, made a coat, and put a piece of bunny rabbit fur on the collar for her.

She'd been a little surprised when her cousin told her some things about Mama that she hadn't known, but afterward, she thought she shouldn't really have been. Putting up a front to be like others had been a large part of May's persona, as was pride. Or maybe May hadn't wanted her family to know things hadn't been quite what she had hoped for in her new life.

After her initial shock at discovering that she'd left her native land to marry an American, which had probably seemed like an exciting, glamorous, romantic adventure, only to run into unexpected racial prejudice, May had become even more reticent and shy. She didn't make friends easily, and she became suspicious of people. All this Cynthia began to comprehend after her mother's death when her mother's best friend told her about it.

When she and Papa had their late conversations about her, they began to see that neither of them had ever really known her. May had been an enigma to them both and perhaps, had always put her relatives in Scotland above her husband and child, considering the ones she'd left behind as her real family.

As Cynthia wrote that last sentence, she thought, "What did Mama think she was to us, or us to her? She'd categorized us as 'You Americans' when she was annoyed with us. Did she never consider Papa and me her family, and herself as a part of it? It used to hurt my feelings when she said that; did it hurt Papa's, too?"

Al, trying to help, had introduced his new wife to some of the wives of the men he worked with. They'd gone shopping together and to the beach, but she didn't become real friends with any of them until after they'd attended a few company picnics together and made dinner engagements with each other's families.

A friend of Annie's introduced May to a Canadian lady who became her only really close friend, a friendship lasting until the day May died.

Al, who belonged to the American Legion, tried to get May involved with the Ladies Auxiliary, but that turned out to be a real disaster. The ladies were planning a fundraising tea at one of the big houses along the oceanfront which had been offered for the occasion. May volunteered to bake a cake. When she went to the house to deliver it, she was met at the front door by a butler who directed her to a side entrance. May, unfamiliar with how these things were arranged, not knowing that this was customary, was highly insulted. Her Scottish pride took offense at being sent to a side door like a servant. Or did she think it was because of her husband's family? To her, it was a rebuff. She did as she was told, delivered the cake and left. She did not attend the tea, nor did she ever go to any of the Auxiliary meetings again.

In later years, when she'd become acquainted with other ladies and neighbors, she had card parties and little luncheons for friends' birthdays or their visiting relatives, then notified the local paper to have them written up on the society page. She carefully cut the items out and pasted them into her scrapbook.

May told Cynthia little about her life in Scotland. Her mother had been a hard woman. She'd expected her two daughters to do much of the work at home. She earned extra money by laying out the dead, and May, in her early teens, was taken along to help. It must have been horrible for the young girl.

May's mother had favored her boy over her daughters. She'd left a pot on the stove when he was very small, with the handle sticking out, and he'd pulled it over, scalding himself and scarring his face. Undoubtedly, it was guilt for this that made her put him above her girls, but they'd been hurt by it. There'd been no closeness between them and their brother as a result. In May's entire life, she received only two letters from him, one when his second child was born and the second when the child died.

In her teens, May, who'd been taking sole care of their mother who was dying of cancer, left after her mother's death to work elsewhere as a live-in mother's helper. May's older sister had married and had a child before the war. Her husband went off to war, came back, and was killed crossing the street a short time afterward. She moved back to keep house for their father.

The entire family May worked for came down with the flu in the 1918 epidemic. Young May took care of them and did not get it herself, nor did any of them die. Then, to help the war effort, she left them and went to work as a streetcar conductor to free a man for the front. It was while she was doing this that she had met her husband-to-be.

She was seventeen; Al was twenty-six, handsome and dashing in his Chief's uniform.

Had she been excited to get a letter from him? She was at an age when romance holds sway in a young girl's heart, and he was an American. Most Europeans thought America was a rich country. Was that what prompted her to answer his letter and decide to marry him when he proposed? She hadn't had an easy life; the family was poor. Her father was a railroad switchman, a steady job, but not highly paid. Had visions of sugar plums danced in her head? Had she been disappointed and had she kept her disappointment to herself?

Cynthia never saw her parents hug or kiss each other, but she didn't live with them until she was twelve. She never heard them fight or argue either. Mama got angry sometimes for what seemed to Al and Cynthia, no apparent reason. She'd leave, slamming the door, and going for a walk or watering the yard. When she came back, she'd be cool for the rest of the evening and if it was more serious, maybe for several days.

Al went to work and came home, ate dinner, then went out to his garage to work on his radios. May cooked and cleaned, washed and ironed, and did the shopping. She kept a tidy house, was a fair cook, and she sang around the house. If she wasn't happy, was she at least content? Cynthia wondered about that.

"I'm still wondering," she told herself. "Vera told me to write about Papa, but Mama seems to be taking over in this story."

May hadn't been a pack rat as Al and Cynthia were. Her house never had an extraneous item in it... no collections, no knick-knacks, nothing that wasn't useful. Magazines and newspapers were disposed of as soon as they were read. The only items left from her life on this earth after her death were her scrapbook, her piano music, her birth certificate, her passport, and the one-word cable sent by her father.

Al had pasted it in his wartime log. Previously he'd made an entry in the log on the day he met May. The other entries were the birth of Cynthia, the deaths of his parents, the death of Angus, Tee Gee's birth, and his final entry... May's death. After that, nothing. Until Cynthia posted his own death in the log twenty-five years later.

May had lived and died leaving little to mark her time and presence on this earth except for memories and questions for her American family.

CHAPTER ELEVEN

All throughout Cynthia's life, the fact that her grandfather, father, and husband had gone to fight for their country in times of war had been a source of great pride to her. Actually, all the men in her family were patriots... Amos, who had been in three wars; Papa, who had been in one; Ted, who had been in the Marines when she first met him and had been in the South Pacific, Korea, and retired after twenty years of service; Tee Gee, who'd done four years in the Air Force, and May-May's husband, who was in the Coast Guard. There were no chickens or draft dodgers in her family for her to be ashamed of.

She was proud of her grandparents who, in spite of their beginnings, had made something of themselves. They had been hard workers, owned their own homes, and had not been too proud to do what was needed to keep the family together or to do it without any help from others. God knows what indignities they may have suffered in their lives or what their ancestors had experienced, but they blamed no one and harbored no ill feelings. Well, her father had, in that one instance, but he hadn't belabored the subject.

Cynthia had never, in her life with her grandmother, heard

Grandma or her colored friends run down white people in any way. Often in her life, both as a child and as an adult, she had heard whites say terrible things about Negroes... dirty, smelly, stupid, lazy, liars, thieves... and she had sat there, one of those whom they were discussing, hiding behind a white facade, saying nothing. She was none of those things, neither had her grandparents been, their friends or her father. She would be squirming uncomfortably inside herself for listening and not speaking out.

"I'm a coward," she told herself. "A grown woman afraid to open her mouth in her own or another's defense, for fear of the consequences to my family and, let's face it, to myself."

When Cynthia heard the young people who call themselves Blacks complaining because of discrimination or never having had a chance, looking for something to blame their failings on besides themselves and using society as a scapegoat, she thought, "What nonsense. That's just an excuse. Where is the Black pride they talk so much about? Why do they drop out of school and blame society when they can't find a job when it's nobody's fault but their own that they have no education or training, can't read or write, or even speak good English?"

Cynthia's mother had come to this country with a Scottish accent. She set right about to change it. There were a few words that gave her away and Cynthia always thought she didn't correct them on purpose because she was proud of her Scottish ancestry. She also gave up drinking tea, switching to coffee. And she joined her husband's church. If she was going to live in America, she was going to become an American. She knew more about American history than most Americans do.

As Cynthia was growing up and learning things about her country in school, she was constantly surprised to find that May already knew about them and more.

May often said, "When in Rome, do as the Romans do," and "If we went into other countries, they wouldn't change their ways for us. It would be up to us to make the change."

Here in this country today, we cater to other nationalities who come here. It wasn't done when Cynthia was going to school. The Japanese and Mexican children in her classes were taught English and they spoke English. If any allowances had been made for them, she had never noticed. Their own languages were spoken at home, she knew that, so by the third grade they were all bilingual. The Japanese children also went to Japanese school on Saturday to learn their parents' language and their traditions. Cynthia had a Japanese friend in Junior High, so she knew this to be true and she admired Fusa and the other Japanese children in her class for it.

Papa said, "We tend to think foreigners are stupid, but most of them speak two languages, their own and ours, which is more than many of us can do."

Fusa offered to teach Cynthia Japanese. Papa thought that would be a wonderful thing, but for Cynthia, it was more than she could handle. Every letter, it seemed, had a different meaning depending on the way it was pronounced. The lessons lasted only a few days, but Cynthia did learn to count to five in Japanese and a couple of words referring to body parts that weren't very nice.

Neither of Fusa's parents spoke English very well, but the children did. There was a little brother and an older one who was in college. Everyone was friendly and nice to Cynthia, especially Fusa's mother, who invited her to dinner when they were having a dish that was similar to the chow mien served in Chinese restaurants after she learned Cynthia loved it. It was much the same, with bits of meat, bean sprouts, other vegetables, and rice. Cynthia learned to like salty little tidbits of seaweed and sweet, crisp, flat, flower-shaped rice cakes. Fusa showed her that a few grains of rice could be mashed and used for paste and how to fold little purses out of paper. They did their homework together on the big dining table in Fusa's house. The dining nook at Cynthia's was too small. They drew paper dolls and their dresses and walked to and from school together almost every day. They drifted apart when Cynthia moved from the neighborhood and her relationship with Vera grew closer, but they were still friends.

After Pearl Harbor, when Mama told her that Fusa's family had been taken away to detention camps for the duration, Cynthia was horrified.

"Why? What for?"

"Well, they are Japanese, and it was the Japanese who bombed Pearl Harbor."

"But not Fusa or her family."

Papa jumped into the conversation. "We can't trust them. We don't know where their loyalties are."

Cynthia didn't get to argue the point. Papa would just get angry, and besides, she knew in her heart that her parents were wrong.

Fifteen years later, she saw Fusa again. She'd always wondered what had become of her. On an impulse, she looked in the phone book one day for the family name and it was there. She called. When the phone was picked up, she asked if the family had ever lived in Coronado. The answer was yes, so she asked if it was Fusa's family.

The voice said, "This is Fusa."

Cynthia was thrilled and delighted. She told Fusa who she was and asked how she was and if she had come back to live in San Diego after the war. She said she hadn't; she was only on a visit. Cynthia's call had been serendipitous. Fusa was leaving for home the next day.

The family had been sent to a camp in Chicago where she'd met her husband and they'd settled there. Her parents, who were both very old, were still alive and lived in San Diego with her grown-up little brother.

Vera was supposed to come over that day, so Cynthia called her and stopped to pick up Fusa on the way. They lunched together, catching up on all that had happened to them in the years gone by. Fusa had a daughter. Her brother had gone into the U.S. Army and been sent to Europe and was now a teacher.

They looked at Cynthia's annuals and her photograph album which had a picture of the three of them on their graduation day from Junior High with their arms around each other. They posed for another one just like it. It was a wonderful day.

Fusa died a short time before their 50th High School reunion. All but one of the Japanese students who had been in classes with Cynthia since grade school had died while they were fairly young. Cynthia wondered about that. Could the stresses they'd been exposed to during the war have been a contributing factor?

CHAPTER TWELVE

Al and May were married on October 9th, 1920. It was Amos's seventy-sixth birthday and four days after May's twenty-first. Cynthia was born ten months later, on the eighteenth of August, in the back bedroom of the house which later became 'the big house' to her when she and her grandparents moved into the remodeled tiny little radio shack sometime before she was three.

Cynthia was weaned early from the breast to the bottle and her mother went to work at a department store in San Diego as a sales-clerk. Shortly after that, Al and May rented a house between Third and Fourth on J, about as far as one could get from between Eighth and Ninth on B in Coronado, unless one were wealthy enough to purchase a home on Alameda or Glorietta Boulevard or the ocean front. They rented with an option to buy, which they did.

The little house on the twenty-five-foot lot cost $2,000 in 1923. It had one bedroom, a small living room, and an even smaller dining nook, just big enough to hold a round drop-leaf table and four chairs from a set of six.

When company came, a library table in the living room with a leaf was used and the other two chairs came out from their places, one beside the piano in the living room and one from a corner of the bedroom. The house had a small bathroom, an equally small kitchen, and a large back porch with a lot of windows called a sunroom. All it had in it, however, before Cynthia went to live with them, was a chest of drawers, a refrigerator, and a washing machine, which were the newest thing in appliances at the time. May had a passion for buying the latest thing. She wasn't going to keep up with the Joneses; they could keep up with her.

Cynthia grew up in her grandparents' house, feeling left out of her parents' lives and wondering while still small why she was singled out for so much unwanted attention when she was with her grandma and, when older, by herself. No one paid attention to her when she was with her mother, but her mother didn't take her along often in Coronado. They would go to San Diego for dental appointments, to buy new shoes, or to go to the movies, but after Cynthia was old enough to go to the beach by herself, May didn't want to be seen with her in the summer. Cynthia would spend the whole day at the beach and get very tan.

Once she asked when May was getting ready to go out, "Can't I go with you, Mama May?"

"No," May replied. "You let yourself get too dark and I don't like being seen with you."

Cynthia was disappointed but said nothing.

Even when she was very young, Cynthia sensed that there was a coolness between her mother and grandmother. It was in the tone of their voices when one spoke of the other to her.

One Sunday, Cynthia told her mother something she had heard Grandma say to Grandpa about her. May was very angry. Papa was angry too; he scolded Cynthia for telling Mama something Grandma should not have said.

"Little girls shouldn't repeat things that people say about other people," he told her.

When he took her back to Grandma's that evening, he scolded his mother too. One good thing that came of it was Cynthia learned very young not to carry tales and the lesson stayed with her all her life.

Another visiting Sunday, to get her mother's attention, she called her by her first name. May looked shocked. Al did too. He took Cynthia aside.

"Little girls don't call their mothers by their first names," he said.

"Why can't I? Grandma does, Grandpa does, and you do too."

"Because she's your mother, that's why, and it just isn't done."

Cynthia considered. May was her mother, she knew that, but... "Alright," she said. "Then I will call her Mama May."

Her parents looked at each other.

"Is that all right with you?" Al asked May.

She thought for a moment, then nodded her head. So Cynthia called her mother 'Mama May' from the time she was four until she was twelve. Then she dropped the May.

"To this day," she thought to herself, "I don't know why I was reluctant to call my mother Mama when I was little. I dropped the May when I was twelve because other kids thought it was babyish."

She'd always called her father Papa. From the beginning, May called him Papa to her. It was the European way. So, "Papa" it was until the day he died. Vera called him Papa; all Cynthia's other friends down the years called him Papa, too.

After he died, Vera told Cynthia that she had loved to come to their house for dinner when she was little because Papa had always been so much fun at the dinner table. He was, but Cynthia knew Mama didn't really approve of it. Vera told Cynthia that she had loved Papa too because he had been like the father she had never known. Cynthia was deeply touched to know that. If it had been anyone else, she would have been jealous, because Papa was hers and hers alone. But not Vera; never would she have been jealous of Vera.

Once, after she had gone to live with her parents, Cynthia did or said something that made Mama flare up. Papa came in at the end of it and asked what it had been about.

"Oh, 'she' said or did something," Cynthia told him angrily. (Whatever it had been, she could no longer remember).

"You don't refer to your mother as 'she,'" he said. "She's your mother and you will respect her no matter what she says or does."

"Alright," she said, sulkily. She was going into her teens, a time when children start asserting themselves. She wondered now if she and Mama might have gotten along better if she'd lived with them in her earlier years... maybe not. Not if Mama hadn't wanted her. There was a coolness between them that was never really reconciled.

Papa's pet name for Cynthia had been Thum, and sometimes Thummy because she'd sucked her thumb until she started school. He held her up at parades so she could see, read the funnies to her on Sunday, and the words on the screen at the silent movies. He sharpened her drawing pencils for her with the pocketknife he always carried in his pocket. She loved to watch him do it, turning it just so, making neat scallops, and handing it back to her with a perfect point. He made kits for her with newspaper and thin sticks. He called her to the garage when he needed someone to hand him a tool or help with other little things as he puttered with the car or his radios. Once, he told her that if she wasn't around and he needed her, all he had to do was think about her and pretty soon she'd show up.

He'd had a way of thumping her on the head with just two fingers. He did it hard, but somehow, she knew it was his way of telling her he loved her, although he never said it in so many words, not once in his entire life. After he died, Cynthia asked her daughter, May-May, if, when Grandpa had thumped her on the head, she'd known that he was telling her he loved her.

May-May nodded, "Yes."

Mama never told Cynthia she loved her. She'd had no pet name for her. It was Cynthia or, if she was angry, her whole name, Cynthia Ann... the tone of her voice telling Cynthia just how annoyed or angry she was. Mama also had a 'look' she used when company was present or they were out visiting. Cynthia, on the receiving end of 'the look,' knew that she was going to get a lecture later on her behavior and maybe the cool treatment for a while. Of the two, the cool treatment was the worst. Sometimes she got it without knowing what it was she had done to pique Mama. It could last from a day or two up to a week. May closed into herself and did not communicate. She'd answer questions curtly, saying only what was necessary.

Cynthia thought to herself, "I think she used the treatment on Papa, too, because sometimes we both seemed to be on the receiving end at the same time."

There was nothing overt in May's manner toward her daughter, but she never hugged the child, pulled her to her, or kissed her. When Cynthia would kiss her mother goodbye before she left to go back to Grandma's, or if she was leaving on a date when she was older, May would lean away and turn her cheek for the kiss.

Besides singing around the house, May played the piano. Not well, but Cynthia didn't know that until she was older and took piano lessons herself. She thought Mama and Papa did everything well. She loved hearing Mama sing and Papa whistle.

"What's that, Papa?"

He'd say it was from one of the shows that came to San Diego he'd gone to see as a young man. He'd sing the words, tell her the plot and what had been done during the *entr'actes*. He had total recall and loved music.

When Cynthia was in her forties, she bought an electric organ, took lessons, and went to some night school classes. She never learned to play as well as she would have liked, but she credited her parents for her love of music and what little talent she had.

They had taken her to the movies when the great Wurlitzer organs had come up from the pit, filling the theatre with the rumblings and tootings of their magnificent sounds. She'd asked for piano lessons but grew to hate them, seldom practicing if she could manage not to. It was the organ she loved, and when she got one, it was a dream come true.

In her room at her Grandma's were Papa's Victrola and all his records and books. She spent hours on cold or rainy days reading his books and playing the records. He had opera stars, Alma Glück, Caruso, classical music, and songs from the operettas of Victor Herbert and Rudolph Friml. There were Strauss waltzes, Sousa's marches, tangos, fox trots and two-steps, and the popular songs of the early 1900s, "My Merry Oldsmobile," "A Bicycle Built for Two," "Get out and Get Under"... so many she could no longer remember them all. All had disappeared when her grandmother died, and May had cleaned out her house.

Her mother's repertoire, which was extensive too, had included Scottish and Irish songs, WWI songs, songs by Stephen Foster, patriotic songs, and Mexican songs: "La Paloma," "Juanita," "Marcheta," "Ramona," "Estrillita," "La Golondrina." She was also as fond of as many light classics as Al was.

May was very partial to movie musicals, and after she'd been to one, the next time she went shopping she'd go to the dime store and buy the sheet music from the last one she'd seen. Cynthia still had it all. Mama often sang.

"Oh, my pretty quadroon,
My flower that faded too soon,
My heart's like the strings on my banjo,
All broke for my pretty quadroon."

It must have been an old song because Cynthia had never heard it before or since.

Why had Mama sung that particular song? Had it been for her? As near as Cynthia could figure, not being good with fractions and not knowing anything for certain about Grandpa and Grandma's backgrounds, Papa likely had been an eighth, an octoroon, and she, Cynthia was probably a sixteenth, her children, thirty-seconds and her grandkids, sixty-fourths. The black drop was getting smaller, not that it mattered to anyone but herself.

In Coronado, as far as most everyone was concerned, she'd been a nigger and still would be to a racist, white skin or not. It still rankles after all these years.

CHAPTER THIRTEEN

After Cynthia's parents moved from the family home, Annie and Amos's exchequer took a downward turn. Al was now a married man with a wife and child. They were buying their first home, so May was working, first for the department store and later for a dentist friend of Al's from the radio club.

Annie, wanting to increase their income, made the decision to mortgage the front house and make the one-room radio shack larger, adding two bedrooms and a bath, for herself, Amos, and the child. She discussed it with Al, who was less than enthusiastic. He tried to discourage her, but Annie was a woman with the courage of her own convictions. Against his wishes, she made the arrangements, and it was done. Later events would prove that Al's instincts were right; her decision had been a great mistake.

For about five years all went well. The furnished house never sat vacant for very long before a new tenant moved in. Some of the tenants didn't mind if Cynthia came into their side of the yard, which was separated from the house in the back by a lathe fence with a gate. A boardwalk went from the front door to the back house through both yards, down the side of the front house and on out to the sidewalk in front of the lot, which Annie retained the right to use whenever she wanted to go directly to the sidewalk in front and not down the alley.

Other renters didn't want Cynthia on their side of the fence, and she had trouble with this. She knew the house belonged to her Grandma and Grandpa and that she had lived in it when she was younger. She thought it belonged to her, too, so why couldn't she go into the other yard?

After being chased out a few times, since she was an obedient child most of the time, she did what she was told. She did throw tantrums sometimes when she wasn't allowed to have her own way. If Grandma wouldn't buy her a balloon or an ice cream sandwich when they were going by the dime store, she'd throw herself down on the sidewalk, kicking and screaming until poor Annie, to avoid any more of a scene, gave in. A mistake Cynthia made sure never to make with her own children.

Cynthia's big palm tree was in front of the lot. She spent many pleasant hours under it with her picture books, coloring books, and crayons, watching the world go by. She ate the dates that fell on the ground and, if she was really hungry, asked Grandma to fix her a piece of bread with butter and brown sugar on it or some of her homemade satsuma plum preserves, fig jam, or loquat jelly.

Some of the tenants stayed just a short while, for the summer months. Others came only for the warm winters, so she adjusted to the arrangement and played in the vacant lot next door when the front yard was forbidden to her. When the wild oats were high, she'd stamp out a circle in them and lie in the middle of it. All she could see was the sky and no one could see her. She'd stare at the sky, losing herself in the ecstasy of her golden feeling, watch the clouds making pictures, chew on sour grass, and observe the insects living there in their own private world, like she was doing, too.

Another girl the same age lived across the alley, one house down, who had cousins that came over to play with her. Occasionally they let Cynthia play with them until they decided to go into the house.

Cynthia trailed along hopefully, but as the mother held the door open for them, she'd say, "I'm sorry Cynthia. I can't let you come inside. You'll have to go on home now."

Disappointed, she'd trudge on back to Grandma's or to her vacant lot. Marian's mother was friendly with Grandma; they often stood in the alley together talking. She was nice to Cynthia, speaking kindly and seeming sorry, but she never let the child come into her home. Not ever, except when Cynthia took small May-May, age five or six, for a visit to show her off thirty years later and was welcomed.

She spent a lot of time sitting on the floor by Grandma's sewing machine, quietly playing with a doll or coloring, more often asking questions. It was in this way she learned what little she knew about her grandmother's early life and her father's birth. When Annie got tired of answering her or needed to concentrate, she'd send her outside to play.

She made mud pies, chased butterflies, followed bees from flower to flower, watched the red ants as they busily streamed in and out of their hills in the dirt, plucked strawberries from the garden, or climbed into the loquat tree, where she could sit and eat the fruit in season. She was happy enough but very lonely.

Sometimes she took the saltshaker and tried to sneak up on the little sparrows. It was said that if you put salt on their tails, you could catch one. It would be fun to have a bird for a friend. She was so lonely much of the time, always wishing she had someone to play with like Marian did.

Once tenants moved in with a baby and a nanny. When the baby was sleeping or if the family was away, the nanny would come out to sit on the back porch. She was very nice to Cynthia, calling her over to talk. On Cynthia's fourth birthday, the nanny gave her a baby doll with a cloth body and a composition head. It said "ma-ma" when it was turned forward and back. Cynthia was thrilled! She'd liked the nanny; now she loved her for giving her the doll. When the family moved away, she never saw the nice woman again, but she named the doll Nanny.

Another time, a couple with a French maid moved in. The maid liked Cynthia, too. She was often alone, and the house wasn't large, so when her chores were done, she'd sometimes invite Cynthia to lunch with her. She taught her how to eat an asparagus spear, laying it across the fork and using a forefinger to daintily guide it into the mouth just so. That wasn't how Cynthia ate them, but she was fascinated by the elegance of it. She gave Cynthia strawberries with the stems on to dip in powdered sugar or with real cream poured over them. Once she offered crackers and black caviar. Cynthia didn't like it... too fishy and too salty. The maid told Cynthia if she would look for snails for her, she'd pay a nickel for twelve nice big ones.

"What do you want snails for?" asked Cynthia.

"I want to eat them," she said. "We eat them in France; they are very good. We call them *escargot.*"

Cynthia couldn't believe it. Eat those slimy things? Ugh!

"After I prepare them, I will give you a taste," she said.

Cynthia politely declined.

When she told Papa that the maid had wanted her to find snails so she could eat them, Papa laughed. He told her that when he'd been in Paris, he and a shipmate had gone to a sidewalk cafe and ordered snails because they had heard they were such a great delicacy. When they came, the two Americans sat looking at them wondering what to do next. A *mademoiselle* at the next table showed them how to take the special pick, spear the snail, dip it into the sauce, and pop it into the mouth. "*Voila!*"

So Al speared a snail, dipped it into the sauce and popped it into his mouth, "*Voila!*"

When he bit down on it, it was very tough and gristly, and it jumped over to the other side of his mouth. He chased it from side to side, then grimly swallowed it while making a face. The *mademoiselle* laughed merrily and asked him if he wanted the rest of them and he said, "no."

She indicated that she would like to have them, so both of the young men gladly gave theirs to her and watched as she ate them with great enjoyment.

"I didn't think they were the same kind of snails that we have here though," he told Cynthia.

The maid asked Cynthia to bring her mushrooms that grew so profusely in the side yard too. She showed her which ones to pick and which to avoid. Cynthia told Papa this too.

"You can't really tell about mushrooms unless you're an expert and the deadly Amanita, which can kill you, looks just like a good one," he told her. "If she offers you any of those you find for her, don't eat them."

So Cynthia didn't find out what mushrooms tasted like until she was grown, and she never found out how snails tasted at all, ever, and felt no great loss over it.

A family with several children rented the house on two separate occasions and Cynthia was allowed to come in and play. That was nice, but after the second stay, she never saw them again. Between them, a Navy officer and his wife moved in. They had been all over the world, the lady told Cynthia, and had collected seashells every place they went.

"Would you like to see them?"

Cynthia nodded, of course she would. They went inside and Cynthia was stunned. Lined along the walls of the living and dining rooms were glass front cases, just like in the Natural History Museum. On the shelves were seashells the likes of which she had never seen. And so many, too. She "oohed" and "aahed" while the lady told her all about them and the different places from which they had come. Then she asked if Cynthia would like to have some of them to start a collection of her own. Of course she did! So they went into the back bedroom where there were chests of shallow drawers with shells in them laid out on cotton. She took a box, put some cotton in it and began to pick out shells.

"Would you like one like this? This is a cowrie. On the island where it came from, they used to use them for money."

"Oh yes." Cynthia was fascinated.

She continued asking and putting shells in the box, telling their history to Cynthia, until the box was filled.

"Do you think you can remember all those names?" she asked.

"I don't think so," Cynthia said, shaking her head.

"Then would you like me to put their names on little slips of paper for you?" And she did.

Cynthia kept the shells until she was grown. They were one of the few things her mother hadn't thrown out. Over the years the slips of paper were lost, but she remembered most of the names and she gave the shells to May-May when she was old enough to appreciate them.

CHAPTER FOURTEEN

"This book is taking on a life of its own," Cynthia thought as she began what might be chapter fourteen or might not. She'd decided some of the earlier chapters should be switched around. Sometimes her memory got ahead of itself, and she had to go back to fill in what she had forgotten when it surfaced.

Thirteen chapters and so far she hadn't gotten into the meat of the matter, her own story, the main reason for the book.

As she wrote, her thoughts dipped into the distant past, then leaped ahead to the present... memories of her life from childhood to young adult, through wife and mother, to old age, and back again with little continuity.

The first decade had been awful... she hadn't understood things that happened, or how or why they related to her, or the reason for any of it. In the second, she'd had to face the reason and try to accept it; that had been the hardest of all. Why, why, why? Had been the central theme of her life. In her bed at night, lying in the dark, she had cried out in silent anguish night after night, "Why God? Why me?" God didn't answer and now, all these decades later, she wondered why she'd never asked her parents anything about herself.

"It must have been because they didn't ask me or tell me anything, so I thought they didn't want to talk about it, so I kept it all inside myself."

For the next forty years she had lived on a cusp with one foot in one life, and one in another. A juggling act, frank and open with some friends, cautious and closed with others; always consumed with fear of being found out and guilty for being afraid, feeling dishonest, disloyal, often paranoid, fearful of what disclosure would do to her kids.

Now, in her last decade, if she was going to live past three score and ten to complete it, she was more open but still careful. Old habits are hard to break. The television talk shows and the news told her that prejudice and hatred still reign in many peoples' hearts. She was testing the waters, one toe at a time. She could call herself Black with only a little flinching in some inner core. It was like the common four-letter word that begins with an 'f.' She'd never been able to say it and then it began to be said on cable TV and written in books. It has always shocked her to read it or hear it. She didn't use it herself, but she probably could now if she had to for some reason. When a barrier is lifted and something once taboo becomes commonplace, one becomes inured to it.

"Saying 'I'm Black' is not too much different now from saying 'fuck you'," she thought, then she erased that once forbidden four-letter word, put it back, erased it, laughed, and put it back again, thinking, "Maybe I'm not crazy anymore. Sane at last, sane at last, thank God, I'm sane at last... maybe. At least I can face the fact that I'm Black and am not ashamed of it anymore. I still hate the word and I may have that damned Black drop, but I'm white on the outside and that definitely has its advantages."

So this is the story of "Little Black Cynthia," who was too stupid to know she was Black and didn't want to be when she found out she was.

Thirteen chapters, the first Black History Month, the Historical Society with their plans for an exhibit, and the phone call that shook her up. Then the reason for their interest in her family, primarily her grandparents, which led to writing about them. Then, from the birth of her father and how he met her mother, to herself, descriptions of her parents and her relationships with them and of the town and the times she'd lived in.

"If this were a Victorian book," she thought. "About now, I would say, 'Gentle reader, I beg you to bear with me. I have digressed at length but am now going to impart to you what it was like to live on both sides of the fence in my life, from my point of view, both as a child and as a neurotic adult'."

As she worked on the book, her old enemy insomnia reappeared. She'd watch TV until she got sleepy, take herself gently off to bed, say her prayers, and lie there waiting for the blessed oblivion of slumber. Insidiously, thoughts began sneaking in... a word or two at first that should be changed to avoid repetition, a paragraph that would read better or be more explicit in its meaning. Something she'd left out would creep into her mind, grow into a page, and go on and on until it created another chapter. If she didn't get up and write it down, it would be gone in the morning. She was old and needed her sleep. She began having headaches in spite of her high blood pressure medication.

She'd be reading or watching the tube and something would trigger a memory.

"This must stop somewhere," she told herself. "I have pages and pages still to be typed, edited, and collated. I can't spend every waking moment on this book. It will never end, and I'll die before I get it all on paper. No, come to think of it, that one psychic years ago told me I'd live until I finished writing. But a psychic told Mrs. Winchester she'd live as long as she heard the sound of hammers, so she kept adding rooms to that famous old house with staircases going nowhere and doors that didn't open anything and she died anyway. You can push off the inevitable only just so long and comes the day of reckoning, no matter what. Me or the book. I wonder which will end first?"

CHAPTER FIFTEEN

Cynthia, before she started school, was always hanging around Grandma, asking questions. She had no one else to talk to and no one to play with. They went into the chicken yard to feed the chickens and gather eggs and into the garden to string a trellis for green beans, plant potato eyes, and seeds for beets, carrots, tomatoes, lettuce, green onions, and strawberries. Strawberries were tiny and sweet then, not like the big tasteless things in the stores today.

Around the edge of the vegetable garden were pansies, violets, freesias, and sweet alyssum. Cynthia loved the sweet little faces of the pansies and violets and the fragrant scent of the freesias. She got up early to look for spiderwebs sparkling with dew-like diamond-studded lace. Fairy rings of tiny toadstools like elfin umbrellas. Silvery snail tracks glistening on sidewalks. The air so fresh, so clean. Each morning was a new delight.

Grandma surely had what's called a green thumb! In a flower bed outside the back door were zinnias, snapdragons, star asters, African daisies, marigolds, bachelor buttons, larkspur, petunias, and Queen Ann's lace. Cynthia loved that name, and she loved the pastel colors and the scent of the sweet peas that climbed the lathe fence in the alley.

By the side of the garage that had been built for the tenants who had cars, grew asparagus fern, four o'clock, and a castor bean tree. The latter two were poisonous Papa told her. Morning glories, a bougainvillea, and a trumpet vine cascaded over the fence on one side from the yard next door. On Grandma's side, there was a honey-suckle and a Cecil Brunner rose. Cynthia loved the little pink rose-buds and made bouquets of them with fern for her dolls or to put in a jelly jar of water for the kitchen table. Farther along were hibiscus bushes in shades of red and pink. Geraniums would grow from pieces stuck into the ground. The tenants who came from the East Coast, where they were kept in pots and tended carefully like hothouse plants, went into ecstasies over them, taking cuttings back home when they left. There were nasturtiums all over and canna lilies clustered along the lathe fence on the other side of the property.

Cynthia hopped around when Grandma was weeding or watering.

"What's this, Grandma?" and the old lady would tell her, naming cinerarias, begonias, phlox, chrysanthemums, statice (dry and papery, also called everlasting flowers). Every house they visited had a bouquet of statice and people put them on the graves at the ceme-tery. Bright green smilax put out its tendrils in all directions. She knew all their names by the time she was five.

She was a curious child, asking questions about everything under the sun except herself.

"Maybe that was the reason why Grandma would send me off outside and Mama would tell me to go out to the garage and see Papa? Well, Grandma did tell me I was a pesky child," she remem-bered as she wrote about the garden.

"Grandma, why do they call four o'clocks four o'clocks?"

"Because they start closing up at four o'clock."

"They do? How do they know it's four o'clock?"

"They just do. Now run along and play. Can't you find something to occupy yourself besides asking me so many questions?"

Cynthia didn't know how to tell time herself yet, so she checked, running into the house to ask, "What time is it Grandma?" and going back outside to look. Sure enough, she saw that four o'clocks did indeed begin to close around four o'clock, just as the morning glories did, and they opened up again in the morning. She marveled that flowers knew what time it was and wondered how they could tell when they didn't have a clock.

Along the foundation of the front house grew shameless pink naked ladies on their tall leafless stalks. Lantana bushes made a divider between their yard and the vacant lot next door alongside the walkway of the front house. Everywhere, California poppies flourished, in yards and in the vacant lots with other wildflowers... Johnny jump-ups, Indian paintbrush, buttercups, and others whose names she never learned or has forgotten. She loved them all.

Alongside the front porch was a big hydrangea bush with blooms the size of a dinner plate. Alongside that was a whale vertebra that Amos found on the beach. It was like a little stool, just the right size for a small child to sit on. What happened to it? Had it been left there? She didn't know but wished they had kept it.

The air was busy with butterflies... yellow, white, black and yellow, orange and black, smaller ones that looked like Monarchs but weren't. Honeybees, bumble bees, dragonflies, moth-like millers, and grasshoppers proliferated. Overnight, tomato worms as big as a man's middle finger appeared from nowhere. She found out by poking one that they could bite. They didn't have teeth, but their mouths were hard and jagged. June bugs as big as the first joint of a man's thumb, dive-bombed, crickets chirped, filling the night with their song and swarms of moths fluttered around the street and porch lights. Things that looked like overgrown mosquitoes, that Grandpa had called gallinippers, flew around, sometimes landing on people, and of course, there were mosquitoes, too. In the summer Cynthia's legs were always covered with scabs from scratching bites.

All around the yard and the lawn were snails, sowbugs, quick spiders, earthworms, gophers, and gopher snakes. In the vacant lot were horned toads and ant lions… some people called them earth babies. They were very ugly. Occasionally a scorpion would get into the house, or a centipede. The grounds of the two houses seethed with life. In the trees and on telephone wires were blackbirds, mockingbirds, orioles, and sparrows. Hummingbirds came to the flowers in the beds and on the bushes by the dozens. Where are they now? Did we wake up to what Rachel Carson said too late? Cynthia hadn't seen a butterfly other than the common white or yellow ones, or a bumble bee, a dragonfly, or a grasshopper in their neighborhood for a long time and there are new birds, different birds, in the area now… doves, crows, blue jays, and Mexican parrots.

On her birthday, Annie would go into the garden and pick a bouquet. She'd put on her long black coat and hat, pick up her big black satchel and she and Cynthia would go visiting. Grandma had many white friends, as well as two colored ladies like herself who also lived in Coronado. Some white ladies asked them in, others invited them to sit on the front porch to visit. The bouquet was for whomever they were going to see that day unless they met a friend on the way. In that case, the flowers were a gift to them.

Annie would present them saying, "Today is my birthday and I would like for you to have these."

The recipient was always pleased, so Cynthia thought it was a nice thing her grandma did, especially on her own birthday. She couldn't remember anyone doing anything nice for Grandma on her birthday. No birthday cake, no candles, no one singing "Happy Birthday to You" like Mama always did for her. Once her mother had given Grandma a coat… had there been other presents? She didn't know. She did remember a time Grandma's friend, Mary Burney, had come from San Diego on Grandma's birthday with a small gift. They'd known each other for a long, long time, since before Papa was born. Had they come to California together? Had they known each other before that? There was so much she didn't know, wished she did and had no way to find out.

When did the chickens disappear? It was after she started school. She knew they hadn't eaten them all so Grandma must have sold them... the white leghorns and Rhode Island Reds. A new regulation said no livestock inside the city limits.

After Amos died, many other things changed. Grandma didn't seem to do or want to do as much as she had before.

After the chickens were gone, eggs came in a paper bag with the grocery order, half a dozen at a time. Grandma phoned in the morning, and it would be delivered later on. The bill was paid at the beginning of the month after the rent and the pension check came in. Sometimes, when Cynthia was older, Grandma sent her to the store for half a dozen eggs with orders to carry them very carefully. Even so, sometimes one or two would get broken; a six year old would forget to walk carefully and start skipping with the pure joy of being alive on a beautiful, sunny summer day.

After electricity was installed, there was no longer a need for cleaning and filling the lantern and trimming the wick. Grandma also got an electric iron. Had that been a gift from Mama and Papa? Perhaps.

Cynthia still got her baths in the washtub and the kitchen was still heated with the blue enameled coal oil stove, which is now in Cynthia and Ted's garage. She wondered if one could still buy fuel for it. So many things had changed in her lifetime and so many things had disappeared forever.

Grandma read the newspaper every day, very slowly, running her finger along the line of print, her lips moving as she whispered the words to herself. She read from her Bible every day too. It was always on a little table beside her rocking chair in the corner of the kitchen. She pushed her glasses up on top of her head when she finished reading, forgot what she'd done with them, and wandered around the house trying to find them.

"My glasses, my glasses. I can't find my glasses. Have you seen them, Cynthia?"

Cynthia had been watching, trying not to giggle. "They're in your hair, Grandma."

Both laughed as she reached up, found them and put them on. "I must be getting old," she'd say. Well, she was. She'd been sixty-seven when Cynthia was born. Losing Amos when she was seventy-one was a shock from which she did not recover. It was a while before anyone noticed, except Cynthia, and the changes were so gradual she adjusted to them, accepting them as normal. Children are adaptable.

Annie was a God-fearing Christian, friendly and kind to everyone. If she ever had been abused or treated with disrespect, she never said, and Cynthia never saw it happen. People had liked her grandmother. Men tipped their hats to her and asked, "How are you, Mrs. Hudgins?" Women stopped her on the street to ask about the family and to chat. Cynthia never heard anyone call Grandma by her first name, ever. She read when she was older that that was a mark of disrespect by whites toward people of color.

Madame Schumann-Heink, the famous opera singer of the day, when she was in residence between concert tours, often sat on the front veranda of her big house on the corner of Eighth and Orange. If Annie and Cynthia walked past the house and she was there, she'd hail them.

"Mrs. Hudgins, Mrs. Hudgins, wait!"

She was a big lady, no longer young, but she'd hoist herself up from her chair, walk down the steps and the front walk to join them and chat. Cynthia hopped around until she got bored and started pulling on Grandma's skirt.

"C'mon Grandma, let's go. C'mon."

The famous lady meant nothing to her, not until she was older.

Women lose their identity when they marry. They become somebody's wife or mother. They are called Mrs. So and So, or Mom, Grandma, Honey, Dear, Sweetie... maybe Dingbat by some, or the old ball and chain, which was jokingly used in those days. To their kids' friends, they are Tee Gee's Mom or your mother. Their friends call them by their first names or a nickname, but after their friends die, who are they? Who knew Grandma's name was Cynthia Ann besides her family, now that she was old? What had her mother called her, Annie, Cynthia, or a pet name? Papa called her "Mother." When Mama spoke about her to Cynthia, she called her Grandma too. Who had she been to Amos? In letters Cynthia had from her grandfather to her grandmother, he addressed her as "My dear wife" and once as "Old Lady." To Cynthia, her only other name was Mrs. Hudgins, the same as Mama. That was all Cynthia had ever heard her called by anyone.

Cynthia couldn't understand why people liked everyone in her family except her. When she was old enough to go around by herself alone, clerks wanted to know what she was doing in their stores. "Grandma sent me. She said to say she needs a spool of number 50 white mercerized cotton thread," or "I lost my skate key and I need another one. I have money, see?"

She wondered why people so often told her, "Cynthia, you don't belong here. Why don't you just go on home?"

She didn't understand why, in some stores, clerks followed her around watching her, or why grown-ups and teachers, after she started school, seemed to think she wasn't telling the truth when she was.

"If only someone had warned me," she mused. "Explained it to me or even questioned me. It would have saved me a lot of grief. It wouldn't have changed anything, but at least I'd have known the why of so many things that happened that bothered me and made me so unhappy. Did Grandma think Papa told me? Did Papa think that Grandma would? Did they think that because I looked white I wouldn't have any problems? Another thing I'll never know."

Because she'd kept everything to herself, her grandparents and parents had lived and died without ever knowing that her color and appearance hadn't protected her from prejudice and discrimination. In a big city, perhaps it might have, but not in a town as small as Coronado was then.

CHAPTER SIXTEEN

Like Mary's little lamb, everywhere that Grandma went, Cynthia was sure to go... uptown to pay the grocery and utility bills, visiting, across the bay to San Diego on the streetcar and the ferry to make the mortgage payment, shopping at Marston's or going to the cemetery until the day Grandma fell. Everywhere they went, people stared at them, the old colored lady and the little girl who looked white. All the old timers knew who they were and made certain that newcomers who didn't know wouldn't mistake them for nursemaid and charge. The newcomers were fascinated, staring with disbelief and whispering. Cynthia noticed all this interest even when she was very small. Grandma didn't seem to or paid no attention. Cynthia said nothing, asking no questions, but she wondered what it was that made people look at them.

One of the white neighbors they went to see lived on the same block, in a big two-story house. She had false teeth which she'd drop down on her tongue, move around and click back as Cynthia watched, fascinated and goggle-eyed in amazement. The lady had a grown daughter who looked old to Cynthia... all grown-ups look old to small children. The three women sat at the kitchen table and talked while Cynthia stood by Grandma, listening until she got bored, then wandering over to a parrot in a large cage nearby, she'd stand, coaxing him to talk. He knew a lot of words, but he was old and stubborn, speaking only when it suited him. Warned to keep her fingers away from the cage because he was a biter, and because he had a nasty-looking beak, she was very careful. She liked to visit this lady because sometimes she got a cookie and, when the strawberry guavas were in season, if she got too bored and fidgety, the lady let her go outside and eat some off the bushes in the backyard.

"Not too many now. We want to make jelly."

The daughter, who Cynthia thought was an old lady too, was a telephone operator. Cynthia didn't know the disembodied voice which answered when the receiver was lifted was someone she knew. She'd come in from kindergarten and, if Grandma wasn't there she'd panic, running terrified through the house looking and calling, then out into the yard. Coming back inside, she'd run to the phone, pick it up and say, "Hello?"

The voice answered, sounding annoyed, "Cynthia, what is it you want?"

"I came home, and Grandma's not here."

"She probably just stepped out for a minute, and she'll be back soon. Hang up now."

It knew her name, and sure enough, Grandma would come in shortly, having stopped on the street to speak to a neighbor or taken a minute to run out and get a spool of thread. The phone was a mysterious and magical thing to the insecure little girl. When she was older, she asked Grandma how the voice on the telephone knew her name. When she found out who it was, she was surprised.

The town was small, and not many people had telephones. When the receiver was picked up, a light on the switchboard lit up and the operator knew from its location which customer was on the line. It was still intriguing, but not really magic. After she started school Cynthia realized there wasn't really any magic except in fairy tales… not for her, anyway, and maybe not for anyone.

Down the street on the opposite corner lived another white lady. Her son, who had moved to another state, had been a friend of Cynthia's father when they were young. They had a common interest in radio, which drew them together. In the lady's kitchen was a marvelous wood stove. It usually had a fire in it, no matter what the weather, unless it was very hot outside. On days when it was too warm in the kitchen, the two old ladies would move into a nearby sun porch to visit, leaving Cynthia alone with the stove, which she never tired of looking at.

It was enormous, shiny black with gleaming metal trim. She walked from side to side, leaning down to look at the blazing fire through the windows in the doors, of which there were several. It was mesmerizing. She wished they had one like it, but Grandma's stove was only an ordinary gas stove. Not interesting at all.

Sometimes they went to see a lady the same color as Grandma, maybe not as old. She lived in a nice house with a front porch closed in with glass to let the sunshine in. She and Annie would go into the kitchen to talk while Cynthia stayed in the living room with a magical thing called a stereopticon, which had a full box of the double photographs that were used with it. When they were placed in a holder on the contraption, they became three-dimensional and it seemed one was right in the streets of the cities, the parks, or whatever was in the picture. It was fascinating. When Cynthia got tired of looking at all the pictures, she would run around the living room, which was very dusty, flapping her arms like wings, stirring up dust motes and watching them swirl in the rays of light that came into the dark room from the sun porch.

Grandma's handyman was an old man the same color as her. He made repairs on the front house for her and spaded the garden… whatever was needed. They often visited him and his wife in a funny little box-shaped house made of stone just down the street from the park on Orange Avenue.

There was one man, lighter than any of them, who was always in bed in the tiny living room. He was very, very ill. Cynthia could see that; he was so thin and frail. One day, when he seemed a little better, he called her over.

"Come talk to me."

She went to him and, not knowing what to say, stood by the bed, looking at him. He asked her name, how old she was, and what grade she was in at school. She told him she was in kindergarten, then asked him his name. He told her only a first name.

"What's your last name?" she asked.

"I never had one and I never had a home, either," he said.

Cynthia thought this was very strange. "How come you don't have a last name?"

"Nobody ever gave me one," he said. Then he told her he was dying.

Cynthia didn't know what to say to that. She stood regarding him, while she thought about it and was relieved when Grandma stepped from the kitchen to call her away from bothering him. She never knew the circumstances of why he lived with Grandma's friends, why they took care of him, or when he died. She never saw him again after the day he'd wanted her to talk to him, but she never forgot him, only his name.

The handyman, Mr. Ellis, had no hair on his head at all... no beard, nor any eyebrows or eyelashes. She never said anything, but she was curious. One day, as she hung around watching as he worked, he took off his old felt hat to wipe the top of his bald head with the bandanna he kept in his pocket.

"I don't ever have to get a haircut," he told her. "And I don't have to shave either."

Cynthia had come to that conclusion on her own, but he'd opened the door for her, she asked, "How come?"

"I had scarlet fever when I was a boy. All my hair dropped out and never grew back. I don't have any hair anywhere on my body."

Cynthia was too young to know that men had hair in other

places on their bodies than the obvious, but she did notice he didn't have any on his arms either. Papa did, and so did other men she'd seen.

Mr. Ellis had a chronic runny nose which she found fascinating. He'd pull out the bandanna from his back pocket to wipe it, but a clear drop would start gathering again. She watched fascinated, trying not to stare as it grew larger, bouncing as he talked until it was just about to drop. Somehow, he always knew and out came the bandanna in the nick of time. She marveled at that... just once she'd have liked to see it drop.

These were the only colored families that Cynthia knew who'd lived in Coronado. She learned that there had been others, but she wasn't aware of them at the time. She only knew the ones she and Grandma went to see. Except there was one other man...

THERE WERE no colored children in school with her at all, other than the Mexican and Japanese, whom no one seemed to harass like they did to her. When she was in high school, a boy showed up who appeared to be younger than she was. If he'd been behind her in school, she'd never seen him. She wondered if he might have had any of the same problems she did, but she also knew that boys were different. It had always been the girls who were mean to her, not the boys. All the boys did was win all her marbles and beat her at mumblety-peg when they let her play with them at recess. Later on, they whispered about her to each other when she walked down the aisle at the movies or passed them on the street, but that was after they were all older.

The other man didn't have a wife, or, if he did, Cynthia never saw her. He was very light, but he had Negro features, freckles and kinky reddish hair. He spoke or nodded to Annie on the street, and she nodded back or replied coolly. It was obvious that she didn't like him much. He had a way of looking at Cynthia that made her feel uncomfortable, even when she was a very little girl. She didn't like him at all.

When she was older, if she was alone when she saw him, she looked away or crossed the street, trying not to be obvious about it, and she spoke only if she couldn't avoid it. He always looked at her with the same sly smirk on his face. She couldn't figure out what it meant until she was older.

"He must have thought I was trying to pass," she decided when she was in her teens, knowing about herself and what others thought about her. The look and the smirk had become even more obvious then, like he was saying, "I know what you're up to, Missy. You may be fooling other people, but you're not fooling me."

She'd been puzzled. She wasn't up to anything. She'd never lied to anyone about herself; what would be the point when she knew someone would tell them anyway? He certainly should have known that there was no way, in Coronado where everybody knew who she was, that it was possible for her to be getting away with anything. It made her angry to think that he could set himself up to judge her without knowing her, only knowing what she was. She wondered if he had ever even seen her mother or her father. There were others who hadn't, who didn't know Al and May were white. She'd found that out after an art exhibit when she was in the sixth grade. The next day, someone had asked in an incredulous voice, "Was that your father with your mother last night?"

Had they been surprised to see a handsome white man in a business suit, white shirt and tie, instead of the big black nigger that one of Vera's mother's friends told people he was?

May went about in Coronado by herself and Al worked in San Diego. After Cynthia started school, they didn't go out around Coronado together. Papa stopped going to the movies with Mama and Cynthia and didn't go to school on Parents' Nights. He took Mama to the store on Saturdays for the weekly grocery shopping but sat in the car with the dog to wait for her. He spent most of his time at home out in his garage and didn't take walks by himself or with Cynthia anymore. He kept a low profile, avoiding being seen with May or Cynthia after she started school. She wondered now whose idea this had been.

Many people knew who Mama was because she'd always come to anything at the school in which Cynthia was involved. In the fourth grade, after a Parents' Night, someone asked if that was her mother she'd been with the night before.

"Sure," Cynthia answered, surprised at the question.

Now all these many years later she thought, "I may have been smart in some ways, but stupid as hell in others. People must have thought my parents were colored like Grandma."

Cynthia had never thought about this before. She knew Grandma was colored, but she and Papa weren't. She'd seen nothing unusual about it; it was just the way things were.

The girl who'd asked if it was her mother she'd been with had also said, "She's pretty." It was true, and May was always nicely dressed. She looked like the lady she definitely was. It was very important to her to look and be like everyone else. She was a little vain. Was she also a little insecure?

After she'd been at the school, she'd ask Cynthia the next day if she'd looked nice.

"Yes, Mama May."

"I always look nice, don't I?"

"Yes, Mama May."

"Did anyone say anything about me to you?"

"No."

May looked disappointed.

People often told Cynthia she had a pretty mother, but for some reason still unbeknownst to her, she'd never told her mother that anyone said she was pretty.

May was a pretty woman. She had blue/gray eyes, which looked even bluer when she wore that color, as she often did. She had dark hair and a clear, fair complexion. After her death, whenever her friends talked of her to Cynthia, they always remarked on how pretty she was, her nice skin and her lovely blue eyes.

May had a nice smile, even white teeth, a wide forehead, a strong slightly square jaw, and a prominent, but not unattractive, nose. She was intelligent. She could be witty, and she spoke with the sweet musical lilt of so many Scottish women.

Shortly after May's death, Cynthia was in Marston's at the glove counter one afternoon. The salesclerk asked about the lady who was usually with her. "Was she your mother? She always looked so nice when she came into the store."

May would have been pleased. She'd have smiled her little closed-mouthed pussy cat smile, so like Vivien Leigh's when she'd played Scarlet O'Hara and asked, "Oh, she said I looked nice?"

"And I'd have told her yes," thought Cynthia. "I'm sorry that I never did before, the other times."

THE LAST TIME Cynthia saw the man with the peculiar way of looking at her was after May-May was born. He hadn't been young; she hadn't seen him in years, so she was taken aback. She would have thought he was dead if she had thought about him at all.

She'd stepped aboard the bus and there he was, sitting on the side seat behind the driver like he'd always done. Their eyes met. If she was surprised, so was he.

He dropped his eyes to the baby in her arms as she dropped her coins into the box and asked rudely, "Where in the world did you get that?"

She was stunned momentarily at both the question and the tone of his voice.

"From the usual place," was all she could think of to say. Feeling stupid, she turned to look for a seat. She knew she was red with embarrassment, both at his question and her dumb answer. "What did he expect to see me with," she wondered. "A pickaninny that I found in a cabbage patch?"

Vera's mother, who was a dressmaker, once had a customer who told everyone she knew, after she saw Vera and Cynthia together, that Cynthia's father was a big black nigger. She thought Vera shouldn't be associating with Cynthia and said so, wanting to be sure not only Vera's mother knew, but everyone else too, what Cynthia was. She admitted she'd never seen Cynthia's father, or her mother either, but when Vera and her mother told her it wasn't true, she didn't want to believe it and continued to tell anyone who would listen, the whole time she lived in Coronado.

As Cynthia thought about this she wondered if that man had thought it too. Then she started wondering about the colored families she hadn't known when she was young. Had any of them had children? Her grandmother's friend with the dusty living room had a son, but he was grown. Cynthia had seen him around town, a light brown young man in a chauffeur's uniform. It was possible that colored children had preceded her through school, or younger ones had come after, but since the town was so small and she'd never seen anyone of color on this street who wasn't an adult, she was positive that she had been the only child like herself in the school at that time between 1925 and 1933.

The school was laid out in the shape of the letter H. The auditorium/gymnasium, the kindergarten room, and offices were in the cross bar. On the south end grades one and two were on one leg, two and three on the other across the playground from them. It was the same on the north end with fifth and sixth, and seventh and eighth grades. The younger children and the older ones were kept separated, each having their own playground area. Even when the whole school was in the auditorium for some special thing, a holiday program, a school play, a talk from the police chief on traffic safety or drugs, a slide show on the evils of tobacco with x-rays of smokers' lungs, or a talk by Belle Benchley of the San Diego Zoo, Cynthia had never seen a dark child or a light that looked Negro. She knew all the Japanese and Mexican children and their younger siblings, so she had to conclude that she had been the only child of her particular ancestry in attendance at the time.

"I could be wrong," she told herself. "But I don't think so."

Papa had preceded her in school and even had some of the same teachers. He often spoke of playing games with the other boys... run sheep run, or anty-anty over, (a ball was thrown over the pitched roof of the old wooden schoolhouse, which was still standing on the grounds when Cynthia started kindergarten, to be caught on the other side and thrown back) along with spinning tops, playing marbles, and mumblety-peg. He still had white friends whom he had gone to school with. If he had ever been beaten up or called names, he certainly didn't tell Cynthia and she didn't tell him she had either.

CHAPTER SEVENTEEN

When Al and May had moved away, leaving Cynthia behind with Grandma, it had been a trauma that stayed with her all her life. It didn't matter that they came nearly every night to see her for a few minutes or that they sometimes took her to a movie with them, then brought her back to Grandma's. It was not enough either that Papa came every Sunday after church to take her to spend the day with them and return her to Grandma's in the evening. She wanted to be with them all the time.

Once, when she was six or seven, they'd taken a trip on Al's vacation and were gone for two weeks. Two whole Sundays with no Papa coming to get her. She knew the way from the route Papa drove, so, by herself, she walked to their house. She tried the doors, but they were locked. She sat on the front stoop wishing they would come home while she was there. Papa had taught her to whistle, and she spent the time whistling every song she knew as loud as she could so the sound would fill the emptiness she felt inside. When she could see by how low the sun was in the sky that it was getting late, she trudged back to Grandma's, disappointed, with feelings that she had no name for then... abandoned?... bereft?

Mama and Papa came back bearing small gifts, but the pleasure they brought was not enough to fill up the emptiness she'd felt while they were away.

Their neighbors had seen her sitting on the front stoop all that Sunday afternoon and told Al and May about it. They questioned her. They hadn't realized that she knew the way to their house by herself. She was scolded for worrying her grandmother, unaware that Annie, who likely had dozed all afternoon in her rocker, had not missed her, had not even asked where she'd been.

Feelings of abandonment and loneliness stayed with her all her life. Common sense told her that Ted had to stand duty or even go off to war before they married. Nevertheless, although she had heard Papa predicting it for years, Pearl Harbor was something she hadn't bargained for, nor had anyone else. She felt abandoned again after Ted left for the South Pacific.

The cases in the news in the nineties about custody of children who had been given away and are now wanted back are very upsetting to Cynthia, reminding her of the King Solomon story of the two women fighting over a child. You can't rip a child apart and give half to each one who wants to claim him, but in essence, this is what is being done. There can be no real love or concern for the child involved, only selfish and self-serving possessiveness. The insecurity, the feelings of being unloved, unwanted, or of abandonment by the parents who have had him since birth will be with him all his life, causing insecurities that will create problems with his relationships with others and leave scars on his spirit that will never heal.

When Cynthia, watching the news on television, saw children taken from the arms of the only parents they'd ever known by people who were strangers to them, to be carried away screaming, it tore her own heart in two.

BOOK TWO

CHAPTER EIGHTEEN

In December 1926, when she was four and a half, Cynthia started kindergarten. She'd been excited about what Grandma and her parents had told her, but when she walked into the room, looked around, and saw children she didn't know, more than she had ever seen at one time, she was scared. She clung to Grandma's long black skirt and screamed not to be left there alone. The other children stared, but Cynthia was terrified. She didn't care what anyone thought about the way she was behaving. She often threw tantrums with Grandma when she didn't get what she wanted and to leave this place and go right back home was something she wanted.

It was a standoff. She wouldn't release Grandma and she wouldn't stop screaming. She'd been left behind once before and she wasn't about to let it happen again. Finally, the teacher told her that her grandmother didn't have to leave and found an extra chair for the old lady to sit on, putting her in full view. Cynthia allowed herself to be seated, sniffed for a while looking down at the floor, gradually calmed down, and started sneaking peeks at the other children as she listened to the teacher.

At the first recess, she went out reluctantly, not knowing what to do. She recognized the girl from her block and her cousins, who she sometimes played with, but when she went over to join them, they ignored her and walked away. She sat on the steps by herself until the bell rang for them to file back in. She looked for Grandma, didn't see her, and panicked. She let out a howl that resounded through the room and turned to run. She was going back to Grandma's! The teacher grabbed her arm to show her that in the meantime, Grandma had moved to another location. She calmed down, breathing hard, her heart pounding in her chest, and allowed herself to be seated again.

This went on the whole first week. No amount of coaxing or explaining made any impression on her. Her grandmother had to sit on a kindergarten chair where she could be seen until noon each day when the children were released. The second week, Cynthia agreed that Grandma could go home when she promised she'd be waiting right outside the door when the noon bell rang. Because she was the only child who had someone there each day, the other children began making fun of her, catcalling that she was a big baby. So in another week, she agreed that if the others came and went by themselves, she could too. She began walking to and from school by herself, gaining confidence as the weeks passed.

Recess was still a problem. No one wanted her near them.

"My mother says she doesn't want me to play with you," they said. Or "Get away from me. I'm not supposed to have anything to do with you."

She stood off to the side or sat on the steps, watching as they interacted with each other, wondering why their mothers didn't want them to have anything to do with her.

She grew to love the time in the school room. The teacher was pretty, and she was nice. They played circle games. She put records on for them, read to them and taught them little songs and dances. Some days she handed out musical instruments... a triangle, tambourines, wooden sticks to clack together, and a drum... and they marched around the room as she played the piano. The ones with no instruments clapped their hands. Each time they did this, someone who hadn't had an instrument before got a turn, while Cynthia continued to clap. Once she asked if she could have a turn with an instrument too.

"I'm really sorry Cynthia, but you can't have one. I'm sure you can see that there just aren't enough to go around," the teacher said. Cynthia nodded, but she was disappointed. The marching was fun, and the teacher had seemed really sorry, but everyone else got a turn, why didn't she?

She didn't look forward to recess. There was little to do for her. She watched clouds as they moved across the sky, wandered around looking at the bushes and flowers that were planted on the grounds, and the birds and insects that were on them or nearby, or found a stick and drew in the dirt, amusing herself in this manner until it was time to go back inside. She was used to being by herself and she kept her feelings hidden. She wished the others would play with her and she didn't really understand why they didn't, but she had to accept it. What else could she do?

The semester passed and it was June. School was over. In the fall, when they went back, they would be in the first grade. Everyone seemed to think that was wonderful.

One day that summer, Annie and Cynthia went to visit a friend in the city, a very old lady who was the mother of a longtime friend. There were several children of various colors playing about, some of them darker than Cynthia's grandma, all of them darker than Cynthia, and a couple of younger colored ladies.

The children accepted Cynthia immediately, drawing her into a wild game of hide-and-seek in the house. They ran into closets, and hid under the beds, galloping and thumping and banging doors. The younger women visiting with the two old ladies occasionally called to the children to quiet down and not make so much noise. It was a wonderfully happy day for Cynthia; she'd never had so much fun with other children before.

Later that summer, she asked Grandma, "Can we go and visit that lady who had all the kids again?"

Grandma told her the old lady had died, so she never saw the friendly children again. She also never forgot that day.

These dark children had accepted her and let her play with them, and she didn't look like them. She went to school with kids who looked just like her and they wouldn't play with her or let her get near them. It was very strange. What could be the reason? She couldn't understand it.

During vacation, the neighbor girl and her cousins let her play with them sometimes, as they always had. Then they would decide to go inside, and her mother would send Cynthia home like she always did. She was nice about it, and she liked Cynthia's grandma... Cynthia knew that. Cynthia decided it was just her that no one liked and wished she knew why.

She'd go on home like she'd been told to do and play by herself with her fleet of Tootsie Toy cars in the little village she'd made by the side of the house with her Tinker Toy sticks, empty matchboxes, rocks, and twigs, her doll and baby buggy, and her little red wagon. She sat under the palm tree in the front yard with her coloring books or went into her haven, the vacant lot, to commune with her golden sparkly feeling. She saw her mother and father every evening when they came by to check up on her and Grandma. Sometimes they took her to the movies and Papa always came for her every Sunday after Sunday school to take her to Mama's for the day. Heaven to her would have been to live with them, but she didn't ask them why she couldn't.

September was just around the corner. She'd daydreamed in the vacant lot, climbed the loquat tree and eaten the fruit, chased butterflies in the yard and helped Grandma in the garden. She'd been by herself most of the time, but happy enough. She'd spent long intervals looking at the sky, waiting for her glorious feeling. It had come often, filling her with such elation that she wanted to run and tell anyone who would listen, but there was no one to tell and no words to explain it. She just knew everything was going to be wonderful someday and she couldn't wait to go back to school. She was so sure someone would want to be her friend this time.

Grandma sewed new dresses, knitted a sweater, and crocheted hats for cold days to keep her head warm. Mama took her to town for new shoes and underwear. At the dime store, Mama bought her a red pencil box with a pencil sharpener, an eraser, a ruler, brand-new pencils, bright crayons, and a pair of scissors that didn't cut very well. There was also a thing called a protractor with shapes cut into it to trace. Everything was wonderful and she loved it. She spent a lot of time taking everything out and putting it back, just so, several times a day, making sure the Crayolas were in rainbow order. She asked Papa what the protractor was for, so he showed her how to use it to make circles and divide them into pieces like slices of pie.

Cynthia was excited and happy as she went off by herself to join the other children in the first grade decked out in her new clothes and carrying her wonderful pencil box. She couldn't wait to meet somebody who was going to like her and play with her, who'd walk with her and be her friend and whose mother wouldn't mind.

CHAPTER NINETEEN

Schools were regimented in the twenties. Maybe not all of them, but Coronado's grammar school was. Classes were large, between thirty and thirty-five kids with one teacher. The teachers were firm... some would say they were very strict. They set the rules and the children obeyed or sat in the cloakroom in a corner for a while to consider what they had or had not done... chewing gum in class, shuffling their feet, squirming, whispering, anything causing a disturbance. Repeated offenses meant a trip to the principal's office for a lecture or a notice to the parents.

The children ran to gather around their teacher every morning when the bell sounded at five minutes to nine to pledge allegiance to our nation's colors as they were raised. Then they marched in an orderly fashion to their classrooms with the teacher in the lead.

AT THE DOORS of the room, they separated to line up again, boys at one door, girls at the other, then filed in quietly to their seats. Seating was alphabetical for everyone but Cynthia who was told to sit in the rear corner of the room until the fourth grade when she told her teacher she couldn't read the blackboard from where she sat.

In the line at the door, the sneaky harassment began. Her hair was pulled; she was pushed, shoved, and tripped. When she objected, turning around to complain, she was "spoken to," or sent to sit in the cloakroom for a while, but her first real inkling that all was not going to be well for her was at the first recess.

Among the things they'd been told that morning was to go directly to the bathroom at recess so they wouldn't have to raise a hand later in class to be excused; to sit quietly in their seats while monitors passed out paper and materials, backs straight, hands folded in front of them on the desk, looking straight ahead, and when the bell rang for recess, to file quietly out of the room and walk, not run, to the restrooms.

When the bell rang, they filed out, but then ran pell-mell to line up at the bathroom doors for their turn and, when finished, ran off to play in the time left. The remaining girls in the line blocked the entrance when Cynthia reached it, telling her it wasn't her turn and forcing her back to the end of the line again and again. At the same time, they grabbed at her clothing, pulled her hair, and sometimes knocked her down, kicking at her. There was a new girl egging them on.

They'd been told to return immediately to the classroom when the bell rang, but Cynthia had to wait until after the others left. This made her late and the teacher kept her after school to warn her about it. After that, she ran back with the others, raising her hand later to be excused. After a few times, she was kept after school again, told this must stop, and that she must go to the bathroom at recess. That was that. So she wet her pants in class; the others knew it and made fun of her. When she got home, Grandma scolded her. She was ashamed, but she didn't try to explain. The teacher didn't want to listen to any excuses, so what was the use?

At the second longer recess, there was enough time to wait until everyone else had left before going into the bathroom. She'd still have time to run out on the playground, but all the equipment, swings, rings, and seesaws were in use, and no one would let her take a turn. She'd get at the end of the line, but when she was next, she was pushed away by the one behind her.

"It's not your turn. It's mine. Go back to the end of the line."

It was just like it had been in the bathroom line, but when they knocked her down on the playground, they kicked dirt at her too. Seeing it was pointless to argue, she went off by herself, as far away from them as she could get. She tried to lose herself in looking at the sky, hoping her feeling would come, but it seemed to have left her.

The new girl in the class had singled Cynthia out, but not to be friendly. She was bigger than any of them, squat, solidly built, freckles all over a homely face, dark reddish hair cut in a Dutch bob. She appointed herself Cynthia's chief tormentor and was the ringleader of several others. She wouldn't let anyone take pity and let Cynthia into the bathroom or to play on any of the equipment. There were some who would have played fair, but she wouldn't allow it and no one wanted to go against her.

Cynthia was always the last one to file out at the end of the day because of the seating arrangement, so the bully and her cronies waited for her just outside the door. She tried to run past them, but they tackled her, knocking her face down into the dirt and rubbing her nose in it. They pulled her arms up behind her back and made her say, "Uncle," or "I give up," but she wouldn't do it. She wasn't going to give them the satisfaction. She'd scream in pain and yell at them to leave her alone and let her go, but it was to no avail.

They called her names, spat on her, and hounded her until they grew tired of the game and decided to let her up. She never let them see her cry; she refused to give them that satisfaction too. She cried after she got away from them, wiping the dirt and tears off her face with the hem of her dress before she entered the house when she got to Grandma's.

Once she asked if she could leave by the hall door.

"No," the teacher said. "Rules are rules, and I can't make an exception or everyone else will want to do it too."

After that, Cynthia braced herself every afternoon for her ordeal. They were bigger than she was; she was small for her age and skinny. She tried to stand her ground, but it was no use. They were at her from all sides, circling like wolves for the kill. There were others who stood and watched. They didn't join in, but they egged the others on, and no one tried to stop it.

All this was happening right outside the open door of the school room as the teacher sat inside grading papers or preparing the next day's lesson. She never came out or interfered.

Cynthia hoped each day that she would come to see what all the screaming was about, but she didn't, not until the day they pantsed her.

She howled with shame and anger, screaming, "Give me back my pants! Give them back to me."

Behold, the teacher appeared. She ordered the others to let Cynthia up and leave her alone from now on when they were on the school grounds. Cynthia got up, clutching her underpants in her hand and went to Grandma's. When she got to the alley, she used them to wipe her face, put them back on, and, holding her head up, went into the house as usual.

After the gang left Cynthia alone when they were on the school grounds, she found a number of ruses to avoid them as they waited for her across the street or down the block. She started off in different directions, going home by roundabout ways and down alleys. The game ceased to be fun when she managed to escape them for days at a time so that they had to give up and go home.

There were others who, at recess or walking to and from school, taunted her verbally, calling her names. Although she wasn't afraid of them, she was just as hurt and confused by it. She talked back to them when they said, "*My* mother says I can't play with you because your grandmother's a nigger."

"She is not!" Cynthia shouted, stamping her foot.

"My mother says you're a nigger too," from another.

"I am not!" Cynthia would yell in angry frustration.

"Why is your grandmother so dark then?"

"She's just tan; she's out in the sun a lot."

This was true but Cynthia had a few doubts about it. She wasn't going to let them call her grandma a nigger.

Grandma did spend a lot of time out in the yard tending her flowers and the vegetable garden, and Cynthia, who was olive, got very tan in the summer. She wasn't certain about what she was telling them, but she still didn't believe what they said was true.

When six-year-old Cynthia looked into a mirror, she didn't see anyone who looked like a nigger to her. Grandma didn't look like a nigger to her either. Grandma wasn't dark brown or almost black like the colored ladies who came from San Diego to work in Coronado who people called niggers and who looked like the African people in *National Geographic* magazine. Grandma looked like her white friends, except she was light brown and she talked like they did, so people could understand her. All of Grandma's friends were either white or light brown like she was. Mama and Papa were both white, so why did the other kids call her a nigger? She couldn't understand it. They were just being mean and nasty she decided, and she wondered why.

It would begin again.

"Why do you live with your grandmother and not your mother and father?"

Cynthia didn't know. She had wondered about that too, but she never asked, and no one ever told her.

"It's because she wants me to," she told them. That had been partly the truth, she learned years later, although she had since realized there had been a little more to it than that.

"Well, *my* mother says it's because they don't love you."

"They do too!" Cynthia would yell, but she wasn't sure. If they loved her, why did she live with Grandma and not with them? She was afraid to ask because she was afraid of the answer. Maybe it was true. She thought about it a lot and it frightened her. Sometimes some of the girls would feign friendliness on the playground. A group would beckon her over, smiling, and Cynthia would go, pleased that they wanted her to join them. But when she got close enough, one might throw a handful of dirt in her face, or they'd all run off laughing. They called her over to seesaw with them only so they could jump off and let her drop. They snatched her papers, tore them up, and scattered them. They got her beautiful pencil box and ground everything into the dirt, ruining it, and there was nothing she could do. She was outnumbered. She became distrustful of them all and stayed as far away from them as she could.

Cynthia started the first grade with such happy expectations, but she ran into a situation that was incomprehensible to her. Never having been warned, she knew no reason for why she was singled out for physical abuse and name-calling. What had made it even more bewildering was that a classmate who had played with her before they started school together had turned against her too. They joined in with the others teasing, pushing, dirt throwing, name-calling, spitting at her, keeping her out of the bathroom and off the playground equipment, and aiding in the destruction of her things.

She never cried where anyone could see her. She cried at night in her bed, alone in the dark, praying to God for an answer, with her tears welling up and rolling down the sides of her face until she finally fell asleep.

CHAPTER TWENTY

Cynthia grew to dread getting up in the morning to go to school, never knowing what the day would bring. She stayed away from everyone at recess, wary of anyone even looking her way. She wished she didn't have to be there and that she could go home, but she'd been told it was the law; she had to go to school. As she listened in class, she drew pictures in her notebook until the teacher noticed what she was doing and told her to put the pencil and notebook away and pay attention. This was the way she paid attention, so without that concentration point she'd get bored and sit looking toward the windows and daydreaming, but she did her work papers and always listened when the teacher was instructing them.

She learned to stay away from the bathroom until everyone had done their business and left and she didn't try to get in line for the swings or bars and rings, shaking her head no for the seesaw, knowing what it was they wanted to do.

She had learned, going home through alleys to avoid her nemesis, that people threw interesting things into the trash. Papa gave her a stamp collection Amos had started for him. The Navy people had friends in foreign lands, and she found stamps to soak off the envelopes and put in the stamp book Mama had bought for her at Kress. She knew it wasn't considered very nice to be picking through other people's trash cans, but it was interesting.

She looked forward to vacation when she could do as she pleased, sleep late, get the magazines the tenants left on the back porch to cut out the Dolly Dingle paper dolls, and play Papa's records. She could spend time in her vacant lot and under her palm tree whenever she wanted to, not just after school and on Saturdays.

A Navy family moved into the house on the other side of the lot. They had a little girl younger than Cynthia and the mother asked if Cynthia could come to play with her daughter. She was nice; she gave them cookies and brought them cool drinks of lemonade or Kool-Aid. One day she came to the back door.

"Come inside. You haven't had your cod liver oil this morning," she called.

Her daughter ran to the door. Cynthia stayed where she was.

"You can come in, too, Cynthia, if you'd like," and she held the door open.

Cynthia, surprised, went in and followed them into the dining room where the mother took out a silver spoon and a box like Mama's and returned to the kitchen. She poured the oil and held the spoon out for her child while Cynthia watched curiously.

"What does it taste like?" she asked.

"Haven't you ever had any?"

Cynthia shook her head. The woman seemed surprised.

"Would you like to taste it, then?"

"Uh-huh." Cynthia nodded.

The woman started to go back into the dining room, changed her mind, turned back, and, pulling out a kitchen drawer, took an everyday spoon like Cynthia's mother used, poured oil into it, and offered it to her. Cynthia made a face when she tasted it.

"Don't you like it?"

"No. It tastes awful.

"But it's very good for you. You should tell your grandmother to get some for you."

Cynthia was appalled at the thought. No way would she ask Grandma to get any of that stuff. Grandma already had a lot of nasty things she used when Cynthia was sick. Enough was enough! Grandma apparently thought if medicine didn't taste terrible, it couldn't do any good. This lady must have thought the same way.

Cynthia was not only curious, she was observant. She'd noticed that the girl's mother used a good spoon for her daughter, but not for her, and she wondered about it. Was that something that mothers only did for their own children? She stored the experience away and didn't think about it again until she remembered the episode. The lady had been very nice, and she was the first mother to ever let Cynthia come into her house, if only just for a few minutes. She probably had no idea that the child would notice the minor discrimination.

From her older perspective, Cynthia now knew the reason, and also why other people never let her into their homes. The town was small, and a woman had to live with what others in the neighborhood would think and say and perhaps condemn her for. Papa had told Cynthia the old Navy rule, "After me, you come first." It had sounded selfish to her, and she knew selfishness was a sin, but one has to live within the rules of convention. She learned to understand and forgive, but not to forget. After that summer, Cynthia never saw the nice mother and her child again.

It was the Navy's custom to send their people back and forth across the country... two years here and two years there. She'd always wondered why and still does. It seems kind of dumb to send a man to do the same job clear across the country when moving his family is expensive and disruptive. Cynthia had heard Papa growling about the governmental waste of taxpayers' money ever since she was old enough to understand what grown-ups were saying.

The entire time she was in school, she'd been in classes with many of the same children at two-year intervals. They'd come to the area, attend for two years and leave when their fathers received orders to go elsewhere. Others came once and were never seen again.

SOMETIMES ON A SATURDAY, when she was small, Papa went for a walk and came by his mother's. When he left, he'd take Cynthia along. He walked very fast, so she had to skip to keep up with him, at the same time asking a million questions about everything she saw or thought about which he'd answer and expound on. He'd stop on the street to talk to people he knew, then continue to the garages on Orange Avenue and the radio shop.

One time he was standing with his back to her at one of the garages where men hung out to talk about cars, baseball, politics, and the economy, engrossed in a conversation with a friend. Suddenly, a man standing near her whom Cynthia didn't know, reached out with both hands, putting one on each side of her head, and lifted her clear off the ground. He held her up a second or two and set her down again. It scared her; she ran to Papa and pulled on his arm.

"Papa, Papa, that man picked me up by my head."

Al turned, "What? Who? Who did that to you?"

Cynthia pointed. She could tell by the look on Papa's face that he was very angry. He marched over to the man. "God damn you. Don't you ever do anything like that to my daughter again! You just keep your hands off her. Understand?"

Taken aback, the man said, "Sorry. I didn't mean no harm. It didn't hurt her."

"You God damned fool, you could have damaged her spinal cord!" Al turned, and taking Cynthia by the hand, walked off. Cynthia wasn't hurt, just scared, but Al was very angry and very upset. "Don't let anybody pick you up by the head, ever. You could have been crippled for life."

She hadn't let him do it but said nothing. She could tell Papa had been scared too.

This memory came back after Cynthia felt she had written everything she could remember about Papa when she was little. It shocked her. Papa had not been a hugger or a kisser, only a head thumper. He got angry whenever she did anything dumb she could have been hurt by.

"Jesus Christ! Don't you ever stop and think for one God damned minute before you go off half-cocked and do some damned fool stupid thing?"

Cynthia knew he wasn't really mad at her, just mad because she might have been hurt doing whatever the stupid thing had been. She was given to doing things on the spur of the moment, without thinking, and she knew it. She didn't mind when Papa yelled at her. It meant he cared about her, didn't it?

Now, this remembrance had popped up and as she thought about it, she realized that Papa had cared about her enough to risk his life for her. It had been in the early twenties. Everyone in town knew who he was, what he was and where he lived. Exploding at a white man like that in the South in those days of Jim Crow could have gotten him tarred and feathered or worse, beaten, or tortured and killed. He had jumped into the situation with no thought for himself, only for his little girl.

"It's true," she thought. "Actions do speak louder than words. Papa may have never told me that he loved me, but I was sure he did. I think now, looking back, that Mama did too, in her cool Scottish way, but it isn't enough. I needed to hear it, to feel it in ways I could understand so that my reactions to what I didn't understand wouldn't have caused so much damage to my feelings of security and self-worth. I grew up feeling unloved and always lonely. In my old age, I'm haunted still by these feelings. Even with a husband, children and friends, I sometimes feel empty."

Cynthia's capacity for love was like an old bucket. The salty tears of her early childhood had rusted out the bottom so it could never hold enough to make her feel anyone, even Vera, had really loved or wanted her. Her head knew, but not her heart.

She'd never seen Papa as furious about anything in her life before or after that day. All the men had stopped talking — shocked, frozen, and staring – when Papa had cursed at the man. No one had said a word while she and papa were still within hearing distance. He'd stormed off, almost dragging her by one arm and making her run to keep up with him. She knew he'd been scared for her. Had he been scared for himself, too? Maybe that was why he quit going for walks. She didn't remember him ever doing it again after that day.

CHAPTER TWENTY-ONE

With some trepidation, Cynthia started off for the second grade. She looked around the first day and saw children who'd been there the previous year, including a new boy who had moved into a house on her block not long before and whom she already knew was mean. She didn't see the hateful girl. Although Cynthia's tormentor was indeed gone, she'd left a legacy of petty meanness to a few of the other girls which, while not quite as bad as the year before, was still mystifying to her.

The teacher was a friend of Grandma's whom Papa had had when he was in school. She had a reputation for being very strict, little escaping her notice, but she was not usually unkind. As before, Cynthia couldn't get into the bathroom at recess or play on any of the equipment, but the girls had lost their leader and their harassment was less than before, so she was grateful.

The boy who lived on Cynthia's block was seated in front of her, so he'd try to trip her as she returned from collecting homework, kicking at her or grabbing at the paper in her hand, and, as usual, if she objected, causing a disturbance, it was she who was sent to the cloakroom, not him. When she was allowed to come back, he'd give her a wicked grin.

Cynthia, hopping around in the wash tub one cold Saturday night as she got her weekly bath, burned her arm on the kerosene stove nearby. Grandma put salve on it and a bandage. Monday at school, while papers were being returned, it was itching so she lifted the bandage to look at it just as the boy was coming back to his seat. He smirked at her and suddenly, reaching out, ran his fingernail down the middle of the quarter-sized burn. Cynthia screamed and started to cry. In a flash, the teacher was there.

"That's no way to behave in class, young lady," and grabbing her firmly at the back of the neck, marched her to the cloakroom. Blood was running down Cynthia's arm, but the teacher didn't notice. She sat Cynthia down hard in the little chair in the corner and, with another admonition about behaving in the classroom, turned and left. Cynthia sat there crying quietly. Her arm really hurt.

She dabbed at the blood with the hem of her skirt as she thought, "It isn't fair. It isn't fair. I don't do anything and I'm always the one who gets in trouble." When she stopped crying, she got angry. She hated that boy; she hated them all.

When she got to Grandma's she had to tell what had happened because of the blood on her dress, but Grandma put more salve, a fresh bandage and that was all.

One Saturday before school had started, Cynthia was walking up the alley eating a piece of bread and butter. As she walked past the boy's house, she saw a cat crouched down in the weeds in his back-yard. She went over to it and to her horror discovered it had been tied to a clothesline pole by a wire around its neck. The hair was all worn off and the skin was raw. It smelled her bread and strained to reach it.

"Oh, you poor thing. Are you hungry?" She began tearing off pieces, which it ate ravenously. She went running back to Grandma for more bread and told her about the cat. Grandma was shocked and went up the alley to talk to the boy's mother. She came back with the cat in her arms.

It was a Halloween cat, black with yellow eyes, quite young, and already pregnant. Cynthia named her June and called her Junie. Junie had one kitten, a little gray boy cat, and Cynthia named him Smokey. While Smokey was still nursing, Junie got pregnant again and later died having three more kittens. She was too young and had been undernourished for too long. Life had not been kind to her and Cynthia, who had loved her, was unkind too.

Mama and Papa had taken the kittens and raised them with diluted evaporated milk in a doll's bottle. They also had the help of the family dog, Bingo, who licked them tenderly and let them curl up alongside him. Mama bathed them too and put them into the oven turned low with the door open, to dry.

Papa had been taken with the pretty little striped female, but Mama said no females. People didn't take their animals to the vet to be spayed and neutered as they do today; money was tight. The little female and one of her brothers were given away and both came to a bad end. She was hit by a car, and he was killed by a dog. Papa was angry at the damned fools who didn't have sense enough to keep kittens safely inside until they were old enough to fend for themselves. Mama kept the other brother, a fluffy black male. He was named Buster and lived until Cynthia was out of high school before he had to be put to sleep.

Cynthia, whose problems at school kept her filled with frustrated anger and hatred, was lonely, sad, and unhappy with no one to talk to. She loved Smokey with all her heart, but what she did to him was unforgivable. She wanted to play with him like she had seen in the pictures of children with puppies and kittens dressed up like dolls in the books her Grandfather in Scotland sent her. One day she dressed him in doll clothes, much against his will, and put him into her buggy. He wanted no part of this game and kept jumping out. She began to get angry. He jumped out again and she picked him up and threw him on the ground as hard as she could. He lay there, unmoving, and when he came to, crept about crying piteously. She was frightened and ran for Grandma. When she came, Cynthia lied and told her he had fallen. Grandma knew better, but Cynthia stuck to her guns, lying, feeling shame and fear, remorseful for what she had done to the kitten she loved, but she did it again a few days later. This time he was really hurt badly. Mama and Papa questioned her, and she lied to them too. He got better but was unable to nurse. Poor Junie's milk soured in her teats. Her belly was swollen and sore and she had trouble moving about. Cynthia hated herself for what she had done to Junie's baby and to June. Smokey got well, but he had trouble swallowing, which was painful to watch. One day she came home from school, went looking for him, and couldn't find him. She asked Grandma where he was.

"Your mother came and took him to the pound to be put to sleep," she said.

Cynthia was sick with the shame of what she had done. She knew she was responsible for Smokey's death. She had been meaner to him than that nasty boy had been to Junie and what she had done to Smokey had hurt Junie too, probably helping to cause her death. She knew then that she must learn to control her temper. Even though she was only six years old, she learned.

When she was grown, she threw things in anger when she couldn't have her own way, but never again anything alive. She grieved for Smokey over the years and had many other cats, sometimes six at a time, hoping to make it up to him in some way. She knew God was supposed to forgive her and she hoped that little Smokey had, but she knew she could never forgive herself for what she had done to him and Junie for as long as she lived.

At recess, Cynthia had noticed the third-grade children run into their wing of the building before they came back out to the playground. She investigated and found another bathroom there, so when the bell rang for recess, instead of fighting with the girls in her class, she slipped away to that one. The older kids paid no attention to her, and she could stay as long as she pleased. This worked fine until one day a teacher came in and, finding her washing her hands, demanded, "What are you doing in here, Cynthia? You belong over on your own side, not in here." She was very angry. Cynthia tried to explain, but the teacher wouldn't listen and as she walked out, said, "If I find you in here again, I'll have to send you to the principal's office." But Cynthia continued to go there. Luckily, she wasn't caught and it was well worth the risk.

The second grade wasn't quite as bad as the first had been because she kept to herself. The name-calling went on, but not the physical harassment. It made her mad, but most of the time she pretended she didn't hear it and when report cards came out, she was promoted to the third grade. That summer the boy moved away, and she never saw him again, but the scar on her arm remained there until she was well into middle age before it faded and disappeared.

CHAPTER TWENTY-TWO

O n foggy nights, lying in her narrow cot in Grandma's house, Cynthia could hear the bells on the ferry boats sounding at regular intervals as they plied their way back and forth across the bay and the foghorn from the lighthouse on Point Loma, sounding its mournful warning. On stormy nights, she could hear the waves crashing against the great rocks of the wall that her grandfather had helped build. There was something comforting about it. As she listened, it kept her thoughts from straying to the troubles that plagued her days at school.

Before she went to sleep, she always made sure her closet door was closed. Otherwise, she imagined things were inside looking out at her that would come out and do mean things to her when she fell asleep and could no longer protect herself. She never let a foot or hand hang over the side of her cot either. The thing that lived under there might grab it and pull her into its black nothingness.

After she began having trouble getting to sleep at night, she'd lie there thinking, wondering about what the other kids said and did to her, and how grown-ups acted when she was around. When she did sleep, she had recurring nightmares. She'd be running from people who wanted to get her and hurt her. In one area, she could fly. She jumped into the air, made swimming motions with her arms, and landed on a telephone pole where she sat, looking down on her tormentors like a treed animal with a pack of hounds circling the ground below, frustrated and angry because they couldn't reach her, yelling and calling insults. She was safe but wished they would go away so she could come down.

In another dream, she was running, running, while some people chased her until she collapsed from exhaustion and lay dying. They gathered around looking down at her and she lay feeling pleased that she was going to die and then they'd be sorry and ashamed of themselves for being so mean to her.

Her fear of the dark lasted until she was twenty-six years old when she was alone with Tee Gee in Guam and Ted had duty every third night. The generator that gave them their electricity was shut down at 10 PM and on moonless nights it was pitch black inside and out. She couldn't let Tee Gee know she was afraid and have him be frightened too; he was only six years old.

His bedroom was on one end of the Quonset hut and theirs was on the other. On the duty nights, she let Tee Gee sleep with her, both for his company and to have him near if anything happened. The Quonset had no doors or windows that could be locked for protection, only screens on the windows and hooks on the front and back screened doors. Mama wrote telling her that she'd read in the *Saturday Evening Post* that many civilian workers in Guam were felons from prisons in the States who were working for time off on their sentences.

"Keep your doors and windows locked," she'd said, not realizing what the climate was like in Guam. Cynthia never let her mother know that she didn't have any doors or windows that could be locked, and it would have been like living in a steam bath if they could.

She put her biggest butcher knife and a hammer under her pillow when she and Tee Gee were alone. At that time, their Quonset at the end of the housing area was the only one occupied. The nearest others were empty or under construction. A main road that went across the island to the camp was only a stone's throw from the back porch and truckloads of Marines or civilian workers went by constantly.

She was scared to death anyway and ashamed of herself for it. Then, one black night, she held her hand up in front of her face and couldn't see it. She wiggled her fingers and brought them right up almost touching her nose and still couldn't see them.

She laughed to herself, "It's so dark that if one of Mama's felons broke in, I couldn't see him and he couldn't see me either. I can find my way around here in the dark because I know where all the furniture is, and he'd be falling over it. If one comes in the front door, Tee Gee and I will run out the back, and if one comes in the back, we'll run out the front."

This was a reassuring thought, so the next day she put her arsenal back in the drawers and never suffered that paralyzing terror of the dark again, except once in a while. If she was alone and stayed up late to watch a scary movie on TV, she'd be afraid going down the hall to bed in the dark, telling herself as she went how silly she was.

She still suffers from insomnia, and she still has to have closet doors closed at night. She still never lets any body parts hang over the edge of a bed, but Tee Gee never knew his mother had been terrified of the dark, the mother who'd reassured him that there were no tigers in the woods in North Carolina or under his bed either, when he was four years old.

"Oops," Cynthia said to herself after she'd written about the melancholy sound of the fog horns when she was growing up in Grandma's house. "I forgot to write about Coronado's smells."

There were three distinctive aromas for Coronadoans. Low tide was the first because it happened the most often. It still does.

Then there was the fishy aroma wafting across the bay (against the prevailing winds for some unknown reason) on the nights they were canning the last catch. The canning industry is gone from San Diego now, so this one is a thing of the past.

Number three was the Citrus Soap Company's fragrant contribution to the atmosphere. Every Thursday night they processed lemon peels and other ingredients... the Lord only knows what... to make laundry soap which was sold in a box with a big yellow lemon on the front. The soap smelled as nice as one might expect, but the processing didn't... it stank.

"It was wonderful soap though and if they were still making it, I'd still be buying it." Cynthia smiled to herself as she thought about it.

CHAPTER TWENTY-THREE

Cynthia's beloved vacant lot had sold the summer that she was waiting to go into the third grade. Two small stucco houses would be built on it later in the year. At the same time, one of the three rentals across the alley had been vacated and the owner came to clean and have some painting and small repairs done. He was living in the vacant house while the work was going on and would often stand in the alley talking to Annie. If Cynthia, who was seven going on eight, wandered over he'd reach in his pocket and give her a nickel. She thought he was a very nice man, considering him to be a friend of Grandma's.

One afternoon, Grandma called her from her nest in the wild oats.

"I'm going to run to the store for something and I'll be back in just a jiffy. Will you be all right while I'm gone?"

"Sure, Grandma," Cynthia said and went back to her daydreaming. She was standing in the lot hoping her golden feeling would come when she heard the man calling to her. She went over to see what he wanted; she had no reason to fear him.

"If you'll come and do something for me, I'll give you a quarter," he said.

A quarter! Cynthia knew that was a lot of money, more than a nickel or even a dime. She went willingly, like a lamb to the slaughter, trusting him.

He took her across the alley to the vacant house while she wondered what it was he wanted her to do, excited at the prospect of getting a quarter. When they went inside, a man she knew was a friend of Papa's was on a ladder, painting a wall. Papa and he had been friends with each other for a long time. He looked at her and he looked at the man she was with.

"You ought to be ashamed," he said.

Cynthia thought he was talking to her, and she didn't know why she should be ashamed. She wasn't doing anything wrong. The man, who had her by the hand, said nothing and, opening the door to another room, took her inside and shut the door. It was a bedroom and because the house was rented furnished, there was a bed in it. He picked her up and laid her on it, pulled up her dress and started to take off her panties. Suddenly she was frightened, objecting as she tried to pull away.

"There's nothing to be afraid of, and remember, I'm going to give you a quarter if you're a good girl." He started unbuttoning the front of his pants and Cynthia began to cry.

"Hush, hush. I'm not going to hurt you," he told her, but she was very, very scared. She wished Papa's friend would come in so the man would stop whatever it was he was going to do.

"To this day," Cynthia thought, "I still can't think about what that man did, and I wouldn't want to tell anyone about it either. He didn't hurt me just like he said, but the things he did and the things he made me do were nasty. They made me feel dirty and ashamed."

Afterward, he buttoned up his pants, took her into the bathroom and washed away her tears with a damp washcloth.

"Now, don't tell anyone what we did, you hear?"

Cynthia shook her head.

"If you tell anyone, it'll just cause trouble and you don't want that, do you?"

Cynthia shook her head.

"So, do you promise never to tell?"

Cynthia nodded her head. She would have promised anything to get away from him and get out of that room.

"I told you I'd give you a quarter, didn't I?" he said reaching into his pocket.

She nodded.

"Well, here it is." And he handed it to her. Then, taking her hand, he opened the door and they left the room.

Papa's friend, still on the ladder painting, gave them a hard look. "You ought to be ashamed," he said again. This time Cynthia was sure he was talking to her, and she *was* ashamed. She couldn't wait to get out of that house and back to the safety of her vacant lot.

"Remember your promise," he said as he let her go.

Cynthia ran across the alley where she sat in her nest, clutching the quarter in her fist, breathing hard with her eyes shut tight until she began to feel better. Pretty soon Grandma came back. Cynthia ran to her and opened her hand to show the coin.

"Look Grandma, I have a quarter. See?"

"Oh, wherever did you get that?"

"The man across the alley gave it to me."

Annie had no reason to mistrust the man either and she asked no further questions. Cynthia didn't know whether to be glad or not. She had made a promise to him, and promises weren't supposed to be broken. If Grandma had asked her anything else, she would have told somehow, even though she didn't know exactly what to tell or what words to use.

There was no repeat performance. Had her father's friend threatened to expose her molester? Had he decided he'd been foolish to let a third party know what he had done and that it would be foolhardy to try again?

The work done, the man went away, and Cynthia never saw him

again. Nor did she want to. She was distrustful of all men after that and had an aversion to face-to-face body contact with them. When she was older, she loved roller skating with a boy at the rink because they were side-by-side, but she never learned to dance well and didn't want to. In high school, she and Vera would go to old-time dances which were mostly polkas and schottisches, with no close body contact.

If they went to a public ballroom, she'd say, "No, thank you. I don't dance," when she was asked and spend the evening watching Vera, who dearly loved to dance. An ironic twist of fate led Vera to marry a man who didn't know how to dance and Cynthia to marry one who had gone to dances as often as he could before he met her.

As Cynthia had been writing about that awful man in her life, she wondered why her father's friend had told no one in her family... not Grandma or Papa or Mama. Had he even spoken to the man who had molested her? He was of Mexican ancestry. Perhaps he'd been afraid to say anything to a white man who was fooling around with a little girl who had not been hurt and who was, after all, part colored and not worth risking his chances of finding more work, not in those hard times when he had his own family to worry about.

As Cynthia grew older, she was wary of men, even the ones she knew were friendly with her parents. There was something in the bold way men looked at her and put their hands on her when they pulled her to them, telling her what a nice big girl she was getting to be, while feeling or patting, appearing to be friendly when she knew they were not.

She was suspicious of all men by the time she was in high school. There was one who did odd jobs for Mama and pulled up alongside her in his car as she walked home from school or the beach.

"Hop in, honey, and I'll give you a lift home."

From another, whose house she walked past on the way to and

from school, it was, "I have something interesting in my garage I'd like for you to see. It'll just take a minute."

Cynthia, once burned, was more than twice shy. She had a pretty good idea of what they had in mind or wanted her to see, and she had already seen more than she ever wanted to see again.

She'd politely tell them, "No thank you. I have to get right home; my mother's expecting me." Or "Thanks, just the same. I like to walk."

She kept all of this to herself, never telling anyone about it. She learned to ease away or keep her distance while still being polite and friendly, afraid that if she spoke out or pulled away and hit them, she'd be the one who got into trouble. She knew from past experience that people didn't believe her, and she didn't know how to tell her parents about men they knew and probably trusted. Most important of all, she didn't tell because the things they whispered in her ear as they fondled her made her feel dirty like it was all her fault.

When she was older, she and Vera discovered they'd both had the same problems with the same men. Laughing about it as they compared notes, she realized the fault had been with the men and not her, but they had managed to make her feel ashamed and guilty anyway.

When she had a daughter of her own, she felt guilty about it but warned her not to go into any of her friends' houses if the Daddy was home and the Mommy wasn't there. When she was walking home from school, she must never accept a ride from any of the neighbor men with no kids or from the ones who did have kids if they weren't in the car with him.

THE WORK WAS BEGUN on two houses on the lot next door and was completed before school began that fall. A Catholic priest moved into the one right next door to Grandma's, with his widowed sister and her grown daughter. The daughter was a schoolteacher, and in September, when Cynthia started third grade, she learned that her next-door neighbor, Miss Ballard, was one of the two fourth-grade teachers.

Miss Ballard and her mother, who was a seamstress, were not very friendly toward Cynthia or Grandma. They were coolly polite and pleasant enough, but Cynthia, sensitive to attitudes, knew they didn't like her or Grandma very much. Cynthia didn't like them very much either, but how Grandma felt, she didn't know.

"I expect Grandma was as tuned in to attitudes as I was," Cynthia thought to herself as she wrote about it. "Maybe even more so. I'm sure she probably had a lot more experience."

The priest, Father Maddox, was a very nice, friendly man. He spent a lot of time in his backyard, which had been laid out in a criss-cross pattern of narrow cement walks with blocks of grass and flowers in between, reading his breviary. He would walk back and forth and across in a regular pattern every morning and afternoon when the weather was fair. He was always nice to Annie, stopping her to talk briefly and ask how she was, and to Cynthia too, before resuming his meditations. Cynthia wondered about him. Did God answer Father Maddox's prayers? He didn't answer hers. Grandma was always reading the Bible too and Cynthia wondered, did God answer Grandma's prayers? Once she had looked at Grandma's Bible. The print was very small; the pages were thin and flimsy and there weren't any pictures. She wondered if God would answer her prayers when she learned to read and could read His book.

CHAPTER TWENTY-FOUR

During the summer before Cynthia entered the third grade, a jungle gym with bars and rings was installed on the playground. Everyone was excited about it. Cynthia couldn't wait to try it. Forgetting how it had been before, she ran with the others to get in line, but they pushed her back until both recesses were over, so she didn't get a turn either time. The next morning she made up her mind no one was going to do her out of her turn. Emboldened by her decision, she got in line, pushing back at those who tried to shove her away until she was next. She was reaching for the bar when a girl named Maggie pulled her back and pushed her.

"Go back to the end of the line where you belong. It's my turn now, not yours."

"It is too my turn." And Cynthia, angry, pushed Maggie back hard. Maggie fell, hitting her head on the metal framework. She was momentarily dazed and there was blood! Someone ran screaming for the teacher and when she came, they all began screeching, "Cynthia did it. Cynthia did it. It was all Cynthia's fault. Cynthia wouldn't wait her turn. She pushed Maggie."

Cynthia was appalled. She hadn't meant to hurt anyone; she only wanted what was fair. The other girls were making it sound like she had hurt Maggie on purpose.

"It was too my turn," she said, starting to cry, but the teacher, after sending someone to get a damp paper towel, told her to go to the principal's office.

She sat for a while in the outer office that day before the principal came out and gave her a lecture on playing fair and waiting her turn.

"Why did you do it?" he asked.

Through her tears, she told him it had been an accident. "She pushed me first. It was my turn, but the other girls never let me take a turn on anything. They always push me back to the end of the line. It isn't fair."

He had asked a question, so she gave him an answer. She was frightened that he would tell her parents. Mama would be angry and scold her for being such a stupid ass and Papa would give her his usual speech on going off half-cocked and doing something stupid.

But maybe he had listened to her and maybe believed her because nothing else was said about it, by anyone. Maggie came back to school a day or two later and she didn't say anything either. After that, however, Cynthia didn't try to get in line for anything again. She started staying in the classroom at recess, reading or drawing, until the teacher found her there one day and told her she should be outside playing with the others.

"They won't let me, and I don't want to anyway."

"Cynthia, you must go out for recess whether you want to or not; it's the rule." But she said it kindly.

So she went out, but she sat alone on the steps with her tablet, as far away as she could get from the rest of them, drawing Betty Boop or paper dolls. Soon some of the girls came drifting over until she'd have a cluster of them watching. They'd tell her she was good and ask if she'd draw a doll for them. She was pleased and obliged, hopeful that they'd become more friendly, but they still didn't walk home with her or invite her to join them when they played tag, jump rope, hopscotch and jacks. She wasn't going to ask and be rebuffed, so it was just another disappointment she learned to live with.

"It must be me," she decided. "There's something awful wrong with me and no one wants to be my friend because of it. I only wish I knew what it was, and I could change it so then they'd like me and let me play with them." When she was in bed at night thinking about it, her throat would tighten, the tears would come, then anger and more tears. So when Cynthia was eight years old, she was miserably unhappy, distrustful of other children, frightened and confused by her feelings. She wished she'd never been born. She wished she could die, but she didn't know how.

When they entered the room for the first time that year, they were surprised. The rows of old desks had been removed and replaced with separate chairs which had a writing arm and a drawer under the seat. Then another surprise. They were going to study about Alaska and the teacher asked for permission from the office to arrange all the desks in a circle around the walls so they could build an Eskimo village in the middle of the room. They were excited and clapped their hands in delight. It was okayed and, overnight, the teacher made a snow scene with plaster of Paris on some sort of base. The children brought things from home, little figures and suitable items to contribute to the theme. They read about Alaska and Eskimos all that first semester. In art period, they drew pictures of Eskimos and Eskimo life; in writing period they wrote stories. It was a wonderful way to learn and lots of *fun*!

They learned to read in the third grade. One day Cynthia looked at the page and suddenly it wasn't single words to be sounded out letter by letter... she could read the whole word, then the whole page. She was excited and couldn't wait to tell Papa. From that moment on, books became her friends. She didn't miss as much not having anyone to walk home with or talk to; she wasn't quite as lonely after she learned to read. Books opened a door for her into a world of fantasies where dreams came true, good people were rewarded, evil people were punished for their evil ways, and the prince and princess got married and lived happily ever after. She would get so lost in a book she didn't want it to end; she didn't want to have to come back out into the real world. She hoped and prayed that someday she would live happily ever after like in the fairy tales she loved, but she was not as certain about it as before. Maybe it happened only in fairy tales. Her golden sparkly feeling came less and less often. The invisible doorway that opened to a magic world was going out of existence and she knew it.

One day the teacher passed out applications for library cards to be taken home for their parents to sign so they could borrow books from the library. She explained how books could be selected and taken out, seven at a time, how long they could be kept, and about the two cents a day fine if they were kept too long. Two cents! That was a lot of money and Cynthia resolved never to keep a book so long that she'd have to pay a fine. Later, they went on a field trip to the library for a lesson in using the card index and the Dewey Decimal System. Cynthia could hardly wait until the day when the cards came back, and the teacher handed her the one with her name on it.

She went to the library every day after school, drawing out seven books and returning the seven from the day before. Every day the librarian would look at her with raised eyebrows.

"Cynthia, you didn't read all these books in one day now, did you?"

Cynthia nodded.

"You couldn't have," she said.

Cynthia had, but she knew by the look on the librarian lady's face that she didn't believe it. Cynthia didn't argue the point. She was used to seeing that look. Other kids told lies and grown-ups believed them, but when she told the truth she could always tell when they thought she was lying.

She started the first book on the way home, walking and reading, lifting her eyes only when she was crossing the street. She read with the book propped up while she ate her supper and after she went to bed, she didn't stop but kept on until she finished them all.

Grandma, dozing in her chair, would call out from time to time, "Cynthia, turn that light off and go to sleep."

"Just one more chapter Grandma. I'm almost through."

The old lady would doze off again and when she finally stirred herself to go to bed, she'd tell Cynthia again to turn off that light.

"Okay, Grandma," and she did. But when Grandma started to snore, she turned it back on and continued reading.

It would be very late, sometimes after two o'clock when she finished all the books and went to sleep. She'd sleep so soundly that she dreamed she was up, sitting on the toilet and would wake to find she was wetting the bed. When she got up in the morning, she'd turn back the covers so it could dry before she got into it again at night.

Grandma didn't change Cynthia's bed very often or do much washing anymore. The child surely must have smelled, since she got only one bath a week, was sleeping in a dirty bed and wearing the same unwashed clothes over and over.

Exhausted from her late hours, Cynthia slept so hard she wouldn't hear the alarm go off and started oversleeping. Grandma, sitting up late dozing in her rocker, began oversleeping too. Cynthia took the clock to her room, but she slept so soundly that she still didn't hear it. She'd wake with a start, knowing by the light in the room that it was late and a look at the clock confirmed it. She'd run in a panic to shake Grandma.

"Grandma, Grandma. Wake up. Wake up. I'm going to be late for school."

The old lady would stir herself and while Cynthia was brushing her teeth and dressing, would scramble an egg, or put cereal in a bowl, heat coffee, and make toast. If Cynthia had time to eat, she'd dunk her buttered toast into the coffee and eat her egg or cereal. If the sun was already over the roof of the house and across the alley, she'd grab the toast and run out the door, knowing she wasn't going to make it in time. She scolded her grandmother as she was hurrying to leave the house, mad at her, refusing to kiss the old lady before she left.

"Come back. Aren't you going to kiss me goodbye? At least come back and eat something," Grandma would call, but Cynthia was already partway up the alley calling back, "I can't, Grandma. I can't. It's too late."

She'd run all the way to school and, breathing hard with her heart in her throat, slip quietly through the back door and tiptoe to her seat. A look from the teacher told her she was in trouble. At first recess she'd be sent to the principal's office where she got a lecture on dawdling on the way to school, and that it must stop. She would promise to do better, but of course, it was impossible. It didn't get better; it got worse. She wasn't getting enough sleep. She often had no breakfast at all and sometimes no dinner, either. She was always hungry because when she went home for lunch her time was limited. Grandma, dozing in her rocker, jumped up to fix something. Cynthia poured a glass of milk while Grandma made her a sandwich of lunch meat and cheese or peanut butter and jelly, which she'd eat on her way back to school.

Some nights dinner was very late. She'd do her homework at the kitchen table and read as she waited for Grandma to fix something to eat.

"Grandma, I'm getting hungry."

"Alright, alright. I'll fix something in a minute."

But the old lady would doze off again while Cynthia kept on reading and more time passed.

This went on for some time until finally Cynthia said, "Grandma, it's getting real late and I'm really hungry."

Annie woke with a start. "What time is it?"

"It's almost nine o'clock, Grandma."

"Oh, my goodness," and Grandma would jump up to search the cupboards for something... canned soup, eggs, a bowl of cereal, or bread and milk. If the cupboard was bare, she'd put on her long black coat and grab her satchel.

"Come on. We've got to hurry before the store closes," and they'd hike to a grocery store with a deli that stayed open until nine. They'd buy a quarter pound of cold cuts and a half-pint carton of potato salad and return home. After they ate, Cynthia went to bed, but not to sleep because she had to finish reading the rest of the books so she could turn them in the next day and take out new ones.

The principal tolerated Cynthia. He was polite, but she'd learned from facial expressions and tones of voice who really liked her and who didn't. She didn't understand why it should be, but from the time she was four, she could always tell.

Memories of people who'd gone out of their way to be nice when she was young, she'd kept in her memory and her heart as she grew older. Others stayed in her memory too and in time, she forgave them, but she didn't forget.

To be fair, the principal had no way of knowing that Cynthia's life was different from the other children. How could he? He assumed someone was getting Cynthia up, fixing her breakfast, seeing that she was sent off in time and that she was dragging her feet on the way to school. One morning, when she was much later than usual, almost 9:30, he was very angry. He told her that if she couldn't get to school on time, he'd have to send her to reform school.

Reform school! Cynthia was terrified. She started to cry. She was still crying when he sent her back to her classroom. She cried all morning. Once the teacher sent her to the restroom to splash cold water on her face, but she couldn't stop sobbing. The other children watched her, wondering, but saying nothing.

Reform school! She resolved to do better, but how? Oh, the shame of it! She decided to ask Mama if she could have another alarm clock.

"Why do you need another one?" May asked. "You already have a clock."

"Because I don't hear the alarm and keep on sleeping and it makes me late for school."

So May gave her a clock they weren't using anymore. Cynthia set them both ten minutes fast and to go off five minutes apart. She did better for a while, but the threat of reform school had frightened her, so she began to sleep through both alarms and started being late again. Soon she was unable to sleep at all. She'd lie awake after she'd finished reading, tossing and turning, praying to God to let her get to sleep and to let her hear the alarm so she'd wake up in time. At last, she'd fall asleep from sheer exhaustion, not hear the alarm and be late again. She spent a lot of time in the office the rest of that semester, but she wasn't threatened again. Cynthia couldn't know that it had been only a threat and children were sent to reform school for worse things than being a few minutes late for school. She was still terrified.

Now she asked herself, "Why didn't it occur to Mama to wonder why I needed two alarm clocks, why I was oversleeping or why Grandma wasn't getting me up in time for school?"

A change was on the way, coming soon in Cynthia's life and she wondered about it when she remembered it. Had someone told Mama and Papa that something wasn't right at Grandma's house and, if so, who could it have been? Cynthia thought she knew but she would never be certain.

CYNTHIA, skinny and uncoordinated, was no good at games or sports. The only exercise she got was climbing the loquat tree to eat the fruit when it was ripe and hurrying back and forth to school. When the teacher appointed the team captains for softball, Cynthia was the last one chosen and because she couldn't catch a ball, she was put in the outfield, which suited her just fine. She'd stand around daydreaming until she'd hear them call her name. She'd look around wildly, see a ball coming toward her, see it fall and chase it as it rolled on the ground. When she threw it, it would fall short and be nowhere near where it was supposed to go.

Nobody wanted her on their team for anything until they began having spelling bees in class and sometimes challenged the other third-grade class. It was then that Cynthia began coming into her own. She was a good speller, the best in both classes it was soon discovered. For the first time in her life, it was she who was picked first when the captains chose their teams. It was she who was the last one still standing as the others misspelled words and sat down. It was she who made her team proud when she won for them. Pleased with her because she had won, they clapped with delight while she glowed with pleasure. Her reading stood her in good stead. She could glance down at the spelling list and have it cold. One time, only once, did she lose a spelling bee. Overconfident, she hadn't looked at the list. The word that took her out was 'disease.' She'd spelled it with three e's and sat down, red with embarrassment and shame, to the collective groans of her captain and team.

SOMEONE KNEW that Cynthia wasn't dawdling on the way to school. Someone had seen her charging out the door with a piece of toast in her hand and heard her grandmother calling after her to come back and eat something. Someone knew that things were not quite right in the little house.

Miss Ballard, who had a car, was backing out of her garage many mornings just as Cynthia tore out of the house and took off at a dead run down the alley, desperate not to be late for school again, knowing it was already too late. Miss Ballard surely knew Cynthia's grandma was getting senile and that Cynthia was going to school hungry, but it was a while before someone told Al and May. Maybe they hadn't thought it was any of their business.

Miss Ballard had pulled up alongside Cynthia one morning as she stopped for a second to catch her breath. Leaning over, she wound down the window.

"Cynthia, I can see you are going to be late for school again. I wish I could offer you a ride, but if I did, I'd be playing favorites and I can't do that. You do understand, don't you?"

Cynthia, who *had* hoped that Miss Ballard was going to offer her a lift, was disappointed and anxious to start running for school again so that she wouldn't be any later than she already was, nodded that she understood. Miss Ballard drove off and Cynthia began running again as fast as she could go.

Cynthia lost a library book which, for her, was a terrible thing. Her parents received an overdue notice and Mama questioned her. Had she had the book? She had. Had she returned the book? She thought she had. Had she looked for the book? She had... under her bed, in the bed, all around her room, in her desk at school. No book. She couldn't believe that she'd been so stupid as to do such a dumb thing when she had promised herself that she'd never, ever, keep a book too long. But she had. The book wasn't just overdue; it was gone.

The book was brand new, and Mama had to pay for it. Mama was not pleased. Cynthia was ashamed. Because of her, the number of books that children could take out at one time was changed from seven to two. She and Mama were the only ones who knew it and for that Cynthia was grateful. If the other kids had known, she could never have lived it down.

The change had been a long time coming, but one afternoon when Cynthia came in from school, Mama was there. All her dirty clothes were gathered up and her bed changed. Mama, who had a new-fangled electric washing machine, had taken it all home and when she brought it back that evening to put away, she told Cynthia that the lost book had been in between the wall and the bedding all those many weeks. She'd taken it to the library to see if she could get their money back, but the book had been replaced and they said since she'd paid for it, she could keep it. So she gave it to Cynthia, who was thrilled to have a brand-new library book all her own. Mama was not thrilled.

After that, May came once a week to change Cynthia's bed and bring back the clothes she had taken home the week before to wash and iron. This was the first step of the change that was coming about in Cynthia's life. The rest would follow.

When Cynthia went to Mama's for Christmas Eve that year, Mama had sent her in to take a bath, came in to check on her and was shocked at how thin the child was. She and Papa had decided that Cynthia was old enough now to start coming to their house at lunchtime and again for dinner, after first checking in with Grandma to see if she needed anything from the store. Later, Papa would drive her back to Grandma's for the night.

Cynthia never really knew who'd been the one to tell her parents that Grandma wasn't taking proper care of her, but she had a feeling it had been Miss Ballard. If not directly, then she'd talked about it and someone else had heard it on the gossip grapevine and told them. Her mother and father hadn't really been remiss, she thought as she wrote about this time in her life. Her father had been raised by Grandma, who had undoubtedly been competent and full of energy, and Grandma had come alive for the short time he'd be there in the evenings when he came by to see if she and Cynthia were alright.

"And," Cynthia thought. "The changes in Grandma and my life happened slowly and I adjusted to them. It was normal to me. How could I know anything else? Mama and Papa didn't ask me any questions and I didn't volunteer any information or ask any questions, either. There's no one to blame except unfortunate circumstance."

CHAPTER TWENTY-FIVE

Though Cynthia was often hungry as her Grandma gave up on life, and stopped cooking or doing much of anything else, she was not completely undernourished. There were many things available to her when she played around the yard and in the vacant lot. There was a small Mission fig tree, not big enough to climb, but she was tall enough to reach the figs when they ripened. Papa warned her not to eat the purple skins because they'd make her mouth sore, but she'd already found that out. They had the same stuff in them, he said, that indelible pencils had and every kid who ever put the point of one of those pencils in his mouth knew that they made it sore.

There was a loquat tree in the front yard from which Grandma made jelly. When the fruit was ripe, Cynthia sat in the tree to eat it, throwing the pits down onto the ground. She picked tomatoes as they ripened, eating them straight from the vine. Is there anything more delicious than a tomato eaten out of hand, juicy and warm from the sun? She'd pull up a carrot from the garden, brush it off and eat it unwashed... dirt tasted good to her, perhaps because there were minerals in it she needed.

When the garden died, berries on the Eugenia bushes at school were tart, but not unpleasant; sour grass to chew on grew in the vacant lots and a small, flat, somewhat salty orange seed on a low-growing weed was something else to nibble on. The centers of a hibiscus flower were edible and she sucked the sweet nectar from the honeysuckle blossoms. Once she took a bite of a cactus apple. She was dismayed when she got a mouthful of stickers, but there weren't so many that she couldn't get them all out by herself. She didn't tell Grandma what she'd done, but she told Papa. Someone had said they were good to eat, and he explained that the stickers had to be burned off first. She didn't try that because she'd been warned that she'd be in big trouble if he ever caught her playing with matches.

She'd pluck a Meyer lemon from the small tree that shaded part of the vegetable garden. They were big, easy to peel with segments like an orange, and not as sour as other lemons. They were also a great source of vitamin C, not that anyone knew or cared very much about vitamins in those days. She'd take one to school to peel and eat in front of the other kids while they watched in disbelief, making faces and asking her, "How can you do that?" It made her feel superior to them and she liked the feeling.

When she sat under her palm tree in the front yard, she'd eat the dates that dropped onto the ground. They were not as sweet as the dried ones from the store, but she liked them. When these dainty delights palled, she'd run inside to ask for a piece of bread and butter with honey or brown sugar on it or spread with Grandma's fig jam, loquat jelly, or, best of all, her Satsuma plum preserves. But as time went on, the jars were emptied. She asked Grandma if she was going to make some more.

"No," Grandma said. "It's getting to be too much trouble." All good things must come to an end they say, so that was the end of that.

The natural edibles Cynthia found around to eat may have helped her to keep her from catching more illnesses than she might have ordinarily. She was prone to have a relationship with every bug that flew around looking for a likely host where it could set up housekeeping for the duration, causing her to miss several weeks of school every winter. As for childhood diseases, she was quarantined with measles and chicken pox but didn't get whooping cough or mumps.

All contagious diseases in those days were reported to the Public Health Nurse. Someone from the Health Department would come with a notice and tack it up beside the door. Neighborhood kids walking by hooted and cat-called at the sight of the card and the poor sick child, if she was on the road to recovery, pulled the curtains aside to stick out her tongue or wiggle her fingers in her ears and "N-yah, n-yah, n-yah" back at them.

Each one of Cynthia's children shared their mumps with her after she was grown. Tee Gee, when she was twenty-five and May-May later on. Poor little May-May caught the mumps three times. The first time, when she was about four years old, she kept them to herself. The second time she gave them to Ted right after he'd lost a job, so he was unable to go out looking for another. The last time she gave them to Cynthia, then in her early forties. What a thoughtful child. The only one she didn't share her favorite malady with was her brother, once was apparently enough for him.

When Cynthia got the mumps the last time, one of their friends, thinking it was very funny for anyone as old as she was to get a childhood disease, sent her coloring books and crayons as a joke. Cynthia, who'd always loved coloring as a kid, actually used them to pass the time, enjoying it because now she was much better at it than she'd been back then!

Cynthia may have been underfed, sickly and skinny, but she had a lot of nervous energy. She didn't walk if she could run. She climbed trees and she roller skated everywhere, always as fast as she could go.

When Annie still cooked every day, she made the best bread and rice puddings and custards in the world. She needed to use up the extra eggs from the chickens. She made cornstarch pudding from the recipe on the box and tapioca pudding, which Cynthia loved.

She cooked many vegetables. Unlike most children, Cynthia dearly loved vegetables with the exception of okra and parsnips. Once she had gone with her grandma into the vacant lot and watched her pick a common, dark green, fuzzy-leafed weed.

"Why are you picking weeds, Grandma?"

"We'll have them for dinner tonight."

"Weeds? For dinner? What do they taste like?"

"You'll see."

She had hopped around curious and excited as Grandma picked, washed and put them on to boil. They didn't taste as good as spinach with lots of butter on it. Cynthia was never certain just which weed it had been and she often wondered about one that grew profusely and appeared to be the same. It surely had minerals and vitamins and it was cheap since it was free for the picking, but what she'd had before hadn't been good enough to risk poisoning the family, so she never tried them.

Grandma had fixed okra for them once, boiling them. Cynthia had thought the little green pods were cute and could hardly wait to taste them but boiling them made them slimy. She took one bite and spat it out.

"Oh Grandma, these things are awful," she said, refusing to eat the rest. She never bought them after she was grown either, even after she learned they were supposed to be delicious breaded and fried... too much fooling around to do with a vegetable in her opinion.

Parsnips met the same fate. They looked like pale carrots and she loved carrots. She thought they'd taste the same, but they were flavorless and disappointing. She'd never learned to care about eggplant either. It was another vegetable that had to be fooled with too much for her to bother with.

When Grandma stopped cooking, Cynthia wasn't getting enough of a well-balanced diet to keep a growing child healthy. It showed in the many minor ailments she got, one after the other. Annie loved the child, but she was old. She was tired, her mind was beginning to wander in the past and the present seemed to hold little interest for her. After Amos's death, the simplest things became too much. She'd begun to fail, and it was nearly four years before anyone noticed.

CHAPTER TWENTY-SIX

After the accident on the jungle gym, the harassing and name-calling lessened. Still, no one asked her to play with them, but perhaps someone had spoken to them about fair play and tolerance.

That year she wrote a poem about Indians which was printed in the school paper and made her feel very pleased with herself.

How she longed to learn all the 'pick-ups' in jacks. By watching from a distance, she'd seen the other girls doing onesies and twosies and so on, but she never learned the fancy tricks like Around the World, Double Bouncies and other flourishes. She played by herself on the front stoop of Mama's house, but it wasn't much fun. At school, she'd watch the others jumping rope with two ropes as they chanted:

"Charlie Chaplin went to France,

To teach the ladies how to dance."

There had been more, but she couldn't remember it, and there was another.

"I see London, I see France,

I see someone's (and a name could be inserted) underpants."

Then "Red Hot Pepper" with the two ropes going like sixty. She skipped rope by herself on the sidewalk in front of the house where she also drew hopscotch grids with chalk and went through the motions by herself. Mama gave her the money for jacks, marbles and tops, and Papa taught her how to throw and spin a top as good as any boy. He also taught her how to throw a jackknife over the back of her hand for mumblety-peg and how to hold a marble to get the most speed and force, but she could never master that last. Maybe a girl's fingers are different. The boys let her play with them, but she didn't like dirtying her knife. They tried to split each other's tops too, and she didn't want to have hers ruined. When they played marbles, they played for keeps. So after a few times with them, she gave it all up and contented herself with counting her marbles, spinning her top by herself, playing at hopscotch alone and, when she got bored, going out to the garage and spinning Papa's grinding wheel, making it go as fast as she could, or drilling holes in pieces of wood with his drill press.

Papa taught her how to make a kite with newspaper and thin slats of wood that he cut for her, how to bow it with a piece of string and how to tie lengths of laundry string together with square knots. Then he made her a reel to make it easy to let the kite string out and wind it in again.

One thing she could do alone, did well and dearly loved was roller skating. She skated everywhere, going as fast as the wind and hardly ever falling down. She got her first pair of Union skates when she was five years old and every year on her birthday Mama bought her a new pair. In the meantime, she'd wear out the wheels and have to buy new sets at the hardware store for Papa to replace the old ones with. After she had a pair stolen, Papa took an awl and his ball peen hammer and punched her name on the underneath of each skate with little dots whenever she got new ones. Her things were usually stolen from her desk or the cloakroom, so she quit taking anything to school that she cared about to show around like the other kids did.

The following summer vacation she played for a short while with a child who had moved onto the block. Rumors flew that she'd been rejected by public schools in other cities because she was given to violence when thwarted. It was reported that she'd chased a maid around the house with a butcher knife, scaring the woman half to death. All this information, which had come straight from the intended victim, made a fascinating subject of conversation to the gossipers and filtered down to the children as well.

One afternoon her mother brought her by the hand to Annie to ask if Cynthia would come and play. Why her Grandma had allowed it, Cynthia never knew. Had she been afraid to say no to a white person? Anyway, Cynthia had a playmate, though not of her choice, before the family moved again.

Cynthia soon learned the other little girl may have been different, but she wasn't stupid and indeed had a certain wiliness about her. She knew people were afraid of her and she played on their fears to get her own way by throwing tantrums and screaming threats. She liked Cynthia because Cynthia, who was used to trying to please others, was willing to go along with her so it worked out well enough for both of them. Cynthia had heard the rumor of violence, of course, so when the girl got a certain look on her face, she would capitulate rather than argue since she had no desire to be skewered with a butcher knife.

Later that summer, Grandma's friend with the parrot, who rented rooms, came to Grandma and asked if Cynthia could come and stay with a younger girl who was being left alone in their room while her mother worked at the hotel as a waitress. Cynthia stayed with her and was happy to have a playmate even though the child was younger than herself. It wasn't for very long, however, just until the mother moved into the women's dormitory and the other maids and waitresses who stayed there could watch her when they were off duty. The two of them stayed only once at the dormitory. It was a very stormy day, and they watched the rain come beating down in sheets, the flashes of lightning, and waited for the thunder. Cynthia counted how far away the flashes were before the thunder crashed.

"One and two for each mile," like Papa had taught her to do when she'd been afraid. They watched the storm move across the area and they weren't frightened at all. It had been exciting!

They were good little girls, never getting into any trouble. They played with their dolls and Cynthia, who could read, read stories and drew pictures and paper dolls while they waited for the mother's shift to be over and her return.

When school started in the fall, she was behind Cynthia. They saw each other and remained friendly, but now she had children her own age to be friends with and Cynthia was alone again.

CHAPTER TWENTY-SEVEN

The Depression had begun with the historic crash of October 1929, a few weeks after Cynthia entered the third grade. For years, she had thought it had been the cause of her grandmother's withdrawal from life, but now, as she sifted through her memories, she realized it was losing Amos that did the damage, starting with the slow decline, which had gone unnoticed in its advancement. Her age, the Depression, the loss of rental income which followed, and the cut to the Civil War Widows' pensions were more than she could handle.

Newsboys hawked their papers with big black headlines up and down the streets, even coming into the residential areas with the news. People turned on their radios, listened intently, and talked of nothing else. The fear in the air was a tangible thing, even children sensed it. In the newsreels, as time went on, Cynthia saw men in bread lines, men selling apples on street corners, men bundled up, rubbing their hands and stamping their feet to keep warm as they stood around fires and ten-gallon drums in alleyways in the East. She felt sorry for them. Her life was still relatively unchanged, but she knew it wasn't so for others.

The big house sat vacant. People didn't come to California for the seasons as they'd done before, but the mortgage payments for the borrowed money to enlarge the radio shack went on. President Roosevelt was elected and began making changes to improve the economy... a cut in pay for the Navy with no advancements and reducing the Widows' pensions by a third. This last isn't known to many people; even at the time, it went largely unnoticed.

The area's economy was largely dependent on the Navy payroll. Small businesses dropped by the wayside. There were empty store-fronts up and down the main street of Coronado and in San Diego. When Grandma and her widowed friends got together, Cynthia could tell how concerned they were by the hushed tones of their voices and their worried expressions. They'd been receiving about seventy-two dollars a month, and it was cut to forty-eight. Or was it forty-two? Cynthia couldn't remember, she was barely eight years old. At any rate, it had been a terrible blow for those poor old ladies.

Al's company didn't lay anyone off. There wasn't much of a demand for title searching; property doesn't sell in a poor economy. They kept everyone on, however, rotating what little work there was. This amounted to one week out of the month per employee. It wasn't much, but it helped to keep their people going and was better than the alternative, which was no work or no money coming in at all.

Al bought materials to make a fishing pole and began going up to the sea wall to fish off the rocks. Cynthia clambered around looking for ground squirrels and rats, happy to be with Papa. She knew the fish would be eaten that evening, but she was too young to realize the true desperateness of the situation.

As things worsened, Cynthia's grandmother spent more and more time sitting in her rocker doing little more than reading the newspaper and her Bible and falling asleep. The chickens were long gone; the garden had long since languished and died. She'd stopped sewing for Cynthia, didn't make preserves, and barely cooked for Cynthia or herself.

The two of them went to San Diego once a month to make the

mortgage payment. In the office of the old friend who'd made the loan, Annie opened her satchel, took out a few bills and laid them on the desk.

"I'm sorry, I can only pay the interest again this month," she said apologetically.

Martha Ingraham gave a sigh, pulled open the middle drawer in her roll-top desk, and took out a ledger and a receipt book. As she recorded the amount and filled out the receipt, she'd asked about Al and May, then begin rummaging in her other drawers looking for something for Cynthia. She nearly always had something for her... the bright papers that had been envelope liners or a souvenir teaspoon from a recent trip. When Grandma died, Cynthia's silver teaspoons disappeared with many of her other small treasures... her little red chair, a beloved white leather-bound book of the birthdays of the week with exquisite drawings, also a gift from Mrs. Ingraham, and so many other things she couldn't remember them all. She found it hard to forgive her mother when she learned the teaspoons and the little book were gone forever.

Cynthia knew something was wrong when they went to make the payment, by the shame-faced way Grandma offered the money and the resignation with which Mrs. Ingraham accepted it. When Papa told her he and Mama had to sell Grandma's house to pay the hospital bills and the mortgage after Grandma's death, Cynthia felt a wrench in her heart. From that day on, she hated the word 'mortgage' and tore up everything that came in the mail with the word on it in the return address. After she and Ted got a home of their own when people called from mortgage companies she'd say, "Mortgage is a dirty word to me. Please don't call here again," and hang up.

CHAPTER TWENTY-EIGHT

The Depression and the social mores of the times contrived to keep a married woman in the home. If she wanted to work, her choices were limited for there were few jobs available to her other than trained nurse, office worker (secretary, file clerk, typist, or accountant), waitress, telephone or beatify operator, salesclerk, or household help. If she were able to do something that could be done by a man, she would be ostracized for taking a job away from someone with a wife and perhaps a family to provide for. So she stayed home, cared for the children if there were any, and kept house according to the time-honored written rules set by other housewives.

Few people had one car, let alone two, unless they were well-to-do. Public transportation served very well, and it was cheap. Shank's mare did for many... one foot placed in front of another could take you where you wanted to go and cost nothing.

Some women liked to get out of the house by doing the grocery shopping. In the days of iceboxes, this was several times a week for perishables. They walked uptown, met friends on the street, stopped for a little chat, then walked back home with their purchases. The lady of the house didn't have to leave home at all if she was tied down with a baby or too busy. Men with services of all kinds came around from door to door or if they had a truck, rang a bell, or blew a horn to announce their presence. The milkman, who also took orders for butter, eggs, cream, and whipping cream, and the iceman, who provided the means to keep them fresh, came into the home with their deliveries on a regular basis. Trucks with baked goods or with fresh vegetables from the local farmers came around weekly or biweekly. A knife and scissor grinder man showed up, usually in the spring, with his grinding wheel on his back to sharpen everything that needed it. Then there was the Fuller Brush man with his brushes for every use and the Watkins man who sold coffee, tea, flavorings, spices, and who gave pieces of China as premiums when required amounts of sales were reached. The laundry man picked up the laundry and the cleaning once a week and returned it a few days later. All these services were a great convenience for the stay-at-home housewives in those days, allowing them more free time than perhaps they really wanted which, before the war, they filled with social events... card parties, baby showers, wedding showers, luncheons, teas, or receptions for visiting friends or relatives.

Later on came home parties... Stanley home cleaning products, Emmons Jewelry, and Tupperware. The Avon lady, who called on a regular basis, became a friend so that one felt obligated to buy a little something each time she rang the doorbell. Soon, however, with women moving from the home into the workplace, many of these businesses faded into near oblivion and, in the nineties, the door-to-door salesperson and the neighborhood delivery truck all but disappeared not only because no one was home but the dog or the cat but if someone was in, they're not likely to open the door to a stranger for fear of their life.

CHAPTER TWENTY-NINE

A woman home alone, children in school, husband at work if he was one of the lucky ones, was perfectly safe in the thirties opening her door to strangers. The men of those terrible Depression years came to California, "the golden land of opportunity," with the hope of finding a job and because of the mild climate. They hopped freight trains, made their homes in train yards and culverts, and slept on park benches or in wooded areas. Homeless, hungry, desperate, they would do anything for a handout... mow lawns, wash windows, chop wood, spade a garden. They didn't rape or rob and if they carried a weapon, it was to protect themselves. It was a kinder, gentler time when people cared about other people and tried to help one another as much as they could or could afford.

Cynthia's parents were rich in comparison to these wanderers. They owned a home with a mortgage, a car, a refrigerator, a washing machine, a piano and furniture, and Al was still employed, if only part-time. May didn't have to go to work to help out, but she had to cut corners, change their lifestyle, pinch pennies and live by the rule of the day, "Waste not, want not."

There was always food on the table, if rather spartan. Most weekdays were meatless days... like they would be again during WWII when the best of everything was sent to "our boys overseas." Then the motto changed to, "Use it up, wear it out, make it do, do without."

Food was inexpensive... milk five cents a quart, butter five cents a cube, bread two cents a loaf, and eggs a dime a dozen. Fresh vegetables grown in the county sold cheap... green beans two cents a pound, carrots two cents a bunch, potatoes ten pounds for very little and other things proportionately. Locally grown fresh fruit sold for pennies... apricots, cherries, peaches, strawberries, melons... sweet, juicy, and full of flavor.

When the milk soured, the thrifty housewife made biscuits, muffins, pancakes, or waffles. A simple syrup was used for pancakes and waffles if there was no money for real maple. Sugar and water boiled until thickened served quite well. Later on, maple flavoring could make the simple syrup tastier for those who wanted the flavor and was cheaper than the real thing. Stale bread, if not used as a meat extender or stuffing for Sunday's roast chicken, became French toast or bread pudding. Bananas too ripe? Mash them and make delicious banana bread. Emasculated carrots and celery, softened tomatoes, sprouted potatoes, and onions made hearty vegetable soup, which with bread and butter and a simple dessert of cornstarch or custard pudding, gelatin with fruit, rice pudding, or canned fruit and homemade cookies, made another day's meal.

Bread, at five cents a loaf, was a mainstay of the Depression diet. One did not throw stale bread away. It was usually bought day-old anyway and one had to get there early to get it. Cynthia's grandma took it out to throw to the chickens when there wasn't enough left for anything else.

She served milk toast or torn-up slices with milk in lieu of cereal for breakfast, or toast with simple syrup if there was no flour for pancakes or French toast, or plain toast cut into fingers to dunk in sweetened coffee with canned milk in it. Cynthia thought that last was divine. Bread stretched a half pound of hamburger to the equivalent of a pound for meatloaf or meat patties fried with sliced onions. Meatballs went into a vegetable stew of potatoes, carrots, and onions, or smaller ones into vegetable or bean soup. For dessert, she made custard bread pudding with raisins. Today, some older people will not eat it because it reminds them of the Depression.

Depression cake was made with no eggs, butter, or milk. The same recipe was waltzed around again in the forties and called Wartime Cake... not a delicacy, too heavy, but okay in a pinch.

Bits of the leftover Easter ham shank went into scalloped potatoes for a main dish and the bone was used to flavor cooked dry lima beans to be eaten with cornbread... delicious. After the holiday turkey and its leftovers were gone, the memory lingered on as the carcass was used to make turkey soup. The thrifty housewife satisfied her hungry family at little cost... with meals not fancy, but nourishing. Time-consuming perhaps, but that was a small price to pay. It was the way it was done in those lean and trying times when most women were home all day washing, ironing, cleaning, cooking or baking, and tending to children too young to go to school. It was her job, as it was her husband's to work to bring home the bacon.

One could look down the alley on trash day and see that everyone had one garbage can and one, maybe two, trash cans. There wasn't much to be thrown away then. The pig ranch man collected Coronado's garbage to feed his pigs. Only what could not be sold to the rag, bottle, and paper men or saved for further use went into the trash. Newspapers were used to cover the floor when something messy was being done, to start fires in the winter, to line shelves or bottoms of bird cages, to make a kite or a paper hat for playing soldiers. Paper bags were saved for carrying lunches, wrapping packages for mailing, and making book covers or makeshift Halloween masks if there was no money to buy one.

Trucks came into the neighborhoods with coal or cordwood to sell. Whichever one came first was the one May purchased their winter fuel from. Even when the new house was built some years later, May didn't want central heating installed but used the fireplace in the winter. Cynthia persuaded Papa to install a floor furnace during the first winter of the six years she, Ted, and the children lived with him after May's death because she nearly froze in the cold house during the day. She wondered how her mother had stood it because she'd lit a fire in the fireplace only in the evening.

May had Al bury the garbage in the back yard to enrich the soil and sprinkled used coffee grounds around plants. She saved the string and paper from the butcher and the laundry which were used for wrapping packages to be mailed. The pieces of string were tied together with square knots and made into a ball for flying kites and for other uses. It was cheaper to use to fly a kite than to buy anything new. "A penny saved is a penny earned," and most housewives in the thirties did some or all of these things to save that penny.

In Cynthia's grandmother's time, every scrap of cloth material was saved for making into patchwork quilts. Before that, when the cloth itself was woven by the housewife, no scrap was too small to be used for this... some quilts were utilitarian, others were beautiful works of art with lovely embroidery, so well-made that many have survived until today. Cynthia still has an unfinished top her grandmother started when Al was a boy.

"Honey, have you got something I can use to wash the car?"

"Mom, do you have something I can tear up to use as a tail for my kite?"

"Mama, I need something to make a blanket for my doll."

"Mother, I want to be a ghost on Halloween. Do you have an old sheet I can use for a costume?"

"Look in the rag bag, dear," was the stock answer to all these questions. No well-appointed home was without its rag bag, well past WWII, before the days of prepackaged cleaning cloths and ready-made ironing board covers. Women used rags for sanitary napkins; a box of twelve cost only a dime, but often there would be no dime until payday, if there was a payday.

Everything went into the rag bag... underwear, dresses, men's shirts, worn sheets, and towels. Hooks and eyes, snaps, and buttons were removed for further use; zippers hadn't yet come on the market for home sewers.

A sewing machine was a household must for making worn sheets into pillowcases or curtains trimmed with rickrack or embroidery. Outgrown shirts and dresses were taken apart to be remade into children's clothes, ragged towels cut into squares and hemmed for washcloths. All this, plus mending and patching as well as sewing for the family with new materials, made the sewing machine a necessity for those who knew how to use one.

Throw rugs came from her rag bag's contents too. Bias strips sewn together, after being wound into a ball, were hooked onto a canvas base or crocheted together to make something both useful and attractive. Saving money in all these little ways was a challenge for the homemaker.

As polyester took over the garment industry, rag content paper all but disappeared. The throw-away society got its start with ready-made ironing board covers, treated cleaning, and dusting cloths, and the rag bag began to lose its importance.

Tissues and paper towels replaced handkerchiefs and kitchen hand towels, so they languished in drawers, unused except by the diehards. Socks were forever and didn't need darning, so the darning egg and the sewing basket were relegated to a closet, seldom seeing the light of day again. Every sewing basket had a darning egg used for darning socks. An invisible darn, which was not lumpy, was a fine art but was no longer necessary. Pinching pennies was an even finer art.

Paper that disintegrated over time wasn't used as much. Plastic began replacing it, polluting beaches, rivers, and oceans. The disposable diaper, decorated and elasticized for a perfect fit, is seen everywhere... by the side of the highway, tossed into gutters, going in and out with the wavelets lapping on the shore at the beach, and tossed onto the grass in parks with a trash can only a step away.

Back in those days of the Depression, everything that might be used again was saved... pencil stubs, rubber bands, paper clips, and scraps of wood for the fireplace.

Kids saved foil from cigarette packages because it was said that a large ball was worth a lot of money, but no one seemed to know who was in the market to buy one. They searched in trash cans, along the sides of the road and n vacant lots for soda pop bottles to return for the refund... two cents for a small, five for larger. They scrounged building sites for the slugs that came from metal electrical boxes for play money and scraps of wood to use for building blocks.

Empty matchboxes were neat for storing small items. Several small boxes glued together made a dresser for a doll house, larger ones a storage chest for a collection of little trinkets. Girls saved the pretty paper liners from envelopes to use for paper doll clothes or to cover and line the matchboxes.

Al took apart wooden fruit crates, which stores threw away and were free for the taking, and carefully pulled out all the nails. He straightened them with a hammer on his mother's old flat iron, which he used for an anvil, and saved them in an empty Hill Bros. Coffee can for further use as needed. He cut kite sticks for Cynthia from the box slats and put aside the solid ends. Sometimes the slats ended up as kindling and the ends were split into pieces for firewood to supplement their winter fuel supply.

Once, Al made Cynthia a soap box scooter from a crate. He didn't put the box on the front as was popular with the boys, but made it more like a purchased scooter, using an old pair of her skates for the wheels.

May saved the ends of a bar of soap. When there was enough, she slivered them into a pattered pan she kept for that purpose, poured in boiling water and set it on the stove to simmer just under the boil. This made soap jelly which she used for washing dishes. It was also good for shampoo, but Cynthia usually rubbed the cake of Ivory soap over her head, sudsed, and rinsed. A final rinse of diluted lemon juice or vinegar was used to cut the soap film, leaving the hair silky, soft, and shining. A vinegar rinse, it was said, brought out the red highlights, and lemon, the blond. Since Cynthia's family was all brunettes, she never found out if this was true or not.

"Penny wise and pound foolish," was an even older homily, still in use in those lean and hungry days. It probably wouldn't hurt to train ourselves to heed that sage advice today. Living within our means appears to have become a lost art.

CHAPTER THIRTY

Much of other peoples' problems passed by Cynthia. She knew about the Depression from the newsreels and the way adults talked about it, but she ignored it. She'd had too many problems of her own, too much inner turmoil to pay any attention to or even care about.

As remembrances surveyed when she wrote, she became aware that the members of her family had had their own personal problems, to which she had been oblivious. Since they went back and forth between the two houses, eating in one and sleeping in the other, she hadn't been privy to anything that happened in its entirety in either one. So she could only guess about some of the troubles that existed for those closest to her and how their life choices and the times had affected them. She was drawing conclusions about it now, piecing remembered bits of conversations and happenings together like one would stitch a crazy quilt.

Almost everything she learned about her family had been told to her and was covered in the first part of the book. She had always been an observer and an eavesdropper. She'd learned to keep a low profile, to look and listen, and never to be obtrusive, ask questions or volunteer information unless she was asked, so the book was a jigsaw puzzle of isolated bits of information to be put into their proper places for the whole picture to become evident.

She learned a lot about life in general from the movies. The Westerns of the time taught her that courage, honor, nobleness of character, and good always triumphed over evil. From drawing room comedies she learned that good manners and polite social behavior were the marks of nice people. When she was older, she had read a quotation from Amy Vanderbilt: "Good manners are the oil that makes society move smoothly." It is very true, and we could use some of that oil in our society today.

Musicals, which she adored, furthered her love of music which had already been started by her parents and Papa's long-gone record collection. Their lighthearted romances had the same appeal for her that fairy tales did when she was small, with their happy-ever-after endings. She sat entranced through both showings when she was older, hating for it all to end, wishing she could stay inside forever.

Papa told her of his disappointments... not in so many words, but she'd understood his feelings.

Letters between May and her father and sister had been regular, photos exchanged, and May always sent a postal money order for a pound every month.

At that time, the English pound was a good bit of money, the equivalent of five American dollars. May sent boxes of trinkets and American candy too, and all during the war she had sent used clothing garnered from her friends, along with sugar, raisins, cans of bacon, and tea. She wore her Bundles for Britain pin proudly until Victory in Europe day (VE-Day) and long afterward. Cynthia still had it and, as she wrote she wondered if Mama had managed to send the pound and the boxes during the Depression. Since she was only a sometime visitor in their house until the death of Grandma, she didn't really know.

Years later, during WWII, Cynthia and young Tee Gee went to spend the day with Mama, which they often did during the long, lonely years that Ted was overseas in the South Pacific. They'd stay until Papa came home, have dinner, then Mama and Cynthia would go to the movies, leaving Tee Gee with Grandpa. Afterward, Mama and Papa used some of their precious rationed gasoline to drive them back to their little house.

One day, when Mama answered the door, she said, "I just got a letter from my sister. My father died."

Cynthia didn't know what to say except, "I'm sorry, Mama." Her grandfather had sent the Teddy Bear when she was a baby and the English books for her birthday and Christmas, but she didn't know him. The last time he had sent her anything was when she was twelve years old. She'd never written to him or received a letter from him. He had never sent anything to Tee Gee at all; she would have written to him if he had.

May didn't show any emotion; she delivered her news to Cynthia in her usual matter-of-fact way. The rest of the day went as always. They chatted idly and Cynthia helped with dinner. May told Papa the news when he came home. He told her he was very sorry, that was all. How her father's death had affected May remained her secret. She didn't talk about him or share any memories, but she never spoke of going home again.

"Did Mama love her father as much as I did Papa?" Cynthia wondered, then answered herself. "I'll never know. Her sister is dead; their brother died before she did and Cousin Jean, if she knows anything, never mentioned it."

When Grandpa Amos had died, there was no change at all in Cynthia's young life. Things were much the same as they had always been except, he wasn't there. It was no different when Grandma died. Cynthia went directly to Mama's house and never saw the inside of her grandmother's house again. Nor did she miss it.

Sometime in the eighties, she was told the property was for sale. She called the realtor and made an appointment to see it. He didn't need to know she couldn't afford to buy it. Her grandmother had bought the lots and had the house built for five hundred dollars...

now the asking price was $285,000! The big house seemed smaller than she remembered. Little had been done to it, except a bathroom added on one side between the two bedrooms. It had been a rental for all these years and was in terrible shape, the floors worn, the walls needing paint. It made her feel sick. Then they went into the old radio shack, and it was exactly the same, the garden put back like it was. The palm tree was still there, but the rose bush was long gone.

A short time later, she heard the property had been sold, the houses and the palm tree razed and two townhouses built side by side on the fifty-foot lot.

A wave of sadness washed over her, and tears prickled her eyes as she wrote about it, remembering the days of her youth in that little house and the yard. No matter how bad it had been, it was still her life. She was purging herself of the bad memories that had poisoned her soul, remembering that she had loved her grandmother and her mother, no matter what, and that not everyone in the small town had gone out of their way to be unkind or insensitive. There had been happy moments and people whom she remembered fondly for their kindnesses.

CHAPTER THIRTY-ONE

Before May took over Cynthia's life during the second semester of the third grade, Cynthia caught one cold after another which always went into bronchitis. Sore throats became tonsillitis; she got earaches, sties, gum boils, and canker sores in her mouth and her private parts. When she woke up in the mornings, she had to scrape encrustations from her eyes before she could open them.

Annie treated her with a variety of home concoctions or over-the-counter remedies suggested by the pharmacist at the Central drugstore. Cynthia remembered the doctor coming to the house only once in her childhood and, after looking at her, saying, "Those tonsils really should come out." May wouldn't hear of it. It was said they yanked them out by the roots in those days and she'd heard horror stories of children bleeding to death. She wouldn't allow Cynthia to be vaccinated for smallpox, either. She'd had a beloved cousin who died after being vaccinated and she herself had scars the size of a quarter on both arms. She said her arms had swollen up to twice their size and turned all colors of the rainbow and that she'd been very sick.

The next time Cynthia saw the family doctor who had delivered her, was when she was eleven. May took her to see him because she'd been having one sty after another, her eyes always red with sore pustules, which Grandma opened with a needle run through the flame of a match, then dabbed with cotton soaked in witch hazel.

Once when Cynthia was constipated, Grandma brewed cascara black tea. It tasted vile and Cynthia, gagging and gasping, had made such an awful fuss about it that afterward she got dosed with Castoria, a sweet syrupy laxative made from figs. Cynthia, who had a sweet tooth, loved figs and would have taken the whole bottle if she could. Annie had to hide it after she found Cynthia with a teaspoon and the bottle, dosing herself when she was four.

For colds, Cynthia was anointed with eucalyptus or camphorated oil until Grandma switched over to Mentholatum. Cynthia hated them all, especially the Mentholatum because Grandma, catching her off guard, always smeared some of it under her nose so she could benefit from the fumes... a benefit Cynthia would rather have lived without. For the terrible coughs when she got bronchitis, it was a teaspoon of honey mixed with butter... wonderful... she liked that. Other choices were not so delicious... a teaspoon of sugar with a drop of turpentine... ghastly; a teaspoon of Vaseline sprinkled with salt... yuck! For scrapes and bruises, turpentine, kerosene, or Iodex and sulfur ointments from the drug store. An earache called for warmed sweet oil drops in the ear and the hot water bottle.

For a fever, Cynthia was bundled up to her ears in blankets, which she kicked off every chance she got. Grandma fussed at her that if she didn't keep covered up, she'd get her death of pneumonia. She'd be burning up; so hot and so thirsty.

"Grandma, I'm thirsty. Can I have a glass of cold water? Grandma, please don't warm it, and please, please, please don't put any baking soda in it."

The begging was useless. Grandma returned holding out a glass and Cynthia would raise up eager for the cool water on her parched tongue and throat.

"I warmed it just enough to take the chill off and there's so little soda, you won't even be able to taste it."

It was a patent lie. The nasty warm soda-y stuff was awful. Cynthia refused to drink it, even though she knew she was going to die of thirst.

May, who was always first on the list for anything new, had bought a new-fangled electric icebox just before the Crash. Cynthia, lying in her bed one day burning up with fever, was surprised and pleased to see Mama come into her room. Mama usually stayed away when Cynthia was sick, afraid she might catch it herself. She had brought ice-cold pineapple juice and she poured Cynthia a big glassful, which she guzzled down and held out the glass for more. All the while Grandma was hovering about, rolling her eyes to the ceiling, wringing her hands, and imploring May to stop before she gave that child her death with all that ice-cold stuff.

Then Mama opened both windows all the way, with Grandma imploring her not to. Oh, the cool breeze felt delicious, but as soon as May left, Annie slammed them down again.

Once Grandma took to her bed with the flu which was very unusual; Grandma had never gotten sick that Cynthia knew of, complaining only of her rheumatism. The imp of Satan that resided in Cynthia saw a wonderful chance to get even, to let Grandma see just how awful it was to get warm soda water when you were hot and thirsty. So Cynthia, the dutiful granddaughter, became Grandma's nurse and every chance she got, she fixed a glass of water, warmed it, and put baking soda in it. To her dismay, Grandma drank the stuff down without any complaint, thanking her for taking such good care of her old grandma. When she recovered, she told all her friends how wonderful Cynthia had been.

"If that child hadn't taken such good care of me, I surely would have died. I don't know what would have become of me if she hadn't been there."

So much for revenge. It had backfired, and the next time Cynthia got sick, the battle lines were drawn again.

"It's a miracle I didn't die of dehydration," she thought.

Because of all the germs Cynthia brought home each winter, Annie dressed her to keep warm as she walked to and from school. At first, there were high-button shoes that had to be fastened with a shoe hook. Papa showed her how to do it, a tricky little maneuver requiring a certain amount of dexterity. Then there were long cotton stockings, held up with caps on an elastic belt arrangement. Annie knitted or crocheted wool hats and sweaters. Her talented hands were always busy before Amos died and for a short while afterward. She sewed for Cynthia too, bloomers and petticoats to go under the dresses she made. Cynthia hated those long stockings, the bloomers made of such heavy cotton material (it was almost like canvas!), and the crocheted tam-o-shanters. She'd get to the corner of the alley, take off the despised hat and the garter belt and put them all under a bush. Then she'd roll down the stockings. She had no choice but to keep them and those darned old bloomers on. On the way back, she fished them out from where she'd stashed them and put them on again before going the rest of the way. She complained to Grandma that the other girls wore ankle socks and oxfords, but Grandma paid no attention, so she told Mama.

Mama took her to San Diego to buy oxfords, dime store ankle socks, and cotton panties. Grandma threw her usual fit about pneumonia, but May won out. She took the stockings, the garter belt, the bloomers, and the button shoes away with her to put in the Goodwill sack. Annie followed her every step of the way to the door, bemoaning that the child was going to die of exposure for sure, if pneumonia didn't get her first.

When Cynthia got sick after she started school, the Public Health Nurse, who was also the school nurse, would come to see if the truant was really ill or only malingering.

When she came, Cynthia sensed that she was being inspected and treated with mild distaste. Miss Cody didn't really want to be there, and Cynthia wasn't thrilled about it either. The ordeal for both of them would begin... a battle of wills.

Miss Cody was there to do what needed to be done and Cynthia was determined not to let her do it. Cynthia won out in the end.

Out came the flashlight, the tongue depressor, the bottle of mercurochrome and the cotton swabs on long wooden sticks. She opened the bottle and dipped the swab into it.

"Open your mouth now, Cynthia. I have to see those tonsils."

Cynthia opened her mouth for a second and snapped it shut.

"Open up again, Cynthia. I need a better look."

"No." Cynthia clamped her teeth and turned her head away. She'd had her tonsils swabbed with that nasty red stuff before and it wasn't going to happen again if she could help it.

"Please, Cynthia, you won't get better unless we do this."

"No." Turning her head from side to side.

"Just let me take another look so we can see how bad they really are."

"No."

By this time, Grandma was into the act, pleading with Cynthia to comply, worried about the child and embarrassed by her lack of cooperation.

"Suppose I let you hold the flashlight for me while we did this?"

A new ploy... Cynthia was interested. She agreed and took the flashlight but held it only for the tongue depressor. When the swab came toward her, her jaws automatically clamped shut and she shook her head.

Annie was really upset, wringing her hands and begging Cynthia to please be a good girl. If she didn't let Miss Cody help her, she might die. All this was old hat to Cynthia, who was always being told by Grandma that she might die. She was still here, wasn't she?

Miss Cody had about had it. She started trying to pry Cynthia's mouth open; Cynthia bit her. Grandma gasped and looked appalled. Miss Cody got red-faced with anger; her pale blue eyes blazed. If looks could kill, Cynthia would have died on the spot. She repacked her bag and left, with Annie trailing her to the door apologizing for what had just happened.

After that day, whenever Cynthia was ill, Miss Cody came to the house as was required of her, took her temperature, made sure she was not dying, and left. Cynthia got better without the benefits of mercurochrome from then on. Whenever they passed each other at school or on the street, they eyed each other coldly and did not speak.

ONE SUNDAY AFTERNOON they were driving along Ocean Front Boulevard when Papa pointed at a fishing boat offshore.

"Look, Thum," he said. "See all those seagulls flying around that fishing boat?"

Cynthia looked. She could see the boat, but not the seagulls. She told him so.

"What do you mean you can't see the seagulls?" Papa demanded.

"I'm sorry, Papa. I don't see any seagulls."

Al was getting angry. "Are you trying to be funny?"

"No, Papa. I really don't see any seagulls."

He turned around from the driver's seat and looked as though he was going to slap her, which he did if he thought she was being sassy. May interceded.

"Al, calm down. Maybe the child can't see."

She was taken to the family doctor again for him to take a look at her eyes. He had an eye chart and after he'd tested her, he told May he thought she needed glasses.

So an appointment was made with the eye doctor, a boyhood friend of Al's. He asked if she'd ever had measles. She had when she was six. Afterward, she had seen halos around streetlights. When she'd told Al and May, they'd laughed, thinking she was being cute. She hadn't told them when she'd asked to move closer to the black-board in the fourth grade. She could read what was on it after Miss Ballard let her do it, so it had been okay.

"If I'd gotten her right after she'd had them," the doctor said.

"She'd have only needed glasses for a short time. Now I'm afraid it's too late."

So Cynthia got bifocals when she was eleven. She was teased about them at school, but she could see things that she hadn't been able to see before, so she didn't let it bother her.

CHAPTER THIRTY-TWO

After May took over Cynthia's life, it assumed some order. She was eating better, she quit wetting the bed, and she wasn't sick as often. With the library rules changed because of the book she'd lost, she wasn't reading until all hours of the night and so got more rest and stopped being late for school. She could get up, dress, and fix herself a bowl of cereal or bread or crumbled crackers in milk and still make it to school on time.

She went to Mama's for lunch. After school, she reported in to Grandma to go to the store for her if she needed anything. On the way to Mama's afterward, she'd stop at the school and play on the rings and bars. This was the only time she could get near them and she'd swing by herself, daydreaming as she went back and forth, back and forth, or sit on the teeter-totter, wishing there was someone on the other end. When the five o'clock bell rang for the teachers to go home and everyone to get off the grounds, she went to Mama's for supper. She spent the evening reading and drawing or doing her homework with Papa answering questions for her. Sometimes she and Mama went to the movies; other times Mama would give her a dime to go by herself. She'd skate up town and back again and after the ten o'clock news, Papa would drive her to Grandma's, and she went straight to bed.

Her grandma saw her now for little more than an hour or so each day; it must have been very lonely for her. Did she fix herself anything to eat or did she go to bed with nothing in her stomach, forgetting to eat? With home deliveries, she could call for groceries, or leave a note in a bottle for milk, butter, and eggs from the dairy if she remembered to do it. Grown-up Cynthia, realizing now the extent of her grandmother's senility which had gone unnoticed for so long, wondered about it.

She didn't remember May sending up a plate of food to Grandma except on Thanksgiving and Christmas. Grandma had come to Mama's for these two holidays and was sent home with a plate until Cynthia was five or six, then it had stopped. Had they decided that it was better for an old colored lady not to be seen coming to their house? Who had made the decision? If that had been the thought behind it, it was far too late. The town was too small, and Cynthia had been seen with Grandma for too many years; everyone knew who and what she was. The barn door had been locked after the horse was long gone.

After a time, things picked up a little. Papa went back to more regular hours so when Cynthia went to Mama's for lunch, a man would be mowing the lawn, washing windows, or chopping firewood. These men were the hoboes, tramps, and bums of the Depression. They were homeless or far from home and they rode the rails, as it was called, looking for work. They were honest, polite, and decent men. A woman home alone was not in jeopardy of opening her door to one of them, but she wouldn't invite him in.

With hat in hand, a man would offer to work for a handout. People didn't have much, but they were more than willing to share. There was a camaraderie in those days. "We're all in this thing together"... much like the same spirit years later during WWII when people were all in the same boat, sharing, pulling together, working and praying for the same end. That spirit seems to have disappeared. Instead of one for all and all for one, these days it's all for ME, ME, ME.

May would give a man something to do and when the work was finished and he knocked on the door again, she'd give him something to eat... a cup of coffee with leftovers perhaps, if there were any... a can of soup with bread and butter or a sandwich of lunch meat and cheese. When he finished, he'd knock again, hand back the dishes, and say his thanks. If there was enough, she might fix a sandwich for him to take along and if there was any money, she might give him some small change before sending him on his way.

Cynthia remembered hearing songs at the time about the Depression. "Marching along together," about sharing, and one Mama sang around the house:

Hallelujah, I'm a bum.
Hallelujah, bum again,
Hallelujah, give us a handout,
To revive us again.

When things picked up after Roosevelt became president, there was another song.

Happy days are here again.
The skies above are clear again.
Let us sing a song of cheer again.
Happy days are here again.

— WRITTEN BY MILTON AGER

There were not as many new shoes as before, but Mama continued to send Papa's shirts out to the laundry. She had said he was a white-collar worker and should look the part. She said it proudly because her own father had been a blue-collar worker, poorly paid. A long-sleeved white dress shirt would be picked up, washed, starched, ironed, and delivered back for ten cents. So Al wore three shirts a week, changing into an old one when he came home from work each night and his half-day on Saturday.

Al taught Cynthia how to put a shoe on a piece of shirt cardboard, draw around it, cut it out, and trim it to make a temporary sole when her shoes were worn through. This worked well only when the weather was dry. Sometimes the hole got very big before May took Cynthia to town for new ones, which was a twice-a-year occasion... for Easter and for the start of school in the fall. Two pairs... black patent leather Mary Janes for dress and serviceable oxfords for every day. In summer, Cynthia went barefoot or had a pair of white tennis shoes, called "tennies." She had a narrow hard-to-fit foot, so her shoes had to come from the better stores, Mastron's or Boldrick's, when she needed new ones, even during the Depression.

May had to wear rayon slips and stockings instead of silk. Rayon was a fairly new fabric that didn't wear well. It shrank, melted if the iron was too hot and the seams frayed in the wash. The stockings were thick, the colors ugly and they stretched and bagged. May couldn't afford to buy the French kid gloves she loved, which were white inside. Cheaper American-mades were darker inside and the dyes rubbed off, making her hands blue or black, which she hated.

Al had always rolled his own cigarettes with Bull Durham tobacco and papers, buying ready-mades only occasionally. Cynthia had loved watching him do it, sprinkling the tobacco, pulling the string on the sack with his teeth to close it while balancing the paper, then rolling it, a lick and a twist and it was done. May came home from shopping with a contraption for rolling cigarettes which were supposed to be just like ready-mades, but Al, after trying it out, went back to rolling his own.

There were no more vacation trips either, but none of this bothered Cynthia. She wasn't personally affected by the Depression that everyone talked so much about. She was happier than she'd been in a long while. She saw Papa every day, she wasn't hungry all the time and she got to take a bath in the bathtub almost any time she wanted. Cynthia loved to loll in the hot bath water, blowing soap bubbles with the cake of Ivory soap and hollow wild oat stems she cut ahead of time in the vacant lot next door.

Mama cooked nice dinners and it was very nice to sleep in a clean bed that didn't smell. May was so concerned about how skinny Cynthia was when she first took over, that she began buying Cocomalt to stir into her milk, hoping to put some weight on her. So, for Cynthia, the Depression was a grown-up problem. She skated happily back and forth between her two houses. The only thing she really needed now was a friend.

Lunch at Mama's was usually a sandwich and milk; peanut butter with apricot-pineapple preserves was a favorite, as was pimento loaf and sandwich spread. Sometimes there was tomato soup, to be eaten with soda crackers crumbled in it, or a can of oysters for oyster stew, or one of alphabet vegetable soup. What adult doesn't remember eating that soup and searching for the letters of their name or trying to find all the letters of the alphabet?

She'd skate to Mama's and fix herself a sandwich or open up and heat the soup or make the oyster stew with milk and a dab of butter to eat with little round oyster crackers. There might be leftover Jell-O from the night before for dessert or a piece of Mama's sponge cake with raspberry jam between the layers. Maybe a package of Lorna Doones or Hydrox cookies.

Mama's house was always immaculate. She'd be cleaning and much too busy to stop to fix Cynthia's lunch, but that was all right. Cynthia didn't mind. She'd had to fix her lunch at Grandma's for the last couple of years.

Dinners were simple... boiled spaghetti with melted pimento

cream cheese stirred into it with a salad of lettuce and sliced tomatoes, navy beans cooked with a ham bone or bacon and eaten with
ketchup, scalloped potatoes with tidbits of leftover ham, macaroni
and cheese, or potato soup. Always with bread and butter and milk
for Cynthia.

May tried to have something special for Sunday... meatloaf, the
hamburger stretched with several slices of bread, and the next day,
cold sliced meatloaf with potato salad; a small, rolled roast and hash
from the leftovers for Monday; fried chicken, Swiss steak, sometimes
a ham shank. On Fridays, fish, either what May had bought at the
market or what Papa caught off the rocks at the sea wall. Or she'd
make salmon patties with leftover mashed potatoes and a ten-cent
can of salmon. Fish on Friday was a Scottish custom May brought
with her from home, not a Catholic caveat. May had been a Presbyterian before she married Al.

Potatoes were cheap and May fixed vegetables of all kinds.
Cynthia liked all the ones Mama cooked except brussels sprouts, but
she ate the bitter things anyway because Papa did. He put ketchup
on them, which helped, and a child who has gone hungry for long
periods isn't overly picky about what's on her plate.

May usually baked a cake for Sunday, sometimes made pudding,
apple cobbler or peach in season, Jell-O, or frozen mousse. Al could
have lived forever without mousse, but he ate it to please May. The
recipe came with the Norge refrigerator and May was trying out all
the variations. Sometimes, for dessert on Sunday, she'd send Cynthia
and Papa to the Sweet Shop to hurry back with a pint of Hage's ice
cream before it melted. Refrigerators in those days had only a small
compartment for ice cubes with no storage space for anything else.
The mousse that May was so fond of was made in the ice cube trays.

Once in a while Mama gave Papa and Cynthia a chop and fixed
something else for herself, a couple of soft-boiled eggs or fish roe
boiled then fried. Young Cynthia thought Mama was fixing something special and keeping it all for herself and wished she could have
it too. She didn't realize that there'd only been money enough for

only two chops and Mama had given them to her and Papa. It was the way of European women, she now knew.

Mama was not very loving, but she was a conscientious wife and mother, keeping a tidy house, doing all the right things, and tending to the needs of her husband and daughter while still keeping to herself.

CHAPTER THIRTY-THREE

Every Sunday for as long as she could remember, Cynthia had attended church with Grandma and afterward, Sunday School by herself. She sat wiggling and squirming alongside Annie, wishing she was someplace else.

Grandma, scolding quietly, whispering, "Sit still and stop fidgeting. You must have worms."

Church was torture for the child except for the singing. She loved the singing.

The first Sunday of every month was communion Sunday. It was the worst. Cynthia called it "long church" and hated every minute of it because it seemed to last forever and sometimes, she was afraid it would.

The two of them always sat in the last row of the church. Cynthia usually ran ahead, wanting to sit closer, but her grandmother would call her back.

"No, we'll sit here."

As the preparations for communion began, everyone moved up closer to the altar except them. Cynthia longed to stand in the line and taste whatever it was the minister was offering his flock. It was something delicious, she was sure because everybody wanted some. She was hopeful, each time the ceremony began, that this time she and Grandma would get into the line too, but they never did, not until the last person had been attended to and was leaving. Then the minister would beckon, and Annie went to him.

"Can I come too, Grandma?"

"No, you stay right where you are and wait for me."

Cynthia asked Grandma why she couldn't go up and take communion too, but Annie told her it was because she hadn't yet been confirmed.

"When can I be?" she wanted to know.

"Not until you are twelve years old."

Cynthia thought that was an awfully long time to wait.

After the services, Annie went home, leaving Cynthia to attend the children's program of Bible stories, memorizing the Ten Commandments and the Catechism. Cynthia and a girl from her class at school usually sat together, side by side on little chairs which were circled on the lawn on nice days and inside the parish house when the weather was bad.

During the week, the other girl more or less ignored her, but in Sunday school they got the giggles, earning them the name "giggle boxes" which they thought was hilarious. If it got too much for the teacher, she sent them to the kindergarten class to shame and embarrass them, but they thought that was even funnier, leading to more giggling and frowns from the adults.

For Cynthia, church and Sunday were something to be endured until she could go back to Grandma's and sit on the curb at the corner of the block to wait for Papa to come and take her to Mama's for the rest of the day. This was the high point of her week and her life.

. . .

ANNIE DIED in the spring of the year that Cynthia would turn thirteen. The first Sunday after the funeral, she asked her mother, "Do I still have to go to church and Sunday school?"

"Not if you don't want to," May said.

"I don't," she answered, and didn't from then on except at Christmas and Easter when she and Mama went to the special programs and services together, leaving Papa at home with the dog and cat, his crossword puzzles, and his occult books.

May liked to go to missionary meetings. Sometimes they'd be in a tent down by the ferry landing and sometimes they were in the Masonic Temple. There'd be a talk by someone who'd just come back from a faraway place with slides of the poor benighted heathens who lived there and for whom the collection plate was passed afterward. This was followed by singing before the evening ended.

"Shall We Gather at the River?" "Work, for the Night Is Coming," "Onward Christian Soldiers"... These affairs weren't formal like a church where she had to sit still and not sing out so loud, so Cynthia sang at the top of her lungs and had a lovely time. Worshipping this way was fun. She really did love God, but she didn't understand Him. He was supposed to be there for everybody, watching over them, hearing and answering their prayers, but He didn't seem to be there or listening when she talked to Him and she wondered why. You were supposed to beware of his wrath but was He so mad at her that He wouldn't answer, like when Mama got mad and wouldn't talk to her, and she didn't know why either? He was supposed to love everybody no matter what, wasn't He? Didn't He love her?

Papa came every Sunday unless he and Mama were on a vacation trip or away for the weekend. On the Sundays that he didn't come for her, she felt lost... there was nothing to do, nothing to look forward to. She could hardly wait for them to get back.

When Al brought Cynthia back with him on Sundays, May put her in the bathtub and washed her hair until she was old enough to do it herself. Then Papa read the funny papers to her until she learned to do that for herself, while Mama cleaned up the bathroom and did other small chores.

When May was done, she'd say, "Let's go for a drive."

This was the signal for Al to jump up, saying that something needed to be adjusted on the car before they could go.

"Why does he always have to do that?" May asked of no one in particular. Then she'd get out the curling iron, turn on the gas burner to heat the iron and curl Cynthia's hair to pass the time while Al adjusted the timing, checked the carburetor, made sure all the spark plugs were doing what they were supposed to do, disconnected the battery from his home-made charger, checked it and the radiator, the oil and the tires.

Cynthia loved having Mama curl her hair. May was always very careful to keep her finger between the iron and Cynthia's scalp so's not to burn her, but if she did, she was truly sorry. It made Cynthia feel like Mama did like her.

When Cynthia was beautified, Mama turned off the burner, put the curling iron in a safe spot to cool, and sent her to the garage to tell Papa that they were ready. He'd take off his overalls, come in, wash his hands, and finally they'd be off.

Usually, they drove down the Strand to Imperial Beach to a chicken ranch where May bought fresh eggs for the coming week and often had a chicken killed for their dinner that evening. Then they'd return, letting the dog out to run for exercise. There was little traffic on the two-lane road so they went very slowly while he ran alongside, occasionally taking a side trip to chase a ground squirrel.

Another Sunday they might continue around the Strand to stop at the Broadway pier and go on a tour of some foreign ship having an open house for the public, then go back to Coronado on the ferry. Two or three times a year they'd go visit an old school friend of Al's who owned the Few Acres dairy farm in Bonita and on the way home they'd stop at a roadside stand for vegetables and fruit in season.

There were many small truck gardens in the backcountry of San Diego in those days and in Mission Valley where the shopping center is now. The fresh produce tasted so much better than the fruit and vegetables imported into the city these days, picked too soon, kept in cold storage, shipped in from miles away... no comparison.

Sometimes they'd take a drive to Coronado and onto North Island. Anyone could go aboard a military base without question in the days prior to WWII. They might go aboard one of the aircraft carriers which were always open to the public on the weekends.

"Our tax money gives us the right," Papa said, so Cynthia had been aboard the Langley, the Saratoga, the Lexington, the Yorktown, and the Enterprise.

Sometimes they went to the world-famous Balboa Park where, when Cynthia was small, she'd ride on the merry-go-round and the miniature train. Sometimes they went into the museums... Art, Natural History, or the Museum of Man, then attend the afternoon concert on the world's largest outdoor organ, all of which were free. A drive out to Point Loma took them to the old Spanish Lighthouse. Other options were Scripps Aquarium, the Presidio, or the Mission in the valley. Once they drove to San Juan Capistrano, but it was a little too early for the swallows and May was disappointed.

A Sunday drive might take them across the border to Tia Juana, as it was called and spelled then. They'd look around the stalls in the bazaars before going into a bar. Mama would give Cynthia some change to play the slot machines while she and Papa had a drink. Other times they'd leave her in the car while they went to the Foreign Club where she was not allowed when she was small. She was told to keep the windows up and the doors locked, and Papa would come out from time to time to check on her. She'd play with her doll, color in her coloring book, or draw pictures while she waited and watched the people passing by. Some smiled at her and she smiled back. Others would motion to her to wind the window down but, still smiling, she'd shake her head no.

When Al and May came out, May would be flushed and smiling. They'd cross the street to the Longest Bar in the World so Cynthia could look at herself in the long row of mirrors that distorted her image like the ones in amusement parks, which Cynthia loved. She'd go down the long row, stopping to look at herself in each one... short and fat, tall and skinny, big head on a short body, and so on. She laughed so hard tears came to her eyes and her tummy hurt. After that, the family would go to the Marianna for a steak dinner and, because she'd been a good girl, Mama would let her have an apricot or peach cordial as a treat. It was alcoholic, but they were in Mexico, and one wouldn't hurt she said. The mirrors and the thick, sweet, fruity cordial in the cute little stemmed glass made up for the long wait in the car.

When she was almost twelve, she went into the Foreign Club with them to watch the Mexican dancers and hear the music. A pretty girl only a little older than herself came out to dance alone. Smiling, skirts swirling, castanets clicking, she kept dancing up to Cynthia, showing off for her. Cynthia, pleased with the attention, kept her head down while looking up sideways and smiling shyly.

The girl's name was Margarita Cansino. Years later she was known to the world as Rita Hayworth.

Just before her twelfth birthday, Mama and Papa took her to the races at Agua Caliente. In the gift shop, Cynthia admired a silver ring with a Mexican opal which Mama bought for her as an early present. May did things like that, unexpectedly surprising Cynthia and making her very happy. She still has the ring after sixty-two years (at the time of this writing).

Cynthia thought it would be exciting to see a horse race but to tell the truth, she found it rather boring. There was no room in the stands, and she couldn't really see anything.

Suddenly, Mama said, "Look! There's Clark Gable."

Cynthia stood on tiptoe and sure enough, she saw him.

"Here, go and get his autograph," Mama said, looking in her purse for a piece of paper and handing it to Cynthia. Cynthia was horrified.

"No, Mama, I don't want to."

"Of course you do. He's a big movie star. Don't you want to have his autograph as a souvenir?"

"No, no. I don't want it."

"Yes, you do," said Mama, giving Cynthia a push to start her off.

Reluctantly, Cynthia picked her way through the crowd in his direction. She was hoping he'd be gone when she got there, but he wasn't. He was standing in the middle of a group of friends, laughing and talking.

She went slowly up to him, held out her piece of paper, and said, "Please, Mr. Gable, may I have your autograph?"

He gave her a big smile and said, "Sure, kid. Where's your pencil?" Cynthia was dismayed; she didn't have one.

"I don't have one," she told him. He gave a big laugh.

"Look," he said to the group around him. "This kid comes up and asks for my autograph and she doesn't even have a pencil."

Everyone with him laughed and Cynthia was so embarrassed she could have died. She turned and left. When she got back Mama asked, "Well, did you get it?"

"No."

"Why not? Didn't he want to give it to you?"

"He would have, but I didn't have a pencil and they all laughed at me."

"He didn't have a pencil?" Mama was surprised.

Papa was a draftsman, and he always had a pencil in his coat pocket with a pocketknife to sharpen it. It apparently hadn't occurred to May that all men didn't do the same.

"You'd think a big star like him, when he knows people are going to ask him for his autograph, would have sense enough to carry a pencil," she said.

When Cynthia remembered this, she realized it was Mama who'd wanted his autograph and sent her to get it instead of going to ask him herself. May had a way of pushing Cynthia into things which embarrassed her on more than just this one occasion.

"She had no idea of how insecure and shy I was," Cynthia told herself. "She wasn't unkind, just unobservant."

When Cynthia was eight, Mama took her to the opening of the newest Fox theatre. Oh, it was something. Searchlights on the sidewalk in front of the building turned up into the sky, flashing their beams back and forth to let San Diego know that the latest thing in movie theaters was now open for business. People waited on the sidewalk for the doors to open as others lined up to get their tickets and wait with them.

At the appointed time, the doors were opened by the ushers and the crowd began streaming in to "ooh" and "aah" at the plush interior, before moving out of the lobby to find their seats and get settled.

Cynthia had forgotten how old she'd been when this event had occurred and also what the movie had been, but while she was remembering the times Mama pushed her into things she hadn't wanted to do, there was an article in the San Diego Union about the opening with both the year, which was 1929, and the name of the film. It had been, *They Had to See Paris* with Will Rogers.

There was a drawing for a new Ford car that evening. At the appointed time, the house lights came up and a man in a tuxedo came out on the stage. Behind him, came others pushing a cage on wheels with all the ticket stubs. Someone began turning the crank to mix them all up. The man walked over to a microphone to announce that the drawing was about to begin and to ask if some little girl in the audience would like to come up and draw the number for the lucky winner.

Mama poked Cynthia with her elbow. "Stand up. You go down and do it."

"No!" Cynthia was horrified at the thought.

The audience stirred as people looked around, but no other little girl stood up. The man called out again, "Surely there's some little girl out there who'd like to make someone happy by drawing their number for a brand-new car."

"Get up, get up, you do it." Mama was poking her again.

Cynthia slunk down trying to become invisible as others around them leaned forward or turned their heads looking at her and smiling.

He tried a third time; still, no other child stood up. Mama grabbed Cynthia's arm, pulled her to her feet, and pushed her out into the aisle. Cynthia could have died. She stood there wanting to turn and run, but he'd seen her.

"Here's a little girl who's going to draw the winning ticket for us. Come on down, honey."

So she went. Reluctantly, is an understatement. Her feet felt like they were made of lead. When she got to the stage, someone helped her up the steps and led her to the cage. The turning stopped and a little door was opened.

"Now just reach in there honey, feel around and get a ticket, pull it out, and hand it to me."

She did. He read off the number and someone gave a whoop.

"Here we are. We have a winner. Come on down and get your new car."

The winner was a sailor. The number was verified and everyone on the stage shook his hand while Cynthia stood to one side watching. When the tumult died and the audience calmed down and stopped clapping, the man came over to Cynthia, handed her a box of candy, thanked her, and someone led her back to the steps and helped her down. She went back to Mama.

"Did the sailor thank you?" Mama asked.

"No."

"He should have given you a tip, after all, you won him a new car. And he didn't even thank you?"

"No."

"Well, what did they give you?"

"This box of chocolates."

May looked at it and snipped. "Humph, this isn't a very good company. With all the money they make, you'd think they could do better than that."

May liked good candy. She had a sweet tooth, but not for junk. When she went to a matinee, she went to a candy store near the corner of Fifth and Broadway that carried homemade candies. She bought a little bag of something she liked and if Cynthia was with her, she shared it during the show... Jordan almonds, Turkish delight, jellied orange slices, chocolate-covered raisins, nonpareils, vanilla creams, and chocolate-covered ginger, which was her special favorite. She also favored Whitman's Samplers and usually bought one for herself at Christmas. She always seemed a little disappointed that Cynthia had a taste for ginger, too.

"Are you sure you really like this?" she'd ask as she proffered the bag, and Cynthia took a piece.

When they got back to the house, the bag would disappear. Even after Cynthia was living with them permanently, the bag was never seen again. May had told Cynthia that her mother had hidden candy from her and her sister when they were young, so it would seem she had learned to be selfish while still a child.

Cynthia's sweet tooth when she was very young was for anything that tasted sweet, so she'd been very happy to have a box of chocolates all her own, but May's discriminating taste had rubbed off on her, leaving its mark.

When they got on the ferry, May said, "Let's open the box and see what this stuff tastes like."

So they did and Mama was right. It wasn't very good, but Cynthia ate all the rest of it anyway.

CHAPTER THIRTY-FOUR

To Cynthia, Christ Church in Coronado was the most beautiful place in the world, an imposing structure of great ivy-covered, rough-hewn, gray granite blocks. The inside was handsomely appointed. Beneath the high peaked ceiling, polished wood pews glowed in the colored rays of light coming through the stained-glass side windows.

The church was never locked. Sometimes, on a weekday, she'd go in alone just to look around, run her hands along the backs of the smooth wooden pews, and sit quietly up in the front feeling the almost tangible presence of Him in the peacefulness and silence.

She never went up to the altar level, nor did she do anything disrespectful. She went into other churches too, just to look around and see what the difference was between Episcopal, Methodist, Presbyterian, and Catholic. There was none that she could see, but none of them compared to her church... its serene and holy ambiance and its quiet beauty were a panacea to her soul.

She wondered, where is God? Could He be behind the door on the right of the apse that the minister came out of on Sundays? This was supposed to be His house, but it wasn't big enough for Him and all the angels. Besides, He was supposed to live in Heaven, too. Was there even room enough for His palace and all the angels up there with all those stars so close together? Did he come to Coronado just for the season like the people who rented Grandma's house? How could He be in all of the churches all on Sundays and live in them and be in Heaven too?

She finally decided that God must be like Santa Claus, who, even though he had a fat tummy, could squeeze through tiny chimneys and who, on Christmas Eve, went into the houses of all the children in the world and who knew all about you when you were bad just like God did. She imagined God and Santa Clause being like the pictures of the puffy-cheeked clouds representing the four winds in her story books. They were invisible, but you could feel them even if you couldn't see them, so you knew they were there.

Once, when she asked Papa about dying, he told her that when people died, they just moved into another dimension or onto another plane and they weren't really gone.

"We can't see them with our eyes because they are vibrating at a different rate of speed. It's like the radio; you can hear the station only when the dial is turned to the same frequency."

After that, she'd decided that Santa Clause and God were on stations people couldn't turn to, but, because they were special, they could tune to any frequency they wanted. It was sort of comforting. From that time on she burned her letters to Santa Clause in the fireplace so the words she wrote would go to him with the smoke. It was silly to put her letter in the mailbox when the mailbox wasn't on Santa's frequency. She still said her prayers beside her bed on her knees every night, wondering if God was tuned to her frequency.

Papa told her that he and his friend, Charlie, had pumped the bellows when they were teenagers for the organ in Christ Church on Sundays for Miss Fenton, who was Cynthia's piano teacher and a dear friend of the family. When Miss Fenton needed air to play the organ, she'd rap on the wall and the boys would begin pumping. It was hard work, especially in the summer in that hot little room behind the pipes. Cynthia never knew if he and his friend had been paid for doing it or not, probably not.

It was hard for Cynthia to reconcile the God of her Sunday School class, who was supposed to be compassionate and caring and whose Son said, "Suffer the little children to come unto me," with the same God who made dire threats, saying, "Beware. For I, the Lord thy God, am a jealous God," and warned about incurring His wrath. She preferred the friendlier version. "Ask and it shall be given. Seek and ye shall find."

She was a little child, wasn't she? Nightly, for years, she begged Him for an answer to her woes and for a friend, but there was no answer. He finally got around to her when she was ten, when she got both in one package... Vera, who told her the reason why people didn't like her and who was her dearest friend until her death on January 17, 1992. Perhaps Cynthia's wait for an answer to her prayer had been so long because God had to find just the right choice for her... someone as lonely as she was.

It took so long for Him to answer Cynthia that her faith in Him was shaken, and she became ambivalent about Him. This was the reason she didn't want to go to church anymore after her grandmother died. To this day she tells people she's an agnostic Episcopalian.

On the wall behind the wide altar area in Christ Church is a large beautiful stained glass window depicting Jesus leaning on his staff with his hand raised to knock at a paneled door. Once, when she was small, Cynthia noticed the door had no doorknob.

"Grandma," she'd whispered. "The door in the picture doesn't have a knob. How is Jesus going to get in?"

"The door can only be opened from the inside. It represents your heart and if you don't open your heart to Him, he can never come inside," Grandma whispered back.

Cynthia thought about this on long church Sundays as she sat beside Grandma looking at the window. She felt sorry for Jesus knocking and knocking, left outside, maybe forever, or maybe even told to go away. It happened to her all the time. She knew how it was not to be invited in and be told to go home.

God's house was one place she wasn't ordered to go home from. More than once, the minister, and twice, the Bishop, both of whom knew who she was, had come into the nave, found her there, and asked what she was doing.

When she told them, "Nothing. Just sitting here," they'd suggested kindly that maybe she should run along now. She hadn't been ordered to; it was her choice, but the spell had been broken by their entrance anyway.

Years later, when she and Ted eloped to Yuma to get married, at the last minute she decided against a Justice of the Peace and said she wanted to be married in an Episcopal church, surprising herself. When the minister asked why she'd wanted to be married in his church, she said, "Because my grandmother would have wanted me to," surprising herself again.

SHE NEVER REALLY GAVE UP BELIEVING THERE was a God; she needed to feel there was someone, somewhere who, like Santa Clause, had a list with her name on it. She argued the point with Vera who, claiming she didn't believe in God, still blamed Him for everything bad that happened to her. Cynthia did turn her back on Him once for six years after the death of her mother. It had been so unexpected and at such an early age.

"How could you?" she asked Him. "I asked you to take care of her for me." She went into a decline but began to recover when one day she realized God had answered her mother's prayers, not her own.

CHAPTER THIRTY-FIVE

Every time a new girl came to school, Cynthia wondered if maybe she'd be the friend she so desperately wanted. Sometimes one was for a short time if they happened to walk home in the same direction. Then it would happen. Other girls called her over and the whispering and looks began. Cynthia watched, knowing the outcome and wondering why afterward. The new girls, instead of joining her or asking her to wait up, hurried ahead or lagged behind to walk with someone else or avoided looking at her to start off alone on the other side of the street. It was the same old story. No one wanted to walk with her or be her friend... not the girls she had been with in earlier grades and not the new girls either... and she still didn't know why.

She'd take Grandma's hand mirror and sit in front of the dresser in her room looking at herself from all sides. Did they see something she couldn't see? She didn't look like a nigger, that couldn't be it. What else could it be? What did their mothers tell them about her that made them say, "My mother says I'm not supposed to play with you," or "My mother says I can't have anything to do with you"?

Grandma caught her looking at herself, gave her a scolding about being vain, took the hand mirror from her and turned the dresser mirror to the wall.

When Cynthia first entered Miss Ballard's fourth-grade room, she looked around to see if there was anyone who might be for her, but there was no new girl. However, after the children were assigned to the seats... Cynthia in a seat in the back of the room as usual... Miss Ballard said she had an announcement to make. A new boy would be coming in presently and she wanted them to know he had a speech problem that made it difficult for him to talk. She said that he couldn't help it and she didn't want to hear anyone making fun of him or teasing him about it. Did they understand? They all nodded in agreement and, to their credit, no one ever teased him that Cynthia ever heard. That same year, the name-calling that Cynthia usually endured stopped and the other hassling too.

"I wonder," she thought. "If one of the times I was out sick, did Miss Ballard talk to the other kids about me too?" Had she only imagined that Miss Ballard hadn't liked her next-door neighbors; that it was her nature to be coolly polite and detached like Mama? Miss Ballard, Cynthia had decided as she wrote, was likely the one who had passed the word to someone that Grandma wasn't doing a very good job of taking care of her granddaughter... if not to Cynthia's parents herself, then to someone else who told them.

A year later, in the fifth grade, when Vera was the new girl, Cynthia figured that this one wasn't going to be any different from the rest of them. She was distrustful at the beginning of their relationship, certain that any day Vera would turn out to be a false friend, but it never happened... not ever.

It had started in the third grade with a slight change in attitude toward Cynthia, both from the teachers and the other kids.

"It was probably because of the spelling bees and the poem printed in the school paper," she told herself as she wrote. But by this time she had put up a wall between herself and people. She didn't speak unless spoken to or if the other person smiled at her. It had hurt too much when she made the first friendly overtures to be ignored or rebuffed, to have people be nice until someone told them the secret about her.

She'd become a loner, her accomplishments ignored by her teachers who seated her in the back of the room and hadn't called on her no matter how wildly she waved her hand when they asked for answers.

"Did they think that because I was part colored that I wasn't worth wasting time on? It's possible, I guess, now that I have read a little about it and know the mindset of the Jim Crow days... that Negroes were more like animals, less than human, had no souls and were capable of all the other degrading things they said and thought besides."

SOMETIMES, after she started the fourth grade, someone would walk part way home with her if there was no one else around. But Cynthia was wary... once bitten, twice shy. She was polite, keeping herself aloof, knowing from past experience that it was only for the moment and wouldn't last. Still... she did seem friendlier...

Reading and sleeping late on weekends and in the summer so as not to have to face the day and going to the movies were Cynthia's escape from the vicissitudes of her life. A shorter day was easier to get through. Once she had learned to read, she read everything... the cereal box on the breakfast table, the advertising cards on the street-cars and the ferry, the Burma Shave signs by the side of the road on Sunday drives. She got so she could even read them backward. She devoured fairy tales, with their promises of a handsome prince and a happy-ever-after life. She discovered the Oz books of L. Frank Baum and the collie stories of Albert Payson Terhune. She read all her father's books in the bookcase that was in her room at Grandma's... Poe, Hawthorne, Kipling, and Twain.

· · ·

IN MISS BALLARD'S fourth grade class, Cynthia began to realize that she was smart. She was good at English and still the best speller. She was the fastest reader too. She could hardly wait for their readers to be passed out so she could take hers home and read it cover to cover. When class reading was assigned, Miss Ballard said, "Read the story starting on such and such a page and when you finish, close your book, fold your hands, and sit quietly until the others are finished."

Cynthia, who'd already read the story, read it again, closed her book and folded her hands to wait. Miss Ballard looked up and whispered, "Cynthia, you didn't finish reading." She nodded her head that she had, but Miss Ballard said, "Read it again," so Cynthia read it again, closed her book and folded her hands to wait. Miss Ballard looked up again, frowned, and indicated that Cynthia should continue reading. Cynthia did, and by her third time through the story, a few others were closing their books and folding their hands. After several times of this, Cynthia knew that her teacher didn't believe she could read that fast, just like the library lady, so she'd just keep on reading through the book and wouldn't close it and fold her hands until someone else did.

Cynthia did okay in school in spite of all her emotional problems. Everything came easy to her except arithmetic. She missed quite a bit of school that year with illness so when they studied long division and later, fractions, she didn't get the hang of it and never caught up. She didn't know she could have asked Miss Ballard for help. For one thing, she thought Miss Ballard didn't like her and she was so used to being unobtrusive, not bringing attention to herself, and staying after school to talk to a teacher would never have occurred to her. You stayed after school only when you had done something wrong.

Once, when they had been assigned to write a poem about something in their lives, Cynthia, who had seen their dog kill a mother ground squirrel and her three babies, one by one, on the previous Sunday's drive, decided to use that for her assignment. She had been very upset by it. She wrote an epic poem of at least a dozen verses and turned it in. When the poems were returned, she didn't get hers back and Miss Ballard told her she wanted to see her after school. When the bell rang and the others left, she called Cynthia to her.

Holding out the poem, she asked, "Cynthia, what book did you copy this from?"

Cynthia was stunned. "I didn't copy it; I wrote it," she said.

"Cynthia, don't lie to me. Don't you know it's plagiarism to copy things from a book and that it's very wrong?"

Cynthia was angry that Miss Ballard thought she had copied her poem and it probably showed on her face. "I didn't copy it. We take our dog for a run almost every Sunday down on the Strand... it really happened."

Miss Ballard gave her a hard look and said, "Alright, you may go now." But she kept the poem and Cynthia never saw it again.

After that, Miss Ballard started calling on her to recite when the others did, to take a turn reading out loud as they did, and to read her compositions as did the others. With the changing attitude of her teacher, the children's attitudes changed too. But for Cynthia, it was too little, too late. She quit doing her best and did only what was necessary to get by. She sat at her desk and drew or practiced writing upside down and backward as she listened to Miss Ballard and watched what was put on the blackboard. She heard the others do their recitations while she waited to do hers. She drew until Miss Ballard noticed and told her to put the pencil and paper away and pay attention. She'd do as she was told and sit daydreaming, losing interest in what was going on around her.

THERE HAD BEEN something else that year that contributed to the changes in attitude as well, but Cynthia didn't learn what it was until after she was grown and married. Her grades were good enough. She did just what she was supposed to do and no more. The grading was gone with letters, Ss and Us, blue or red with, pluses and minuses. Blue was satisfactory; red was not. The pluses and minuses were indicative of very good, good, and average. The Us were below average, poor, and failing. The best thing to get was a blue S-plus; the worse, a red U-minus.

At the end of the day when report cards were passed out, the children ran out screaming, waving their cards in the air. Then they began comparing.

"I got all blue S-pluses. What did you get?"

Cynthia, knowing she wouldn't be asked, started walking home. She showed her report to Grandma, who wasn't very interested, then showed it to Mama when she got to the house. Mama looked at it and signed it. Cynthia showed it to Papa when she got home. Her card was usually all blue, with maybe a plus or two. The only below average was in arithmetic, which apparently didn't matter much to anyone. Cynthia took it back to school and that was it.

Miss Vance, the music teacher, began taking an interest in Cynthia that semester too. She came to the classroom to teach the children basic music once a week and lead them in singing. Several times in the next few years, she asked Cynthia to come to the music room after school. Cynthia didn't like being singled out for this special attention, but she dragged herself unwillingly to the appointment as asked. The little talk was the same each time.

"Cynthia, I know you have it in you to do better than you have been doing. Your grades are average, but I know they could be much higher. I'd like to see you making more progress in bringing them up. Will you promise that you'll at least try? You have so much potential, and I hate to see you wasting it. I'm not scolding you; I only want to help you. Do you understand?"

Cynthia liked Miss Vance, who was always nice to her, but she was wishing she was somewhere else. Standing first on one foot and then the other and waiting to be excused, she nodded her head that she understood. When she was free to go, she took off without a thought about anything Miss Vance had said or why she had said it.

CHAPTER THIRTY-SIX

Cynthia's self-esteem had been knocked down and stamped into the ground until the fourth grade when it began putting out a few small leaves and tendrils. She already knew she was a good speller and a fast reader, now the other kids knew it too. And she had a talent for writing. A few more of her things were put into the school paper, so, her own opinion of herself improved. She didn't realize until years later that the wall between herself and the other girls, which they had erected in the first place, had been built higher and stronger with bricks and mortar and her own pride. She'd been guilty of one of the seven deadly sins, all of which are harmful to the self.

Papa had told her, when she came to him to ask if she could do something she'd seen the other kids do that he didn't approve of, "Do you have to do something just because some other damned fool Tom, Dick, or Harry does it? Would you jump off a cliff because someone else did? You don't want to be a sheep, with no mind of your own, do you?"

"No," she said. Of course, she wouldn't be dumb enough to do something like jump off a cliff just because someone else did. If the fire engine went by with the other kids running after it, she'd turn in another direction.

They hollered, "C'mon, c'mon, there's a fire."

But Cynthia ignored them, keeping her face expressionless and letting them go running willy-nilly like idiots. She'd tell herself, "I don't have to be like them. I'm not like those other Toms, Dicks, and Harrys who go to gawk and get in the way when it's none of their business. I'm not a sheep," and she felt the stirrings of personal pride growing within her.

Miss Ballard was an excellent teacher. When she taught English, she went all the way... part of speech, the rules of punctuation, diagraming sentences, how to begin creating a story, how to build it to a climax, and end it... comparing it to climbing a mountain to reach the top and then come back down. She taught that the most basic rule of good writing was to tell who, what, when, where, and why. She had them take turns reading poetry out loud to show them the elements of rhyme, meter, style, accent, beat, and more. She explained poetic license and alliteration.

Now, from her grown-up overview, she was even more sure Miss Ballard had been behind the earlier change in her life and had put a stop to the name-calling and harassment as well. She wondered, "Had Miss Ballard been an angel in disguise?"

She'd talked to them about good character, cleanliness, courtesy, honesty, and the still small voice of conscience, which she said everyone had. Then she asked them, "Have any of you heard it? Do you know what I am talking about? Raise your hands if you do."

Every hand in the room went up.

Teachers in those days didn't have pre-prepared lessons and tests to be passed out to the class. They made their own tests on paper with an indelible pencil, then printed them on a hectograph, which was a layer of gelatin in a frame. The hectograph was a precursor to the mimeograph machine, which Cynthia first saw and used in high school for the three years she was the art editor of the school paper, *The Echo*. Many years later, the son of a friend who worked on the paper, now renamed *The Islander*, heard she had once worked in it too and laughingly called it, *The Stone Age Gazette*. It was very funny, but still, she was a little rueful about it. She was only thirty at the time and hardly as archaic as he seemed to think.

TEACHERS CAME EARLY and stayed late, working at their desks after school grading papers and preparing the next day's lessons until the five o'clock bell rang for everyone to be out of the building and off the grounds. Often, they would ask a child to stay after school to help them carry materials from the storeroom to the classroom or to carry papers to and from the hectograph, also in the storeroom. This was considered a great honor, as was erasing blackboards and taking erasers outside to slap together to get rid of the chalk dust. Cynthia was flattered when she was asked to help do these things by her fifth- and sixth-grade teachers.

CYNTHIA REALIZED that Miss Ballard had been a teacher *par excellence* after she was grown when articles in magazines had titles like, "Why Johnny Can't Read," or discussed how children were being rushed through schools before they had learned what was required to be passed to the next grade and that high school graduates were having to take "dumbbell" classes because they weren't scoring well enough on college entrance exams.

There hadn't been much money for the schools during the Depression. Children were told to treat new books with respect and were shown how to open them carefully for the first time... a little from the front and a little from the back so as not to break their spines because their parents paid for all their books, pencils, paper, and crayons with their taxes. They were warned not to be wasteful with the supplies, not to damage the books in any way... no dog-earing pages or marking in them... and to be very careful not to lose them because they couldn't be replaced.

Teachers had to be innovative with their lesson plans, often bringing materials purchased out of their own pockets. Miss Ballard brought notepaper and envelopes for lessons on the proper way to write a letter and to address an envelope. She brought checks, deposit, and withdrawal slips from a bank so they could learn to do all the things connected with having a personal checking or savings account. She followed this by asking them to bring in a quarter, dime, or nickel and invited a man from the bank to come to class with account books to start savings accounts for them which they could add to whenever they wished.

They were taught architectural symbols and how to draw to scale, after which graph paper was handed out and they were asked to draw a plan of their house with all the doors, windows and electrical fixtures in their proper locations, using so many squares of the paper to a foot. Today, some would surely take offense at this, calling it an invasion of privacy, but for the children in Miss Ballard's class, it was a wonderful learning experience.

They studied American history and government, learning about our system of checks and balances, the Boston Tea Party, Nathan Hale, Patrick Henry, Paul Revere, and the battle of Monitor and Merrimack. They read about America's inventors and their inventions, as well as about Luther Burbank, the famous California horticulturist and other famous people of the day. She taught the history of the flag, called "Old Glory" in a poem they read, along with the proper way to display it, fold it, and dispose of it. They learned to always treat it with respect for what it represented. The lives of George Washington and Abraham Lincoln, whose portraits hung in every room of Coronado's elementary school, were included in their lessons and each child had to memorize the Preamble to the Constitution and Lincoln's Gettysburg Address.

In art period, they did soap carvings, bringing a cake of Ivory soap and a paring knife to class (imagine a room full of kids with knives in their desks today! The teacher's life would likely be in jeopardy and the lives of the other children as well)!

Blueprint paper was supplied, and they went outside into the sunlight to make prints of leaves and other items. When they took a sack lunch to the park, as was done occasionally when the weather was fine, to draw trees and flowers, they were expected to clean up after themselves and leave no trash behind. In the classroom, neatness was an absolute must.

Besides the Preamble and the Gettysburg Address, Miss Ballard asked the class to memorize the capitals of the States, the principal rivers of the world, and the exports of other countries. She also had them draw maps of the countries they were studying and take turns reading epic poems out loud like, "The Midnight Ride of Paul Revere," "Barbara Frietchie," and other classic stories. There were many other things as well, they had learned so much in Miss Ballard's class that Cynthia couldn't remember it all, sixty-four years later.

Once a man had come with pictures of teeth, their composition, and their different names. He handed out small tubes of Colgate's toothpaste and a child's toothbrush, then asked the children to sign a contract promising they would take good care of their teeth to take home to their parents.

The life of the honeybee was accompanied by a film. The children filed quietly out of the room, went across the school grounds, back into the building and upstairs into the dome, where there was a small windowless room with folding chairs where educational films and slides were shown. There had been a film on the life of the ant, as well as other insects then and in later classes.

The evils of tobacco were exposed by a man who came with an easel of lung x-rays of smokers and non-smokers. All the classes were gathered in the auditorium for it. It made such an impression on Cynthia that she never smoked though Papa did and, for a while, Mama did too. Cynthia heard men asking for a pack of "coffin nails" in stores and she could never understand why in the world people of today seem to be so naive about the dangers of smoking; she and her classmates had learned of its risks when they were nine and ten years old.

The Chief of Police came to the auditorium to speak to all the children about bicycle safety and, another time, about the horrors of opium, other drugs, and alcohol. In those days, many children believed that if you took an aspirin and drank a Coca Cola it would make you drunk. No one Cynthia knew had ever tried it and she was afraid to. Fear was a wonderful deterrent. That, and having to face your parents if you had done something wrong, kept most children on the straight and narrow.

Every child in Coronado knew the name of every officer on the police force because it was so small, and every policeman knew almost every child by name as well. The wayward child couldn't get away with anything. Even if they'd wanted to, by the time they got home their mother already knew about it. Coronado was a safe place too because of its separation by the bay from the mainland and the length of the Strand, both of which made escape almost impossible. A phone call would intercept a perpetrator on the other side of the bay if he took the ferry or in Imperial Beach before he could get all the way around the Strand.

The first murder ever occurred when Cynthia was in junior high. Two new children had come to the school. A short time later, they were no longer there. The news flew... they and their mother had been arrested for killing their father. No one knew why. Had it been a case, like those so often today, of wife and child abuse? No one ever knew. Then, when Cynthia was in high school, a lady her mother was acquainted with was shot to death by her estranged husband in the beauty shop she owned. It was Coronado's second major crime; the whole town was in a state of shock and disbelief. How could anything like that happen in Coronado?

. . .

THUS PASSED Cynthia's fourth year of school which had been two semesters with many changes for her. After this summer she would be going into the fifth grade, another year of change, but she didn't know that. All she was looking forward to was vacation... going to the beach, running from body surfing in the ocean to swimming in the bay, and back to the ocean for lying in the hot sun or the hot sand. Other kids she knew would be there too, but she didn't join them, nor did they ask her to. She'd be all by herself all day long, but happy to be able to do what she wanted to do and not what someone else expected of her.

CHAPTER THIRTY-SEVEN

When she went to Mama's for lunch one day, Cynthia found Papa home. This was unusual. The Depression had made changes in his work schedule, but things were easing up after the country's initial shock and he had been going to work every day, even if only for a few hours. May was in bed... even more unusual... Mama was never sick.

"What's wrong with Mama?" Cynthia asked. "Is she all right? Is she sick?"

"She did something for you," was all Papa said.

Cynthia fixed her lunch as usual and went back to school, wondering what Mama could have done for her that had made her have to go to bed. She was not to find out what it was until she was grown, married, and had Tee Gee.

During WWII, when Ted was in the South Pacific, Cynthia and May began to be the friends they never were. Cynthia was growing up. They'd meet at Marston's department store, shop and go to a matinee a couple of times a month, getting to know each other and enjoying themselves. At least Cynthia did, and May must have, or the arrangement wouldn't have continued.

One afternoon shopping, they decided to go to a spiritualist church and have a psychic reading instead of going to a movie. When it was May's turn, the reader said something ambiguous about a son.

"If you know what I mean?" he asked. Cynthia turned to look at her mother; May looked mildly shocked.

"What was that about?" Cynthia wondered as Mama nodded her head yes, she knew.

The rest of the reading was a blur except when Cynthia told the man her husband was overseas, he said, "Your husband will come back when the snow flies if the snow flew here. Do you understand?" Of course she did. He meant in the winter.

But that winter passed, and yet another. Ted was away twenty-eight months in all before coming home on a thirty-day leave and not to stay. It was in December, so they had a Christmas together and a New Year's Eve, which was their fourth wedding anniversary. They had been married a little less than two years when he had gone away, and it was a long time afterward before Cynthia realized what that psychic said had been true. Ted had indeed come home when the snow would have flown if they hadn't lived in California. It hadn't been the next winter, as she'd expected it to be and had been disappointed.

As they left the church after the reading, Cynthia sensed that May was prepared for her question.

"What was that about a son? You had me, not a boy."

"I got pregnant after you and had an abortion," Mama said. "The baby would have been a boy."

"Oh," was all Cynthia could think of to say. Never would it have occurred to her to press May for more information, so she didn't learn the whole story until she asked Papa about it after her mother died four years later.

"Mama told me that she had an abortion, but that's all she told me. Was that the time I came home from school and she was in bed?" she asked Papa.

"Yes. She didn't want to have another baby because of the Depression when money was so tight and we already had you."

Cynthia had her doubts about that being the real reason. Had it really been enough for Al, or had he just gone along with May's decision for whatever reasons of his own?

"There are three other possibilities," Cynthia told herself. "Mama wasn't maternal. She left me with Grandma. She did all the right physical things after she took over my life, but she held me off at arm's length, so I never felt loved. Maybe it was all she was capable of, but it wasn't enough; I needed more. Maybe she was afraid that if she had another child, she might not be lucky enough to get a white one, even one as white as me. I knew that sometimes she was ashamed of me. I got very brown in the summer. She was afraid when I was pregnant with Tee Gee. She didn't say anything, but I knew. She told me she could take me to someone who would do an abortion if I wanted her to. I said no and she let it drop, but she stayed at the hospital the night Tee Gee was born to see him before she drove home around the Strand at four o'clock in the morning, alone."

Papa had left earlier because the streetcars and the ferry quit running at midnight and he had to go to work the next day.

Her thoughts continued. "The final reason could have been because I was a breech birth. The doctor came to Grandma's house, but the nurse was late. I had already been delivered when she got there. Papa told me he helped as much as he could, but at last the doctor had to turn me with his hands and no anesthetic, while all he could do was stand and watch. It must have been a terrible ordeal for all of them, especially Mama. Maybe she didn't want to go through that again and probably Papa wouldn't have wanted her to."

Al often told Cynthia she was the last of the Hudgins. She never knew if it pained him to know that the son who could have carried on the family name had been lost to him forever, but she never heard any bitterness in his voice. Nevertheless, she would always wonder.

"Mama's decision left me an endangered species," Cynthia

thought... "Like the last of the curlews. And why did Papa say that she had done it for me?"

Al told Cynthia that May had gone to the doctor, the one who'd delivered her, and told him she wanted an abortion. He'd tried to talk her out of it, but she'd said, "Give me the name of someone who will do it or I'll do it myself with a knitting needle." He must have known that she meant it and Al must have known it too. May was strong-willed and stubborn. Al deferred to her on most things because it probably made for peace in the family and Cynthia knew too, that her mother would have had her own way, one way or another. She had proved it later with her untimely death.

CHAPTER THIRTY-EIGHT

Papa told Cynthia how to take a timed test when she told him they had been having them in her class and sometimes it was hard to get all the questions answered in the time allowed

"There's a trick to it," he said. "You're taking too long. When you take a test, don't waste time on the ones you don't know the answers to right off. Skip them and go on. Get all the ones you can, then go back and work on the ones that take longer until the time is up."

Cynthia started doing this and did much better. She had learned a valuable lesson because one morning when the children walked in, there was a packet on each desk. Curious and excited about anything different, some started to pick theirs up.

"Don't look at what's on your desks just yet," Miss Ballard told them. "We have to talk about it first." She explained that they were achievement tests sent out by the State to find out how much the children knew and that each section of the test would be timed. Everyone was to get out a pencil and sharpen it so there would be no delays after the tests began.

When the flurry of pencil sharpening was over and all had

returned to their seats, she said, "Don't open your booklet to look at the first page until I tell you to, then wait until I say 'begin' before reading the first question, and when I say 'time,' you will stop immediately, even if it's in the middle of a word. This is very important. Do you all understand?"

Everyone nodded.

"Alright," Miss Ballard said. "If you're all ready, we will start. Now, begin."

Cynthia went through the different parts of the tests like Papa had told her, answer... skip... move on... last question, go back again, and again, as many as there was time left for.

When she told Papa about the test, he asked how she thought she'd done.

"I got almost all of them," she said. "All the reading and English and most of the others too, but not so good with the arithmetic."

"Did you go through the test the way I told you?" he asked.

"Yes, and it really helped."

"Good," was all Papa said, looking pleased. "You probably did okay."

Just how well Cynthia had done on the test was something Mama would be told and tell her some thirteen or fourteen years later after Cynthia was grown and Tee Gee was a toddler.

"I met Mr. Birth, your high school English teacher, on the streetcar last week," Mama said one day when Cynthia and Tee Gee had come to spend the day while Ted was overseas.

"Oh? How was he? I always liked him. All the girls did."

"He was fine. He asked about you and I told him you were married and had a little boy. He said he was glad to hear about you and to say hello for him. He also told me that you had been one of his best pupils and he had often wondered about you because when you were in the fourth grade you took a state test that had been sent to Sacramento; it was sent back to the school because they thought a high school student's test had gotten in with the fourth grader's by mistake. He said that all the teachers knew about it and that they had been watching you from then on."

"Really?" said Cynthia, as she thought, *I wish I'd known that sooner. I'd have tried harder.*

"He told me that you had one of the highest IQs in your high school graduating class, too," Mama said.

"Really?" was all Cynthia could find to say a second time.

Afterward, when she thought about it, it explained so much; Miss Vance's little talks, and her teachers from fifth grade on who seemed to take more of an interest in her than any had ever done before. She realized she had let them all down. She had given up and quit trying to excel. It hadn't been very important to her when no one else seemed to care one way or the other.

Not long after that, Cynthia met Miss Andrews, her fifth-grade teacher, as they were boarding the streetcar.

They sat together and in the course of their chat, Miss Andrews said, "You know, Cynthia, you used to sit in the back of the room drawing. I thought you weren't paying attention, but whenever I called on you, you knew the answer."

Smiling to herself as she remembered, Cynthia thought, "I knew I did, but I didn't think any of my teachers knew. Someone should have told me sooner."

CHAPTER THIRTY-NINE

As Cynthia relived her memories, she knew that, in one way, it had been a wonderful experience growing up in Coronado in the second and third decades of the century. The school was a very good one and the teachers were truly dedicated. When she got back to college in her forties, she'd been surprised to learn from her young associates that some of what she'd been taught in elementary school was the same material they were there to learn.

Surprised, she'd asked them, "Didn't you do this in grade school?" and been dumbfounded when they'd said they hadn't. She couldn't believe it. She was taking music, art, and English and it was the same information she'd had when she was just a kid. The same stuff was still being taught when she'd attended the business college May had shipped her off to after high school. That was what had been so disappointing to her then, not to be learning something new, just rehashing the same old same. She wanted to stay with it this time and get her degree, but fate had other plans for her.

Her appendix acted up and she was hospitalized for surgery. When she'd recovered and gone back, Al suffered a stroke and she'd dropped out to take care of him. After he died, two and a half years later, she gave up on the idea. She was nearly fifty and she was tired.

Coronado was a multi-layered community. There were the very wealthy and well-to-do families, some of whom lived there year-round and some who came from back East only for the summer or winter seasons, though not as many of these as before the Crash. Then there were the Navy officers and their families who rotated in and out in two-year cycles, along with the middle class and those who were newly poor as a result of the Depression.

Al and May were between the two latter classifications. Cynthia, though not invited to any homes, grew up seeing these distinctions of society as they were then... expensively dressed ladies shopping or going about their business, who lived in the big houses on the ocean front or on the bay side, who drove around in expensive cars, and the people like her parents, who owned or rented more ordinary houses of different sizes, who did their shopping in the city because it was cheaper to take the ferry and the streetcar than to pay the jacked-up prices in the Coronado stores.

The wealthy owned yachts or sailboats which they kept at the Boathouse. They played golf and tennis or had horses stabled near the golf course, where the show ring was. They were seen around town wearing the garb of their particular sport... golfing tweeds and cashmere sweaters, white tennis or boating outfits, sometimes their riding gear, beige jodhpurs, black jackets, cravats, and derbies.

The ladies shopped in the simple pastel shirtmaker dresses with sweaters to match, spectator pumps, and strands of real pearls. They dined at the hotel and had their photos taken at Lou Goodale Bigelow's studio where, if they were somebody, their pictures were displayed in the window for a time. Some of their children attended a private school on the grounds of the hotel, then the girls were sent to Bishop's in La Jolla and the boys went to the San Diego military academy. These contemporaries mingled within their own circles of wealth and prestige.

Some of the wealthy ladies and the Navy officer's wives did

volunteer work as Gray Ladies for the Red Cross at the hospitals, the small one in Coronado and the Navy hospital in San Diego. They wore Red Cross uniforms and drove new Packards with the Red Cross insignia everywhere they went, including grocery shopping, so they could "see and be seen," the local housewives said smirking, but probably envious of the freedoms wealth made possible.

AMONG CYNTHIA'S mother's friends, divorced women were looked at askance and whispered about since divorce was considered the woman's fault. It was a man's world, mothers told their daughters, so it couldn't have been him; it had to have been her. If she were widowed or divorced, had children and worked, it was understood, but not necessarily condoned. If she was married and had children and worked, there was outright disapproval. Why wasn't she home taking care of them and making a home for her husband like a good wife should? If she was an artist or 'arty' in any way, she was Bohemian, possibly immoral and therefore suspect. A widow or divorcee could be looking for another husband, possibly yours, so beware!

Being different in any way made one a pariah. Folks would be polite to their face but talk about them behind their backs. They were not socially acceptable; society's rules were rigid and unbendable.

Being a good wife had its rules also. Monday was wash day, and the first load should be on the line by no later than nine in the morning. Tuesday was ironing day and so it went throughout the week... certain things on certain days. Thursdays, ladies called on their friends or friends came to call on them. Anything was an occasion to break the monotony for the bored housewives. They planned their little social get-togethers, or went shopping together or to a matinee as long as they were home before the children came in from school and dinner was being readied when hubby came home from work.

. . .

THE BAY WAS empty Monday through Friday each week. The ships went out off Point Loma on maneuvers. Navy wives went to the Officer's Club on North Island or to the hotel to sit around the swimming pools and sun themselves. They played the popular games of the time... 500, Mahjong, and Bridge while their colored maids cleaned the house and cared for the children too young to go to school. The maids sat in the park with their charges in the early afternoon. In the late afternoon, they were seen waiting for the streetcar or walking back down to the ferry landing to go to their homes, where they had to do the same things they had been doing all day for their own families.

In the twenties and thirties, running a home... cooking, cleaning, washing, ironing, caring for the children, entertaining, and being available for her husband in the bedroom... was what a woman did in exchange for security, a roof over her head, food, clothing, and maybe some spending money of her own. She was really lucky if she got a friend and companion who cared about her as a person, enjoyed her company, listened to her, laughed with her, and didn't consider her merely an adjunct to his life to make things easier for him by doing all of the above without complaint so he could concentrate on his own interests and pursuits.

From conversations over the years with other women in the different places where she and Ted had lived, Cynthia learned that most married women her age or older had settled for the roof, the food, and the clothing. The children and what went on in the bedroom were part of the bargain. They didn't enjoy sex because they were afraid of getting pregnant, especially if they already had one or more children. The ones who said they liked it were looked at askance by others.

"Over-sexed," they'd whisper with raised eyebrows behind her back.

By tacit agreement, if you were 'nice,' you didn't like sex. It was a thing to be tolerated in exchange for the badge of respectability. It was expected that a 'nice' girl would remain a virgin until her marriage else she be considered 'damaged goods' by the man who married her.

Old fashioned? Yes, but that was the way it was.

If a wife really loved her husband, he was good to her and the children and loved her too, sex was a gift she could give him to show he was appreciated. If it made him happy, she was happy too. Otherwise, it was something to be tolerated while praying another child wouldn't be the result.

In those pre-pill times, a married woman who had children wasn't remiss not to be keen about sex. Children kept you tied down. It was frowned upon to have children and work outside the home or to allow anyone other than a relative to care for the child if you did. A good wife did the things that a good wife did according to the rules of the day and had no life of her own to speak of except possibly in the world of imagination.

Sex was always risky. The diaphragm wasn't completely safe and was messy to boot. The rhythm method was extremely 'iffy' unless her monthly periods were as regular as clockwork. Women marked their calendars and watched them closely, breathing a sigh of relief if they made it safely through the month.

Husbands didn't want to use a rubber, as condoms were called then because they said it was like taking a shower with a raincoat on. They were more reluctant to have vasectomies, pre-supposing their wife might die. What if they remarried and the new wife wanted to have a baby? That manhood thing was a major consideration for them too. Divorce and the possibility of another marriage weren't that much to worry about then because divorces weren't as easy to obtain as they are now and were frowned upon by society, especially where the woman was concerned.

Doctors refused to do a tubal ligation on a woman of child-bearing age unless another baby would be detrimental to her life or health. Abortions were illegal and dangerous. More than one woman, tired of being burdened with too many children, tried to abort herself with a knitting needle or by allowing a midwife or a defrocked doctor of dubious reputation to do it then bled to death or died of infection. Every time a husband and wife had intercourse, it was like playing Russian Roulette for her.

All this changed with the advent of the pill when young women, no longer having to fear getting pregnant, were more relaxed about sex. The bondage of the marriage license and becoming someone's maid were kicked aside for sexual freedom and independence. Now the fear of AIDS keeps many virtuous and the condom is the preferred method of avoiding both pregnancy and disease. Even so, in the heat of the moment, caution is often thrown to the wind.

Unfortunately, television commercials showing happy young mothers playing with smiling, cooing babies in adorable nurseries lure young girls into thinking that a baby is like a real live doll. Since there is no longer a stigma to illegitimacy, they want one, unaware that babies cry, spit up, get sick, and go through a lot of diapers before they are potty trained.

Sometimes they get pregnant on purpose, not knowing that a baby isn't always happy nor a real live doll, but a responsibility, limiting their freedom to do as they please and making them grow up too fast. If they have the baby just to get on welfare because it sounds like a lot of money, they'll find it isn't the bonanza it seems. It's not for clothes and having fun, but for necessities... rent, utilities, food, baby clothes, and medical care... the real facts of life.

CHAPTER FORTY

Some holidays were different back before Pearl Harbor. WWII changed many things... customs, lifestyles and lives. Families were separated, some never to be together again. Women went to work in numbers larger than ever before. Stores began staying open evenings and Sundays; movie theaters, bowling alleys, and coffee shops stayed open all night. The Coronado ferry and the streetcars which had stopped running after midnight, ran 24 hours a day. Strangers exchanged news, hopes, and feelings with each other on the street corners as they waited for the light to change, or on streetcars and the ferry.

We'd just been through a Depression, so we were used to doing without. Nothing was too difficult to handle if it was for 'our boys,' and winning the war was the most important thing in everyone's life.

"When all this is over, we'll all be together again and it will be wonderful."

But nothing ever went back to the way it had been before the "Day of Infamy" when Japan caught us with our pants down.

Most of the holidays have now been changed from their actual day so workers can have a three-day holiday to party, get drunk, drive, and kill others as well as themselves. When Cynthia was young, a day off from school in the middle of the week was special, something to look forward to. If a holiday fell on a weekend, it wasn't the same because weekends were days off anyway and the kids felt cheated.

Christmas is still Christmas. Santa Clause still exists for children, and we still remember that the birth of Jesus is the reason we celebrate. We still mail out cards, perhaps not as many as before because postage has become so expensive. We still put up decorations, exchange gifts, and families come together. We spend more money because it's more commercial now, but otherwise, it's still the high point of the year, especially for kids.

Decorations were made during art period to put up in the classroom and kids made presents for their parents. Pen wipers of felt for their fathers, match scratchers to hang by the stove or the water heater for their mothers, and desk calendars for them both.

Mothers bought handkerchiefs, scented soaps, bath powder, boxes of stationary, or candy for the children to give their teachers. This is not allowed today because someone decided it smacked of bribery, which was not likely in those days when honesty was the best policy and people prized their reputations.

On the last day before Christmas vacation, after the Christmas program, each teacher had a party for their class. Out of their own pockets, they purchased Dixie cups of ice cream and gave each child a candy cane as they went out the door to head for home.

The holidays were very exciting... a party, no school until after New Year's, the trip to the city to see the department store Santa, the Christmas program at the school and the one at the church, where each child got a small gift, Santa at the big tree on Orange Avenue on Christmas Eve, calling most children by name as he handed out net stockings of hard candy and little booklets of Christmas carols or *The Night Before Christmas*, mail deliveries hourly all day long, store clerks, and people on the street calling,

"Merry Christmas," to friends and strangers alike. Everybody was so happy and friendly.

At home, the decorations, the tree, the presents, the dinner, and the drive around town to look at the lights and other peoples' Christmas trees in their front windows. Christmas time was wonderful!

CYNTHIA ALWAYS GOT some presents from Santa and some from Mama and Papa. Santa left a huge net stocking full of wonderful small toys and trinkets. In the packages under the tree would be a dog, a game, drawing tablets, a new set of watercolors, and crayons from Santa. Mama and Papa gave her socks, panties, a new dress and petticoat, a new sweater... useful things.

Cynthia believed in Santa until she was six going on seven. That year she caught on. She'd written a gift list, which she didn't give to Mama, but put in the fire and watched it curl, burst into flame, and go up the chimney in a puff of smoke. Mama asked her about it.

"Why didn't you give it to me to mail for you?"

"Because Santa Claus is magic. It will get there quicker. The smoke will go to the North Pole and tell him what I want."

"Oh," May said.

Cynthia never got the electric train she yearned for that year or any other year, even after she'd told Mama what she wanted after she knew there wasn't a Santa.

"Electric trains are for boys, not girls," May said and Cynthia got dolls instead. Dolls were nice, but she didn't play with them much. She had a wind-up train she dearly loved, which was always breaking because she wound it too tight to get all the mileage she could out of it. Papa patiently repaired it and scolded her as he handed it back.

"Now don't wind it so damned tight. One of these days I may not be able to fix it."

She'd be careful for a while and then break the spring again. She gave it away when she was twelve to a boy visiting the neighborhood who was the same age, hoping it would make him like her. He couldn't have cared less and she regretted it for the rest of her life.

She learned the truth about Santa on Christmas Eve at the big tree. When he handed her the stocking saying, "Merry Christmas, Cynthia," she recognized his voice. She ran back to Mama.

"I know who Santa Claus is. He's the man at the service station!"

"Oh, is he?" was all May said.

That night she feigned sleep on the couch in the living room. She heard Mama whisper, "I wonder if she's asleep yet." She felt Mama leaning over her, so she kept her eyes shut and breathed slowly.

"Okay," Mama whispered and she and Papa tiptoed into their bedroom. Cynthia heard rustling noises and a musical tinkling sound followed by a *shhh*. When they came back, she sneaked a peek and saw them putting wrapped packages under the tree.

Christmas morning she tiptoed in to ask Mama if she could open her presents now as she always did.

"Alright, but be quiet. Papa's still asleep." Mama stayed in bed too.

This time she looked closely at all the tags with her name on them. She'd never noticed before that Santa's handwriting was the same as Mama's distinctive Scottish hand or that his presents were wrapped in the same paper. The musical tinkling she'd heard was a push top. The handle worked up and down and the top spun around, making a bell-like sound. She loved it, but now she knew what the other kids said about Santa Claus was true. It made more sense than one fat old man visiting all the children in the world and going down chimneys. She kept up the pretense for another year, then told May that she knew he was just pretend.

"Oh," was all May said.

EASTER IS STILL THE SAME. The Crucifixion and Resurrection of Christ have not yet been forgotten. Eggs, Easter baskets, bunnies, and chickies are still symbolic gifts, although we don't sell dyed live rabbits and chicks anymore. A good thing, since they seldom lived very long, dying from being loved too much or not enough... neglect a cruel mistreatment.

A new Easter bonnet, a new outfit from head to toe, then going to church for the Easter program where each child was given a pansy plant to take home made Easter special. That and exchanging baskets with the boys on the block where her parents lived and with the daughter of one of her mother's friends.

When Cynthia was little, May gave her a plant every Easter, telling her it was 'her' flower. Cynthia never knew why it was 'her' flower, but it made her happy. That Mama thought she was special.

May went all out with Easter baskets. The baskets she put together for Cynthia to deliver to her friends' children had grass, dyed eggs, all sizes of sugar and chocolate eggs, marshmallow bunnies and chicks, and tiny cotton ones... and always a big chocolate rabbit wrapped in printed foil. When Cynthia came back with the baskets she'd gotten in exchange, May inspected them, deploring the cheap junk that other people put in their kids' baskets, especially the gaudy candy eggs with marshmallow insides that she and Cynthia both hated because they were too sickeningly sweet.

FOURTH OF JULY was more exciting than Christmas or Easter to Cynthia. Mama gave her $2.50 on each of the two paydays before the holiday to go to Perkins for her fireworks. When she came back with the bag, May inspected it to see what she'd gotten. Cynthia loved the noisemakers... the firecrackers and the bombs. Mama liked the cones that sprayed a fountain of colored sparks... Mt. Etna, Mt. Shasta, Roman candles, and sparklers.

"Is this all?" she'd ask. "Why didn't you get more of the pretty things I like?"

"They cost more, and I like the ones that make noise and so does Papa."

"Oh," May would say.

During the next two weeks, she'd slip Cynthia another fifty cents or so from time to time with instructions to get more of those cone things. May loved this sort of display because it reminded her of the ones at home for Guy Fawkes Day, which was celebrated on November 5th in Scotland, and the king's annual birthday celebrations.

The evening of the Fourth was another night Cynthia spent at her parents'. The first firecrackers and bombs would be heard intermittently after dark, making it difficult for an excited child to get to sleep.

The next morning, bright and early, all the kids in the neighborhood would be in the vacant block across the street, setting off their firecrackers. Cynthia did hers in the vacant lot next door to the house. Papa lit her punk with his cigarette lighter and warned her never, never to light a cracker in her hand to throw like the boys did, and if she put a can over a big one to watch it fly up in the air, never go to it until she was certain it was a dud and to stand far enough back so the can wouldn't hit her in the head when it came down. Punks were given free, several for each purchase. They lasted a long time and had a nice smell.

Cynthia was always careful, was never hurt, and she didn't know of anyone else in Coronado who was either, although there were always stories of damaged eyes and fingers blown away in other parts of the country in the paper the next day.

After a supper of hot dogs, potato salad, and baked beans, as soon as it was dark enough, they'd walk up the block to a vacant lot next door to the two other families with the younger boys Cynthia played with occasionally... the ones Mama invited to her birthday parties and she exchanged Easter baskets with. They'd have their own display with their sparkly fountains, Roman candles, rockets, sparklers and burning houses made of cardboard that shot sparks out of the chimney then caught fire and burned slowly to the ground. Things called snakes sent off black stuff squiggling and writhing out when lit, and red devils, about the size of a quarter but thicker, sent out sparks when ran along the sidewalk. These were okay, though Cynthia never bought but one of each.

May reminisced about the wonderful displays in Great Britain.... The king and queen in outline, the Union Jack, ships, cars, trains, and all manner of things. No one could imagine it then; it sounded so unbelievable. These displays built on the framework are common-place now but weren't in the twenties and thirties in the U.S.

Shortly before nine o'clock, everyone in Coronado walked or drove to Coronado Heights overlooking Glorietta Bay to watch an hour of public fireworks. So close to the onlookers, so beautiful, and so loud! May hated the noise and covered her ears, but Cynthia and Al would count the booms, shouting with delight, "OOH, that was a good one!"

When it was all over, with the American flag still drifting down at the last, they'd go home for watermelon and then off to bed. Another glorious Fourth was just a memory.

MEMORIAL DAY WAS parade day in San Diego. After the parade, the family went to the cemetery to put flowers on the two graves, then drove back to Coronado around the Strand. It was not a happy day, remembering all the men who had died in WWII, but the parade with marching bands and all the horses made it a special one.

The Civil War Vets were dwindling; the few that were left rode in cars, but the American Legion was still going strong, still marching along together on their own two feet.

WHEN CYNTHIA WAS SMALL, still living with her grandmother, she knew that there was a flag folded into a triangle in one of her grand-ma's dresser drawers.

"Why is it all folded up and we don't use it on holidays?" she asked. Grandma told her it was the flag that had been given to her at

Grandpa's funeral because he had been a soldier in the Civil War. After Grandma died, Al took the flag and put it in a drawer of the chest on the back porch where Cynthia slept when she first went to live with her parents. When they moved to the larger house, Al unfolded it. The material was so rotten he took it outside and they had a respectful flag burning.

The flag that was given to Cynthia at her father's funeral went into a drawer for a while, then she said to Ted, "That flag is going to rot away like my grandfather's did. Why don't we fly it until it wears out? I know Papa wouldn't mind." So they did. It didn't last long... apparently the government doesn't spend any more money on the honorary flag used on the coffins of veterans than they have to.

ANOTHER PATRIOTIC HOLIDAY whose name has been changed is Armistice Day. Originally intended to honor the day the Armistice for WWII was signed, it has been changed to Armed Forces Day to combine the end of all our wars into one occasion.

"No reason they couldn't have separate holidays for V-J Day and VE Day as well," Cynthia thought. "Those two-wars-in-one were just as deserving of their own special day as any other."

"Apparently, no one know cares when our boys came home from Korea, which some never considered a war, or Vietnam, which undoubtedly will never be over for the families of the MIAs as long as they live."

The two birthdays of our most famous presidents, George Washington and Abraham Lincoln, have been combined and are now nothing more than a day for shopping in stores having big holiday sales. Children no longer know the true meaning of what is now just another day off from school.

THERE WERE special days that were not official holidays that the children looked forward to, Valentine's Day and Halloween. Valentine's Day was never a special day to Cynthia. At first, when a teacher made a 'mailbox' by covering a carton with red and white ruffled crepe paper and construction paper hearts, Cynthia had been excited. Mama bought a jar of paste and a box of materials for making cards with beautiful things to work with... white lace paper doilies, gold paper lace and ribbon, push-out pre-cut cupids, hearts, and flowers... everything one could wish for. Cynthia worked carefully, cutting and pasting to make her cards as pretty as she could. She saved the best ones for her teacher and Mama, Papa, and Grandma. She put them in the envelopes, wrote the names of everyone in her class on them, took them to school and dropped them into the box. She could hardly wait until they would be passed out just before school let out on that day.

Finally, the moment came. The teacher selected a "mailman" and it began. Cynthia sat squirming with excitement, waiting for her name to be called as she watched the piles of cards growing on the desks around her. The first time, and the others that followed, if she was lucky, she got three or four and one from the teacher, but the ones she got weren't nearly as pretty as hers. She was disappointed to the point of tears. When she was in the fourth grade, along with a few more from other girls, she got a couple of the penny ones that had verses on them that were supposed to be funny but were really cruel. They weren't signed, but she knew they were from the boys. That day, when she got to Mama's after school, she took her little handful with her. Before, only Grandma had seen the few cards she'd gotten and hadn't paid much attention, but Mama was interested.

"Oh, are those your valentines? How many did you get?"

Cynthia handed them over. Mama looked at each one.

"Are these all you got?"

"Uh-huh."

"Did any of the others get more than you did?"

"Uh-huh."

"Oh," May said with a funny look on her face. "Some of these aren't very nice, are they?"

"Uh-uh."

The next year May asked Cynthia if she wanted to make valentines to take to school.

"I like making them, but I'm only going to take ones to school with me for the girls who gave me ones last year and for you and Papa and Grandma and one for the teacher."

"Alright," Mama said and gave her the money to go to Perkins' to buy a box. Somewhere along the line, the custom was dropped. Cynthia didn't miss it.

CYNTHIA'S BIRTHDAY CAME NEXT, in August. May always had a party for her, going all out with decorations. Paper birthday tablecloths, napkins, crepe paper nut cups which she filled with jellybeans, crackers with paper hats inside, horns, blowers, balloons, and confetti. She had games like pin the tail on the donkey, or punch cards with things to do, prizes, and booby prizes. Then there was opening the presents and last of all, birthday cake and ice cream. Everyone had a good time and went home carrying something. Cynthia knew all the children who came bearing gifts, but they were not close. They lived in the neighborhood and were younger or older than she was, except for the daughter of her mother's friend. No one from school was ever invited; there was no one to invite who was a friend. No one from school invited her to their parties either, but she heard them talking about them before and afterward. The children who came to her parties didn't have parties. She remembered being invited to one only once. The only parties she attended were her own.

HALLOWEEN WAS nothing then like it is now. There was no Trick or Treat. That came west with the people who migrated here to work in the aircraft factories during the war. All kids did was soap or paraffin windows, especially the storefronts up and down the Avenue. They chalked sidewalks or rang doorbells then ran to hide. They wore things from the rag bag or their mother's or father's old clothes; they draped themselves in old sheets to be ghosts and painted their faces with make-up or soot, or, for five or ten cents, bought a cheap stiffened gauze mask. Others bought ready-made cambric costumes... gypsies, skeletons, witches, ghosts, or pirates were the choices back then, each with the same sort of mask included.

May frowned on soaping windows or using paraffin, but she let Cynthia have chalk. She walked with her around the block so she could ring doorbells and run. This made Cynthia wildly excited... being out after dark with other children running up and down the streets in costumes, peering at each other to see if they knew who it was, hiding behind a bush or a fence while someone inside the house opened the door, looked around or shouted, "Who is it out there? Show yourself."

Cynthia was beside herself, making herself as small as she could as she hid, trying not to giggle and give herself away. Many years later, when Tee Gee was born on Halloween, Al wondered if she'd been so excited about Halloween because she knew somehow that someday it was going to be an important day in her life. Perhaps.

No one ever did anything more than harmless tricks... stealing and hiding someone's front gate or porch decorations or knocking down a fence already starting to fall over... until Cynthia was in high school. Someone put a garden hose into a mail slot and turned the water on. The people were out and came home to a terrible mess. Someone told and the girl was apprehended, suspended from school or sent to juvenile hall because, for a time, she wasn't seen around. Shortly afterward, the family moved away.

In those days, the names of boys who got into trouble were printed in the daily paper. The most serious thing a child could do was bring shame to the family name. This kept most kids on the straight and narrow because if they got into that kind of trouble, they knew there'd be hell to pay at home. Public opinion was hard to live with in the thirties in a small town where the family's good name was considered an asset above all else. It was the middle of the Depression, and a good reputation was about all some families had to be proud of.

Kids were told, "If you get into trouble at school, you'll be in a lot worse trouble when you get home." Spare the rod and spoil the child, the credo of the Victorian Era, was still in effect when Cynthia was young.

Al said, "The quickest way to reach the brain is from the end of the spine." However, he spanked Cynthia only once, using the little silver-headed cane he'd bought in Rio. She'd come in very late from school with her shoes soaked from stamping in puddles and wading in the gutter. It was nice to have shoes with soles and not cardboard inserts and she'd had a lovely time. However, it was at that time that a little girl was found dead in Balboa Park later, was still missing and they'd been frightened. She knew that now, but at the time she thought it was because of getting her brand-new shoes all wet.

Al was a slapper, not a spanker. May used her tongue and the fly swatter. Grandma cut a pepper tree switch... and did they ever sting on bare legs! Cynthia had her share of punishments and Al was right, the quickest route to the brain is a good smack across the mouth for sass and on the rear for more serious offenses. There are some who would disagree but think about the unruly and disobedient trouble-makers that many of our teenagers are today.

Papa said Cynthia didn't have to love him, but by Jesus Christ, she was sure as hell going to respect him. She did both and still does —with all her heart and soul and being.

PERKINS' was the place to go for party supplies, seasonal decorations, and toys... kites in March, tops, jacks, jump ropes, and marbles. Each had a month when they were what is called "hot" these days. Someone would be the first and soon everyone was doing it. Mama bought everything for Cynthia in San Diego or gave her the money to go to Perkins'. Cynthia played with them by herself, which wasn't much fun, but if she took anything to school it was usually stolen from her desk at recess.

Perkins' shop on Orange Avenue was the mecca for children with refund money from a returnable bottle, a penny found on the street or a gratuity for an errand run for an adult. It was a dark little store run by an old couple, both white-haired and wearing glasses, who lived upstairs over it.

The shop was jam-packed with the small things that delight a child's heart... metal clickers, whistles, yo-yos, chalk, crayons, drawing tablets and pencils, celluloid kewpie dolls of all sizes, little metal cars, penny candy, and bubble gum.

Mothers went to Perkins' if they didn't want to make the trip to San Diego for party supplies at Woolworth's or Kress... invitations, candles for the cake, nut cups, jellybeans, party hats, snappers, paper tablecloths and napkins, streamers, balloons, confetti, and party games. They stocked seasonal decorations too... Halloween costumes, masks and noisemakers, paper mache jack-o-lanterns, Easter baskets, grass and all kinds of candy eggs and chocolate figures, decorations for Thanksgiving and Christmas, valentines, fireworks, and flags for all the patriotic holidays.

Mr. and Mrs. Perkins were nice to everyone, friendly and helpful. It was the only store that Cynthia could go into whether she had money or not and not feel someone's eyes watching her every move. She could look and finger to her heart's content and they never asked her to leave or told her to go home.

Mahala Hudgins Brigman, mother of Amos Hudgins, Richmond, Missouri, 1890s

Amos E. Hudgins, 2nd Kansas Colored Infantry Regiment, Union Army, 1863-65 (Courtesy of San Diego History Center)

Amos Hudgins and Cynthia Ann "Annie" Hudgins, Topeka, Kansas, 1874
(Courtesy of San Diego History Center)

Annie Hudgins and son Algernon "Algie" Hudgins, Logan Heights, San Diego, 1897. (Courtesy of San Diego History Center)

Amos, Algernon and Annie Hudgins, Julian Street house, Logan Heights, San Diego, 1896. (Courtesy of San Diego History Center)

Annie Hudgins, Coronado, 1927
(Courtesy of San Diego History Center)

Elderly Woman Struck By Automobile

In what was termed by local police as an unavoidable accident, Mrs. Cynthia Hudgins, 80 years old, of 845 B Avenue, was struck by an automobile last Thursday evening at Ninth and C, and after emergency treatment at the scene of the accident, was taken to the county hospital by the city ambulance. The car is said to have been driven by J. H. Alexander, 1033 Encino Row.

Mrs. Hudgins' injury consisted of a fractured hip, and but for her advanced age would not be considered particularly dangerous. Reports from the hospital indicate no change in her condition.

Coronado Journal, June 7, 1934

Services Last Saturday For Mrs. Hudgins

Funeral services were held last Saturday at the Benbough mortuary for Mrs. Cynthia Ann Hudgins, of Coronado, who died June 27. Mrs. Hudgins, who had resided in Coronado for more than thirty years, was struck by an automobile on May 31, sustaining injuries from which she never recovered.

A native of Kentucky, aged 80 at the time of her death, she came to California from Missouri with her husband some forty-five years ago. For some years the Hudgins lived on a government claim in the El Cajon valley.

One son, Amos A. Hudgins of Coronado, survives the deceased. Interment was in Mount Hope cemetery.

Coronado Journal, July 5, 1934

Algernon and May Hudgins, 1920

Algernon and Cynthia Hudgins, 845 B Avenue, Coronado, 1921

Algernon "Algie" and May Hudgins, circa 1930s

May, Cynthia and Algie Hudgins, 1934

Cynthia Hudgins, Graduation day, Coronado High School, class of 1939

Vera Smith, Cynthia Hudgins and Fusako Tsuneyoshi, 1935

Vera, Cynthia and Fusako, 1965

Cynthia Hudgins Gibbon and Theodore "Tee Gee" Gibbon Jr., 1943

Theodore "Ted" Gibbon, Cynthia Hudgins Gibbon, and Algie Hudgins, 1941

Cynthia Hudgins, B Avenue, Coronado, 1928

Annie and Cynthia Hudgins, 845 B Avenue, Coronado, 1927

BOOK THREE

CHAPTER FORTY-ONE

Every summer as soon as she was old enough to go by herself, Cynthia went to the beach alone. Even after she met Vera she went alone because Vera didn't like the beach. She sunned on the sand alone and swam in the bay alone until she got old enough that boys from San Diego, not knowing about her, began to notice her when she was fourteen and fifteen and made friendly overtures. They were short-lived when they learned she was younger than she looked or someone told them about her. There were a few who hadn't minded though.

At eight, she'd learned to swim when Papa took her water wings away with one hand and tossed her into the bay from the float into twenty feet of water with the other. She came up spluttering and gasping for air to discover that he was right, she didn't need those "God damned things" anymore. By age nine she was going to the beach by herself every day during summer vacations. She'd sleep late, grab a piece of bread and peanut butter with jam or fix a bowl of cereal, drink a cup of coffee with top milk and lots of sugar, put on her suit, get a towel and with a, "Bye, Grandma" she'd be off to spend the day until the sun was well past the meridian and the shadows lengthening before heading back, first to Grandma's, then to Mama's. She body surfed in the ocean, tanned in the sun on the sand, then ran across to the bay to dive in and rinse the sand off, always alone.

Cynthia thought May had been irresponsible in allowing her to go alone to swim in the ocean and the bay until one day a letter came from Vera. They had been reminiscing in their letters about their youth and she was surprised to read that Vera had thought all the summers they hadn't been together that Cynthia had been at the beach with other friends.

"What other friends?" Cynthia wrote back. "You were the only friend I ever had then. Didn't you know that? I was never with anyone until I was sixteen. I was always alone except for that one summer with Marie."

Certainly, many other kids from school went to the beach in groups and alone. She'd seen kids from her own class, some of whom she'd known nearly all her life, but they weren't friends. They might say hi, that was all. They didn't ask her to join them, and she certainly didn't ask them if she could.

After she sent her letter off to Vera, she thought about it. Mama had looked after her welfare in so many other ways it was strange that she'd let her go to the beach alone. Had she thought, like Vera had, that Cynthia was with other kids and that they watched out for each other? That was never true until she was in her teens. There were no lifeguards in those days on the beach or at the bayside. Cynthia made sure when she had kids of her own that they never even walked to school alone, much less go unaccompanied to the beach, even though the world was a much safer place for children then than it is now.

It was about this time that Cynthia decided she'd rather be a boy than a girl. It seemed to her that boys were nicer than girls. They didn't say and do the mean things to her that the girls did. They'd let her spin tops with them and play mumblety-peg or marbles, which she wasn't very good at so she'd lose them. She wasn't very good at anything really if it required coordination... not jacks or jump rope or hopscotch, only roller skating and swimming. She watched the other girls playing their games and practiced at home by herself, but it wasn't much fun. May let her buy jacks and marbles and jump ropes as they came in season and kites, too, until Papa taught her to make her own. May must have thought that Cynthia was playing these games with other girls at school, but of course, she wasn't, and sooner or later someone would steal them from her desk at recess or before she got back to school for lunch.

One summer day when Cynthia was nearing eleven, May came up to Grandma's to collect her laundry and change her bed, bringing with her a pair of boy's trunks a friend had given her. She showed them to Cynthia, who was thrilled.

"Now, I don't want you wearing these to the beach until we can get you a halter," Mama said.

"I don't need a halter. I want to wear them now."

"You heard what I said."

Cynthia nodded, but as soon as May left, she put on the trunks, threw a towel around her neck like the boys did, and avoiding Grandma, left the house. Cynthia was not given to minding Mama as well as she did Papa. She often wondered about that after she was grown and decided it was because Papa usually gave her a good reason why she shouldn't do something while all Mama did was say, "Don't do it," which made her curious to see why she shouldn't.

It was early, not many people were out. Cynthia spread her towel and leaned back on her arms, face to the sun. After a bit, she looked down at herself. She looked different. There were soft round bumps she hadn't noticed before... not very big, but there. Her chest wasn't as flat as it used to be. She was growing a bosom!

Suddenly she was very self-conscious. All she had was her towel to cover up with and she'd have to walk back home on the street when more people were out and about. Momentary panic overcame her, but just as she realized she had a problem she heard Mama's voice behind her.

"I thought I'd find you here. Didn't I tell you not to wear those trunks yet?"

Caught in the act of downright disobedience, Cynthia was wary. Mama was going to be mad, but even so, Mama's voice was heaven to her ears. She was relieved.

"Yes, Mama May," she answered.

"Get in the car and be quick about it," May said as she herded Cynthia toward it. When they got back to Grandma's house, Mama didn't say anything, but she confiscated the trunks and Cynthia never saw them again.

Even though it was impossible for her to be a boy now, she asked Mama if she could get a boy's haircut for the rest of the summer so her hair wouldn't be so sticky all the time from salt water. It was all right and May gave her a quarter to go to the barbershop.

After she got the haircut, she wangled a couple of dollars from Mama for a pair of boy's jeans and a shirt she'd seen advertised on sale at the Hub in San Diego. Now, maybe she wasn't a boy, but she could pass for one. She was very pleased with her new look, and she kept her hair cut short off and on for most of the rest of her life because it was easy to care for.

Later that summer, having spent the night at her parent's house for some reason now long forgotten, she took the family dog, a fox terrier named Bingo, to the beach with her. There were no leash laws then and he ran along beside her as they walked down the main street leading to Tent City. Suddenly, appearing from nowhere, a German Shepherd attacked Bingo who was less than half of his size. On the dog's heels came four or five grown men to watch the fight. Cynthia was scared beyond belief. Her dog was going to be killed right in front of her eyes. Bingo was doing his best to defend himself, but the shepherd had him on the ground on his back going for his throat.

"Stop them, stop them!" she screamed. "He's killing my dog!"

Not one of the men moved. They stood watching, egging the shepherd on, so Cynthia made a dash into the middle of the growling, snarling, snapping melee and grabbed Bingo in her arms. Jumping back, she kept turning away from the shepherd who was still intent on killing the terrier, jumping at her, trying to reach him until one of the men called the big dog off.

"You God damned fool, kid. Don't you have any better sense than to jump into the middle of a dog fight? You could have been all torn up."

"I don't care. He was going to kill my dog. He was killing my dog and you weren't doing anything to stop it. You all were just going to stand there and watch him do it!"

She stamped her foot and glared at them, still cradling Bingo in her arms like a baby.

"My God," the man said. "You're acting like a girl. You're not a girl, are you?"

"Yes, I am," Cynthia said as she looked angrily around at all of them. She was furious and still scared.

"Gosh, I'm sorry I swore at you kid. I thought you were a boy."

"Well, I'm not," and Cynthia stomped off to put as much distance between Bingo and herself and them as possible.

Swearing didn't bother Cynthia. Papa swore all the time, taking the Lord's name in vain on a regular basis. But he was a nice man; he would never have stood and watched one dog kill another for the fun of it. She set Bingo down and looked him over. He seemed to be all right. As the two of them went on, she was thinking, "I guess I really don't want to be a boy after all. It's too late now anyway, but if that's what some men are like, I don't want to be one."

Afterward, she felt a little smug, feeling that she had put those men in their place and kind of proud of herself for the way she'd rescued Bingo.

There was still an experience to go that summer. The hotel put a float in the ocean about a hundred and fifty feet out. It was secured to the shore by a rope with cork floats. Cynthia sat in the sun watching the big kids go hand over hand through the surf to the float, where they lay sunning themselves before diving off to swim back to shore. It looked like fun.

"I'm going to go out to it," she told Papa when she told him about the raft.

"No. I don't want you to even think about trying it. You're not that good a swimmer and it's too dangerous," he said.

It didn't look all that dangerous to her and she thought she was a pretty good swimmer. The next morning, after deciding to do it anyway so she could tell Papa he was wrong, she got up from the sand and went to the rope. It was much bigger around than it had seemed from a distance, more like the hawser they used on ships. Her hands barely went halfway around it, but it seemed safe enough; she'd just hang on real tight. She started out. It went well as long as her feet touched the bottom, but just as she realized she was out over her head, a wave came, lifted her up and, as it broke, jerked the rope right out of her hands, rolling her over and over every which way, slamming her onto the bottom and knocking the wind out of her. She was swallowing sand and salt water and she didn't know which way was up. She was terrified.

"Oh, God. I'm going to drown and my folks will never know what happened to me," ran through her mind.

Just then, by the grace of God, she felt a hand touch her shoulder, grab a bathing suit strap and haul her up out of the churning water like a kitten being held by the scruff of its neck. She'd noticed some high school girls just ahead of her as she went into the ocean. They wore the black bathing suits with the Red Cross lifesaving medallion on the skirt. She knew who they were; she'd seen them around Coronado many times over the years as they were all growing up. She hadn't had time to cry out, but luckily one of them had looked back just as she went under and came back to save her. She felt herself being dragged to the beach by the strap and dumped unceremoniously on the sand just out of the reach of the surf where she lay coughing and gasping, trying to catch her breath.

"Are you all right?" her savior asked. She nodded that she was.

"I wouldn't try that again if I were you."

She looked up. "I won't." Then she put her head down on her arms to lie there and recover. The girl turned and went back into the ocean to join her friends who were still in the water, watching.

The girl should have gotten a medal for a bona fide lifesaving rescue, but Cynthia went home and never said a word. Papa would have given her a lecture on foolhardiness, using his stock response to whatever she had done that was so foolish he couldn't believe it of her. She knew it by heart.

"Jesus Christ," he'd say. "Don't you ever stop and think for one God damned minute before you go off halfcocked and do some damned fool's stupid thing? I thought you had more sense than that." What more he might have said, knowing that she'd done something even after he'd told her not to, she couldn't begin to imagine.

Fifty years later, she looked up the girl's family name in the phone book. The wife of a brother answered and when she heard the story, gave Cynthia the name of her sister-in-law. Cynthia wrote a belated letter of thanks for her life, apologizing for not telling anyone so a medal could have been awarded. She received a letter in reply. Her rescuer didn't remember the episode but wrote that she was glad Cynthia had written and that she'd been able to help her. Cynthia disobeyed Papa only three times in her life. The near drowning was the second time.

THE FIRST TIME, she'd asked him if he could put a bar up in the side yard for her like the ones at school. She could only play on those after school when no one else was on the playground, but she didn't tell him that. He looked around the yard, found an old broomstick, sawed it off to fit the space and nailed it up for her. As he walked away, he told her not to hang by her knees on it because it wouldn't hold her. That was the exact reason she had wanted a bar, so he'd no sooner turned the corner of the garage than she got on it and hung by her knees. He was right; it wasn't strong enough. It broke with a crack and she fell on her head. There was blackness and flashes of light like she'd seen when the ice truck hit her. He heard it break and came running back to pick her up and carry her in to his mother, who put her in bed for the rest of that day.

By the time Cynthia was sixteen, she and Vera had found a number of things to do in the summertime together... window shopping with imaginary money, going to old-time dances then to roller skating rinks, and dating the young servicemen they met there. Cynthia deserted her old friend, the beach, for other pursuits with not much guilt or sense of loss... the relationship had been one-sided anyway.

CHAPTER FORTY-TWO

Bingo, the family's fox terrier, was Cynthia's second dog. They'd bought him on a ride around the Strand one Sunday when Al saw a sign for fox terrier puppies. He'd had fox terriers before and was fond of the breed. Cynthia was eight and Bingo was six weeks old. She'd held him in her arms all the way back to Mama's house from Imperial Beach and from then on, he was her dog.

After he was grown, he'd been allowed to run loose all over Coronado. There were no leash laws then, so he'd follow the mailman on his daily route, coming home when all the mail was delivered. When he learned where Cynthia was each day, after she'd met him on his way back to Mama's a time or two, he began waiting outside her room when it was time for school to let out, and they'd go together to check in at Grandma's then on to Mama's.

He had a fascination with rolling in dead, smelly, rotten things. Once he came home smelling of horse manure... he'd found his way into the stables near the golf course. Another time he'd been down on the beach and found a lovely dead fish to roll in. May, who'd never owned a dog before, didn't understand the thing. She'd beaten him before bathing him, breaking a yardstick over him each time. This wasn't quite as brutal as it sounds because there were free yardsticks given out at the hardware store and the lumber yard and were very thin. The third time was the charm. It was decided that a fence was needed to keep him from his delightful habit.

A trip to the lumber yard was in order for posts, and to the hardware store for rolls of wire. Al borrowed a surveyor's instrument from the company and the next Saturday Cynthia held the pole as he sighted the boundaries of their lot, drove the pegs and strung string to mark the places where the posts would go. The holes were dug, and the posts put into place with cement while Cynthia again assisted to be sure they were set perfectly straight before the wire was nailed into place.

Bingo was unhappy for a while, but he was a good dog; he didn't try to dig under or climb over the fence. He soon learned when it was time for Cynthia to get back from school. She'd see him waiting at the gate, wiggling with ecstasy as he spotted her cutting across the vacant block in front of the house. At the last moment, he'd run off to search the ground and the woodpile for a stick to "horse" with, jumping up and spinning around, running off and back again until she opened the gate, and he ran to give it to her to be praised and patted.

He went everywhere with Cynthia in the summer and on weekends. After she got her bicycle, she'd put him in the basket to go to the beach or to the store for Mama. People laughed and pointed to see a dog in the bicycle's basket. Seeming to know he was the center of attention, he'd loll his tongue out and grin at them.

If she had the money for an Eskimo Pie, she'd share it with him or if she bought popcorn at the gleaming red and brass popcorn wagon parked by the bleachers in the summer in Tent City, they'd share that too. She painted his nails with Cute nail polish when it first appeared on the market.

Cynthia gave May manicures too, but May couldn't have been as pleased as Bingo was when they told him how cute he was after his manicure. He'd wriggle with delight looking up at them, holding up a paw and grinning from ear to ear, his eyes shining. He was a happy dog and smart too. He was Cynthia's pal from the time she was eight until she was seventeen when he developed a tumor and had to be put to sleep.

The love of a dog is unconditional. Cynthia never had to wonder how Bingo felt about her like she did with people. She was everything to him and she felt the same way about him. Hadn't she waded into a fight with a dog three times his size when she was ten years old to save his life? She knew he would have done the same for her.

Her first dog, brought home in Amos's pocket shortly after she was born, was named Prince, a giant orange fox terrier. He followed her everywhere when she began to crawl and then to toddle. If she wasn't around, he could be found lying in the garden swing in the side yard. A passing neighbor, seeing him there, told Annie that he didn't know why they called him Prince when he should have been called Prince Useless! The name Useless stuck and Prince was dropped, but Useless proved himself a Prince when Cynthia was four and a half years old.

Annie took Cynthia for a walk every afternoon, usually going to the sea wall about three blocks at the most from the house. This day she was sewing clothes for Cynthia because she'd be starting school after the first of the year when Cynthia wanted to go for their afternoon walk.

"Grandma, can we go for our walk now?"

"Not now. I'm too busy. We'll go tomorrow."

Cynthia didn't want to wait until tomorrow. She called Useless, told him they were going for a walk, and they started off. It took a while because they had to stop and look at bugs in the vacant lots in the next block and at horned toads and down gopher holes to see if they could see a gopher. That day they looked down a hole just in time to see a gopher snake go by at the bottom of the hole. It was a big one too, took a long time to go by.

Finally, they arrived at the sea wall and were going to walk a ways down Ocean Front Boulevard before heading back when a police car pulled up alongside them.

"Come on Cynthia. Get into the car and we'll take you home."

"No. Useless and I are going to finish our walk first."

He got out of the car and started toward her. Useless, who had been sniffing around the rocks for rats or ground squirrels, came running over and, putting himself between his girl and that man in the uniform, began barking. A few people came wandering over to see what was going on, forming a circle around Cynthia. Useless got hostile. No one was going to get near his charge. He circled her, barking and growling, and no one tried.

The impasse continued for a while as the crowd grew. Someone must have called Annie, or perhaps she'd guessed where Cynthia had gone, because presently she showed up, took Cynthia in hand and, with Useless following, they started back.

From that day forward the excursion was referred to as the day Cynthia ran away or the day she got lost.

"I did not run away," she'd say every time. "Useless and I were just taking a walk and I wasn't lost either!"

Needless to say, Useless was the dog of the hour. He was still called Useless because usage had made it a habit, but to all concerned he was the Prince of a dog he'd originally been dubbed.

Unfortunately, Marian, the neighbor girl, teased Useless one day when he had a bone and he bit her. Her mother raised such a fuss about it that Useless was put to sleep. Cynthia grieved for Useless for a long time because he'd been the only real friend she'd had until Bingo came into her life when she was eight.

This was another thing Marian had conveniently forgotten on the day she called Cynthia after she'd seen the article in the paper about Cynthia's grandparents during that first Black History Month. She'd forgotten not only that her mother never let Cynthia into their

house or that she, too, had helped to keep Cynthia out of the bathroom in the first and second grades at school, but that she hadn't
listened when Annie kept telling her to leave Useless alone because
he might bite her. By not paying attention to what Grandma said,
she'd been responsible for his death.

CHAPTER FORTY-THREE

Swimming in San Diego Bay was not healthy in the twenties and thirties. The exercise was, but the bay itself was polluted. People back then had good immune systems; they didn't sanitize everything and worry about germs as much as they do today. No signs were ever posted saying "No swimming allowed." Cynthia never heard of anyone getting really sick or dying from swimming in the bay and besides, her grandmother used to say, "Everybody eats a peck of dirt in their lifetime," or something like that.

The Navy ships in the harbor dumped raw sewage directly into the Bay. It was not uncommon to be swimming and have a human turd bob up right in front of your face. Cynthia got trench mouth from swimming in the bay at least three times that she could remember when she was a kid.

"My mouth is real sore, Papa," she told him the first time.

"Let's have a look-see," he said, then. "Oh, that's trench mouth. Let's go into the bathroom and I'll show you how to get rid of it in case you get it again."

He took a small glass vial with purple crystals in it from the medicine cabinet, drew a glass of water and dropped a pinch of the crystals into it. The water turned a beautiful pale violet.

"Here swish this around in your mouth for a few days until it gets better. Now don't use too much. It's permanganate of potash and it's caustic."

It worked fine and in no time the soreness was gone. The next time she got it, Cynthia fixed the solution herself, putting way too much in the water, making it a deep royal purple.

Telling herself, "It'll probably make it go away quicker because it's stronger," she took a big swig and knew immediately that she'd made a terrible mistake. She spat it out right away and rinsed her mouth, but it was too late. She could feel the skin on her cheeks, the roof of her mouth and her gums hanging in shreds. She looked in the mirror and was very frightened, but she didn't say anything to Papa... she knew exactly what he'd say, and he'd have no sympathy for her either.

"God dammit, don't come crying to me. Didn't I tell you to be careful with that stuff? It serves you right."

Fortunately, the damage wasn't permanent, but she had a bad few days, afraid her teeth would all fall out and then Papa would really be mad at her. She knew it was only because he cared about her welfare, but it was still scary when he yelled.

That wasn't all the Navy dumped into the bay, to the anger of Coronado residents. Mess cooks, at the end of the week or month, would toss unused food overboard because if they hadn't used their quota, they'd be shorted the amount of the extra for the coming period. It was difficult to estimate how much would be needed because the number of men who stayed aboard for meals varied. It was not at all unusual to see whole loaves of bread still in the wrapper, cubes of butter, or whole fruits and vegetables floating in the bay as one rode on the ferry. Money was hard to come by, people were going hungry.

May stormed, "Here we are in the middle of a Depression, making do to make ends meet with hardly any money to buy necessities while the military is throwing perfectly good food away and there's not a thing we can do about it"

May wrote letters when she was angry, but whether she wrote to the Commandant of the Naval District or not, Cynthia didn't know. She did know that in the worst of the period after the crash, on Thanksgiving, when May read in the paper that the prisoners in the jail were going to get a turkey with all the trimmings for the holiday, she was furious. She wrote a letter to the supervisor of the county jail, telling him in no uncertain terms that it was a crying shame that decent, honest people had to make do with what they could for the holiday while thieves and other felons were going to have a wonderful dinner. As a result of her letter, and possibly complaints from others, the prisoners that year got a dinner, but it wasn't turkey with all the trimmings. That was the year that Cynthia came to the house from school to find her mother crying. When Papa came home, she asked him about it.

"Mama is crying because Thanksgiving is coming Thursday and all we're going to have for dinner is beans with ketchup," he told her. They said grace over their bread and butter and beans with ketchup, reminding themselves that there were probably others who weren't as lucky as they were.

Governmental waste was one of Cynthia's father's pet peeves... that, and deficit spending. Back in the thirties, when the national debt was a pittance compared to what it is now, Al warned that if a line wasn't drawn, it would do nothing but get worse... and he was right. Al was a conservative Republican, isolationist, hawk.

If he hadn't already had his stroke and died, thought Cynthia, the state of our country today, with the governmental waste, the size of the national debt, our interference in other countries' politics and wars, the billions we give to those who won't lift a finger to help themselves and the people in charge running the country, who Papa would have called "this God damned fat-headed politicians in Washington who can't tell their asses from their elbow," or "those God damned bleeding heart liberals," would do him in for sure.

As she wrote about Papa, Cynthia found herself smiling. She realized she was beginning to think just like he had when she was young and didn't understand how what went on all the way across the country in Washington, D.C. could have anything to do with them or why he and Mama got so angry about it.

CYNTHIA's personal experience with governmental waste was when she went back to college in her fifties. In an art course she was taking, the assignment was for a poster which the instructor wanted to be done with poster paints. Cynthia still had the materials from her short-lived time at Washburn College when she was young, but when she got them out, the paints had dried up and she didn't want to buy new unless she had to. Her neighbor next door, who was a schoolteacher, had four children.

"Perhaps his kids have some paint I can borrow," she thought, so she went to ask.

"Sure," he said. "We've got lots of it. I'll bring you some." He brought five mayonnaise-size jars of the powdered kind to be mixed with water... the three primary colors, and black and white.

"Oh, my goodness," she said. "I just need a little bit, not that much. I'll return it when I'm finished."

"Keep it," he said. "I've got lots more. The teachers take some of it and the rest of it is thrown out at the end of the school year. If we don't use it all, they short us for the coming year."

"That's a shame," Cynthia said, shocked. "Some of those kids I go to college with don't have much money and are hard-pressed to buy supplies. Sometimes they have to ask the instructor for more time until they can afford to get what they need. Why can't they give it to the college or to someone else who could use it, instead of just throwing it away? Or have a yard sale and sell it?"

"It probably wouldn't be allowed, and they're not set up to do it anyway if it was."

"I guess not," she agreed. "Too bad."

The vagaries, rules, and regulations of bureaucracy had been another of her father's favorite soapbox subjects. "God damned bureaucratic red tape," he called it.

She told her neighbor about how it had been with the Navy and the wasted food during the Depression. All he could do was shrug and agree that it was a terrible waste of the taxpayer's money. Little did they know that it was going to get much worse over the next couple of decades.

CHAPTER FORTY-FOUR

When Cynthia went off to the fifth grade, she had no high hopes there'd be a new girl who would be the friend she'd prayed for for so long. She'd given up expecting it to happen, but this was the year her prayers would be answered. God had finally found the right someone for her, decided that Cynthia was the right someone for that other someone and that the time was right to bring both little someones together to become friends for a lifetime.

The new girl was Vera. She'd come to California from Chicago with her family, an older sister and brother and her mother who, because of the Depression, had lost everything and was looking for a new beginning, as were so many others at that time. Her brother joined the Navy, her sister became an Arthur Murray dance instructor, and her mother started a dressmaking and alteration business in an apartment over a store on the main street.

The news was passed around in class. "There's a new girl in the other fifth grade!"

Cynthia looked around at the first recess and saw the new girl standing with a little group of four or five other girls. At the same instant, to her horror, she saw that her old enemy, who was in the group, had spotted her and was bearing down on her full speed ahead.

"Oh Lord," she thought. "She's back!" Her first instinct was to run and hide. Frantically, she looked around then realized there was no place to go, not enough time to go anywhere anyway and nothing she could do. She stood her ground, bracing herself, her heart in her throat, breathing hard as the other girl determinedly bore down on her.

She arrived, eyes glaring and, thrusting her face right into Cynthia's, demanded, "Do you like the new girl?"

What shall I say? What shall I say? Cynthia asked herself as she stared back into the grim, wickedly expectant face. "If I don't say what she wants me to, she'll probably beat me up." She realized the other girl had grown taller and stockier than herself and looked meaner than ever.

"Uh... I don't even know her," Cynthia said.

"Well, do you like her or not?"

"Uh... no," Cynthia said. Knowing her enemy, she hoped it was the right answer. It was, and she breathed a sigh of relief when the bully turned, lumbered off back to the other girls and pointed back toward Cynthia, who knew she was telling them what she'd just said because they all turned their heads to stare in her direction. Cynthia carried the guilt of her cowardice for years after she and Vera became friends, long after marriage and children, until they were both in their sixties. She wrote the whole story to Vera, who had moved to Oregon by then after her husband, Wood's, retirement.

"I'm sorry," she told her. "I've felt like a traitor all these years for saying it, even though we hadn't even met yet."

Vera wrote back that she didn't remember anything about it. She'd been too nervous that first day at a new school to pay any attention to what was said to her by anyone about anything.

Vera had been just as insecure, and just as shy and self-conscious as Cynthia was. She, too, had lived with a grandmother until the old lady, whom she loved dearly, had died. Her mother, who was a divorcee with a dressmaking business, had farmed her out to a sister who had two children of her own. The aunt was not unkind to Vera, but she favored her own children over her, continually reminding her how lucky she was and how thankful she should be to have someone like herself to care for her... a burden which should never be laid upon a small child. It made her feel unloved and unwanted, just as Cynthia felt. Vera was also left-handed and, in school in Chicago, had been forced to use her right hand, causing her to stutter. This cleared up in a year or so after she started in Coronado's school where no attempt was made to change her natural bent.

Vera was very fair, inclined to be a little plump, with a round face, large blue eyes and light brown hair. She was not unattractive, but she had a slightly receding chin and her canine teeth protruded, crowded because of her small jaw. All these things had made her very self-conscious. She was convinced she was fat, stupid, and ugly and that no one could ever like her. All this she shared with Cynthia as they became friends. Cynthia shared little about herself, not to Vera and not to anyone else.

The relationship didn't get off the ground immediately because another girl in Vera's class lived right across the hall from her in the same apartment building. The two girls walked together and allowed Cynthia to walk with them until they reached the place where they turned to go their separate ways. On days when the other girl had something else to do or someplace else to go, Vera walked all the way to Cynthia's grandma's before going on home. As time went on, they'd go from there to Vera's apartment to stay awhile or, after checking with Vera's mother, walk to Cynthia's mother's house. Vera loved to listen to Cynthia do her piano practice. Then they would walk back to the school, which was a halfway point, and separate. As the friendship grew and they spent evenings together or went to the movies, loathe to leave each other, they'd make the walk from one house to the other, back to the school again and again, many times before they finally said good night. It seemed they never ran out of things to talk about and never tired of each other's company, but it didn't become the close relationship that it grew to be over the years until after graduation from junior high when Maggie, the other girl Cynthia had been unsure of and very jealous about, moved away. Cynthia, always cautious, always fearing rejection, began to trust Vera more than she had anyone before.

Vera and Maggie had a game they played several times a week and on those days they'd turn toward home, leaving Cynthia to go her way alone. She accepted Vera's apologies with good grace, but since she'd been left out of things so many times before, she always expected it to be the same old rejection. She wished that she'd be invited to join them, and Vera seemed genuinely sorry that they were not including her. Even so, each time Cynthia waited to see if this was going to be the last time she'd be allowed to tag along, she was more relieved than she cared to admit when it wasn't. Later, she was to learn that one reason she wasn't asked to join them was that the other girl's mother didn't want her in their apartment. Vera's mother, on the other hand, may have had some trepidation when (Cynthia learned later) her customers asked why she let her daughter associate with that little nigger girl, but she didn't try to break them up. She seemed glad that Vera had someone, as did May after the first few times Vera came to the house. Even though May expressed disapproval of Vera's mother early in the girls' friendship because she was a three-time divorcee, she accepted Vera.

While the two mothers never became close friends, they were cordial, stopping to chat when they met on the street, but no more than that, even after May was asked to be one of Nancy's Godmothers. Cynthia, of course, was the other, eleven years later.

Many years after that, not long before her death, Vera's mother thanked Cynthia for having been such a good friend to her daughter. Cynthia was deeply touched. She felt it had been the other way around; Vera was a good friend to her and her mother had allowed it, which was a lot to be said in her favor.

Vera finally told her that the 'game' had been a pretend knights and ladies, King Arthur sort of thing that she'd been afraid to include Cynthia because she was such a cynic, she'd probably have laughed at them for playing such a silly game. Cynthia had to admit to herself that it was true; she probably would have. There were many things over the years that Cynthia never told Vera about herself, indeed had never told anyone until now as she was writing about her life, so Vera had no way of knowing why Cynthia was the way she was.

Nancy told Cynthia once, as they spoke of her mother after Vera was gone, that Vera had loved Cynthia but hadn't always understood her. Cynthia laughed.

"No, I guess not. I expect that may be true of some of my other relationships too. I kept it all inside. I didn't even understand myself."

"Only now," she thought. "Is it all beginning to fall into place as this book progresses? I loved Vera too and I'm glad I was able to open up and tell her so before she died."

THE TWO GIRLS buddied every school year, but when summer vacation started, they went separate ways until their sophomore year. Vera was very fair, burned easily and was self-conscious about her "fat white legs" so she wouldn't go to the beach with Cynthia.

For Cynthia, the beach was her life. She was often alone, but sometimes she met others her age who came to Coronado from San Diego or other places on vacation with their parents. They didn't know about her and so were friendly for those short times... ships that passed in the night. Every so often, someone from school would hang out with her for a while. It was only a stop-gap for them both, understood without saying. When school started again in the fall there'd be a "hi" as they passed each other in the hall, but it was over. That was the way it was and Cynthia accepted it, telling herself she didn't care to protect her feelings and reminding herself of part of an old song she'd heard. "Got along without ya before I met ya, gonna get along without ya now." Still...

Even with Vera, it was that way for a long time on Cynthia's part. She sometimes hurt sensitive Vera's feelings with her callous remarks and had to apologize, feeling genuinely sorry.

Cynthia's mother, Vera's mother, and Vera didn't have the protective insulation (or was it a hard shell?) that Cynthia had developed by the time she was nine. They trusted people and were often hurt. Cynthia trusted no one so she wasn't disappointed or, if she was, even a little, she didn't let it show. If someone turned out to be nice, it was like receiving an unexpected gift that never failed to surprise and please her since she always expected the worst.

As for Enid Wood, Cynthia's arch enemy, somehow, they never crossed paths again that year or ever. Cynthia never knew what had happened, if the family had moved away or they just managed not to see each other on the playgrounds or the streets. Maybe the changes that had been happening for Cynthia worked their magic on Enid, too, so that her vendetta against Cynthia no longer gave her pleasure. As far as Cynthia was concerned, Enid wasn't missed and was soon forgotten, not to be remembered again for over sixty years.

Vera and her family lived in the apartment for only a couple of years. Her brother came home from the base from time to time to spend the night. Jackie, her sister, married and moved out. Now that there was an empty bedroom, Cynthia was allowed to spend the night with Vera in the Murphy bed in the living room occasionally, while her mother slept in the other room. So it was that Cynthia learned what the secret was that she had wondered about for so long.

The two were growing closer. One night, when they were having one of their long conversations about nothing and everything and Vera had been telling her about her earlier unhappy years before they'd met and that she'd never had a real friend before, Cynthia opened up a little.

"I've never had a real friend before either," she said. "No one has ever wanted to be my friend because there's something terribly wrong with me and I don't know what it is."

Raising up on her elbow to look at Cynthia in the light coming into the room from the window, Vera said with surprise in her voice, "Cynthia, you really don't know the reason why people don't like you?"

'No. Do you?"

"Yes."

"Well, what?"

"It's because your grandma is colored."

Cynthia was stunned. She didn't know what she was going to hear, though she was prepared for whatever it might be, but that certainly wasn't it. Her jaw snapped shut; she lay there with her teeth clenched, her eyes wide open in a state of shock, her head in a whirl of confusion. Finally, she opened her mouth.

"But what's that got to do with me?" she asked.

"White people don't like colored people," Vera answered.

"But I'm not colored; I'm white."

"Not to white people," Vera said. "You're still a nigger to them."

"But how can people not like people for something they don't have any control over?" Cynthia was trying hard to understand.

"I don't know, but that's the way it is."

"You're white and you like me. How come?"

"Because you're my friend."

Then, because Cynthia didn't say anything else, after a short while, Vera turned over and went to sleep. Not Cynthia. She lay there staring into the semi-darkness for a long, long time, her mind in turmoil, trying to fathom what she had just heard. All the things she'd wondered about for years had suddenly become understandable, but still, it made no sense at all.

"So, that's what it is," she thought. She must have been stupid not to have figured it out for herself before. She wasn't ugly; she didn't smell. Grandma was colored. Papa must be colored too... but he wasn't. He was white like she was and like Mama. Now that she knew what people thought, it explained the whispers, the pointing, the snubs, the spitefulness, and dirty tricks, why she was followed in stores and told to go home, why no one wanted to sit with her at the movies or had wanted to be her friend. There wasn't anything wrong with her except she was colored. She didn't want to accept it. She was white; she was not colored. She would not accept it.

"I'm not, I'm not,' she whispered to herself as Vera snored gently beside her. "I don't want to be I won't be. I am not!"

But in her mind, her heart and her soul, she knew it was true.

That night changed Cynthia's life, her way of thinking about herself and everything from that day forward. Vera and she never spoke about it again, nor did she say anything to anyone else except when she felt she knew someone well enough to tell them herself, taking the risk of being rejected, feeling that she should tell before someone else did it for her, which infuriated her. But she had to take that chance. She was unable to live her life as a lie, letting anyone she cared about think she was something she was not... what she hadn't wanted to believe, what she hadn't wanted to be. After all the years of resistance and denial and telling herself other people were lying about her and wondering why, she'd just had to come face to face with it... that it was true. It was really true and nothing she could do or say could change it or make it not be so.

CHAPTER FORTY-FIVE

Cynthia's life improved in almost every way after she entered the fifth grade. She had a friend... only part-time, but Vera hadn't turned and walked away as others had. They were together more than she'd been with anyone else before her. The two had an on-again, off-again relationship for a while, depending on their schedules and other interests... if Vera was going to play 'the game' with her neighbor, if Cynthia had to go to Grandma's and then straight to Mama's to help her bring in and fold the wash, or if it was her day to go to the artist's studio, the stamp and coin club or French class, all offered by a sixth-grade teacher after school for those who were interested, which Cynthia was.

They didn't see each other during the summer because Cynthia went her own way, which was to the beach. What Vera did, Cynthia didn't know. They might meet on the street and stop to talk for a minute or wave to each other from a distance. When they met again in the fall, they picked up where they'd left off. This never changed, no matter how long their separations were. When they were older and Ted got orders, they wrote regularly and there was never any sense of strangeness when they were able to be together again.

Some of the other girls had begun making friendly overtures, trying to be nice, but Cynthia was merely polite, no more. She let no one get too close to her. She was still testing Vera, still a little unsure of her, still waiting to see if she'd back off as had happened so many times before.

Her teachers of the fifth and sixth grades and supplemental classes in art and music appreciation, sewing, and cooking, began taking an interest in her, calling on her to recite, pinning up her best artwork, and asking her to read her essays and poetry out loud to the class, earning her respect from her peers for her abilities. All of this was nectar to her spirit, which had been deprived of attention and appreciation for so long. Having a friend was the icing on the cake.

She didn't take home much homework. After the fourth grade, the old arrangement of alphabetic seating wasn't used. The children could sit where they chose and Cynthia chose to sit in her familiar place in the back corner of the room where she could daydream, draw, and doodle without being noticed for long periods of time. Until she got caught, she'd work on her homework too. Sometimes in the later grades, a teacher would allow a little time for beginning the assignment before they took it home, so Cynthia usually managed to get most of her work done one way or the other before the bell rang ending the school day.

When Papa came home, he'd help her with anything she hadn't finished or had trouble with, then play checkers with her. Together they worked rebuses that were in a magazine he bought and one that Cynthia's piano teacher gave her as a gift. If he went out to the garage, she tagged along to keep him company and help in any way she could.

"Hand me that thingamajig over there, will you, Thum?" And she would.

They laughed at the same jokes and cartoons. They both loved mystery stories, trying to beat each other in guessing whodunit first. They asked riddles and recited nonsense rhymes to each other, and he answered every question she could think of to ask in ways she could easily understand. This included trying to explain eternity with one of his vast repertoire of little rhymes.

"Little fleas have lesser fleas
Upon their backs to bite 'em,
And lesser fleas and lesser fleas
And so ad infinitum."

He kept chemicals in the garage which he warned Cynthia about. Pointing to a small bottle, he recited,

"Little Johnny used to drink,
But now he drinks no more.
For what he thought was H_2O,
Was H_2SO_4."

"Do you know what that is?"
"No," she said.
"Sulfuric acid. It's poison."
"Oh," she answered.

It was a great way to teach, and Cynthia never forgot anything she learned from him.

Al was given to talking about his day at the dinner table, telling all the news about his co-workers, what they had said or done, repeating the latest jokes that had gone around the place, and who'd walked by and stopped to chat on the street at his corner at noon that day.

Cynthia, when she remembered this story, thought she'd been there at the time, but it was probably because he told it to her later since she was only six and still living with Grandma.

One evening, he told May he'd been walking to the ferry with a friend he met up with each day as usual. They'd run into another fellow coming along First Street whom his friend knew. They'd stopped to chat and Al was introduced.

"What are you doing out so early this morning?" the friend had asked the man.

"Well, I'm planning on flying across the Atlantic," he told them. "So I've been practicing staying awake for long periods of time. I just spent the night walking around the Strand from San Diego."

A few pleasantries and they parted ways, the tall, thin, younger man to finish his walk and the other two to go on to work. Al told May about it that evening.

"I think that's about the most dim-witted thing I've ever heard," he'd said. "That guy must be nuts."

Weeks went by. One day, the newsboys were calling out the latest, their huge headlines screaming about a solo flight across the Atlantic Ocean just completed by a young man named Charles Lindbergh.

"Look at this," Al had said. "That's the fellow I told you about awhile back who I met down on First. I thought he was a fat head without a lick of good sense, but I'll be a monkey's uncle, he actually did it. I'll be damned. Who'd a thunk it was possible?"

This was one of Papa's little jokes. He said 'thunk' was the past tense of 'think.' He also said that a 'myth' was a female moth and so many other plays on words that Cynthia couldn't remember them all. This was one of the reasons Vera had loved to come over to their house for supper. Al loved to show off because it tickled both girls. He'd make one of his little plays on words to Cynthia, then ask her, "Did you get that, Thum?"

"Yes, Papa," and she'd grin at him. He'd smile back with the smile that lit up his face and showed his nice white even teeth.

Oftentimes, in the garage, he'd tease her with riddles or recite limericks and nonsense poems the whole time she was with him. Cynthia recited these things to friends on occasion and recently, a neighbor told her, "You should write some of the things your father told you down before they get lost forever."

So here's one:

A long time to come, I remember it well,
A maid by the side of a poor house did dwell.
She lived with her father and life was serene.
Her age it was red and her hair was nineteen.
Now this maid had a lover, who nearby did dwell,
A cross-legged ruffian and bow eyed as well.
Said he, "Let us flee, by the light of yon star,
For you are the eye of my apple, you are."
"Oh, no," cried the maid, "For it t'would be a disgrace."
So saying, she buried her hands in her face.
By this action the ruffian to anger was made
He silently drew out the knife of his blade.
He slit the throat of the maiden so fair
And dragged her around by the head of her hair.
T'was then her old father appeared, it appears,
And gazed on the sad scene with eyes in his tears.
He rushed at the ruffian and told him to bolt,
Then drew a horse pistol, t'was raised from a Colt."

— AUTHOR UNKNOWN

CYNTHIA WAS DELIGHTED.

"Say it again, Papa. Say it again." He did and she said it with him helping her through it the first and second times. She did it alone the third time and she has never forgotten it.

Papa was so much fun to be with and she loved him so much. Every minute she spent with him was very special.

"If it hadn't been for Papa and Vera," Cynthia told herself, "I probably wouldn't be as sane as I am. Being lonely and feeling unloved can make you crazy."

MISS ARLEN, their teacher, had saved her money to visit Greece on more than one occasion and had fallen in love with the country. It was a major subject in their curriculum that year. They read all the Greek myths, *The Odyssey*, and *The Iliad*.

As it had in Miss Ballard's class, a lot of reading was done in Miss Arlen's class about the Revolutionary war and its heroes, and many poems too... works of Longfellow, Coleridge, Holmes, Scott, and nearly everything that Poe had written, both poetry and stories. Cynthia liked Miss Arlen and Miss Arlen liked her. She talked to Cynthia about Greece and about her schoolwork. No teacher other than Miss Vance had taken this much interest in Cynthia when she was in their class and Miss Arlen didn't lecture like Miss Vance had done, making her feel uncomfortable. When Cynthia took an autograph book she'd received as a birthday gift to school, Miss Arlen wrote in it:

"The isles of Greece, the isles of Greece,
Where burning Sappho loved and sung,
Where grew the arts of war and peace,
Where Delos rose and Phoebes sprung."

Following it with, "Dear Cynthia, I hope you will remember the time you spent in my class and our studies about Greece."

Cynthia never forgot Miss Arlen or the poem. She had a special place in her heart where she kept the memory of people who had been nice to her when she was young and Miss Arlen was one of the first.

She was sorry to leave Miss Arlen behind when the two semesters ended and she passed into the sixth grade, but Miss Andrews was another very good teacher, very innovative in her methods of instruction and also very kind to Cynthia.

It was decided to have an art show in which the whole school would participate in the spring of their second semester that year, so Miss Andrews taped sheets of butcher paper over the two blackboards while she explained that the sixth grades were going to do wall murals in art period. One-half of the room would be in

competition with the other, with everyone in the class participating.

"Who do you want to decide what your mural is going to be and
start it?" she asked after lots were drawn to see which side would be
first.

"Cynthia, Cynthia. Let Cynthia start it," everyone on her team
shouted. Cynthia was in seventh heaven; no one had wanted her on
their team like that for anything except the third-grade spelling bees.
Using the colored chalks provided, she drew a swan on a lily pond
while the whole class "oohed" and "ahhed." She was so proud of
herself; she could have burst. Then the others took over, adding
trees, clouds, flowers, birds, and butterflies. It was going beautifully
until the last boy got up and, using black chalk, began filing in the
background with it.

"What are you doing? You're ruining it," the kids hollered. Even
the teacher was upset.

"Why are you using black?" she asked.

"Because I want to," he said.

Once started, nothing could be done about it, so he had to finish.
Of course, the project was ruined and the other side of the room took
first place when the murals were judged.

Other individual artwork selected by their teachers was
displayed for the exhibit which was held on the week of the annual
Parent's Night so mothers and fathers could see what their children
were doing artistically as well as academically. It was from that art
exhibit that Cynthia got the chance to work in a professional artist's
studio once a week when school started after summer vacation that
year.

Mrs. Mack, a wonderful lady and talented block print artist,
encouraged Cynthia and let her use anything in her small studio as
long as she replaced the materials she used. This was fine with May
and Cynthia had to clean up after herself, which was fine with her.
Cynthia learned block printing, as well as having some of her other
work critiqued. For the next few years, she earned Christmas gift

money by making and selling block-printed Christmas cards to friends and neighbors. Al took orders from the people he worked with. The cards sold for fifty cents a dozen so, Cynthia didn't make a lot of money, but what she made went a long way at the ink store.

The block print, on torn-edged rice paper, was pasted onto a torn-edged folded paper cover which, because it was open on two sides, could be mailed for a penny less than if it were sealed. Pennies were still important; many people tucked the envelope flap inside the cards they mailed because it was cheaper.

Mrs. Mack, needless to say, went into Cynthia's memory bank of special people she would never forget for their kindness.

MISS ANDREWS AND MISS COLE, the two sixth-grade teachers, were both very special ladies. Miss Andrews was older than Miss Cole, who was fresh out of teachers' college. Young, petite, and a little plump, she didn't seem much older than the girls in the sixth, seventh, and eighth grades. She didn't eat her sack lunch in the teacher's lounge, but sat with the girls on the school steps, unpacking a rather sumptuous array of goodies which no doubt was the reason for her plumpness. The girls loved her; she was so cute and so much fun. From their point of view, she was one of them.

A NEW GIRL came to school later in the first semester. She was in Vera's room, but she met Cynthia on the playground and they hit it off. She walked to Mama's one day with Cynthia and acted very strange when Cynthia introduced her, asking her a lot of questions about her family, where she lived, what her father did, and where she'd lived before coming to Coronado. Cynthia was embarrassed; she didn't understand why Mama was being so nosy. The girl's name was Ruth and her last name, which Cynthia could no longer remember, was different than any she had heard before. Ruth never walked home with Cynthia again, nor did she invite Cynthia to walk with her.

One day she said, "I'm going to my Girl Scout meeting. Would you like to come with me?"

"Sure," Cynthia said. "Is it okay for me to come along?"

"I don't know why not. If you like it, maybe you can join too, and we can go to the meetings together."

"Okay then." It sounded good to Cynthia, so off they went.

The meeting was held in the Parish house of Cynthia's church where she went with Grandma and had gone to Sunday school for as long as she could remember. It was their church. It would be all right.

It was the Friday before Mother's Day, so the girls were seated at a long table with materials laid out for them to make cards for their mothers... construction paper, scissors, paste, stickers, and lengths of ribbon. They set to work, while a couple of women, whom Cynthia had seen often at church, worked in the kitchen preparing refreshments.

"What do they give us to eat?" Cynthia whispered.

"Hot chocolate with marshmallows and cookies," Ruth whispered back.

A short while later, the girls were called to line up for the treats. Cynthia got in line with Ruth a little way behind her. It was Cynthia's turn next, but the woman serving stopped, staring at her in obvious surprise.

"Cynthia Hudgins, whatever in the world are *you* doing here?'

"Ruth invited me to come. She said it would be alright and that I could maybe join the Girl Scouts too."

"Well, it isn't all right, and you can't join. You don't belong here at all. You'd better leave right now and just go on home where you do belong."

Cynthia was stunned. She flushed, embarrassed to be where she wasn't wanted and ashamed to be told to leave in front of all the other girls. She felt sick to her stomach, so she turned and left. Ruth came running out after her.

"Why are you leaving?"

"They don't want me here. They told me to go home."

"But why? You haven't finished your card and you haven't had any refreshments yet."

This was months before Vera told Cynthia why people didn't like her, so Cynthia knew only that she'd been told again, as she had so many times before, that she wasn't welcome and she didn't know why.

"I don't know and I don't care. I can't go back. I'm leaving like that lady told me to."

She walked on, fast, holding her head up, tears pricking her eyes. She didn't want Ruth to see her cry.

"Well, bye then. See you on Monday," and Ruth went back inside.

Cynthia walked on, looking down to hide the tears. "What's wrong with me? Why doesn't anybody want me around? Those girls are girls I go to school with and they've never liked me either." She couldn't understand it, but she went to Grandma's like she was supposed to before going to Mama's, drying her eyes, acting like everything was just fine, never saying anything to anyone about what had happened.

IT WAS LATER that year she was asked to join the Camp Fire Girls and much later, years in fact, before she figured out why Mama had acted so funnily the day Ruth had come to their house.

Miss Cole and Miss Andrews were Camp Fire Girl leaders. Possibly feeling Cynthia would benefit from the association with other girls, they asked Cynthia to join. When May said they couldn't afford the dues just then, the two teachers decided to split the fee and pay them for her. Vera joined, too, to be with Cynthia, but by mutual consent, they dropped out. Their parents couldn't afford to let them go to camp or do some of the other things that cost money and the other girls were stand-offish. They decided: Why should they stay where they weren't wanted when they could be together and not feel left out of anything?

Cynthia had gone into a house with some other kids she'd met who came to school in the seventh grade... two brothers and a sister. The oldest boy took a shine to Cynthia. So did his little sister, and their mother hadn't minded that they became friends. Another boy lived next door to them and they all played street games together, Cynthia included. On this day, they'd all traipsed inside with him when he went to get a glass of water. Unbeknownst to Cynthia, the boy's mother was a customer of Vera's mother... the very one, she learned later, who told people that Papa was a big, black nigger. She had many little knick knacks and figurines around on her tables, which fascinated Cynthia. Her mother kept a much more spartan house. As Cynthia looked at the collection, she was aware that the woman never once took her eyes off her, watching her every move. Then, she began questioning Cynthia in much the same way May had quizzed Ruth.

"Whereabouts do you live?"

"On J Avenue."

"Here in Coronado?"

"Yes." *Where else would I live?* She thought.

"Who does your mother work for?"

"My mother doesn't work for anybody. She stays home."

"She doesn't work for anybody and she stays home? Well, what does your father do, then?"

"He works for a title company in San Diego."

"Oh. Is he the janitor?"

Why does she think Papa is a janitor? Cynthia was puzzled, but she answered politely, "No. He's a title searcher."

"A title searcher?" The woman seemed very surprised, which puzzled Cynthia even further.

The boy was ready to go back outside, so they left with Cynthia wondering why his mother had asked so many nosy questions and if she thought she was going to steal or break some of her pretty things.

Ruth hadn't stayed in school very long. By the end of that one semester, she moved away and Cynthia never saw her again. When she was much older and remembered those inquisitions, she realized that Ruth had been Jewish. She knew by then that many people didn't like Jewish people, had nasty names for them and said things about them, just like they did about Negroes. Now she knew why Mama had asked so many questions, like Robbie's mother had done with her that day. Mama hadn't liked Jewish people either.

"I'm surprised at Mama," she thought. "You'd think that having been on the receiving end of prejudice herself, she'd be more understanding and compassionate about others. How strange."

After she knew, she realized that Robbie's mother had thought Mama was somebody's live-in maid and that Papa, because she thought he was a big black nigger, couldn't possibly have a white-collar job. Handsome, intelligent Papa... somebody's janitor. What a ridiculous thought. It would have been funny if it hadn't been so insulting. But Robbie and his mother had moved away long before Cynthia later learned from Vera that he had been killed in the war.

It was a long time after Vera told Cynthia why no one liked her and before she remembered all these things that had happened and the reason for them, but it took a longer time to sort them out and place them in some sort of perspective, trying to make sense out of them and even when she had, she didn't really understand it.

CHAPTER FORTY-SIX

Hatred. What a nasty emotion. It not only hurts the person who is hated and called names (or worse) but also hurts the one who does the hating. It is like a boomerang, returning to erode their souls, making them less than human.

Cynthia knew why her mother didn't like Jewish people. She'd heard the story more than once. Mama was introduced, by a mutual friend, to a Jewish lady who owned a dress shop in San Diego. She liked the lady, so she started buying clothes from her and they became good friends, she thought. The clothes were very expensive, so she bought them on time. May liked nice things and kept up with the latest fashion by buying a complete outfit in the newest color and style for the season. Cynthia remembered a year of the color teal and another of Empress Eugenie style.

Then came the Depression. Al wasn't working regularly; they were making a house payment, buying a car, and had to eat. May went to the shop to tell her friend that she couldn't afford to make as large of a payment on the last things she'd purchased, but she would pay as much as she could, as soon as possible and as often as she could. She left the shop confident that her friend was understanding and that it was taken care of. She was wrong.

The woman immediately went to Al's company and garnished, from what he had coming, the full amount of what was owed on May's account. When Al came home and told her, May was shocked. She felt betrayed. She was hurt and angry. She never went back into the store again and from that day on she had nothing good to say about Jewish people.

A Jewish landlord was behind the loss of Vera's mother's dressmaking business in Chicago, which caused the family to make the move to California. Mrs. Smitts had a small factory in a building owned by him and when the Depression hit, business dropped off, so she was hard-pressed to keep up with the rent. One day she went to the shop and found it padlocked. The owner wouldn't open the door even long enough for her to get inside and remove her personal belongings. She lost everything... all of her sewing machines, tools, and supplies. Because of what one Jewish man had done to her mother, Vera disliked them, painting them all with the same brush, which people are wont to do.

Cynthia didn't like hearing her mother and Vera and other people expressing that hate, although she could understand how their experiences caused them to feel that way. Her own experience, years later when she and Ted were in Guam in 1947, was a positive one.

Mama died suddenly, unexpectedly, while Cynthia was in Guam. She'd felt that something might be wrong with her mother, but May kept things to herself. Cynthia didn't know for sure that anything was amiss, but she told Mama she wouldn't go to Guam to join Ted if she might need her.

"Your place is with your husband," Mama said in her positive way which said, without words, that the subject was closed.

When Cynthia stepped off the plane, the first thing she asked Ted was, "If anything should happen to my mother, can I get back to the States?"

"Sure, no problem," he told her, but she continued to feel uneasy, especially when Mama's letters came, and she saw that her handwriting was deteriorating.

May died ten months later.

Cynthia was cooking supper on the kerosene stove in the Quonset hut kitchen when the generator ran out of gas as it often did, leaving their end of the housing area in near darkness. At the same moment, a young enlisted Marine knocked on the door.

"You have a message at the message center," he told Ted and left.

Luckily, Ted had a civilian friend, an old friend of the family, who worked in Guam. He owned two surplus jeeps and let Ted and Cynthia use one. Leaving Tee Gee with a neighbor, they took off for the camp, arriving just as colors blew. They had to stand at attention and wait, with Cynthia thinking the ceremony would never end, knowing in her heart something had happened to Mama.

Ted read the message with Cynthia looking over his shoulder. The words jumped at her; in one glance she read them all.

"Mama passed away painlessly, 6 PM, Sept. 7. Al." He'd signed it in that way to avoid any confusion with Ted's parents, but Cynthia had known from the moment they were told there was a message, who it was for and what it was going to say.

"Oh my God. Poor Papa is all alone. I have to get back to him." But there was nothing they could do that evening. The generator came back on; she served dinner and put Tee Gee to bed. A few people dropped by with condolences and offers to help in any way they could. News travels fast on a small station and even though Cynthia didn't know some of them at all, Ted did.

Early the next morning, Ted started out to arrange a military flight back to the States. He came in at noon with bad news... she could leave on a military plane only if he had orders and he didn't, not yet, although they knew they were to go back to the States soon, to the east coast again. She had written to Mama with the news. The letter came two days after she'd gotten back home, so Mama never knew they wouldn't be away the full two years.

Ted went off again to check commercial flights, coming back with more bad news. To fly commercial would be $700 one-way for her and Tee Gee to go home to Papa. They couldn't afford it. They had some money, but not that much and payday was still a week away. She would need money; Ted would need money. It was impossible

They went back to the message center and were lucky enough, weather-wise, to get through on a short-wave call to Papa. A Ham operator in La Jolla acted as a relay for them while Cynthia told Papa she couldn't come. Al broke down and cried after he hung up, the neighbor who had the phone told her after she got home.

That morning, Elsa, a neighbor up the dirt road, had come to the house and taken over... answering the door, making coffee for callers while Cynthia packed, hoping somehow to be able to get back to Papa. Another neighbor took Tee Gee to play with her little boy. Elsa was Jewish. Before she married her husband, she'd owned a restaurant which she sold after the marriage, so she had money of her own. When she heard the bind that Cynthia was in, out of the clear blue sky and the goodness of her heart, she said, "I'll lend you the money for the plane fare."

"Oh, I could never borrow that much money from anyone," Cynthia told her. "But I sure do appreciate the offer."

"Well, I really mean it," Elsa answered. "I know how you feel. I lost my own mother not too long ago."

Cynthia was deeply touched. She'd known Elsa only four months and Elsa was prepared to lend her an unbelievable sum of money. She knew she couldn't lend someone she'd only known for four months money except maybe some change or a couple of dollars not hundreds of them.

Ted came back exhausted. He'd been to every Commanding Office on the island and the news was good. The Commanding General of the Marines had signed the necessary papers so that Cynthia and Tee Gee could fly back to the States on MATS, the Military Air Transport Service, but they wouldn't be able to come back.

That evening Cynthia finished packing. After the next-door neighbor called them over for soup and sandwiches, they started off, stopping by Elsa's to thank her for everything and to say goodbye. Everyone had been so kind when they were practically strangers, but it was Elsa's kindness that had made the biggest impression on Cynthia.

They corresponded for a while and then a letter was returned. Cynthia lost track of Elsa, but she went into Cynthia's memory bank of people she would never forget, where she remains to this day, as does General Craig who signed the papers so she could leave the island, thus setting a precedent for other emergency situations. Years later, Cynthia was able to thank him personally.

She and Ted were attending a Marine Corps Birthday Ball when someone said, "Oh look. There's General Craig."

"My General Craig?" she asked Ted. "The one who signed the papers so I could leave Guam?"

"Yeah, that's the one."

She went over to him and told him briefly about what had happened while she was in Guam and how grateful she was that he had signed the release so she could go home to her father. She couldn't tell if he had any memory of it at all, but it gave her a lot of satisfaction to thank him. It had meant the world to her to be there for Papa.

After she got back home, she told Vera about Elsa, what she had done and what she offered to do.

Vera shrugged. "Well, I guess they're not all alike," was all she said.

CHAPTER FORTY-SEVEN

Vera and Cynthia were never in the same room, nor did they share a class together except for one semester of drama in their senior year. Vera took only the classes necessary for graduation; Cynthia took the classes needed for entry into State College. Their interests were different except for drawing, paper dolls, and wanting to get married before they were twenty-five because they didn't want to be old maids. Cynthia was the more active of the two, roller skating and going to the beach, while Vera liked to sew exquisite doll clothes with tiny hand-made buttonholes, teensy hems, and delicate stitchery for a small doll she had. Cynthia was envious, but it wasn't her cup of tea. She went on to learn to sew for herself later and did better finishing than Vera did on her clothes. Then Vera was envious of her.

Fifth grade through junior high years were hard to remember time-wise; so much had happened in those years. It seemed like she and Vera were always together, but she'd also had other acquaintances, developed an unrequited crush on a new boy in the sixth grade, disobeyed Papa, and nearly drowned at the beach. Her grandmother died. She moved to her parent's little house on J Avenue and yet, in retrospect, it seemed she and Vera were not apart that much.

In those years, Cynthia had a real boyfriend in the seventh grade, developed a sixth sense about staying away from older men with overly friendly intentions, had her first period and spent a lot of time with Papa in the garage... helping him, listening to him, learning from him... and was a Camp Fire Girl for a year or two. How could so much have been crammed into just four years? Time, they say, is only an illusion and doesn't really exist, sometimes flying, sometimes dragging itself slowly by.

"Anyway," she thought. "I couldn't have been with Vera as much as it seems we were together and done all those things she wasn't interested in too, but we were and I did. Our time together was special. We laughed a lot, but we were serious too. We drew; she sewed while I watched. We dreamed out loud together. We talked about boys and we discussed the mystery of God up one side and down the other as we walked back and forth between our two houses dozens of times each day. We could talk endlessly, and we could be together all evening saying little. Time must have been elastic then."

SIXTH-GRADE GIRLS WERE TAKEN to the auditorium by the school nurse for a 'sex education' lecture where they were told about menstruation. They were about to become young ladies and were given booklets from a sanitary napkin company with a title like, What Every Young Girl Should Know. That was it.

They learned nothing about procreation or where babies came from. Some girls thought it was from your belly button, some from where you went to the bathroom, which was disgusting to think about, but they had no idea of how a baby got there in the first place. Maybe the French kissing they talked about in hushed whispers was what did it. It was one theory... yuk! They made faces as they discussed that possibility.

A short time afterward, when Cynthia came home from school, May handed her a library book from the library.

"I want you to read this," she said. Cynthia scanned it, saw the first part of it said the same things they'd been told by the nurse.

She said, "Oh I already know all about that," and handed the book back.

"You do?" May said with a peculiar look on her face as she took the book, but she said nothing more and that was the end of that.

It was Cynthia who told Vera that babies didn't come from those other places, but from a separate place in between the two places you did your business from. Vera opened her big blue eyes wide.

"How do you know?" she asked, shocked.

"I took the hand mirror and looked," Cynthia told her.

Vera was even more shocked. "You didn't!" she said.

"Yes, I did."

"How could you do such a thing?" Vera asked even more shocked still.

"Because I wanted to find out, that's why," Cynthia said. Vera never got over it that Cynthia would take a hand mirror and look at her bottom to see where babies came from. Still, neither had a clue as to how a baby got in there in the first place to come out from anywhere at all, except that boys caused it.

It was this combination of innocence and ignorance that kept a girl on the straight and narrow back then. When Vera and Cynthia started dating in high school, they usually dated together and nothing untoward was allowed because who knew what might make you pregnant... the most shameful thing a girl could do to her family and her own reputation. Why take chances with so much at stake?

Many young men got their faces slapped for French kissing or being too handsy. Nowadays, if a girl slaps a boy for being 'fresh,' she'd probably better be ready to duck because he's likely to slap her back. Young women have lost respect for themselves, so why should men respect them? It has always been up to women to set the rules of behavior and decorum which keep men civilized.

Dating was a lot of fun back then with tickling and giggling and smooching, the girls saying, "Oh you!" and "Stop that!" as the boys tried to unfasten the hooks on a bra through her clothes or cop a feel.

Vera and Cynthia were 'nice' girls, even though when they went to high school, they dated young servicemen... considered not something a nice girl should do. They knew they were talked about and considered tramps, but these young men were gentlemen, which was more than one could say about high school boys, one of whom had to marry his girlfriend because he got her pregnant. It was also assumed by their contemporaries that Vera and Cynthia were 'queer,' which the two of them also knew because they were always together. In high school, their drama teacher had paraphrased "Oh wind, if Vera comes, can Cynthia be far behind?" which got a big laugh adding fuel to the whispers about them. It's a bit strange that the girls could be thought to be two different things at once, things they knew next to nothing about. It must have made fascinating conjecturing for the busybodies with little else to do but gossip. Cynthia was used to it, but Vera was not.

When they were older and looked back on their years in Coronado, Cynthia remembered them fondly. She had always loved Coronado, but Vera didn't. She hated everything... not being included in school affairs or invited to parties, not having any other friends. Cynthia had been inured to this before she'd met Vera so, now that she had a friend, she didn't need anything else; she didn't care. Poor Vera never realized it was her friendship with Cynthia that had made her a pariah too.

CHAPTER FORTY-EIGHT

Before Cynthia met Vera, unless she went with Mama, she sat alone at the movies. As soon as she was old enough, Mama gave her the dime to go by herself for the Saturday kids' matinee. Other kids standing in line might say 'hi' and make space for their friends, but not for her. She had to go to the end of the line. When she got inside and looked for a seat, no one asked her to sit with them. Mama liked to sit on the side right on the aisle in case there was a fire so she could get out quickly. Cynthia did that too. Kids slid by her to sit in the same row, but not in the seat beside her. It was always empty.

When the film broke, as it did often in those days of silent films, the other kids would hoot and whistle, clap their hands, and stamp their feet until the break was repaired. Not Cynthia. The lesson Papa had taught her about not being like every other Tom, Dick, or Harry, had made its point. She would not join in the racket like the rest of them. It gave her a certain amount of smug satisfaction not to be like them... still, she kind of wished they would accept her so she could join in too. Being different wasn't much fun.

When Vera came into Cynthia's life, she had someone to go with and to sit with her. Vera didn't always have the dime to go because her mother's business was iffy. When Vera had the money for the evening show, they sat together, giggled together, whispered about what was happening on the screen, clapped their hands and stamped their feet along with the adults when the film broke. It was fun.

THE MOVIES TAUGHT Cynthia about life in those times. From the kid's shows, she learned about honor. The cowboy hero in the white hat was noble, decent, honest, and always a gentleman with the ladies. He was cheered when he came on screen, while the villain in the black hat was booed. Drawing room comedies, popular in those times, taught her about polite social behavior... tablecloths and candles, gentlemen sending flowers, bringing candy, lighting ladies' cigarettes, and opening doors for them. Sex, which the girls knew nothing about, was when the hero picked up the girl, carried her into his bedroom, and kicked the door shut. In the next scene, it was morning, and she was fixing breakfast wearing only the top of his pajamas. What had happened in the interim was a romantic mystery.

By this time, some of the girls at school were being friendlier toward Cynthia, but it was too little, too late; she kept herself aloof. She didn't need them now; she had a friend. It was different with the boys... they changed. Not that they had ever been friends, but they had tolerated her, not harassed or called her names.

In the sixth grade, at the first recess, there was a new boy from the other class on the playground with a group of other boys. She took one look and was smitten. He was lean and tan and had dimples when he smiled. Her heart flip-flopped in her chest.

At the next Saturday matinee, he came down the aisle to sit beside her. Oh, happy day! When some other boys behind them called him, he excused himself, saying he'd be right back. As she looked after him, her heart sank. They were whispering and looking at her and she knew he wouldn't be back.

From then on, when she walked down the aisle at the movies by herself, she'd hear rustles and whispers from the boys.

"There goes the nigger."

She held her head high and pretended not to hear, but it was a knife in her heart. Once she heard a voice she recognized, the son of a friend of her grandmother's whom she had been in classes with since they were in kindergarten.

"There goes old nigger nose," he said. She felt sick. When she got home, she took the hand mirror and looked at her nose from all angles. It didn't look flat or broad to her, but she began to hate her nose. The more she worried about it, the bigger it seemed to be. It haunted her. She didn't say anything to Vera who would have told her it wasn't true. She knew that the two of them had always given each other moral support. Vera, who thought she was dumb, would say to Cynthia, "You're smarter than me. You draw better and write better than I do. I guess I'm just stupid."

"You are not stupid. I don't have any use for stupid people. If you were stupid, I wouldn't have you for a friend."

Cynthia wondered now, all these years later, who had planted that seed. Had it been the aunt Vera had lived with or a teacher who had forced her to use her right hand when she was a lefty, so she stuttered and was probably laughed at or teased by the other kids?

Vera would have told her the truth nicely, but Cynthia was so hurt and self-conscious about what she'd heard that she didn't tell her because she was afraid of what she'd hear. She knew Vera would say, "Well it is a little big, but it isn't bad. You still look okay." So she suffered in silence until the boys started noticing them and asking for dates when they were older.

"I know I held a lot of things back from Vera," Cynthia told herself. "But I don't think she ever held anything back from me. Sooner or later she'd say, 'I never told you this but...'"

CHAPTER FORTY-NINE

In the second semester of the seventh grade, they took turns in class reading *Ivanhoe* out loud. When they'd finished the story, Miss Andrews came up with what turned out to be a wonderful idea.

"How would it be," she asked. "If we made a part of this story into a play and gave a puppet show?"

A collective murmur of interest and approval went through the room.

"We can't do the whole book; it's too long. Let's decide what part to use, then we'll all vote on it and write the play together."

So it was that the whole class participated in writing the dialogue and deciding on the action, calling out what the characters would do and say until all agreed. Then Miss Andrews divided them into groups of three to make the characters needed for the excerpt in the book they'd voted on using.

Each one in the group made a head for their character, molding it out of clay, covering it with paper mache, letting it dry, cutting it off the mold, piecing it back to gather, painting it, then gluing on yarn for hair. Cynthia's trio of herself and two boys drew the jester and her head was chosen by the class as the best of the three when they were completed. The boys made the hinged bodies and controls out of wood in shop class; the girls made the costumes in sewing class. The stage was built by the boys; the curtain was made by the girls. For the scenery and backdrops, they all participated in deciding what to use, bringing things from home to complete the costumes or the stage sets. This took the whole spring semester, with everyone in the class doing something with the project... working on the marionettes or the stage sets, polishing the dialogue, memorizing lines, prompting, rehearsing... anything and everything needed for a stage performance. Everyone got hands-on experience or helped with learning many skills and how to cooperate while working with others to achieve a goal in the process. All of them profited from it.

They were ready. The marionette handlers knew what to do; the stage crew knew what to do. The first performance was the dress rehearsal to which they invited the other sixth-grade class. It went off better than expected. The following Friday evening, parents came by invitation to the performance. It was a rousing success, followed by refreshments of hot cocoa and cookies made by the girls in cooking class.

Everyone had participated in a variety of learning experiences, individually gaining a great sense of accomplishment in the process.

"Who gets to keep the puppets?" someone asked. "Three of us worked on each character."

"You can draw lots like we did for the characters," Miss Andrews suggested. Cynthia won the jester, but when she moved from Grandma's to live with her parents, it was another of her treasures that Mama threw out with everything else from the old lady's house.

"That must be the reason I'm such a pack rat," Cynthia thought to herself as she wrote about it. She never got rid of anything that belonged to her own kids without asking if it was okay with them first.

CHAPTER FIFTY

Cynthia's days had become busier in the seventh grade... going to the studio, staying after school for Camp Fire Girls, the French Class, and the stamp and coin clubs. On most days, she was getting to Grandma's later than before. One day, when she was very late getting there, it was nearly time for her to be at her mother's to set the table for dinner. If she was late, Mama would be annoyed.

Grandma was waiting anxiously at the gate for her.

"You need to go to the store to get some food for Pinky."

Pinky was Cynthia's orange tiger cat she'd brought home from her father's friend's dairy farm when they'd gone to visit one Sunday, and she'd found a litter of kittens in the hayloft.

"I haven't got time, Grandma. I'm already going to be late by the time I get to Mama's."

"But it'll only take a few minutes with your bike."

"I'm sorry Grandma. I just can't. Mama will be mad at me."

She hopped back on her bike and rode off with the old lady calling after her to please come back.

"I can't. I can't," she hollered as she turned onto the street from the alley and went out of sight. She felt bad about not going to the store, but she'd do almost anything to avoid having Mama be angry with her.

After dinner that evening, Mama gave her the dime to go to the new movie at the theater. Barely into the feature, she heard the siren. It was close by; everybody in the theater turned their heads to listen. Then it stopped and they turned back to the show. Cynthia gave a shrug, thinking, "Well, it's got nothing to do with me," and turned back to the screen.

She stayed later that night to watch the cartoon a second time before cycling back to Mama's so Papa could drive her to Grandma's. As soon as she opened the door, she knew something was wrong. Papa wasn't asleep in his chair; he was standing in front of the fireplace. Mama was sitting on the couch facing the door.

Cynthia thought, "Oops. I'm late and they're mad."

She expected to be scolded, but as she closed the door behind her Mama said, "Grandma's been hit by a car."

"You're kidding," Cynthia said, surprised because it wasn't what she'd expected to hear.

"Would I kid about a thing like that?" Mama said and Cynthia knew it was true. Suddenly, she had a premonition.

"Where did it happen?"

"At the corner of Ninth and C, in front of the Episcopal church. She went out to get cat food."

Cynthia felt sick; she knew it had been her fault.

"Is she still alive?"

"Yes, but she was badly hurt and she's in the hospital in San Diego."

"I heard the sirens," Cynthia said. "But I didn't think they had anything to do with me. She wanted me to go to the store for her, but I was late. I didn't have time."

Cynthia learned about the sin of omission in a way she never forgot. She had been the cause of her grandmother's accident and she felt guilty about it for the rest of her life. Not only that, but her cat had gone hungry that night and the next day too before anyone remembered him. From that day on, whenever Cynthia was at home with her family and out and about and she heard sirens, she was uneasy until everyone was safely home again. The bell had tolled for her once and she hadn't listened. It wasn't going to happen again if she could help it.

Their old next-door neighbors had moved into a house on the corner where the accident occurred. They'd heard a scream and the sound of squealing tires as a car braked going at a high rate of speed. A Navy officer's son, out joyriding in his father's car without permission, doing 60 miles an hour on a residential street, hadn't seen the old lady until it was too late.

Annie had been cutting kitty-corner and so was out of the streetlight's range. In her long black coat, she'd have been nearly invisible. She'd seen him coming and, knowing she was going to be hit, screamed in terror. The skid marks told the story. She'd been thrown fifteen feet, suffering internal injuries and head trauma. She was taken to San Diego's County Hospital instead of the Coronado Hospital, which was a block and a half away, and Cynthia's parents hadn't been notified by the police about the accident until just a few minutes before Cynthia walked in the door. Al and May were still in a state of shock. Cynthia spent the night on the couch at her parent's house that night, never setting foot inside her grandmother's house again until many years later.

May was furious about not having been notified about the accident sooner and about Annie's having been taken to the County Hospital like some indigent itinerant. As soon as possible, she arranged for her to be returned to Coronado's hospital where she lingered for weeks before dying of her injuries.

The boy wasn't arrested. There was no trial. In the town paper, the local police called it an 'unavoidable accident.' The death certificate didn't mention any injuries, stating only that the patient had died from complications of old age. She would have died soon anyway, the doctor who did the autopsy said, because she had a brain tumor. The family knew that couldn't be true. She had taken no falls, complained of no headaches, hadn't been disoriented, had any dizzy spells, or passed out. There had been nothing whatsoever to indicate that anything was wrong other than the forgetfulness of old age.

The whole thing was swept under the carpet because Coronado was a Navy town and the boy's father was a high-ranking Navy officer. This is what May believed, and all her friends agreed. Annie was an old colored lady of no consequence to anyone but her family and her few remaining friends. The boy got off scot-free and his parents sent no condolences, nor did they offer to help with the medical expenses. To do so would have been an admission of guilt on her son's part. Al and May had to sell his parent's home to pay the doctor, the hospital bills, and of course, the mortgage he'd warned his mother against.

"The whole thing was a sad miscarriage of justice," Cynthia thought. "I wonder if that boy ever gave a thought to what he did to an old lady and her family. He was older than me, so he could be dead by now if he wasn't killed in the war. I wonder if he went to meet his Maker with a clear conscience... probably so."

While Annie lay dying in the hospital, someone broke into her house and stole a bond box with the family papers in it. Why anyone would think an old lady on a Civil War Widow's pension who owned a house that had sat for months with a 'for rent' sign on it would have anything of value was hard to understand. A couple of nights later, the box was thrown back through a closed window, breaking the glass, with all the papers intact. The only things missing were the three gold nuggets Amos had brought back from his otherwise fruitless trip to the Yukon.

SCHOOL WAS LET out for the summer shortly after the accident. Cynthia went by the hospital every day on her way to the beach and again on the way to Mama's to see her grandmother. At first,

Grandma recognized her, but as time passed, she lay there with her eyes closed, moving her lips as though whispering to herself, unaware anyone was there.

The hospital didn't like Cynthia coming in and out through the front door, so they moved the old lady into a small back room barely large enough to hold the single bed and a night table. It had obviously been used for storage and for deliveries because it had an outside door. The superintendent told Cynthia she could come down the side of the building and use the door, which wasn't locked in the daytime, to see her grandmother anytime she wanted without having to come in through the front. They were nice enough about it, but Cynthia got the message.

Twelve-year-old Cynthia was alone with her grandma when she died. The hospital phoned a neighbor to tell her parents they should come at once, death was imminent. When they got there, Al took one look at his mother lying on her back with her mouth open, breathing hard, the terrible sound filling the room, and told May he'd better get to town to file some legal papers because it must be done while Annie was still alive. Mama reached into her purse and took out her car keys.

"I'm going to drive Papa to the ferry and I'll be right back," she said to Cynthia as they walked out the door.

Cynthia sat watching her grandmother, listening to the awful breathing. Each breath, as her chest rose and fell, was such an effort it seemed it would tear her apart. It was horrible.

Suddenly, Annie opened her eyes and rolled them upwards toward the head of the bed like she saw something there, but there was only the blank white wall. At that same instant, a nurse entered the room and the awful breathing stopped, leaving the room deathly quiet. The nurse took one look and went back out. She came hurrying in again with a hypo, swabbed Annie's arm with a wad of cotton and stuck the needle in. Cynthia, watching, thought it went in like a hot knife slicing cold butter. It made her insides squirm. Then, picking up Grandma's wrist and feeling for a pulse, without looking at Cynthia, "She's gone," the nurse said, turned and left the room.

A moment later the latch clicked and the door opened. Cynthia thought it was the nurse coming back, but no one came in. She got up to close it, thinking it may not have latched before, but she looked out both ways to be sure, saw no one, shut the door, and sat back down. Another minute passed, the latch clicked and the door opened a second time. No one came in. Cynthia got up and closed it after looking around as before and sat down again.

The third time it happened, she thought, "What's the matter with this door? Is the wind blowing it open or something?"

Making sure it was firmly closed this time, she sat again.

How long she sat there beside her dead grandmother, she didn't know. She felt nothing; her mind was blank. The next time the door opened, Mama came through it with the nurse behind her. They stood talking quietly beside the bed while Cynthia sat watching, hearing nothing until Mama said, "Come on now. We're going home," and they drove back to the house on J.

That evening was very quiet. Mama fixed something for dinner and they ate half-heartedly, without conversation. Papa sat in his chair, not working the crossword puzzle, staring into space. Mama washed the dishes and then sat in her chair, holding a magazine in her lap, idly flipping the pages, but not reading. Cynthia went into the back porch sunroom where she kept a few things for the times she was at the house. She lay on the floor, idly doodling, while over and over the thought ran through her mind, "Grandma's dead and it's all my fault. She's dead because of me."

When the doorbell rang and the former neighbors, the ones who'd heard the whole thing, came in, it was a welcome diversion. They'd brought their son, Leroy, whom Cynthia didn't like very much. The feeling was mutual; he didn't like her much either, but they'd been thrown together because of their parents' friendship. They got out her train and played with it as the adults conversed quietly in the living room. There were no other callers.

. . .

CYNTHIA COULDN'T REMEMBER ATTENDING her grandmother's funeral. Had there been one? Had Mama asked her if she wanted to go and she said no? She couldn't remember anything at all and yet she remembered her grandfather's funeral when she was only four.

Grandma was old. Most of her friends were gone and the ones remaining were as old as she. Maybe Al and May had decided to have the body prepared for burial and interred because it would be best to get it over with as soon as possible.

"Mama's doing," Cynthia thought, remembering and realizing she'd never given it any thought before. She knew only that Grandma was laid to rest beside her husband with the G.A.R. head-stone with Amos's name on it centered between them.

Cynthia recalled telling Papa about the strange happening with the door and how Grandma's eyes had rolled up as she looked at the blank wall at the head of the bed. He had been very interested and they conjectured about what it might have been. Had Amos come to his wife as she lay dying to be with her when she passed over? Or was she watching her departing soul?

Something similar happened when May died. Al told Cynthia about Mama's last day when she came home from Guam to be with him. The cat had been lying at the foot of the bed all afternoon as the day wore on. He woke up, just before the end, stretched and, when he looked at the wall above May's head his eyes had widened, his tail puffed up and he'd leaped off the bed to go running down the stairs like something was after him. May opened her eyes, looked at Al, said "bye," and was gone.

IT HAS BEEN SAID that if one has reviewed their life and is prepared to leave the body, the enlightened soul departs through the top of the head at the site of the fontanel, which, in occult circles, is considered to be the third eye. While Annie lay whispering to herself, had she been reliving her life, preparing herself to leave it?

May knew she was going to die soon. She'd known she had possible cancer and refused to have a hysterectomy long before Cynthia left for Guam. She'd made a vow after her mother's death that she would never be operated on for cancer and she'd told the doctor not to tell Al or Cynthia. Cynthia thought her mother was going through the change when May complained of not feeling well, although she'd felt uneasy leaving to go so far from home to join Ted. She told her mother that if she thought she might be needed, she wouldn't go, but Mama had said, "No, you go. Your place is with your husband." Cynthia never argued with Mama.

The next ten months before she died, May removed all traces of herself from the house... selling her piano, jokingly telling her friends that she was trading it for a harp, and getting rid of all her personal papers. Maybe the cat was frightened because he'd seen May's soul leaving her body. Al and Cynthia both knew now that May had been preparing to die.

May drove up every evening during the time her mother-in-law was in the hospital to feed Pinky. Cynthia wondered now why her mother hadn't brought Pinky back to the home where his life with them had begun when it became obvious that the old lady wasn't going to get better. Pinky had been so tiny that May thought it would be better if she took care of him before she let Cynthia have him at Grandma's, so he'd lived for a couple of months in the house on J.

When May went to feed Pinky the evening of the day Annie died, he was nowhere to be found when usually he was waiting to greet her. She looked for him and called, but no Pinky. She went up every evening for about a week and asked around the neighborhood, but Pinky was gone. Cynthia didn't remember being upset when Mama told her. She must have been in some sort of limbo after her grandmother's accident and death. Pinky was gone and she hadn't gone to see him or even asked about him.

Months later, when she was on her way from school to her mother's, as she walked past a house half a block away and around the corner, she saw an orange cat sitting on the fence.

"That cat looks just like Pinky," she thought and went over to feel his tail. Pinky had a distinctive break at the end of his tail and there it was. The cat was Pinky, but he didn't seem to remember her. Well, no wonder. He'd been left alone all day for weeks except for the short times May had come to feed him and it had been months since Grandma died.

She told Mama that Pinky was sitting on the fence at Hugo's house. She knew Hugo; he played with the boys she had played with when she was younger. Mama went to talk to his mother and when she came back, she told Cynthia that Pinky had come to them as a starving stray and they'd taken him in. They liked him and wanted to keep him.

"I told him they could," Mama said. Cynthia agreed.

They were all amazed that Pinky, somehow knowing about Grandma's death, had gone looking for the house he'd lived in as a small kitten. He'd gotten so close before giving up... just around a corner and another half a block and he'd have made it.

This unusual ability to find a former home is not uncommon in cats, nor is the knowledge about death, followed by running away. A similar thing happened with Al's cat on the day he died. Cleo had lived in Cynthia's house since day one of Al's stroke. Ted and Cynthia didn't allow their cats to go outside except into a special enclosure, so that was the rule for Cleo for two and a half years.

The evening of the day Al died and all the next day, every time Cynthia went to the door to let the dogs in or out, she'd had to fight to keep Cleo from getting outside to run off. Then she quieted down and stayed on with her owner's family, living to be nearly twenty years old and never trying to get out of the house again.

CHAPTER FIFTY-ONE

The chapter on Grandma's accidental death was gone. Cynthia had worked on it for two whole afternoons. One to write, one to edit, make additions, and clarify. She'd taken a nip here, a tuck there, as she probed her memories about that time, then spell-checked, made sure the headings were in the right place, saved, and closed.

It hadn't been easy to write, because she'd felt so much guilt for her grandmother's death, and still did. Also as she wrote, she realized she'd forgotten things that had happened in the months afterward.

The chapter was still on the menu, but when she tried to bring it up to add something, it wasn't there. GONE... it was gone. She couldn't believe it. Two days' work and the computer from Hell had swallowed it whole, or chewed it up, not leaving a paragraph, a sentence, a single word, comma, or period to show her chapter had ever existed, and it hadn't even had the grace to burp! She could have cried.

Was this some sort of an omen? Was something or someone

trying to tell her something? Should she tear up what she'd written so far into a million tiny pieces or just round-file the manuscript and forget the whole thing?

At this moment, either one seemed like a very good idea.

CHAPTER FIFTY-TWO

After Cynthia wrote about her grandmother's death, she began wracking her brain trying to remember the rest of that summer. She must have eaten, slept, and surely she'd gone to the beach. Or did she? She couldn't remember. Had she seen Vera or Fusa, who lived just up the block? Her mind wandered around in circles... nothing... then a flicker. Had Mama let her invite Fusa and Vera to dinner on her thirteenth birthday or was it just for cake and ice cream and then the movies? Mama had asked her if she wasn't getting a little old for a kiddy birthday party and she'd agreed, she remembered that. It must have been cake and ice cream and the movies.

That was the summer she'd gone to the races at Agua Caliente and Mama bought the Mexican opal ring in the gift shop for an early birthday present. It had been the year of the doll and the Depression camera from Papa.

Cynthia had seen the doll at Marston's and fallen in love with it. She'd shown it to Mama and every time they went into the store she'd looked to see if it was still there. And it was. It was expensive... twelve dollars and ninety-five cents... a lot of money for those lean times. She knew she was too old for a doll and she'd never really played with them anyway, just carried them around when she was small. But she wanted that doll.

The doll wasn't very big, but she was special. She had honey blonde real hair, a darling little face and a cute dress and a sun hat with green polka dots. She looked just like a beautiful real live little girl in miniature.

"My Lord," Cynthia thought she remembered. "That doll looked like May-May did when she was little. Could I have known that someday I was going to have a little girl who'd look just like that doll?"

Shortly before her birthday, Mama asked if there was anything special she wanted.

"That doll at Marston's."

"Now really, you're going to be thirteen. Don't you think you're getting a little old for a doll?"

"Yes, but I'd really like to have her. She'd be my last doll and I'm not having a party this year."

May considered for a moment, then said, "Alright."

She gave Cynthia the money a few days later. She'd gotten it by selling her wedding ring, but Cynthia didn't know that until a while afterward. Had May seen that Cynthia was having a problem? Had she had some idea about what it might be and tried to do something special to help her quiet, withdrawn, and often unhappy daughter? It would seem so.

"Go and see if it's still there," May said as she gave Cynthia the money. It was, and she came home happy. She didn't play with the doll, but she took very good care of it. She tried to keep its hair nice and took the clothes off to wash and iron them occasionally. Years later, she took the doll to have a new wig put on it and, at the same time, had her old Nanny doll refurbished. Nanny had been loved almost to pieces from being carried around so much when Cynthia was small.

Aunt Vera made some doll clothes and May-May got the doll and the clothes for her eighth birthday. There was something special about the doll... May-May took very good care of her, too. Today, the doll and Nanny are sleeping together in a box in Cynthia's garage. Nanny is seventy years old and the doll is sixty-two. She has a missing finger because one of May-May's friends dropped her, but otherwise, she is still just as beautiful as ever.

Al got into the act for Cynthia's birthday that year, too. Usually, it was May who saw to everything and decided what to buy, but this year he came home with a punch card for a Depression camera. It used regular film and had an arrangement that allowed two smaller snapshots to be taken in the space of a larger one... a money-saving feature, hence the name.

The card had spots on it that were pushed out for a chance to win the camera. Underneath each spot, there was a price, ranging from a penny or so to more, but all for a penny less than a dollar. When all the punches were sold, a master spot was punched out which had the winning number. The person who sold the card sent the money to the company and received two cameras in return, one for the winner and one for the seller to sell or keep for himself. Cynthia had known that Papa had the card but thought nothing about it. Imagine her surprise when, on her birthday, Papa gave her the camera! He'd sold out the card to get it just for her. The ring, the doll, and the camera... What a wonderful birthday that must have been, now that she remembered it.

The camera, like the dolls, rests in the bottom drawer of a dresser in Cynthia's spare room. In the same drawer, to keep it company, are the old bellows Kodak that was used for Cynthia's baby pictures and Ted's mother's old Box Brownie.

CHAPTER FIFTY-THREE

At last, Cynthia was living with her parents. The dream of her life had come to pass but at the cost of her grandmother's life. There is a saying, "Be careful what you wish for; you may get it." She'd gotten the friend she'd prayed for so long and it worked out very okay as time would prove. This wish didn't work out as well. She hadn't realized there'd be a price to pay or that she'd never really feel at home in her mother's house.

After the first few days of sleeping on the living room couch, she'd slept in the barren back porch sunroom on her old bed from Grandma's, using a couple of drawers that Mama emptied out in the chest already there for some of her clothes. The rest were hung in the nearby service closet. No rug was on the floor, no curtains at the high windows. The only other things in the room were the refrigerator and the washer.

Because Cynthia slept late on vacations and the milkman came inside to put the delivery in the refrigerator, May decided to move Cynthia back onto the living room couch, making her feel like the overnight guest she'd always been until now.

When 815 Third was built a couple of years later, the second bedroom was supposed to be Cynthia's, but because it had a balcony, May had other plans. She envisioned herself having tea with her friends on it, so Cynthia was given a studio couch for a bed which had to be made up every night, making her feel like a guest again, and her personal things were to be kept out of sight. The same dresser was put in the back of the closet, with all the drawers available to her now. The rest of her stuff went in there too, either on the shelf or in boxes on the floor. The only other furniture in the room was a student desk with a matching chair, bought unpainted, which Cynthia painted white, and an upholstered slipper chair... Mama's touch. No one ever used it except Buster, the cat. On the desk was a blotter, a covered box for pencils, and a desk lamp... nothing else. The room was to be kept pristine at all times for Mama and her friends' would-be tea parties which never came about when she found it was too much trouble to carry a tea tray up and down the stairs. Still, Cynthia was expected to keep the room looking unlived-in for the next five years she lived there.

Grandma's house had been more of a home, she realized now, although she hadn't thought of it that way at the time. Her room was hers, as was the bed, and there was furniture... a bird's eye maple chiffonier, dressing table and chair, her father's Victrola and record collection, his books on a tall bookcase with enough room for hers too, more closet space than she needed, and shades on the windows.

She'd been lonely there as her grandmother declined. Now she had Mama and Papa, but Papa was at work all day and Mama was always too busy to be bothered with her. She had a room and a bed, her dolls, and a few books, but no place to put them where they weren't in Mama's way. It didn't feel like home to her.

The only friend Cynthia brought to Mama's house was Vera. After the Ruth episode, Cynthia felt her friends wouldn't be welcome, so most of the time the two of them hung out in Vera's Mother's workroom.

Mrs. Smitts had a telephone so after they started dating when they were in high school, this was the number they gave to the boys they met. There was a niche in the stairwell wall for a telephone in the new house, but no telephone was in it until after May died and Cynthia had installed one.

While they were still on J, Cynthia had to stack her art supplies and a few other things she owned from Grandma's house under the bed and the chest. No bookcases or shelves were provided. Anything that spread out or got too messy was thrown out on cleaning day while Cynthia was at school. She'd come home to discover everything except her books and clothes had been thrown out by the trash can. If it had rained, everything was ruined. Cynthia complained the first time.

"I asked you yesterday to straighten it up," May told her.

"But I didn't have time and now it's all ruined."

May gave a shrug. "It was in my way," she said.

All Cynthia had left of her early artwork was what she'd done in high school, her short-lived stay in the Los Angeles business college and a few classes she'd taken at the local junior college when she was in her fifties. May managed to make Cynthia feel that there was no room for her in her house or her life or her heart.

At first, because she felt uncomfortable in Mama's house, Cynthia stayed late at school or went into the vacant block across the street by herself. If Papa was home, she'd be in the garage with him. Later, most afternoons or evenings were spent with Vera or Fusa, her Japanese friend, but early on, when she was still in junior high, she spent evenings with her parents and the dog. May slowly accepted or adjusted to having a daughter living under the same roof. Cynthia had expected more.

Sometimes Mama would ask her to give her a facial or a manicure. Cynthia loved catering to Mama this way, trying to make the procedure as much like a beauty shop as she knew how... a hot towel to open the pores, Lady Esther cold cream (send a dime and get a sample) to cleanse, an egg white mask to stimulate, and finishing up with cotton soaked in witch hazel to close the pores. If Mama was pleased, Cynthia was happy.

The manicures were as professional as Cynthia knew how to do them too... warm soapy water for soaking the fingertips, an orange stick to clean under the nails and push back the cuticle to expose the moon. Large moons were considered an asset. Then the nail polish, which at that time wasn't put on over the moon and was wiped off the nail tip. Cute nail polish came in very few colors... clear, maybe three shades of pink from pale to dark, and bright red for the brave. The manicure was complete when a special pencil was run under the tips to make them look nice and white.

The water heater was lit only twice a week, on Monday for the wash and Saturday for family baths, which was another money saver when compared to these days when hot water is available twenty-four hours a day. Water for washing in the morning and for doing dishes was heated in the tea kettle on the stove on other days.

Before Cynthia went to live with Mama, when she got up in the morning she splashed water on her face, brushed her teeth and that was it. Her first morning at Mama's, May got her up and handed her the tea kettle full of hot water.

"What's this for?" Cynthia asked.

"For your morning ablutions," said May.

"What's that?"

"Washing your face with a wash rag and under your arms and between your legs and your feet. You're getting to be a big girl and a bath once a week isn't enough. You don't want to smell do you?"

This was new to Cynthia. "Oh, no," she said, and it became her daily routine. Later, when Cynthia was older, one day May called it a whore's bath.

"Huh? What's that Mama?"

May laughed. "As far down as possible, as far up as possible, and possible," she said.

Cynthia had to think about it for a minute before she got it. "Oh." And she laughed too.

May cleaned house on Saturday mornings, then took her bath. When Al came home at noon, they went grocery shopping. Then he took his bath, sometimes falling asleep in the tub and taking so long that May checked to see if he'd drowned.

Cynthia put Mama's hair up on Hollywood curlers and combed it out for her when it was dry. Did Mama have some notion that she could be a beauty operator? Cynthia had other plans on what she wanted to do with her life, but May had her own thoughts which took precedence when the time came later on.

On winter evenings, when the three of them were in the living room with a roaring fire, May made hot chocolate sometimes. Using Ghirardelli's chocolate, she'd stir in evaporated milk to make a thick paste, then pour in boiling water. Sometimes they'd have bread and butter with this; sometimes buttered graham crackers. Yummy.

In the summer, Cynthia helped Papa make Hires Root Beer from concentrate. They'd listen for the ice cream man to come by on his pedal cart with the ice chest on the front, ringing a bell. Mama sent Cynthia out to buy Dixie cups of vanilla ice cream for two cents each to make root beer floats. If there was no root beer, they bought four cups because Bingo loved ice cream too. Bingo, waiting for his cup to be opened, grinned and wagged his stub of a tail furiously. Money was still tight, but it was worth more than two cents to see Bingo enjoying his treat.

On occasion, May would stand up, saying, "I think I'll make some fudge." Sometimes it was chocolate fudge with walnuts from the recipe on the Hershey's cocoa box. Another time, it might be penuche with walnuts. Cynthia cracked and shelled the nuts while the mixtures cooked to the soft ball stage, then helped with the beating. May made the best penuche in the world, using a whole box of brown sugar and all of a small can of evaporated milk. She stirred in a good lump of butter and added a teaspoon of vanilla when it came off the stove. When cooled enough to beat, the nuts were added before it was spread onto a buttered platter. Cynthia could have eaten it all if Mama had let her. It was so divine.

May went to bed after the ten o'clock news every evening as soon as Walter Winchell said, "That's thirty for tonight" because she was an early riser. She got up every morning, washed and dressed then put the kettle on for Al, polished his shoes, and fixed his breakfast. After he left, she did the same for Cynthia (though not the shoes; Cynthia had to polish her own). She cleaned the house until one o'clock then changed into a clean house dress and was usually resting on the couch if Cynthia came in early from school.

May lived by the strict schedule of the times. Wash on the line on Monday morning by no later than nine. Iron on Tuesday, dust on Wednesday, Thursday, 'maid's day off.' This was the day she stayed home, did nothing, went visiting, or friends came by.

Twice a month, on the Thursday after payday, she went to the city to shop and go to a matinee. She stopped at Caesar's to bring home ravioli or at the chicken pie shop for chicken pies and coleslaw. Next, it was to Ferguson's, a Scottish bakery, to buy the sweets of home so dear to her heart, but not to Al's. Cynthia liked them though... anything Mama liked, she did too.

May was very fond of sweets, as was Cynthia, whose baby teeth had rotted from too much sugar. After she'd been weaned from the breast, her formula was diluted condensed milk and she took the bottle to bed at night until she was four years old. Grandma had taken it away from her after Amos died. Every penny she was given or found on the street went for penny candy and every tooth in her head had a filling by the time she was in her teens.

Al's taste in sweets was for sugar, not candy. He liked old-fashioned vanilla creams, that's all. Mama's boxes of Whitman's chocolates were safe from him. He loved ice cream, preferring plain vanilla, sprinkled sugar on tomatoes, rolled a leaf of lettuce around a spoonful of sugar like a cigarette and took at least three teaspoonfuls of it in a cup of coffee. In spite of all this sugar, Al died with all his teeth intact.

Cynthia learned to cook in the sixth grade and now that she was living with them, May went to dinner after the matinee and came home later on her day off, leaving Cynthia to cook for Papa and herself. Poor Al had to eat some strange concoctions, one of which was a salad for a ladies' luncheon... leaves of lettuce, a slice of canned pineapple, a banana cut in half and stuck on the end in the hole of the pineapple slice with a blob of mayonnaise and maraschino cherry on the top. It was called candle salad and Cynthia loved it. Al did not; he thought it was silly, but he ate it anyway. She made waffles too, which she loved, but he merely tolerated, and old-fashioned macaroni and cheese with chunks of Tillamook, which he liked. She also made scalloped cabbage, which he didn't like, and lemon meringue pie, which was his second favorite... apple being the first. He was fond of a slice of leftover pie for breakfast. Al had a good digestion, fortunately, liked most things, and Cynthia got hands-on practice in cooking.

May's apple pie filling was delicious, but she couldn't make a decent pie crust. Not that she didn't try. The British didn't make pies with a bottom crust and May's were tough beyond belief. When company came for Sunday dinner, she always made apple pie to please the Americans. When she served it, she always said the same thing.

"You don't have to eat the bottom crust if you don't want to."

No one ever wanted to, so Cynthia grew up thinking this was the way to eat pie until she learned to make crust herself. She'd come in from school and Mama would ask her to make a pie for Papa. While she was mixing the crust, she noticed Mama hovering around, not saying anything, but watching. It made her nervous; she thought Mama was making sure she wasn't doing it wrong. Then one day she learned the real reason.

"Oh," May said suddenly. "I see what you do. You don't use very much water."

May, whose Scottish pride wouldn't allow her to ask, had been watching to see why Cynthia's crust was better than hers. Cynthia, in high school now, turned her head away so that Mama wouldn't see and smiled to herself. By this time, she knew about Mama's pride and sensitivity.

It didn't make a lot of difference that May had learned the secret of a light crust. She still had too heavy a hand. While her crust improved a little, guests still left it on their plates. During WWII, when rubber was in short supply, Al joked that May should dig out her old recipe for pie crust and sell it for a mint of money to the government for tires. To May's credit, she thought it was funny. She didn't laugh out loud, but she did smile the little pussycat smile she sometimes used.

Living with Mama, Cynthia learned things about her... her pride, her vanity, her desire to be somebody, and how she should act and behave so Mama wouldn't get mad at her. She thought she was beginning to know her mother by the time she was in high school. Once, pleased with her own observation, she told Mama that the reason the two of them didn't always get along was because they were so much alike. May had looked incensed, not a reaction Cynthia had expected.

"I'm not anything like you," May flared back, hurting Cynthia's feelings both with the words and the tone of her voice. Cynthia had meant only that she'd noticed she and Mama were both proud and shy and kept their innermost feelings to themselves. She'd been pleased to notice the similarity, which had made her feel closer to her mother.

Once before, when they were still in the house on J, May remarked she didn't know what would become of her if anything should happen to Papa. "I don't know what I'd do or where I'd go," she'd said. May had once said that when Cynthia was younger, she didn't ever want to grow old and that she didn't want to have to be taken care of by anyone either. With a rush of compassion, Cynthia, who was about thirteen at the time, said, "You can always come and live with me, Mama."

May stiffened. She drew herself up and glared at Cynthia. "I would never live with you. I'd die first," she snapped.

As it happened, she did die before that could have come about, but at the time, Cynthia's feelings were hurt. She'd wanted Mama to know how much she loved her. She really did love her and tried her best to please her, but it seldom happened until she was grown and married when May's attitude toward her began to change.

"Mama doesn't just not love me; she doesn't even like me," Cynthia told herself at the first rebuff. The second time, when she was older, she thought, "I've always been rejected by Mama and I guess I always will be."

Before Cynthia left for Guam, May, who knew she had cancer, said, "I worry about Papa if anything should happen to me."

"Don't worry, Mama," Cynthia answered. "I'll always take care of Papa."

That time May had no response and as it turned out, Cynthia kept the promise she had unwittingly made to her mother. After Al had a stroke at age seventy-nine, he'd remained semi-invalid and Cynthia cared for him until his death two and a half years later.

"DID Mama ever care anything about me at all?" Cynthia thought to herself after writing these remembrances. "She didn't usually want to be seen on the street with me, but she came to all the things at school. She called me a stupid ass whenever I did some of the dumb things that kids do sometimes. No matter what I did, it never pleased her except for the manicures and facials and hairdos. But when she let me go alone to San Diego for the first time, she followed me across the street, telling me what to do and what not to do, and then stood watching until I went out of sight. I think she cared about me in her way, but there was no warmth in her caring."

CHAPTER FIFTY-FOUR

Cynthia learned a lot about her parents in the next few years that she'd had no way of knowing before. She'd been with them only on Sundays or holidays the first eight years of her life and in the afternoons and evenings after school for the next three. In the summers, she'd gone to the beach from Grandma's, then back to change, then to her parent's house and back again after ten to her grandma's for the night... a few hours here, a few there each day.

She never saw her parents hug or kiss each other, nor did either of them ever hug or kiss her. She never heard them argue. Papa spent most of his time in the garage on Saturdays and on summer evenings as long as the light held. He stayed up until one or two in the morning before going to bed. Cynthia, on the couch in the living room, heard a few murmurings from the bedroom on the other side of the wall if she was still awake, nothing more. The bedroom door was never closed, nor was it after they moved to the new house three years later.

She'd hear Papa come up the stairs, go into the bathroom to

brush his teeth and come out to stand for a few minutes at the upstairs landing window that looked toward San Diego. Then she'd hear a few murmurs as he got into bed. It was years, long after Mays' death, before she found out Papa was saying his prayers each night as he stood there looking toward the city, still visible then, before the trees grew up to obscure the view.

Al and May were readers. May brought books home from the library for herself and for Cynthia to read when she was in bed recovering from some sickness. She still got sick a lot, though not as often as before. After Papa left in the mornings to go to work, May made up their bed and moved Cynthia into it. She checked on her regularly, bringing her ice-cold pineapple juice and hot soup. It was almost worth being sick to be in that soft, clean bed and have Mama fussing over her.

May introduced Cynthia to the *Topper* books by Thorne Smith. Once Al asked what Cynthia was reading and was mildly shocked. Thorne Smith's books were funny and slightly risqué.

"Should she be reading those?" he asked.

"Most of it will probably be over her head," May said.

It was true. Cynthia thought "Skin and Bones," in which the people were suddenly nude when their flesh came back on the bones unexpectedly, was excruciatingly funny, as was the one where the idol on the mantle switched the married couple so they were in each other's bodies. The sexual innuendos escaped her.

Papa introduced her to H. Rider Haggard, Edgar Rice Burroughs, Algernon Blackwood, and Rex Strout's *Nero Wolfe* mystery stories. He had a small collection of occult books and he studied May's Bible after she went to bed. May had likely given his mother's Bible away.

May brought archeological books home from the library for herself and read her Bible, which had been a gift from her father when she'd left Scotland.

When May-May got married, Cynthia covered her mother's Bible with some of the wedding dress material and ribbon. May-May carried it in lieu of a wedding bouquet with a fresh flower corsage on the top. She felt Mama would have been pleased and she'd have loved May-May.

Al bought *Liberty* magazine for the Cock-eyed Crossword puzzle, *The Saturday Evening Post, Collier's, Popular Science,* and *Popular Mechanics.* They subscribed to the *National Geographic* and May bought *Redbook, Bluebook,* and *Cosmopolitan,* which was much different than it is today. Cynthia read them all.

After the dinner dishes were done, May sat in her chair and read or listened to the radio until bedtime. Papa took a short nap after dinner, then worked the crossword puzzle in the daily paper. Cynthia did her homework, if she had any, read or drew as she sat on the floor between the two chairs in front of the fireplace where her parents sat, looking up at Papa from time to time. Al, looking up to see her watching him, smiled at her, gave her a wink or wiggle-waggle of his forefinger. If she was close enough, he'd give her one of his two finger thumps on the head. She smiled back at him, pleased that he'd noticed her. Mama noticed her only if she'd done something she didn't approve of.

When the evening radio program started, they all listened to "The Firestone Hour," "Fred Allen," and "Fiber McGee and Molly." Papa and Cynthia liked "I Love a Mystery," which was not a favorite of May's. "Chandu the Magician" was the favorite of all the kids of assorted ages in the neighborhood. On a summer evening, when they were playing tag or hide and seek in the vacant block, the games ended when, on hearing the first strains of the program's theme wafting from the open windows, they hollered "bye" and ran for home.

Nights when she was in bed on the couch with Papa staying up late reading and tending the fire in the winter until it burned down far enough to be safe, Cynthia read or watched the fire and both of them listened to the radio. Al kept it turned low so's not to bother Mama, sleeping in the next room. They heard the music of Paul

Pendarvis and his Magic Violin, Henry Buses and his Rippling Rhythm, Wayne King and the Waltz King, and others coming from famous dance halls across the country. Sometimes Cynthia fell asleep before Papa banked the embers and went to bed. From time to time, if she was still awake, he'd read something to her, talk about what he was reading, or hand her his book to read a page or a paragraph. Sometimes they talked idly about things that happened during the day, exchanging thoughts about the music. Their tastes were similar. For Cynthia, it was the special, magical time during the three years before they moved into the new house. There, if she got sleepy, she'd have to go upstairs to go to bed, leaving Papa and the dog, who'd slept on the couch at her feet before, downstairs in the living room alone.

MAY WAS NOT PHYSICALLY ABUSIVE, but she hurt Cynthia's feelings with her criticism and her cool withdrawal when she was angry. She kept Cynthia clean, properly clothed, and fed. She'd bring little surprise gifts from her shopping trips... a new box of crayons or a watercolor set, a drawing tablet, and sometimes new socks or underwear. She loved to go into Quon Mane's, the oriental arts shop, where she bought incense for herself, paper fans, candies wrapped in edible rice paper, or paper pellets that magically opened up into flowers when dropped in water, for Cynthia. But there was an invisible fence between herself and her daughter that Cynthia could never penetrate. May avoided physical contact, never hugging her, only pulling her close when they were taking family snapshots, then letting her go as soon as the shutter clicked. She leaned away from Cynthia's kisses, turning a cheek and not wanting her hanging around.

"Go outside and play," she'd say or "Papa's in the garage. Why don't you go out with him?"

Papa was always glad to see her.

"There you are, Thum. I was just thinking about you."

May could be sweet, but she was like the cactus fruit Cynthia had once bitten into. One had to get past the prickles to find the sweetness and Cynthia hadn't known how.

The first year Cynthia lived with Mama, she asked May on her birthday how old she was.

"Thirty-five," May said.

On May's next birthday, she asked again because she'd forgotten what her mother had said before.

"Thirty-five," May said.

That rang a bell. "Weren't you thirty-five last year, Mama?"

"Oh, was I?" May replied. "Well, I'm still thirty-five and I'm going to stay thirty-five from now on. I don't intend to get old."

Cynthia was shocked and didn't know what to say. How could Mama not get old when everybody got old?

May had played fast and loose with her age for so long, she'd lost count. The year she died she'd told Al she'd be forty-nine on her next birthday.

Going through her mother's things and the family papers after her death, Cynthia found her birth certificate. May was already forty-nine and would have been fifty if she hadn't died a month before her birthday. She smiled to herself at her mother's vanity. She held the paper out for Papa to see. He looked at it and smiled too. There were some things about May they both knew... but much they didn't.

Al had once said that the date of one's death is somewhere in their lives. Cynthia knew two people whose mothers had died on their birthdays and had once been in a restaurant when a woman died while she and her husband were celebrating their wedding anniversary.

Digging deeper into the box of papers that evening, Cynthia found May's passport from before she'd come from Scotland to marry Al. May died on the seventh of September, the date the passport photograph had been taken was on the wall over her head. It was September the seventh. She showed it to Papa.

"Do you suppose that's where the expression about your number being up comes from?" she asked him.

"Could be."

Al had said he thought his number was thirteen because that was the day he'd left San Diego to go to war and a couple of other things had happened to him on that date as well. His number wasn't thirteen; he died on February 2nd at age eighty-one, the same age that Amos had been when he died.

CHAPTER FIFTY-FIVE

Now that Cynthia was living with them in the little house on J and sleeping on the couch, Papa started talking about a larger house. Around that time, because of the Depression, many veterans of WWI were agitating for the bonus which had been promised to them at a later date to be paid early. They marched on Washington D.C. Some of them stayed on with their wives and children, making camps in vacant areas and living in empty government buildings. President Hoover called out the military to chase them off and a couple of men were killed. People talked about nothing else for a time. May was very angry that the government would treat its veterans in such a shabby fashion. The bonus was paid after F.D.R. took office and Al's share was five hundred dollars.

Then began two years of frustration with the CalVet Administration. "God damned bureaucracy and red tape," when Al, a Californian veteran, applied for one of their home loans. Cynthia came home for lunch one day to find Papa in bed.

"Why is Papa still in bed? Is he sick?"

"No," said Mama. "He's having a nervous breakdown from fighting with that damned man at CalVets over the loan for the house." It wasn't really a breakdown; Al was just stressed out, suffering from nervous exhaustion. He'd probably been going without lunches too, taking his allotted time to go to the CalVet office for his daily runaround with the man in charge.

He stayed in bed a couple of days then girded his loins to have another go with the CalVet's office about what constituted a house. Because the family already had one, they hadn't thought a new one was needed. Al came home with a thick rule book and poured over it night after night. Then, taking a tape measure, measured the rooms and drew a plan of the house with all the windows and doors, light fixtures, etc.

"I've got him this time," he said. "That room in the back, because it has all those windows and the back door opening into it, doesn't fit their requirements for a bedroom."

CalVets conceded defeat. Al won out and got the loan.

Al, the civil engineer, designed and drew the plans for the new house.

CalVets said, "No. These are unacceptable." The plans had to be drawn by a licensed architect.

"Jesus Christ, we've only got five hundred dollars. Where in the hell can I find an architect we can afford?"

As it turned out, an older boy of one of the families they'd shared their July Fourths with had just gotten his degree and was a newly licensed architect. Al dickered with him to redraw his plans for a price.

The plans were accepted and then another blow. The Administration would loan money only for the house. The lot was not included. So now a lot must be found... another delay.

Al was getting more and more frustrated. He and May looked around and finally found the back half of a corner lot that the owner was looking to sell. The price was affordable if they could swing a five-hundred-dollar loan. A friend at the office offered to lend it; she would be repaid from the small amount of money left after Grandma's house had been sold to pay off the mortgage and expenses for her medical care and burial.

Now all they had to do was find a contractor who would build the house to CalVet's specifications while staying within the amount of the loan. Al was getting fit to be tied at all the delays and nasty little surprises.

May found the contractor in Coronado. He was another Scot, which gave them something in common and they had known each other for a long time. He agreed to take on the job and at last they were on their way. The ground was broken; the building began.

The inspector from CalVet practically lived on the site of the construction. He watched with an eagle eye every nail, every two-by-four, every type of wiring, and you-name-it that was going into this house that they were going to carry the mortgage on for the next twenty-five years. Al, with his volatile temper, lived in a constant state of frustration with all the nit-picky rules that some "God damned fat head" had thought up just to drive him crazy. It's a miracle that he didn't have the stroke that incapacitated him at age seventy-nine when he was forty-two!

The move was made into the new house on July 4, 1935. Cynthia would enter high school in the fall and a new phase of her life was about to begin.

May had their living room furniture reupholstered, traded the library table for a dining table with a leaf, kept the chairs, bought inexpensive felted fiber rugs for the dining room and the room which Cynthia would sleep in for the next five years. She bought beige silk pongee, and Al, who knew a little bit about sewing, made the curtains for the living and dining room, sewing them on his mother's old treadle machine. Later, he cut it down and put an electric motor on it. Cynthia used it to sew her clothes in high school and afterward until WWII ended and she bought a brand-new New Home as soon as things like new cars and sewing machines became available again.

· · ·

DURING THE ROOSEVELT YEARS, when Franklin and Eleanor were publicly quoted in the press and one or the other spoke at length in interviews or F.D.R. gave one of his famous "Fireside Chats" about the rights of the "common man" and what the government could be expected to do for him, Al roared with anger. Some people might feel Al was about as common as a man could be... middle-class, white-collar worker and mixed race to boot, but Al did not consider himself common and he didn't expect the government to help him with anything he could do for himself. He would have died before taking any sort of handout or welfare, as would proud Scottish May, who also took offense at Eleanor for her references to the "common people."

"Who does she think she is, calling other people common?" she asked. "What makes her think she's any better than the rest of us?" May also stated angrily that she'd never take a nickel's worth of welfare. "I'd die first," she said, and Cynthia didn't doubt it for a moment. By now she'd learned more about May's Scottish pride and the lengths to which she'd go with it.

AL WAS NOT A SELF-EFFACING MAN. He was positive in his beliefs and would not back down in an argument about them. He had opinions and no reservations about expressing them. He disliked Unions, the ACLU, governmental bureaucracy, red tape, deficit spending, and helping all those "G.D. countries who won't help themselves and who borrow money from us they don't intend to pay back." All of these, in his opinion, were "going to be the ruination of this country."

F.D.R. was an anathema to Al. His man was Teddy, someone who walked (or was it talked) softly, carried a big stick, minded his own business, and kept out of the rest of the world's business was right up his alley.

· · ·

CYNTHIA HAD ONCE HEARD him tell his best friend, Ray, in one of their on-going political arguments, that he was a God damned fool for leaning toward Communism as an answer to the country's problems. This bone of contention kept them occupied for years, with neither one changing the other's mind.

"A lot like me and Vera about God," Cynthia thought.

Cynthia had heard him scold his mother a time or two, but he'd never yelled at her, nor had she ever heard him yell or argue with Mama. He generally abided by May's wishes, perhaps to keep the peace and avoid one of her silent treatments? He'd yell at Cynthia though and pound the table if she did or said something he considered stupid.

One might think, knowing these things about Al, that he was a nasty, mean-tempered man, but that wasn't true. He was polite... a true gentleman of the old school, honest, kind, thoughtful, funny, and dear. Eddie Fisher's recording of "Oh, Mein Papa" could have been about Cynthia's father. She loved him with all her heart and he was the most important person in her life and all the world to her. May told Cynthia that Papa was a fine man shortly before her death. No one needed to tell Cynthia that about her father. She'd known it all her life and for all the rest of his as well.

May, who had become a conservative Republican isolationist hawk, both through marriage and osmosis, couldn't abide the Roosevelts either. Al despised F.D.R. He thought the man had delusions of grandeur and was making plans to become emperor of the U.S. if he kept getting reelected.

Early one morning in 1945, when Cynthia and Tee Gee were just barely up, the phone rang. Mama was on the line.

"Well, the old bastard is dead," she said.

Cynthia, who was still half asleep, asked, "What old bastard?"

"F.D.R. He's dead."

"Oh," Cynthia said.

She really couldn't care less. She'd never been as interested in politics as her parents were. She was a fatalist, believing what was going to be was going to be, and one might as well accept it. She was interested only in what was happening in the South Pacific anyway, waiting for the war with the Japanese to end, worrying about Ted coming home alive and the sooner the better for both.

If we hadn't used the atomic bomb that ended the war, Cynthia may never have seen Ted alive again. She wondered how many of the people in the nineties, who think we should never have used it, have or had fathers who may not have been here to father them if we hadn't.

People heard the rumors about what Hitler was doing to the Jews in Germany, but no one had believed it or wanted to. It was just too horrible to think about. "Propaganda," they said. "No human being could be that despicable." When the truth came out, it was still unbelievable.

When Cynthia read Herman Wouk's book *The Winds of War* years later, she was stunned about the happenings in Europe that she knew nothing about. It was like she'd been living in another world. That war had no reality for her.

"All that was going on in Europe happened in my lifetime," she told herself. "And I was oblivious." She could hardly believe it. She felt ashamed that she could have been that self-centered, thinking only of herself, when there had been others alone and lonely, and suffering. The horrors of the holocaust had been a reality, not just rumors and propaganda. But only the war in the South Pacific had held any meaning for her.

CHAPTER FIFTY-SIX

Al could do anything he put his mind to. The only thing Cynthia ever saw him stumped on was spoking the wheels on her bicycle. She had no doubt he'd have figured out how to do it, but Mr. Fleck, their neighbor, knew how and said he'd help. When Al had a problem, he paced the living room floor, turning it over and over in his mind until he figured it out.

They'd bought the car before the Depression. Al took care of it like a baby. He changed the spark plugs, changed the oil, charged the battery with his home-built battery charger, put distilled water in it and tap water in the radiator, adjusted the timing, did something to the carburetor, and that's what Cynthia could remember. There may have been many more.

The Essex was about five or six years old when the ring gear on the flywheel broke. Al went into a garage in the city to ask about repairs. He came home and told May it would cost about a hundred dollars.

"We can't possibly afford that," she said. "Can't you fix it?"

"They told me I couldn't do it myself; it takes special equipment I don't have."

"Oh dear, what will we do? We have to have a car."

"Let me think about it; maybe I can come up with something."

The next day, Al went back to the garage and asked if they could order the ring gear. They said yes, but it wouldn't do him any good. It would be impossible for him to do it himself.

They'd issued a challenge and Al responded like a bull to a red flag. "Order it anyway," he told them. "And let me know when it comes in."

In the meantime, he nearly wore a path in the rug pacing back and forth night after night, turning the problem over in his mind. One night, he snapped his fingers and stopped pacing.

"I think I've got it," he told Cynthia.

The ring gear came and when he went to pick it up, they told him he'd be back. "No, I won't," he replied.

The next Friday he put the flywheel in the little freezer section of the refrigerator. On Saturday morning he asked May to turn the oven on as high as it would go, put the ring gear in it and told her to let him know when it was red hot. It took a while. He kept running in to see how it was coming along. When it was glowing, he took the ice-cold flywheel out of the garage with his work gloves and came back in with a pair of tongs.

"Stand by the door to open it for me when I come back," he told Cynthia.

He got the ring gear out of the oven with the tongs, she opened the door and he went flying out with it. When he got to the garage, he put the hot ring gear on top of the cold flywheel on his mother's old flat iron, gave it a few whacks with a mallet and it went on like it was greased. He let it sit until it had reached room temperature. It was on to stay. He installed it and *voila* it was done. On Monday, he went back to the garage and told them he'd done it, but he didn't tell them how.

Things changed after they moved into the new house. Al rebuilt his workbench, but there was no window for light over it as there had been in the old garage. He quit fussing with his radios; the old neighborhood garage buddies had been left behind.

There was a fence to be built, which Cynthia helped with as she had done before and after that, the new garage sat there with nothing in it except the Essex for the next six years when they traded it in for an eight-cylinder, two-door, blue 1937 Ford, just after Cynthia and Ted's marriage.

CHAPTER FIFTY-SEVEN

Cynthia's grandmother had a mixed garden of old-fashioned flowers in a profusion of colors and sizes. May had a fuchsia bush, set carnation slips along the sunny side of the house, and planted gladiola bulbs in a small plot in the back. She liked flowers but wasn't much of a gardener.

The Coronado Flower Show was one of the big social events of the year. A huge tent was erected for it in the East Park every spring. It became a tradition and it still is. Everyone who was interested in gardening entered their best blooms, vying for the best of the show and other ribbons. May had taken Cynthia every year and they looked at everything. Both were particularly keen on roses.

Being somebody was important to May. Many of the entries came from gardens of people who had gardeners, but that wasn't going to stop her. She told Al, just before Cynthia came to live with them, that she was going to take a prize at the flower show with a rose and she wanted him to prepare a plot in the back yard for a rose garden.

The next time the fertilizer man came by, they bought a load and had it piled by the side of the garage. Al spent one Saturday turning over the dirt and manure in a carefully laid out rectangular bed. The surveyor in him came to the fore. He measured and marked the corners, drove in pegs and tied string to enclose the area so all was neat and tidy, as Cynthia watched and helped when needed.

"Now it has to sit and cool for a while," he said, explaining that manure got hot and would burn tender roots.

Soon afterward, May came home from one of her shopping trips with a paper bag full of grungy looking twigs with their root ends wrapped in burlap and tags on them telling the name and the color of the roses they were going to have when they grew up someday. It was hard to believe that from these sticks would come the miracle of a gorgeous rose, but May planted them, watered, raked, weeded, and sprayed and the miracle happened. The names were as varied as the colors... Herbert Hoover, velvety red dark, Talisman, one of the new roses for that year, a peachy orange and yellow with a touch of pink, other beautiful pinks, yellows, and whites with names now forgotten. The aroma was heavenly.

It took two years, and by that time May was beginning to grumble about the care and feeding of roses. The first year there'd been an honorable mention and a second. She read the gardening columns in the women's magazines and the Sunday paper and went to the nursery in Coronado to talk to them about the best thing to do. She hovered over her possibles like a mother hen.

The next year she had two choices... the Talisman, which she thought would win, and a Herbert Hoover. The Herbert Hoover took the blue ribbon. Al photographed her beaming with pride, holding up her prize winner in its face with the blue ribbon attached. She bought the next issues of the Coronado journal, cut out the list of winners, and pasted it into her scrapbook. By the next year, the new house had been completed, the family had moved, and the rose bed was left behind. May's mission had been accomplished. She went back to carnations and gladiolus, planted another fuchsia which died, and never grew roses again.

"Mama always did what she set her mind to do," Cynthia remembered. "And May-May is just like her."

May-May had missed being born on her grandmother's birthday by just six minutes. May had been gone for four years and so had never known her granddaughter.

May often drove around the Strand and one time she'd had a flat. A nice man stopped and put the spare on for her, but she hadn't liked the situation or being beholden to a stranger so she'd asked Al to teach her how to change a tire. She'd also decided, since Cynthia was no longer riding her bike very much, that she could save gas and get exercise by using it to go uptown to the post office and to pay the bills. Al taught her how to ride, running her up and down the street until she got the hang of it like he had with Cynthia and May pedaled happily around town on her little excursions for several years.

May-May had taught herself to knit and knitted quite a nice sweater. She also used babysitting money to buy a guitar she wanted and taught herself to play. Like her grandmother, when she'd made up her mind to do something, it got done and she had the same way of setting her jaw when her mind was made up and nothing was going to change it.

When May-May was three, Cynthia had given her little behind a swat and sent her out of the small kitchen in their quarters because she was being a nuisance. May-May got as far as the doorway, turned, put her hands on her hips and glared at her mother.

"When I was the Mommy and you were the little girl," she said, "I didn't do that to you." Then she stomped off.

Cynthia was surprised but had to stifle a laugh and as soon as May-May went back outside, she called Papa to tell him about it. He was as startled and amused as she had been.

"You don't suppose she's Mama reincarnated?" Cynthia asked.

"I don't know," he said. "It is kind of funny, isn't it?"

Cynthia thought about it afterward and it was true. Mama had often swatted her on the legs with the fly swatter but had never paddled her on the backside with her hand like she'd just done to

May-May. Believing in reincarnation as she did, it was something to think about.

CHAPTER FIFTY-EIGHT

Now that Cynthia was older, almost in her teens, Mama was letting her go to San Diego by herself to shop or to go to Marie's and soon to the skating rinks at night. When she was by herself on the streetcar, people looked at her and whispered. She'd sit where she pleased, walking proudly down the aisle to a seat she'd chosen while dropping her coins in the toll box. She sat alone unless someone she knew smiled and moved over for her to join them or someone got on who knew her and sat beside her. No one ever told her to move to the rear of the car, though. She'd have been insulted, gotten off, and walked uptown or to the ferry.

She was learning that many men had no respect for her or perhaps women in general, but she only knew about ones she had to be careful to stay away from. It was surprising to her because these men were not strangers. They had been polite to her grandmother; her parents were acquainted with them and did business with some of them.

Vera had the same problems with some of her mother's men friends and a couple of the same shopkeepers Cynthia had to watch out for, starting in junior high when they both were maturing.

Walking home from the beach one day, when she was about fourteen, the son of one of her mother's acquaintances pulled up alongside her in his car. He was a married man with kids, well known around town and liked by everyone.

"How about a lift home, Cynthia?"

The alarm inside her head didn't ring... no prickly feeling at the back of her neck either.

"Okay," she said. "Thanks," and got into the car.

Instead of taking her home, he drove to the water tower, a place she'd never been before, pulled up, and parked. She looked around, interested. She could see parts of the city and ships in the bay she'd never seen from this angle before.

"I had no idea this place was here," she said.

"You haven't ever been here before with boys?" He sounded surprised.

"No," she said. "This is the first time I've ever been here."

"I'm sorry. I've made a mistake," he said and, starting the car, drove her home.

Afterward, she realized he must have thought, like many others did, that she was no better than she should be and he'd taken her to the place where the boys took girls on dates to neck.

She told Vera about it. Neither of them had known about the necking place before. Vera never went there and Cynthia went only one other time. A boy she really liked took her there to break the relationship off shortly after she'd told him about her grandmother. It would break her heart, but she had to tell him, knowing that might be the outcome. She felt bad about losing him, but at least he'd been nice about it, not like the guy who, after standing her up, never spoke to her again if they happened to see each other. She dreamed about him sometimes for a while afterward and wondered if he ever thought about her. She never forgot him, telling herself that it had been his decision, his choice, and his loss.

. . .

By the time Vera and Cynthia started high school and were becoming fast friends, they both had grown ample bosoms and were very self-conscious, wearing loose sweaters and carrying their books against their chests to hide the offensive projections. The two were a perfect match in everything except appearance. Vera was big boned, wide-hipped, and taller than Cynthia. Cynthia appeared slimmer, though both wore the same size.

They made up parodies about themselves, changing the word "ears" in the ditty "Do your ears hang low? Do they wobble to and fro? Can you tie 'em in a knot? Can you tie 'em in a bow? Can you throw 'em over your shoulder like a Continental Soldier? Do your ears hang low?" to "boobs" and then had giggling fits when they sang it.

Both had acne; both thought they were fat and ugly. They walked together, elbows linked, singing, "Give me a man who's a stout-hearted man, who can face and not turn away." There was more, but Cynthia had long since forgotten it. They bolstered each other's egos, shared each other's deepest thoughts and feelings. It was truly a friendship made in Heaven.

They argued, but never fell out over anything with the exception of four episodes Cynthia could remember. Once, in high school, they didn't speak for nearly a week. Vera said something that hurt Cynthia's feelings. Cynthia told her to go to hell and stomped off. They both worked on the school paper, with Vera as business manager and Cynthia as art editor. It appeared that the paper wouldn't come out that week and the school was in a turmoil, buzzing about what was the matter. Neither would discuss it.

Mr. Birch, the counselor, talked to both of them separately. Cynthia was adamant, but Vera, contrite, wrote a note of apology, telling Cynthia how much their friendship meant to her. They met in the hall, said they were sorry and the paper came out to everyone's relief. Cynthia still has the letter in her scrapbook.

The two of them were conscientious about their jobs on the paper. Cynthia did the ads they solicited from the local businessmen, making them more legible than in the past with the use of lettering stencils. They delivered copies to each advertiser when the paper came out, which they learned had apparently been done only hit or miss before. The merchants were happy. More of them bought ads and the paper, which had been in the red, made money for the first time since God only knew when, making everybody happy. It was a terrific boost to Vera and Cynthia's nearly non-existent egos, making them happy too.

The other times one of them got an ego damaged by the other were insignificant, lasting only a few minutes. While still in their teens, window shopping in San Diego, Vera said something that made Cynthia angry. She threw her brand-new envelope purse down on the sidewalk hard, told Vera to go to hell and stomped off. But she had to go back to pick up her purse. They looked at each other, started to laugh, and that was the end of that. The purse was the only thing hurt; it was dinged on one corner.

The third time, they were grown women washing dishes together when Cynthia told Vera to mind her business about something. Vera, picking up her coat, headed for the door.

"Wood, get the kids and c'mon. We're going home," she said.

"I'm sorry. I'm sorry. Don't go," Cynthia said, and Vera put her coat back down.

Number four was almost the same as number three... not a bad record for sixty-one years of friendship.

CHAPTER FIFTY-NINE

Vera and Cynthia went into eighth grade the fall of the year Annie died. Uniforms were now required. Long dark pants, corduroy being the material of choice, and white shirts for boys. Black or navy blue skirts and heavy white long-sleeved middy blouses that had navy blue wool button-on collars trimmed with white braid, worn with a black silk kerchief, folded and tied with a square knot Navy style, for girls. In a school attended by the wealthy and newly poor middle class alike, the uniform code was a social leveler. No one was any better than anybody else... maybe smarter, maybe richer, but not in outward appearance.

When Tee Gee had started school in Coronado fifteen years later while they were living with Papa after May's death, Cynthia made short-sleeved shirts, bought dress pants and oxfords for his first day of school. When he came home, he told her that he'd been the only boy dressed like that and the other boys had teased him.

"What did they have on?" she asked in surprise

"Jeans and tee-shirts and sneakers."

"Jeans and tee-shirts and sneakers? Those are play clothes, not school clothes!"

She couldn't believe it. He had them, but she'd gotten them for him to change into when he came home.

"Okay," she said. "You can wear yours tomorrow. We can't have you looking different, but I can't say I approve of those kinds of things for school."

It was true. She found that out when she walked to the school the next day to meet him, to see for herself. A swarm of children, the boys looking all alike in their jeans and striped tee-shirts, came charging out. She didn't see him at first; they might as well have all been in uniforms. He saw her and they walked back to the house together.

It seemed to her this had been the start of a breakdown in customs and behavior, causing the decline in social graces, moral behavior and respect for law and order that has led to so many problems in our society in the last forty years. A little thing, perhaps an oversimplification, but most things start out small and grow. The weeds of sex and violence in movies and on television have proliferated in the garden of society, leaving no time to stop and smell the roses because of the time it takes trying to eradicate them.

During the worst of the Depression, no one would have allowed themselves or their children to be seen in public in the torn, ragged, and often dirty clothing that young people consider stylish today. Hair was neatly combed, not shaggy-dog unkempt, a rat's nest or "I just got up and haven't combed it yet." Times were hard, money hard to come by, but soap was cheap, only a nickel, and a comb, two cents. No one wanted to look like a hobo, some of whom appeared more respectable then than many people do today.

Uniforms were required in high school until 1937, when it was decided the girls could wear simple, everyday dresses, not what one would wear to a party, on Fridays. The following year they could wear everyday dresses five days a week. It was then that the difference between the girls of ordinary ilk and the ones whose fathers were Navy Officers or wealthy businessmen became obvious. Girls from the moneyed families wore expensive cashmere sweaters, pleated wooled skirts, saddle shoes, and Add-A-Pearl real pearl necklaces, started for them at birth. Others wore what their families could afford. Anyone with two eyes could see the difference in social and economic levels.

Some yearned for the Friday 'uniform' of the girls whose parents had money. These were the girls whose own parents didn't, whose sweaters and skirts weren't as elegant, whose shoes were inexpensive and pearls fake.

Cynthia and Vera didn't try to compete. Cynthia's clothes came from the twice-a-year sale at Lerner's dress shops. Vera inherited lovely dresses from some of her mother's customers. She hated wearing adult hand-me-downs, but they were excellent quality and she wore them well. Her mother's clientele wore custom made or clothing from the finest stores... Lelah Elgin's in Coronado, Marston's, or I. Magnin in the city. Cynthia, who wanted to be a dress designer, knew the difference between cheap stuff and good stuff and was envious as she watched Vera trying on her "new" things.

May began giving Cynthia twenty dollars on her birthday and for Christmas after she started high school. From this largess, which really was a lot of money for the time, Cynthia bought all her clothes and incidentals for the season. A trip to Lerner's, then to Chandler's, one of the less expensive shoe stores, for the after-holiday sales and she was set.

The dime store was her makeup source when May decided she was old enough to wear it, at sixteen. A box of face powder, a Tangee lipstick, Maybelline mascara in its little red cardboard box with a brush, pink liquid Odorono antiperspirant with its sponge applicator or a jar of MUM deodorant, thick green "wave set" in a bottle one could stick a comb down into, and a can of Theatrical cold cream. For a little over a dollar, she was set for a while.

With the money earned from babysitting at twenty-five cents an hour, thirty-five cents if washing dishes was included, ten cents an item for ironing, fifty cents an hour for house cleaning, and, if she was lucky, a little extra for a tip, she went shopping.

Material was ten cents a yard at the dollar store where she'd buy three yards for a new dress or four for a skating skirt. Next, off to the dime store for findings... thread, buttons, snaps, hooks and eyes, materials for a belt and a pattern, all for less than a dollar. She'd replace her cosmetic supply or treat herself to some dime store jewelry or perfume, and, if she had enough, she'd buy a pair of summer sandals, a new pair of huaraches or white tennies, which she also wore to school. She'd walk uptown from the ferry to the shops and back again to save the dime for more to spend. Sometimes May came home from her 'maid's day out' with a sweater, under-wear, or some little something extra for a surprise and saw to it that she had a new outfit for Easter.

Sometime in the thirties, the latest fashion to hit the scene was beach pajamas. Meant for summer wear, they were an instant success and, worn with a big-brimmed, floppy hat... *tres chic.* One piece, low necked and sleeveless, with full legs similar to palazzo pants, they were very cool and affordable.

May bought two of bright flowered material, one for each of them. You stepped into them, pulled them up and fastened them with floppy ties at the shoulder. Cynthia, in her early teens, having gotten over the 'I wish I were a boy' phase, loved hers. They made her feel feminine and she liked the feeling.

Cynthia set her own style, ignoring what the other girls wore, sometimes talking Vera into getting or making some of the same things.

It was in junior high that Cynthia met the two brothers and their younger sister who became close friends for the short time they lived in Coronado, only one full school term and a summer. Then, the following year, she met a girl named Marie whose mother didn't mind that Cynthia wasn't what she appeared to be and allowed her to come into their home too.

Mrs. Adams, the mother of the two boys and the girl who were Cynthia's friends, liked her, sometimes inviting her along on picnics or to the beach with them. After an outing at the beach up the coast one day, Mrs. Adams put both girls into the tub to wash the sand off. Betsy looked at Cynthia in the buff and, surprised, said, "Look Mama, Cynthia's as white as I am under her bathing suit."

"Sure I am," Cynthia said. "Didn't you know that?"

Mrs. Adams said, "Betsy!" in a sharp tone. Cynthia could tell she was not only embarrassed because she turned pink, but from the expression on her face, that she was surprised too. It was a revelation.

"Does everyone think that I'm this tan all over?" she wondered.

She was sorry when Betsy and her two brothers moved away, but she didn't have time to miss them because she'd met Marie, who was the same age as herself. They had a wonderful summer together at the beach, met some boys from Los Angeles, swam in the bay and ocean, and tanned in the sun. Although Marie moved to east San Diego before summer ended, they were able to continue seeing each other because of the transit company's summer passes for kids, allowing them to go all over the city for two dollars and fifty cents a month. Sometimes they rode the streetcars just for fun, getting to know the city well.

Cynthia went to Marie's almost every day and they met two boys and another girl to pal around with, going swimming at Lake Murray and skating at a rink not far from where Marie lived. In the fall, Marie moved to Los Angeles, but she invited Cynthia to come up for a visit after Christmas. They went skating at the Shrine Auditorium and swimming at Bimini, a large, enclosed plunge, with one of the boys they'd met at the beach the summer before. Cynthia decided that skating rinks were "the greatest thing since sliced bread," a common expression of the day after bread slicing machines first appeared in bakeries and people no longer had to slice their own.

That fall, when they started high school, Vera's neighbor had moved away so Cynthia and Vera picked up again as they always did at summer's end. Now there was only the two of them, which suited Cynthia just fine, and the friendship deepened.

The following summer, after their freshman year, Vera went to Chicago to visit the aunt she'd lived with before the move to California, and Marie, who had moved to Hawaii for a short while, came back to Coronado. It wasn't long before they met a couple of boys who were friends. Rob was from San Diego and Chet lived in Coronado with an older brother and his wife. The four of them bummed around Coronado on the days when Chet, who had a job, was free, going to the beach, sitting in the park talking, hanging out around Marie's house, and sharing malted milkshakes at the new malt shop in Coronado. A shake cost only a dime and was enough for two.

One evening the girls were washing dishes at Marie's with Rob keeping them company. The girls had been on the streetcar earlier when two local girls Cynthia had gone to school with for years got on. They sat together whispering, looking at Cynthia and Marie, then started talking to someone in a seat nearby loud enough for them to hear the word nigger. Marie was angry and so was Cynthia.

"They're talking about both of us," Cynthia said. "You're the same color as me (Marie was Italian). I bet they're saying you're colored too. Why do people always think they have to tell other people stuff? Why can't they just mind their own business?"

That was the evening Cynthia decided to tell Rob when Marie left the kitchen for a moment.

"I already knew it," he said.

"You already knew? Why didn't you say something?"

"I was waiting to see if you'd tell me."

"Well, I just did," she said. "But who told you?" She thought maybe it had been Marie.

"That streetcar conductor you know told me."

"Mr. Edwards? I thought he was a family friend."

She couldn't believe it. She was angry, very angry. She was angry at Mr. Edwards and at those other girls and so was Marie when she came back and they talked about it. They decided to get even and the boys offered to help after they told Chet about it the next day.

Chet had the use of a printing press at the place where he worked, so that afternoon, they printed up some cards with the two girls' names on them saying they were liars. The girls put them under the windshield wipers all up and down Orange Avenue. They should have known better, especially the boys, who were older, but...

The next day the police picked Cynthia up as she was walking alone and took her to the station where they began asking questions after showing her one of the cards.

"You and another girl were seen putting these under windshields. Who was the other girl? Whose printing press was it? Yours? No? Well, whose then and where is it? Whose idea was it?"

It went on and on as she sat there, terrified. She wouldn't answer any of their questions, except to say that it was her idea and she wasn't going to tell them anything that would get anyone else in trouble. She was in big trouble and she knew it. What would Mama and Papa say? But whatever happened, she wasn't going to get the others in trouble too, and maybe make Chet lose his job. She just kept shaking her head until finally they gave up. She thought they were going to put her in the jail cell, but they said they'd let her go if she'd go to one of the mothers and apologize. (She never learned why not the other one.) They wouldn't tell her parents and it would be excused.

So she went to the house and rang the bell. The girl's mother opened the door.

"The police told me I had to come and apologize."

"Well, what do you have to say for yourself then, Cynthia?"

"I'm sorry," Cynthia said.

"Why ever did you do such a thing, Cynthia? Didn't you know it was wrong?"

Cynthia did. If she hadn't before, she sure did now. "Because people are always telling other people that I'm colored," she said, wanting the woman to see that she didn't like people talking about her, but it didn't come out right.

"Well, it's true isn't it, Cynthia?" she said.

Cynthia stood there looking at her, her throat so tight she couldn't speak. Emotions impossible to describe were swirling inside her. She hung her head, close to tears.

"Well, alright. You can go now," the woman said after a moment. "I hope you've learned your lesson."

She had. She turned away, tears starting to roll down her cheeks. It was true; she knew it was true, but she didn't want it to be. She didn't want people telling her or other people about her either. It was her business, not theirs. Why didn't they mind their own and leave her alone?

She cried all the way to the house, went in the back door and hurried up the stairs to splash cold water on her face so Mama wouldn't see. What would happen next she didn't know, but she'd have to wait and cope with it then.

The police were true to their word. As far as she knew, her parents never heard anything about the episode and she didn't tell the others about it. She was too ashamed of herself and for what had almost happened to all of them because of her.

When she was writing about it now, almost sixty years later, she thought, "Maybe it was a good thing Mama had such an aversion to telephones. I got away with things she never heard about because of it."

She was realizing she'd been just as prejudiced against colored people, in her own way, back then as others had been. She hadn't wanted to be colored. She'd been a hypocrite too, not wanting to admit to herself that she was. She could like it or lump it... her choice. It wouldn't change a thing.

CHAPTER SIXTY

What else happened in the seventh and eighth grades? Cynthia found it hard to remember. School was no longer the dominating influence in her life. She had Vera and Fusa; she met the Adams kids, then Marie. She was no longer an outcast; she had friends. She had places to go... the after-school clubs and Mrs. Mack's studio. She had to practice the piano too, for her Saturday morning lessons from Mrs. Mack's son, Roy, who was the church organist now. These were the things that had stayed in her memory... having friends and fun, someone her own age to talk to, not being alone and lonely, and being accepted.

She could remember how nice Miss Robb, the Art Appreciation teacher, had been and Miss Vance, the music teacher, who let her be in the elite choral group of a dozen or so girls who sang at school programs and sometimes at businessmen's luncheons. She knew Miss Vance, who had been interested in her ever since the fourth grade, had done it just to be nice.

Cynthia was an alto but couldn't sing the alto parts. She understood harmony from her piano lessons, but she couldn't sightread and strayed off to the melody. It must not have made a difference in the sound or Miss Vance would have asked her to leave. Vera, who sang very well and had sung harmony with her sister, Jackie, hadn't been accepted. She was hurt and angry and never liked Miss Vance after that.

They'd read Shakespeare, a lot of Shakespeare... *The Merchant of Venice, Hamlet, All's Well That Ends Well, A Midsummer Night's Dream,* and perhaps others, forgotten now. They'd had to memorize; "To be or not to be...," "The quality of mercy is not strained...," "All the world's a stage...," and more. They must have done other things as well, but they no longer took precedence in her memories.

She had an essay selected from a city-wide contest that was printed in the San Diego Sun. She was paid a nickel for it and received four tickets to the Fox theater for a special kid's movie. Mrs. Adams was to drive her kids and Cynthia to the theater and May was going to go get them. Cynthia got so wound up and excited about it that on that day she was too sick to her stomach to go. The Adams kids and their mother got to see the show on Cynthia's free passes.

Now that she lived in Mama's house, she had to be friends with the boy next door, Leroy. Their parents played Five Hundred every Saturday night, got a little tipsy on homebrew and went to San Diego to the Douglas Hotel, which had a colored review, the Hollywood Theater, which had burlesque.

Leroy and Cynthia were sent to the movies together on these evenings. Another boy, a friend of Leroy's, usually went along. Joe and Leroy sat apart from Cynthia in the theater and on the way back spent most of the time trying to ditch her. They'd join up again to go into the house so their parents never realized there was no love lost between them.

"Leroy is in the hospital for mastoid surgery," May told Cynthia one day. "It's a very serious operation and he could die. His parents are very worried. Maybe you should pray for him."

Leroy was always doing things to hurt her... pulling her arms up behind her back to make her holler uncle or digging his fingernails into the inside of her wrist until she bled, trying to make her beg for mercy. She wouldn't give him the satisfaction of giving in to him and after a while he gave up, grudgingly admitting that she was pretty brave for a girl.

Pray for Leroy? Cynthia was just glad it wasn't her in the hospital with a mastoid. She'd had enough earaches to last a lifetime. Vera had mastoid surgery before she'd come to Coronado and she had a scar behind one ear. Cynthia hadn't known Vera then so hadn't prayed for her and she hadn't died. Leroy was on his own as far as she was concerned.

Leroy got better. His brush with death hadn't changed him any. One Saturday afternoon, his parents were out somewhere and Cynthia's had gone grocery shopping, he suggested a game which involved tying Cynthia up as she sat on a chair in their sunroom in the back of the house. Then he and Joe ran out of the house calling that they'd be back in a little bit. Time passed and they didn't come back... more time passed... where were they? She called and there was no answer. Then she knew they weren't going to come back. They'd left her there on purpose. She sat there twisting her hands and feet, trying to loosen the rope. The chair fell over. She began calling for help as loud as she could. Then she began to cry. She stopped a while later, lay there scared, then began crying and calling again.

Finally, she heard the car. Her parents were back so she screamed as loud as she could. Papa, on his way out to the garage, heard her, came running in, and untied her. He was furious. Old houses had old electrical wiring that often shorted out, starting a fire in the dry wood. Al was an electrician; he had to be to build radios. He'd warned Cynthia not to leave appliances plugged in, to always unplug them from the wall first and to be careful with the heater in the bathroom if she was in the tub.

"Jesus Christ," he said. "Those God damned fools. The house could have burned down with you in it."

Did he speak to Leroy's father? Cynthia didn't know. All she knew was she didn't like Leroy and she wasn't the least bit sorry when the family moved away to the house on the corner where her grandmother was hit by the car shortly afterward.

After they were in high school, she and Leroy never spoke to each other again. She did feel sorry for his parents when Mama told her he'd been killed in WWII. He was their only child.

When the two of them had been younger, Cynthia, playing alone on the front lawn on a warm summer day when the French windows were open, heard Leroy's mother telling Mama what a terrible liar he was and that she just didn't know what she could do about it. Cynthia didn't know then about her mother's Scottish pride that wouldn't allow her to admit to being less than anyone else, so she was stunned at what she heard next.

"Cynthia has never lied to me. Never," May said.

Cynthia couldn't believe her ears. She knew she had and she thought her mother knew it, too, but from that day on, so as not to shake Mama's apparent misplaced faith in her, she never told another lie except for the polite social kind.

"This casserole is just delicious," (it's really ghastly) or "Oh, what a darling baby!" (the little mutt looks like a chimpanzee). These kinds of lies are a necessary part of our social structure to avoid hurting a friend's feelings.

GRADUATION WAS GETTING CLOSE. One of the teachers thought it would be nice to make a little memory book, like the high school annual, the *Echo*, but on a less expensive scale. It would be mimeographed, have a construction paper cover and be put together with brass paper fasteners. What a wonderful idea, all agreed, and a discussion was held on a name. Someone suggested the *Re-Echo*. Everyone liked it, so the *Re-Echo* it was.

Different students were given assignments for the class prophecy, the class will, etc. Cynthia was elated when she was chosen to write the class poem. It was about remembering and cherishing the memories of teachers and school friends over the years to come. Her teachers thought it was remarkable. Her classmates liked it too. She still has the memory book with her poem on the first page, put away in a box with other school pictures and mementos.

THE SUMMER before she entered high school, she met a boy at the beach who was older than she was by five years. He and his friends knew about her and didn't care. They ran around the beach together, went to Mission Beach, spent hours riding the streetcars to the end of the lines and back, and took long walks around Coronado in the evening. He liked to dance, but Cynthia was too young to get into a dance hall. She liked to roller skate, but he didn't. The friendship lasted for about two years, then fizzled out.

She and Vera were getting older. Cynthia was fourteen now, Vera fifteen. Her sister, Jackie, got invitations to Marine Flying Squadron dances and those put on by various Navy ships in a building in Balboa Park or on the Broadway Pier and she began taking Vera along. She also got invitations to dinner aboard some of the ships in the bay and took Vera to those too, so Vera and Cynthia went their different ways for a year or two... Vera to the Saturday night dances, Cynthia to the Ocean Beach skating rink. They still saw each other every day at school and on some weekday evenings.

Jackie married a Marine she met at one of the dances and moved away. Cynthia had been trying to get Vera to skate, so they went to the rink. She held Vera up until she got the hang of it and found it was almost as fun as dancing. The rink at Ocean Beach became their favorite place of choice. Some of Cynthia's happiest memories center around her time there, both before and after she got Vera interested. She'd been accepted. No one knew about her. There were no whispers, no pointing, no discrimination. She was one of them. It was a friendly rink; one or two others she'd tried hadn't been. She became a part of the group that went to Los Angeles to skate at the Roller Bowl on one of the movie studio lots when Judy Garland and Mickey Rooney had come in to skate for a while. They rented a cabin and spent two days and a night at Laguna with a married couple acting as chaperones and she saw snow for the very first time in her life. They went on Sunday drives and picnics. One of the boys had an old funeral limousine; they called themselves the Cadillac Club. They had parties at some of their homes, where they played "Spin the bottle," "Gossip," "I'm going on a trip and I'm going to take..." and other harmless, funny, party games. Two boys liked her and she dated both of them. Vera introduced her to Ted one evening at the rink, so then there were three. Kids didn't go steady then like they do today. Unless there was an understanding or an engagement ring, they played the field and dated whomever they pleased. She took a chance with the boy she liked the best and told him about herself. He was the one who politely bowed out of the relationship while being very nice about it. The other she'd lost track of after she came home from her short-lived stay in Los Angeles at Washburn College. She never told him. She told Ted about herself and it made no difference to him.

When she started writing the book she asked Ted, "Do you remember when I told you about myself?"

"Yeah."

"The streetcar conductor Mr. Edwards told all the boys he saw me with about me and lots of times, I got stood up on dates because of him. Who told you first, him or me?"

"You did," Ted said.

"Good." She was glad.

Then Ted told her something she hadn't known.

"The first time he saw me on the streetcar after we were married, he told me we shouldn't have any children because they might be colored."

"He did?" At first, she was shocked, then she started to laugh.

"That old busy body. It was probably already too late," she said. "Remember I got pregnant the very first month because of that damned slippery diaphragm that had a mind of its own? What business of his was it anyway?"

CHAPTER SIXTY-ONE

From the time a counselor talked to the seventh and eighth graders about college possibilities and requirements, Cynthia knew she wanted to go to San Diego State. She'd heard they had a very good art program, on par with two well-respected art schools in Los Angeles which were expensive. She could pay for the transit company's student passes and art supplies with babysitting and house cleaning money. The State's tuition was low and she'd be living at home so it wouldn't cost her parents much. It made perfect sense to her.

Maybe the trouble came about because she'd kept her dream to herself. Since she wasn't used to communicating with others, she'd said only that she wanted to go to college and take art after graduation, assuming, because of the Depression, that her parents would know she meant State. It was where most of the local kids went. She'd made up her mind, thinking it was all cut and dried, without considering her mother's penchant for keeping up with (or ahead of) the Joneses and doing what wealthy people did, which was send their kids "away" to college. She'd thought Mama would be pleased that she'd be saving them money, but she couldn't have been more wrong.

May had gone out on her own in her teens. Had she been concerned because Cynthia showed no inclination to do the same? Cynthia hadn't lived with them until she was twelve and May held her off at arm's length. They'd had no heart-to-heart mother and daughter talks. May was totally unaware that Cynthia was too insecure, too unsure of herself, and nowhere near ready to leave the nest... the closest thing to security she'd ever had... even though she was well aware that May was trying to push her out of it. May didn't know Cynthia. How could she? Cynthia was beginning to know Mama, but she was never sure how Mama was going to react to anything.

Cynthia had taken the required curriculum to get into State... one semester of chemistry, two of biology, three of English, two of French, and three of history. She also took typing, public speaking, drama, journalism, four semesters of art, and worked on the school paper for three years.

She and Frank, the boy she'd had the crush on since sixth grade, the one who'd walked away from sitting with her at the movies, were assigned to share a table in chemistry in her freshman year. For four years, if she'd seen him a block away, her heart started pounding in her chest so hard she couldn't breathe. It was common knowledge since sixth grade that he was her heartthrob. She'd been teased about it and probably he had to, but he'd always been friendly toward her when they met on the street or the school grounds. Now, four years later, the fire in Cynthia's heart had gone out. She could work alongside him, talk to him without falling apart, and, to her amusement, he seemed to be just a little disappointed.

During her years in high school, Cynthia had drawings in a county-wide school art contest exhibited in Balboa Park, was appointed roving reporter on high school doings for the Coronado paper, and had some little verses printed in it. Her scrapbook and art portfolio were becoming a source of pride to her. She thought her future was all set and she was happy for one of the few times in her life since she'd lost the connection with her golden sparkly feeling. She had no idea that State was not to be. Mama had been making plans to send her to Washburn College in Los Angeles.

CHAPTER SIXTY-TWO

The dance hall in Tent City had been closed for quite a while. Prior to Tent City's death throes, when Cynthia was small, she remembered hearing the music and seeing people moving about in time to the music. Now, years later, the word was that the handsome old building was going to be reopened as a skating rink. A skating rink! In Coronado! Cynthia could hardly wait.

About that same time, Errol Flynn, the dashing movie hero, disappeared. His not-so-well-known friend, actor Patric Knowles, was also missing. The papers were filled with speculations about the disappearance... Kidnapped? Foul play? Publicity stunt? No one knew.

In the meantime, the rink opened. The two girls kept their skates at Ocean Beach and went to get them so they could check it out. Partway through their first evening, the missing stars came in. They'd taken off just for the fun of it and come to Coronado. Had they been at the Coronado Hotel or had they come down in Flynn's yacht? Cynthia couldn't remember. What she did remember was that they'd come in, watched the skaters for a while, then rented skates and were out on the floor when a "change partners" was called. All the girls who were there that night got to skate with them. Wow! Truth was, the changes came pretty fast as the boys moved up to the next girl in line when the whistle blew, so the moment of glory was short-lived. Neither Vera nor Cynthia had any special memory of anything other than smiling, saying hello, and that they'd gotten to skate with a couple of movie stars for a couple of minutes.

The two of them had spoken to Flynn once before anyway when he'd come down to Coronado on his yacht during the time he was married to Lily Damita. They'd gone to the Coronado Boathouse and were walking out on the docks looking for his yacht. There he was on deck, winding up lines so they spoke to him and he'd answered, completely boggling their minds. His wife, hearing voices, came on deck and joined the conversation. Nothing much was said; the girls were shy. When Flynn and Lily excused themselves politely to go back below deck, they left pleased and surprised that both movie stars had been so charming and friendly to them.

"Weren't they nice?" they asked each other, still flabbergasted at the experience since they'd expected a rebuff.

The rink in Coronado didn't stay open long. There was a scandal. The town buzzed, and rumors flew, but no one knew exactly what had happened except the police and the parents of the girls involved, who kept quiet.

Vera and Cynthia, who many people thought were no better than they should be because they dated sailors and Marines, were happily skating at Ocean Beach on the night of the arrests. Cynthia hadn't cared much for the shape of the old dance floor or the music, having become a skating rink connoisseur of sorts. The kids at Ocean Beach were friends. She hadn't liked skating with boys she knew from school who'd never been friendly and neither had Vera. They'd been uncomfortable in Coronado's rink.

Graduation day was growing closer. Mama came up with the money for senior pictures, the annual, rental for the cap and gown, and fifteen dollars to buy a new outfit for the special occasion.

Cynthia went shopping alone because that day Vera's mother

was making her dress. Cynthia could sew but wasn't experienced enough to tackle a dress-up dress yet. She went to all the stores in downtown San Diego before finding a lavender Princess-style dress with a square neck, short sleeves, and a zipper up the front. To go with it, she bought white medium-heeled shoes with an open toe and a strap around the back. A little was left over so she got a new pair of knee-high hose at the dime store too. She went back to Coronado pleased with her purchases. To her pleasant surprise, Mama was pleased too.

On Ditch Day, a tradition not really sanctioned by the school, the two girls ditched with the other seniors, but since they'd not been invited to any picnics or beach parties, they spent the day together. The two Cinderellas didn't attend their high school prom either. No handsome prince asked them, nor did a fairy godmother appear with beautiful evening gowns or glass slippers. With all the other expenses that May had grumbled about, Cynthia figured they couldn't afford it even if she wanted to go, which she didn't. She and Vera had both agreed they didn't want to go anyway and it wasn't sour grapes, it was true. They had no close relationships with anyone they went to school with.

On graduation night, Cynthia put on her new dress and shoes and her cap and gown. Both Mama and Papa were going to attend so they drove to the school. After the ceremony, with diploma in hand, Cynthia went to her home room, which was seething with girls in pretty dresses admiring bouquets of flowers or *oohing* and *ahhing* as they opened gift boxes. She turned in her cap and gown and was leaving the room when someone asked, "What did you get?"

"I didn't get anything," and she moved to pass the other girl and go into the hallway.

"Sure you did. Didn't you see the bouquet and the box on your desk?"

"Yeah, but I didn't know they were for me."

She'd seen the flowers and thought they'd been laid there by someone else for a minute. She went back. They were for her, a bouquet of beautiful gladiolas... Mama's favorite and a small box with her name on it. Her heart was pounding as she opened it to find a gold Elgin wristwatch. She put it on and held her arm out proudly to the others who came to see her. In her early years in school, some had told her that her parents didn't love her. Now they could see they'd been wrong.

She went out to find Mama and Papa.

"How do you like your present?" asked May.

"Oh, it's just beautiful Mama. And the flowers too. Thank you, thank you."

Feeling like she could burst with happiness, she kissed her mother on the cheek and beamed at Papa. She could tell that all he wanted to do was get out of there and go home, so as soon as she found Vera and they exchanged their gifts for each other, they left.

Cynthia had expected nothing. Still, she should have known that her mother would do what was expected. May always did the right thing, even if not always for the right reason.

CYNTHIA'S annual remains just as pristine to this day as the day they were passed out to those who'd paid for them. She'd waited to see if anyone was going to ask her to sign theirs and then she'd have asked them to sign hers, too. When no one asked, she didn't hang around. She left and went home.

Mama asked to see it and Cynthia handed it over. May turned the pages, saying nothing. When she handed it back, "Didn't anyone want to sign your book?" she asked.

"No, and I didn't want them to."

"Oh," May said.

CHAPTER SIXTY-THREE

Pride. One of the seven deadly sins, but in moderation, essential to one's self esteem. Cynthia had it instilled in her by Papa with his lectures on not being like every other Tom, Dick, or Harry. Mama taught her both by example and osmosis. The pride of the Scots is legend.

One of May's sayings was, "Anyone can shit on my doorstep, but when they ring the bell and ask for paper, that's the last straw." Cynthia felt the same way. She gave no one who shit on her doorstep a second chance. She wasn't rude to the girls she was in school with, the ones who'd tormented her or called her names in the first few years of grade school. She was indifferent, or pretended to be. In high school, when they jockeyed for seats next to her in study hall to watch her draw and ask questions, trying to be friendly, she was polite, but no more than that. She kept herself aloof, not allowing them to get any closer to her than the seat beside her.

She'd learned about hypocrisy, cruelty, prejudice, and hatred from some of these same girls so she was never disappointed in a relationship as Mama, Vera, and Vera's mother had been. She went into any new association with a "wait and see" attitude. If it fell apart, it was no more than she'd expected. If it turned out well, that was fine and dandy.

She walked with her head high, looking people in the eye, but never speaking or smiling unless they did it first.

"My pride hurt no one but me," Cynthia thought. "It put a second fence between others and myself, holding them off at arm's length. They'd done it to me so it was tit for tat. Perhaps some who may have wanted to be friends, now that we were older, were reluctant to make the first move for fear of a rebuff from me, but that's all water under the bridge now. I didn't give them a chance. I didn't erect the fence to begin with; they did, to keep me out. I learned to live with it, building my own fence while telling myself I didn't need them or want anything from them. It didn't hurt them; it hurt me. All seven of the deadly sins hurt the person who practices them. Like hatred, pride is a boomerang."

Fifty years after high school, in 1989, it was Cynthia who, with several other girls still in the area helping, located as many of their senior class as she could, what with war losses and marriages changing names in the years between, for a reunion. To her great surprise, those who came seemed glad to see her and at the end of the evening, gave her a standing ovation. She found herself blinking back tears while she grinned like an idiot.

CHAPTER SIXTY-FOUR

Vera and Cynthia always double dated, feeling it was safer, except on the nights Vera went to Navy dances or to wrestling matches with her sister. On those nights, Cynthia sometimes dated other fellows or went to the rink alone. They had a policy never to go with a guy alone in a car so she had no problems except with guys who tried to get a little too chummy in a dark theater. Once she remembered telling an over amorous sailor to leave her alone when he started getting too free with his hands.

"What did you come in here with me for?" he asked.

"To see the movie. What else?" she'd whispered back angrily, and he left her alone. She made the mistake of walking back down to the ferry with him and he gave her some trouble when they cut through a small park on the way. He didn't get too aggressive so it wasn't anything she couldn't handle. She never saw him again and it was no great loss.

Since she'd met Ted, she'd been going out with him pretty often, but he was on maneuvers on San Clemente Island the night she and Vera met a couple of guys. It turned out, when Cynthia told them her name, one of them knew a fellow she'd dated a couple of times and he'd mentioned knowing her. An alarm should have gone off in her head, but it didn't. To the girls, that was almost like an introduction, and they made a date to meet on the San Diego side for the movies that weekend.

They were waiting in two cars when the girls arrived.

"No way," the girls said, so it was agreed that they'd go to a meeting place, leave one of the cars and all go in the other. Reluctantly, the girls decided it was probably all right and they separated. Neither of them had any idea where it was the boys planned to meet, which was another mistake.

The guy Cynthia was with didn't drive to the meeting place. She wasn't concerned about it because she didn't know which way they were supposed to go until he stopped in an isolated area with no house or a streetlight in sight. It was out on the Kearny Mesa she realized with a shock.

"What are we doing here? Where's your friend and my girlfriend?"

"Take your clothes off," he demanded.

"What? I will not!" She was suddenly angry and frightened too.

"Yes, you will," and he was all over her, pawing and grabbing at her clothes.

She fought back, managing finally to get one of her shoes off, and began beating him on the head with it, thinking it would make him stop. It only made him angry. He got rougher and began choking her. She couldn't breathe...

"My God, he's going to kill me," she thought. "What can I do? What can I do?'

There was no place to run to and she had no money in her purse, only her father's streetcar pass, but she managed to get the car door open and make a break for it with no idea of where she was or which way to go. He started the motor and began trying to run her down. She tripped in the dark and fell. He won.

She got back into the car. Either way, even if she didn't cooperate, he meant business. She had to make a choice between her life or her virginity.

Afterward, she started to cry and couldn't stop.

"What are you crying about? You've done this plenty of times before."

"I have not," she said angrily through her tears. "Not ever."

"Bill told me all about you. He said you did it with him."

"He's a liar. I never did." The streetcar conductor had seen them together. Now she knew what else he'd been told about her.

His attitude changed. He started the car.

"Where are you taking me?"

"Back to your friend."

When they got to the meeting place, he got right out of the car and went over to Vera and his friend who were standing beside the other car, waiting. Cynthia stayed where she was, still sobbing. Vera came over.

"Where have you been? I was getting worried. What's wrong?"

"He... he... raped me." Cynthia could barely get the words out. Vera was shocked. She turned and went back to the two boys. Cynthia heard her tell them to take them back to the ferry.

"Right now!" Vera was furious.

They got into the car and drove back downtown with Vera in the back seat with Cynthia who was crying all the way to the ferry, on the ferry, and as she and Vera walked to her house. Vera handed her in the front door to Papa, who called upstairs to May. When May came down, Vera left to walk on home alone. Al was too upset to offer to drive her.

May herded Cynthia, still crying, up to the bathroom to clean her up.

"What happened?" she wanted to know.

"I got raped." Cynthia was hoping for sympathy from her mother.

"How did it happen?"

"He was choking me. He was going to choke me to death and

then he tried to run me down with his car. He was going to kill me if I didn't let him do what he wanted, so I let him"

"I would have died first," said May coldly.

May's answer shamed Cynthia. She was hurt by it, but at the same time she was thinking, "Maybe you would have died, but I didn't want to."

It took her a long time to get over it and she was even fearful when she was alone with Ted for a while. She will always believe a rape committed with consent is still a rape if one fears for their life. She was seventeen. She made her choice and got fifty-seven more years of living that she might not have had otherwise. When her period started on time, both she and Mama breathed sighs of relief. She never saw Bill, the lying racist, or Dan, the rapist, ever again.

CHAPTER SIXTY-FIVE

The girl graduates were out of school with the summer ahead of them, their last summer of freedom before circumstance (or was it destiny?) changed their lives.

Just before graduation, Cynthia had broken up with Ted. He was coming on strong for marriage and she wasn't ready. She didn't go to the beach that summer; things were changing. The boys she'd known had jobs now, or maybe it was because she was older. She and Vera spent most of their time together and went as often as possible to the skating rink.

Ocean Beach had closed so the girls tried Mission Beach, but it was too crowded. It had been there longer and was better known than some of the others. The Pacific was downtown below Broadway. They'd heard it had a rough crowd, but a great organist... a blind man who was related to one of the couples who had been May and Al's neighbors on J so many years before... but had it only been four years? Why did it seem so much longer?

The girls felt uncomfortable below Broadway, which was considered unsafe, so when they heard of another rink on Fourth Street, just a storefront down from Broadway, they went there. The floor was small, but there was a live organist so they decided to stay.

Cynthia went into Lerner's one day and discovered little cotton knit sweaters in a variety of pastel colors for ninety-nine cents. They had short sleeves with just a hint of fullness at the shoulder, no collar, with buttons up the front. She bought one and took it to the dollar store, where she matched it to some cotton yard goods and made a full skirt. That evening, she wore the matching skirt with the sweater turned around and buttoned up the back. Vera liked it and, over the next few weeks, they used their babysitting money to buy all the colors... pale pink, powder blue, lavender, aqua, and yellow. Vera made matching pompoms to put on the toes of her skates, but Cynthia stayed with Christmas jingle bells which, long before, she'd tied on with a narrow black velvet ribbon. The other girls at the rink copied them and became known as the Palace Pastels. Cynthia and Vera weren't included with them. They were shy; they didn't know how to mingle and were afraid of being snubbed, so they stuck together, which made the others think they were snobs. It couldn't have been further from the truth.

Vera learned what had been the matter after she and Wood, a floor manager at the rink, began going together and she met some of the other girls through him.

"They thought we were stuck up," she told Cynthia.

"Us?" asked Cynthia and they both laughed.

Cynthia's way with clothes had started a fad at Ocean Beach too. On one very hot summer evening, she'd gone to the ladies room to dab her face with a wet paper towel and unbuttoned the front of her shirt halfway up. She'd tucked the back and sides up under her bra, tied the tails in front and gone back out on the floor to create a sensation with her midriff bared. She didn't care; it was a lot cooler. Some of the other girls did the same and by the next summer, blouses had shown up in the stores that were made to be worn that way.

They went to the rink every night whether they had money or not. Boys they knew asked why they weren't skating and paid their way in. But the weeks were flying by. In August, when Cynthia turned eighteen, May gave her five dollars more than her usual birthday twenty because she'd be buying clothes for college at the August sales.

She bought a light blue pleated wool skirt and sweater set to match, a *dirndl* dress with a wide elasticized waist, brown with sprigs of tiny flowers of the same blue as the sweater, a pair of saddle shoes, two pairs of knee-high socks, two pairs of pajamas, a pair of bedroom scuffs, two bras and six pairs of panties, a clutch purse, and some knee-high stockings. She had a dollar and some change left over!

May looked at all of it and approved, then took her to Marston's and bought a black and white tweed Chesterfield style winter coat with a black velveteen collar, on sale for ten ninety-five. Very nice... Cynthia loved it and wore it for years.

The girls were still dating any nice boy who asked them. Then Vera met a Marine she'd seen before at one of the dances with her sister. They dated for a while, but he wanted more than a platonic relationship and she didn't, so he drifted away. Before Pearl Harbor, he'd married another girl because he'd gotten her pregnant. He was shipped overseas soon after war was declared and was killed. His name was Bob and Vera never forgot him. Cynthia had met a Bob too. Hers was a sailor, the one who broke off their relationship after she told him about herself. She never forgot him either. *Que sera.*

Summer was over. It was time for Cynthia to leave. She and Vera were close to tears when they said their goodbyes. Some of the kids from Ocean Beach, who were going to Los Angeles for the weekend, offered to drive her to the hotel near the college where she was to stay until she got signed up and final arrangements were made with the people for home she was going to work for her room and board.

Her new life was about to begin, but it was going to be over sooner than anyone expected.

CHAPTER SIXTY-SIX

Just before graduation, Cynthia had come home for lunch one day and met Mama just coming out of the kitchen.

"Well, it's all set," May said. "You're going to go to college."

"I know," she said. "I'm going to go to State."

"No you're not. I just signed you up for Washburn."

Cynthia couldn't believe her ears. "But I don't want to go to anyplace but State," she said.

"Your tuition's paid and you'll go to Washburn or you won't go to college at all," May told her.

Cynthia knew that tone of voice. She felt sick. She'd never even heard of Washburn. She went into the kitchen, fixed herself a sandwich and poured a glass of milk. She ate without tasting anything while Mama told her all about Washburn, none of it good as far as she was concerned. It was a business college in Los Angeles, but it had art classes too, Mama assured her.

"Why does she think I need to go to a business college in Los Angeles? Even if it does have art classes?" she wondered as she listened.

"If you don't go, they won't refund the money, so you're going and that's that," May said.

May had spoken. What could Cynthia do? She was only seventeen. All her life she'd tried to do what Mama expected of her, to please her. Did Papa want this too? She resigned herself to go if that's what they both wanted.

Cynthia wondered about the money business long afterward. Had Mama lied about no refund? It seemed likely to her now. Had Mama wanted her out of the house that badly? Or had there been a different reason? Did she want to get Cynthia out of Coronado where everyone knew about her ancestry? Perhaps May had known more about her daughter's problems than Cynthia realized. It was possible. That old "debbil gossip" flew around Coronado on winged feet like Mercury. May wouldn't have a phone, but she did have friends. Cynthia learned years later from her mother's friend with the newsstand that, after she'd left for Washburn, some had thought it was because she was pregnant. It should have been scotched by the fact that she came back to Coronado every weekend, but of course, she wasn't always seen. Her mother's friend, who saw everyone and heard all the gossip, told people it wasn't true, but gossipers hate to give up a good story. Cynthia was back in Coronado again in just about the right amount of time, so they probably cackled and said, "See? Now she's had the baby and she's back."

As Cynthia was writing about this long-buried memory, she was beginning to see the enigmatic mystery that Mama had been to her was perhaps less of an enigma and maybe not so mysterious after all. Mama kept her thoughts and plans to herself, like Cynthia did.

So, against her wishes, she'd be going away from Coronado, the only place she'd ever lived, to a school where she'd have to take classes she didn't want... business and industrial art. What did she need or want with that, when she'd already decided on becoming a dress designer? It was going to be a fiasco; she knew it. And it was. The representative from Washburn had come to Coronado, obtained a list of graduates and, calling on the parents, told them their child was the caliber of student wanted there. With neither Al nor Cynthia present at the sales talk, May had fallen for it hook, line, and sinker. Without saying a word about it to Cynthia, she'd borrowed a thousand dollars of Al's life insurance and signed the papers. It was a *fait accompli.*

Cynthia wondered afterward if Mama had consulted Papa or made up her mind and arranged it all without telling him either.

"I wouldn't be surprised," she told Vera, who thought it was terrible. They'd be separated for two years. What would they do without each other?

Vera made her mind up what to do in five months. She married Wood, who was one of the floor managers at the rink. Cynthia had dated him once or twice, a nice fellow, but not for her, and she'd introduced him to Vera.

"I got so lonely with you gone," Vera told Cynthia when she came back to stay a few months later to find things changed.

CYNTHIA HAD SPENT a semester and a half at Washburn, working for room, board and ten dollars a month pocket money for an elderly couple with a Boston Bull Terrier. The school had a list of people who needed household help, and May had thought this was a great idea. It would save them the ten dollars a month cost of a room near the school. Cynthia didn't want to be a mother's helper or a maid either, but she picked the couple, an elderly lady and her son, a man older than Papa, and the dog... she liked dogs... as the lesser of two evils.

SHE NEVER FORGOT her first day in college. After she checked in, she was told where her classes were and given her locker number. She found the locker first, then looked for the room. The art room door had a window at the top, so she stood on tiptoe and looked inside. To her horror, a nearly nude man was on a dais. He had on a green jock strap sort of thing to cover his privates and that was all. She knew what a jock strap was because she'd seen Papa's hung up to dry with his bathing suit after they'd been to the beach. It was underwear, never meant to be seen in public. As far as she was concerned, this green thing wasn't any different.

She panicked. "I can't go in there," she thought. "It's my first class; I've got to go in there. I can't go in there... I have to... I can't... What am I going to do?"

With her thoughts in a turmoil, she turned to go. But where could she go? Back to her locker... out of the school... anywhere away from there. Then she stopped, took a deep breath and went back to the door.

"I came here to take art and this is an art class. I have to go in there."

She turned the knob, opened the door, went in, found an empty seat and sat. From day one she was disillusioned. She didn't want to draw nude people; she wanted to draw ladies with her designer dresses on their bodies. She didn't want to make color charts or color wheels or draw from still life or design playing card backs. She'd done stuff like that almost all her life... in grade school and high school and at Mrs. Mack's.

In high school, Miss Cook, the art teacher, had excused her from most assignments, letting her do as she pleased then critiquing it as Mrs. Mack had done. She hated having to do beginner stuff again as if she'd never had anything to do with art in her life before. She'd expected to have her talent honed, to be given encouragement, advice and helpful criticism, so she was bitterly disappointed. She got little advice and less encouragement, only grades on assignments she had no interest in. What she did learn about bone and muscle body structure changed her style. She was never able to draw people as well as before she went to Washburn.

Business English was a requirement. She'd learned to write letters and address envelopes in the fourth grade. Charm class was a requirement. Everything they take about was the same stuff about makeup, skin and hair care that was in the women's magazines she got at the drugstore. She was learning nothing that she didn't already know. It was boring. Two other girls agreed with her so they began cutting those two classes to go window shopping a couple of afternoons a week.

As they walked back toward the bus stop one afternoon, she saw an Essex the same color as her parents' car.

"That looks like our car," she said to the other two. As it passed, she saw their dog Bing's head sticking out the window on the driver's side.

"Oops! That *is* our car. It's my parents and our dog. I'm in trouble." Her stomach felt like it had dropped down to her knees.

She ran back into the school and called the old lady, who told her that her parents had been there and were gone. She hadn't even asked them to wait. They'd come to check up on her and she hadn't been in class. Oh boy... big trouble!

She took the bus home the next weekend and thought she was being honest about her cutting class while not saying anything about how often she'd been doing it. She got a lecture from Papa about throwing her educational chances away and Mama was pretty cool. The school had sent a report about the skipped classes and that was the reason they'd come. Some people get away with murder and some people get hoisted on their own petard for much less. Cynthia was one of the latter.

She and Vera went to the rink that night and she went back to Los Angeles late Sunday night to discover, in the morning, that her employers had company for dinner the evening before. The kitchen was a disaster... plates carried out to the kitchen and set everywhere with encrusted food on them and the pots and pans not put to soak. She'd been taught to clean up after herself in the sixth-grade cooking class. She set to work and managed to get the kitchen cleaned up, the dishes done, and breakfast prepared before it was time to leave to catch her bus.

After that, every time she had enough money saved, she took the bus to San Diego for the weekend and every time, they did the same thing. She thought it was a pretty dirty trick. Why couldn't they at least scrape, rinse, stack and soak, and not leave things all over the stove and counters and drainboards like a bunch of slobs? She learned to do the dishes for eight in nothing flat and a lot about organization in the process.

After she'd been with the old lady and her son for a couple of weeks, she was so homesick for Coronado and Vera and everything she knew that she could have died. She thought about Ted. He was a link to everything she loved. She knew he came to Los Angeles with a carload of other Marines every weekend he didn't have duty and stayed at his mother's, so she looked for the name in the phone book and called. He was there, but when he came to the phone, he was very cool... who could blame him? She'd kissed him off before graduation; he'd been coming on too strong for marriage. She began to cry. He melted and said he'd come over and they picked up from where they'd left off. He still wanted her to marry him and she still didn't want to get married... not for a while anyway.

As soon as they were seeing each other again, Ted began showing up to spend Wednesday evenings with Cynthia's parents. He'd made dates with Cynthia the same way. He never asked her for a date; he told her they were going to have one.

"I'll see you on Wednesday," he'd say when they got to her doorstep and on Wednesday he'd show up. She'd thought about not being there when he came, but it wasn't in her to hurt his feelings.

He told Al and May that he was going to call them Mom and Pop, which put May in a mild state of shock. Cynthia could tell when Mama told her about it. Mama wasn't used to being told anything. If any telling was going to be done, she was the one who was going to do it... and not the other way around. Cynthia laughed to herself as she wrote about it.

Ted and Cynthia spent Saturdays and Sunday afternoons together on the weekends when he came up to Los Angeles. It helped a great deal, but she was still homesick for Coronado. She missed Vera terribly; she missed the skating rink. She hated school; she hated the assignments. She was growing more miserable by the week, by the day, by the hour.

The old lady was all right and her son was nice enough, sometimes driving her to the school which was near where he worked and thus saving her the bus fare. Their silly dog, Buster, liked her too, but she was desperately unhappy. She began getting colds and strep throats again and then she got really sick. The old lady was concerned when, day after day, she'd stick her head in the door of the maid's room and ask her if she wanted anything... some soup maybe? But Cynthia, too sick to raise her head from the pillow, whispered no. She'd slept, awakened to crawl on her hands and knees to the bathroom and back, then slept again, not caring about anything, not eating anything for days.

The old lady got scared and called the school. The school called the neighbor with the phone. Al and May lent Ted the Essex and sent him to collect her and her things and bring her back. That was the end of that. She was a college drop out. Papa was disappointed and Mama was *not* pleased. She'd said Washburn or no college at all, leaving Cynthia wondering what was next. She was pretty certain that her art career was a thing of the past and she was right.

It was quiet around the house. Mama was coldly distant. Cynthia, still recovering, was in the doghouse... no mistake about it. Jobs were hard to find, and she had no skills. She looked in the classifieds every day, but they all wanted experience. She was ready to go back to babysitting and house cleaning when, one morning she saw an ad in the paper. A vocational school in San Diego, within walking distance of the ferry, was offering a two-semester *couturier* class in dress designing, pattern drafting and finished sewing. It was just what she'd hoped for at Washburn and been disappointed. She showed the ad to May.

The tuition was only six dollars a semester. She could walk to and from the ferry, spending only ten cents a day for the round trip.

She could babysit for the money for the materials needed. She already had sewing equipment from the class she'd taken in the sixth grade and she'd been sewing for herself ever since.

"You already had your chance and you muffed it," May said. "How do I know you won't mess this one up too?"

"Because this is what I wanted and expected to learn at Washburn and didn't," Cynthia told her.

May thought a minute and then said, "Alright. I'll give you the money for the tuition."

Cynthia took a deep breath. "This is it," she thought. "Just what I wanted all along."

And it was wonderful while it lasted. She had as much sewing experience as the others in the class. Her dress designs were as good, her fashion drawings better. She didn't know then that these would be the last drawings she'd do until she went back to college again in her middle age.

The girls in the class were friendly, but she missed Vera, who was no longer a free agent. Vera had a husband now and a furnished railroad flat to care for. May, with her decision to send Cynthia off to college, had not only changed the path of Cynthia's life, but Vera's as well.

MANY OF THE boys she'd known at the rink were gone. The ones still there thought she was going steady with Ted, backed off and didn't ask for dates. Ted was pressing her to marry him.

"What would you say," she asked Papa one day. "If I married Ted?"

"Well, he certainly seems to have your best interests at heart," Al said after a moment's thought.

Cynthia thought about it too and decided to tell Ted she'd marry him after she finished the classes, so they became engaged. One door opens and another closes, or is it *vice versa*?

No matter, some things are just not meant to be. After she and

Ted were married and Tee Gee was born, she stopped drawing. Now she wondered if Mama had noticed.

After May was gone, Cynthia asked Papa about Washburn.

"It wasn't what I wanted," she told him. "It was all Mama's idea. Was it yours too?"

"I'm sorry, Thum," he said. "I didn't know. Mama took care of the whole thing and I thought you and she had talked it over and you wanted it too."

May had done the same thing with Cynthia's plans for her life that she had done with her mother-in-law's earthly possessions after her death.

Between September and Christmas vacation, the girls learned pattern drafting and couturier finishing, making a notebook of muslin samples of bound buttonholes, slot pockets, and different sorts of seam finishes. They covered purchased dress forms with muslin cut and sewn to fit their bodies and stuffed them to size so that shortly after the first of the year they'd be ready to start draping a block directly on a patron. She never finished the class.

After Christmas, she and Ted eloped to Yuma and were married. She got pregnant the first month and when her morning sickness started, although she was a high school graduate and a married woman, because she was pregnant, she was asked to leave.

BOOK FOUR

CHAPTER SIXTY-SEVEN

Vera and Cynthia sometimes went to a Friday night meeting at a spiritualist church in San Diego if they had the money. For twenty-five cents they wrote a question or asked for a message on a slip of paper, dropped it into the basket, found a seat, and waited for the psychic to find their slips and give them the requested message or answer to their question.

At ages seventeen and eighteen respectively, they were interested in marriage. Vera more so than Cynthia... Cynthia had other plans, but she still wanted to know when it would come about. It was the custom then that if a girl didn't get married right after high school, she worked for a while at a job considered suitable for a woman or went to business school, became a nurse or a beauty operator. Becoming an artist didn't fit that criteria; it was too Bohemian. Twenty-five was the age when one was considered to be an old maid... a fate to be avoided at all costs.

Al didn't like Cynthia and Vera going to the church. He didn't approve of dabbling in the occult, although he was interested in it himself and did a lot of reading on the subject. He warned both girls about the dangers of being influenced by elemental spirits, but with the confidence of youth, they didn't believe it would happen to them and it didn't.

When the psychic picked up a slip, she didn't open it. She held the folded piece of paper to her forehead for a moment, then called out a name. When assured the person was there or knew someone by that name, she answered the question or gave the message. Afterward she opened it, read it, and asked if the message had been understood or if the question had been answered. If it was satisfactory, she'd pick up another slip and continue. When she got to Vera's that evening she told her she'd be married in two years. When she picked up Cynthia's, she told her she would be married a year after Vera.

Vera introduced Cynthia to Ted first, at the Ocean Beach rink. Cynthia introduced Wood to Vera when they started going to the Palace, after she'd gone on a date with him. All their lives, when one of them told someone else that they'd introduced the other to their respective husbands, the other would say, "And we're still friends." It always got a big laugh.

Shared laughter was one of the bonds between them and they saw humor in everything. Once one told the other, "We don't have to get drunk to have a good time; we get drunk just being together." It was true.

Cynthia was out on the floor during 'ladies' fast skating,' which she loved, but Vera didn't care for. When Vera was introduced to three Marines by another fellow they knew, she came out on the floor.

"I just met three Marines," she said as she caught up to Cynthia. "And one of them really wants to meet you."

"Okay." Cynthia followed her over to the snack bar, where she was introduced to the man she would marry two years later.

Like Al had known that May was his wife to be when he first saw her, Cynthia knew that she had just met her future husband.

One of the three had a brand new maroon Willys-Knight. They offered to drive the girls home around the Strand and they accepted.

It was a lovely night, with the moon reflecting off the water and the Strand, living up to its name, gleaming like a silver ribbon. They pulled off at the lookout and walked on the beach for a while before continuing on to Coronado. They dropped the girls off at Vera's after agreeing to meet again at the rink. Vera and Cynthia walked to the school as they always did before separating for the night and, on the way, Cynthia told Vera what she knew.

"That guy who wanted to meet me is going to ask me to marry him," Cynthia told Vera. "And I don't want to." She wanted to be a dress designer first.

"How do you know?"

"I don't know how I know; I just know."

It was true, she didn't know how she knew, but she'd known somehow that very first night that marrying "that guy" was in her stars.

So began the routine of Wednesday evenings together until she broke it off with him a few months later before she left for Washburn. Vera, at twenty, married Wood while Cynthia was away on January 17, 1939, two years after the psychic had told her she would, but neither girl realized it at the time. Cynthia, at nineteen, married Ted a year later on New Year's Eve, December 31, 1940. Several years passed before one of them remembered that what the psychic had told them both had come true.

Cynthia put the idea of marriage on hold, even after she'd accepted the engagement ring. She'd finish school first, find a job, work a while, and then she'd marry Ted. These thoughts, as always, she kept to herself.

On the 30th of December Ted came over. "We've been invited to spend this evening with a couple I know," he said.

It sounded right to Cynthia, so they went. The husband was another Marine and his wife worked in the P.X. Her brother, also present, was a Marine too.

They sat around talking and getting acquainted. The couple had just celebrated their first anniversary and had bought a new car. The wife noticed Cynthia's ring.

"Oh, you're engaged. When are you going to get married?"

"Probably after I finish the dressmaking class I'm taking."

The young wife threw a glance at her husband. "Why wait?" she asked. "We've been talking about taking the car on its first long trip. Why don't you let us drive you to Yuma and get you married tonight?"

Her husband thought it was a good idea. Ted was ecstatic; he thought it was a wonderful idea.

"No, no, too soon. I'm not ready yet," Cynthia told them, but they kept insisting while she kept resisting, feeling overwhelmed. Finally, to shut them up, she told them, "Alright, if you take us right now, right this very minute, I'll go."

She'd thought that would put a stop to the whole thing, but she was wrong. Fate... destiny, whatever... took everything right out of her hands at that point.

Ted jumped up. "I can get off tomorrow, how about you?"

The others said they could too. "C'mon. Let's go to the base and get it all arranged."

Cynthia was swept off her feet to get moving. When they got to the base, Ted, who'd just made sergeant, was required to ask permission before getting married. The officer of the day called the commanding officer, who must have been in a holiday mood because he okayed the marriage. No problem with getting off for the others either because the next day, which was New Year's Eve, was only a half-day anyway.

Cynthia was dismayed; she'd hoped they'd have to report in, but "It's all set; let's go," they said when they got back in the car.

"You're not going to welch on us now, are you?" someone asked.

"No," Cynthia said weakly. She'd made a commitment and she couldn't back out now.

"We have to go to Coronado, though, to get the ring. It's at my house."

Cynthia was stalling for time. When they got to her house, she knew Mama would put a stop to this nonsense, but fate intervened again. Her parents weren't home. A note said they'd gone to play cards with friends. These friends didn't have a phone so she couldn't call them. She got the ring and left another note on the table beside theirs.

"Ted and I have gone to Yuma to get married. Will be back sometime tomorrow."

When her parents came home and found the note, May cried to Al, "Get the car. Get the car. We have to stop them."

"Don't be silly," Al said. "We don't know how long they've been gone and just think a minute... They're saving us the cost of a wedding!"

"Oh," May said and went upstairs to get ready for bed. May didn't know, and neither did Cynthia until much later, that if she and Ted had been married in California, their marriage would not have been legal because of a miscegenation law. Did Al know? Perhaps.

After they got to Yuma, they had some breakfast and found a justice of the peace. Ted realized he didn't have enough money for both the license and the ceremony... payday was after the holiday... so they decided to get the license at the courthouse where it was cheaper, then return to the J.P. That was when Cynthia decided she wanted to be married in an Episcopal church.

The minister, after hearing Cynthia's reason for wanting his church, sat them down in a pew to give them a lecture on the responsibilities of marriage. Cynthia was listening closely, not getting the drift, when Ted interrupted.

"Sir," he said. "I'm already in the Marine Corps."

The minister had thought they might be getting married just so Ted could avoid the draft. When he heard this was not the case, he said, "Let's do this then," and led them to the altar.

Cynthia was married in a five dollar and ninety-five cent rust colored wool suit and a pair of black suede pumps. She'd gotten the suit at Lerner's after-Christmas sale with her usual stipend from Mama and the shoes had been on sale too. She took her marriage vows, knees shaking and fighting back an insane desire to giggle throughout the whole ceremony. Ted gave the minister the last of his money and they headed back home.

The newlyweds sat in the back seat of the car. Instead of cuddling with Ted, who kept trying to get her to sit by him or to move closer to her, she sat as far away from him as she could, looking out the window, seeing nothing.

"Oh, God, what have I done? I just promised my life to Ted and now I'm going to be nothing but a housewife and never get to have an art career." She was right.

When they got back to the house, they got out and the others left. Mama saw them coming up the walk and opened the front door. Ted went in first and went upstairs. Mama blocked Cynthia's way.

"Well now," she said curtly. "You've made your bed, now lie in it and don't come running home to me."

"Don't worry, I won't," Cynthia thought and she never did, not even during the war when they could have saved a little on expenses and she wouldn't have been quite so lonely. She chose to stay in the little house in the canyon in San Diego... just she and Tee Gee... because it was the first place she'd ever called or thought of as home.

PAPA CAME in shortly after they got back from Yuma. He'd gotten the afternoon off for the holiday eve. Mama went upstairs with him while he changed out of his suit and when she came back down, she called Cynthia out to the kitchen.

"I don't want you and Ted doing anything until we can get you fitted for a diaphragm," she said. "Papa is going to talk to Ted."

Cynthia and Ted spent a chaste night that night and the next on the studio couch in the room that had never felt like it belonged to her. Now, being in it with Ted, she felt more like a visiting guest than ever.

On the second of January, unpredictable May took Cynthia to the family doctor to have her fitted for a diaphragm. Then, telling her now that she was a married woman, she'd have to stop wearing pajamas, she took Cynthia to Lerner's and bought her two night-gowns. After that, they went to Jessop's jewelry store where May picked out a pattern and bought a set of Gorham's silver-plate, service for six, for a wedding present. Before going back to Coronado, they stopped at the drugstore, got spermicidal jelly for the diaphragm and, when they got back to the house, May gave Cynthia a lesson on how to use it.

That night, when Cynthia went to the bathroom, the battle lines between her and the diaphragm were drawn. The darned thing had a spring and when the jelly was in it, it was slippery. She'd get it just so, and *sproing!* it slipped out of her hand and flew across the room, leaving a greasy mark where it hit on Mama's gleaming white tile. She wiped it away with a piece of toilet paper and tried again, and again, and again, and again. She was getting hot and perspired and frustrated. The thing had a mind of its own and she was never going to be able to get it in where it belonged.

"What's taking so long?" It was Ted knocking gently at the bath-room door.

"I can't get the darned thing in," she whispered and, when he left, the battle began again. Every night it was the same thing. She was using up toilet paper at a great rate and the tube of jelly was almost empty. One night, when it finally decided to cooperate after the usual resistance and slipped into place, almost all the jelly was off it.

"I should take it out and put more jelly on it," she thought. "But oh, God, I just can't go through that again. It's in and the hell with it."

That was the night Tee Gee was conceived because, when it was due, she missed her period. Mama called her into her consultation room, the kitchen.

"You and Ted didn't before you got married, did you?" she asked.

"Oh no, Mama." Cynthia was so shocked at the question that it showed and she could tell Mama believed her. It was the truth; they hadn't.

Truth was, it was almost worth being pregnant, even after the morning sickness started, not to have to use that damned diaphragm again.

When the doctor confirmed that she was indeed pregnant, Mama called her into the kitchen later that day.

"I know a doctor who'll do an abortion. I can take you to him if you want," she said.

Cynthia was horrified. She believed that things were meant to be. She was pregnant and that must be what God wanted.

"No, Mama, I don't want to have an abortion," she told her mother. Later she told Ted want Mama had said about it.

"You tell her you'll do no such thing," he said.

"Don't worry," she responded. "I already told her no."

Was Cynthia finally beginning to grow up? She hadn't let herself be pushed into something she didn't want to do by Mama for probably the first time in her life... and Mama hadn't tried to force the issue either.

CHAPTER SIXTY-EIGHT

It took seven months for the newlyweds to find a place of their own they could afford. On sixty dollars a month, with a baby on the way, the most they felt they could pay on rent was twenty-two fifty. They checked the classifieds every weekend, borrowed the Essex and went looking, hoping this would be the day. As Cynthia began to show, it got harder. Every place they went it was 'no children allowed' as soon as the landlord got one look at her. They didn't have kids yet. The baby was still only a gleam in his daddy's eye, but it made no difference back then.

Then Ted came in with the news that a Marine he worked with said there was a vacancy in the court where he lived and the landlords allowed kids. They went out that evening to the address. It was perfect, close to a streetcar line, clean and furnished, too. It was two dollars and fifty cents more than they thought they could afford, but they told Ted's friend to tell the landlord that they'd take it and went back to May and Al with the good news. May offered to help out with the fifteen dollars a month until Ted made his next couple of rates. Cynthia accepted, while thinking that her mother wanted them out of her house bad enough to pay to be rid of them.

They had been contributing the fifteen dollars a month rations that Ted got for being in one of the first three pay grades as a married man to help you while they'd been living with her folks. Ted brought him a mimeographed list once a month from which they could pick seven dollars and fifty cents worth of staples and canned goods at no charge, on each of the two paydays in the month.

On the list was flour, sugar, and coffee... canned milk, canned fruits, grade B eggs, and cold storage butter... each item with a price. Ted would come in with two bags loaded with the foods May selected for their use. She'd seemed satisfied with the arrangement and Cynthia used the money they saved on rent to buy things at the dime store for when they found a place.

Borrowing the Essex one last time, they moved their clothes, wedding presents received after May sent out wedding announcements, and Cynthia's purchases. Cash gifts from May's best friend and Ted's father had been used for sheets, pillowcases, pillows, bath towels, pots and pans, and a set of dishes. May bought a new vacuum cleaner and gave Cynthia her old one.

The little house had a small bathroom, a bedroom with a double bed and a chest of drawers and just enough room to add a baby crib. A worn carpet was on the living room floor; the furniture consisted of a worn but serviceable studio couch, two wooden-armed padded chairs, and a floor lamp. The tiny dining area had a divider which was a small China cabinet and a drop-leaf table with four chairs. The kitchen had an icebox, a tiny stove, and a sink which also served as a laundry tray.

There were neutral colored monk's cloth curtains on the four windows in the living and dining room areas and on the front door, which were glassed halfway up. The two windows in the bedroom and one in the bath had shades, but no curtains, as did the kitchen window and the back door, which was also glass at the top. Cynthia bought curtains at, where else?... the dime store, as soon as possible with the first fifteen dollars May had given them to help out. Their first cozy little nest. It was pretty nice, after everything was in place and they were settled.

Vera and Wood lived within walking distance so Vera walked down one afternoon to see how things were coming along.

"My mother met your mother uptown the other day and your mother started to cry," she told Cynthia.

"My mother cried?" Cynthia was at a loss for words... Mama never cried. "What was she crying about?"

"She told my mother you'd been living here for over two weeks now and you haven't invited them over."

Cynthia was incredulous. "I thought she was so glad to be rid of me she'd never want to see me again." It was the truth. Her mother never failed to surprise her.

After Vera left, she went across the narrow street in the court to a neighbor who had a phone to call Papa at the office and invite him and Mama for dinner the following Sunday.

"You'll be making Mama very happy, Thum," he said. "She's been hurt that you haven't asked us over before."

Thus began a tradition of alternating Sunday dinners between the two families whenever Cynthia and Ted were in San Diego, until May's death.

CYNTHIA HATED THE ICEBOX. The two landlords, who opened the court, were brothers named Anderson. They also owned a small appliance store in the business section just up the alley and around a corner. Cynthia and Ted arranged to buy a small refrigerator for sixty dollars, on time for five dollars a month. May co-signed for the loan just a little reluctantly, but they never missed a payment. The doctor got another five dollars a month. Cynthia didn't want to have the baby at the Navy hospital. She was going to have it at Mercy, so Mercy wanted five dollars a month too, on their fifty-dollar fee. And oh, yes, they were still paying Jessop's five dollars a month on Cynthia's ring. Water was paid, but they had to sign up for light and gas. Phones were at a premium. They were unable to get one until after Pearl Harbor, when Ted had to be on call.

At the same time, Vera was pregnant too. Nancy was born six months before Tee Gee arrived. Someone gave them the crib they were using for her and then they got another one from someone else. Vera gave it to Cynthia. She bought an unpainted chest for six dollars, which Ted painted, along with the crib, with dime store paint. The crib didn't have a mattress so May offered to get one as her gift to the new baby. Then, after Tee Gee was born, she bought more things for him. Over the seven years of his life before she died, May gave Tee Gee more love than she'd ever given to Cynthia. Cynthia might well have been jealous, if it had been in her to be, but she was too pleased that Mama loved her baby. It was almost like Mama was loving her too, in a way.

In the court, Cynthia was the newest tenant. No one knew any more than that about her. Most of them were service people who didn't have friends or family in San Diego who might know someone who knew someone who knew Cynthia's secret. She didn't have to be always on guard. She was accepted and made several close friends in the time she lived there.

During the war, while Ted was in the South Pacific, she made one mistake. She told a neighbor with a little boy who'd been born a month before Tee Gee, which whom she'd gotten to be friends, about herself. It had been okay, until later when she and her husband separated. She'd let one of his sisters have the baby and had gone to work for Consolidated Aircraft. She moved in with Cynthia and Tee Gee for just a short while before she found another place. Her husband, who was being nasty about the whole thing, was mad at Cynthia for aiding and abetting her. After his wife left, Cynthia got a few harassing phone calls with name-calling. She knew it was him and it upset her. It wasn't long before he stopped. Apparently, he'd told no one in the court, but it had frightened her and she became more careful. She had Ted and Tee Gee to watch out for now, not just herself anymore.

A thought occurred to her with that memory. She'd comforted herself with the thought that she'd never really tried to pass. Still, she had, just by keeping quiet. Well, she knew now that in passing on purpose or just letting it happen the way she'd done, there was no peace... only feelings of guilt and shame.

CHAPTER SIXTY-NINE

The house on Essex Street would be their home for nearly four and a half years. Tenants left and new ones came, but the "Mr. Andersons" never raised the rent on a tenant already in one of their houses. Throughout the war years, when rents skyrocketed until a lid was put on them by the Office of Price Administration, Cynthia paid twenty-five dollars a month. When they moved out, the newcomers would pay thirty.

Both Andersons were very nice men. Usually one or the other was around to fix things or move anything heavy for the women with husbands overseas who lived in the little sixteen-house court, which, because it was down in a canyon behind an apartment building, May called Sleepy Hollow. The name fit.

Because Cynthia and Ted had no phone, her parents couldn't check on her during the last weeks of her pregnancy. Al began coming out on Wednesdays. Foregoing lunch, he caught the streetcar and came to see how she was doing. After the first time, when he asked Cynthia if she could fix him something, she began preparing lunch for him, giving him leftovers or frying a minute steak and potatoes... a favorite. Even after the birth of Tee Gee, even after they'd gotten a phone, and all during the war when Ted was over-seas, Al continued coming. He liked visiting his daughter and she liked having him come to see her too.

Lunch was a hurry-up affair. He'd dash in to eat and run, not wanting to be late getting back to work. He began leaving her the twenty-five cents his blue-plate special would have cost at the greasy spoon where he'd eaten lunch for years, as a tip.

"You don't have to do that, Papa. We're getting along okay," she told him.

"I want to, Thum. I'd have spent it anyway and I know you can probably use it."

That was true enough. Sometimes the tip bought their dinner so she didn't have to use up something else and sometimes it went into the kitty for an evening with Vera and Wood. She picked up a little extra money during that time by sewing on chevrons for the guys Ted knew when they made their next rate, at fifteen cents a shirt. That helped too.

During the war years, Al's weekly visits broke the monotony of his daughter's life, which was mostly one long day after another. There were the weekly Sunday dinners; she and Vera saw each other as often as possible on Woods' duty days, spending the night together at one or the other's houses with the babies sharing a crib. One night, Vera, whose sister, Jackie, and her husband had been renting the house next door to them, complained that Jackie didn't seem to want to be bothered with her.

"You're more like a sister to me," she told Cynthia. "Than Jackie has ever been."

Cynthia was touched. She thought, but didn't say, "And you're like the sister I never had."

Cynthia still had a protective core of reticence and kept her deepest feelings to herself, never telling Vera how much she loved her until shortly before Vera died.

There were morning kaffeeklatches with the neighbors and trips to Coronado to spend the day with Mama. Even so, there were still long stretches of time... dull days and duller evenings with nothing but the radio and books or magazines after Tee Gee was put to bed. As the months dragged on, she began to hate the U.S. Marine Corps and sometimes even God for what she felt was another abandonment.

SHE WAS a week overdue for the baby. The date had come and gone. *Nada.* One morning she decided to paint some large metal cans that already popped popcorn came in. They bought them for the Sunday night get-togethers with Vera and Wood when they played Hearts, penny-ante poker, or Monopoly, the latest game.

After they got the phone, Vera would call on a Saturday morning.

"We've got almost a dollar. How much do you have?" Wood was on the fire department now and earned about a third more than Ted did.

"I think we've got a quarter and some bottles from last week we can return."

"Shall we come over there or do you want to come here?"

They'd send the men out for the popcorn, strawberry pop and root beer, finishing off the evenings with coffee and cake or pie or tin roofs... vanilla ice cream with chocolate sauce and peanuts.

Over the years, they played whatever game was popular at the time besides Monopoly... Yahtzee, Double Twelve Dominoes, Canasta, Samba, Tripoley, Dammit, Scrabble... everything but Trivial Pursuit, which came out after Wood retired and he and Vera had moved to Oregon.

They pooled what money they had, never keeping track of who put in how much. Sometimes they went to the movies with their shared funds, but more often they played games and visited, taking turns at each other's houses with the babies sleeping in the bedroom.

The two men had not much in common but grew closer over the years. They seemed to understand that the relationship between their wives was going to be a part of their marriages whether they liked it or not and luckily, both chose to accept it. For many, many years, holidays, birthdays, and anniversaries were usually spent together whenever Cynthia and Ted were in San Diego... also picnics, outings to Balboa Park, hot dogs and toasted marshmallows on the beach, trips to the zoo, birthday parties for the kids, and always the Saturday evening games. The only holiday they never spent together was Christmas. Wood's schedule oftentimes forced them to open their presents and celebrate Christmas on Christmas Eve and Cynthia was a traditionalist.

CYNTHIA HAD FINISHED PAINTING the cans and was cleaning up the brushes when a neighbor walked by and saw her.

"What in the world are you doing?" she asked.

"Cleaning up. I just painted these popcorn cans. I'm going to use them for kitchen canisters."

"Don't you know you're not supposed to be around the smell of paint when you're pregnant? You'll have that baby tonight."

Cynthia went into the house to go to the bathroom and, sure enough, she had a show. It was followed an hour later by her first labor pain. When Ted came home, he went across the street, phoned the doctor, and called Al at the office. After dinner, Al and May came over to wait.

Around nine o'clock, when the pains were about fifteen minutes apart, May said, "I think it's time we went to the hospital."

Cynthia was prepped and put into a labor room. Ted came in and was fussing over her, wanting to hug and smooch. She was hot and sweaty and uncomfortable. She told him to go away and leave her alone, which he did. He went to the waiting room and fell asleep. She never really forgave him for that... the least he could have done was stay awake. She had to.

A nurse came in and told May she'd have to leave. May said she'd do no such thing; she was staying right there until the baby came.

Finally the doctor came in and, after looking at the mother's progress, said it would be hours before anything happened and he was going home and back to bed.

"You do," May said. "And I'll call you every fifteen minutes so you won't get any rest. You'll stay right here or I'll know the reason why."

He didn't argue. He went into an empty labor room to do his napping. It was a good thing too, because he no sooner got to sleep when Cynthia got down to the business at hand. May left to find Ted. Left alone, Cynthia looked up at the crucifix on the wall at the foot of her bed.

"Please help me get through this, dear Lord," she pleaded, scared to death about what would happen next. The pains were hard and close together, not much worse than the cramps she had with her terrible periods, but with them she didn't have a baby inside her that had to come out. The Christ on the cross hung there without saying a word, but a voice in her head answered.

"He's not going to help you," it said. "This is something you've got to do all by yourself." With a sense of shock, she realized it was the truth.

A nurse came in, checked, said it was time and Cynthia was whisked away to the delivery room. The baby was coming fast. At the very last moment, when someone said, "Here comes the head," she got a little ether and when she woke up, it was over.

"What did I have?" she asked.

"An eight-pound, two-ounce baby boy."

"Just what my husband wanted. He'll be happy, but I was hoping for a girl," she said. *Que sera sera.*

She didn't get to see the baby. He'd already been taken to the nursery. From start to finish, the whole thing had taken just twelve hours. She saw Ted and Mama for a moment as she was wheeled past them in the hall and taken to her room where it took her a while to get to sleep.

. . .

CYNTHIA DIDN'T GET to see her baby until three days later when her milk came in like gangbusters. Her chest looked like an opera star's and was pulsating with every beat of her heart. It was very uncomfortable. Unfortunately, the supplemental bottle given to the babies in the nursery satisfied the as-yet nameless Tee Gee. He was sound asleep whenever they brought him to her and refused to wake up and nurse. Finally, they had to pump her. She was feeling like she might explode and bits of her bosom would be all over the walls and floor, making a terrible mess!

Mama came in just as they were leaving the room with the milk. She told Cynthia, who was curious about what they'd do with it, that it would be used in the nursery for the supplemental bottles, something that could never be done today because of the risk of AIDS or drugs in the donor's system.

On the third day, Cynthia waited anxiously to see her baby. Mama had said the baby was all right; Ted had said little. The truth was that Ted had never seen a newborn before and since the baby had been born on Halloween, his first look had convinced him that Cynthia had given birth to a goblin.

She heard the cart coming down the hall, stopping at the wards, the babies wailing. Finally a nurse came in and handed her a bundle. With her heart in her throat, she undid the blanket and looked to see if all his fingers and toes were there, then she looked closely at the little face. He did *not* look like the baby in the Gerber baby food ads. He was red; his head went to a point on one side, there was a blister on his upper lip, and little white bumps on his cheeks.

What was wrong with him? He wasn't cute; he was funny looking. She'd never seen a new baby before and her feelings were a lot like Ted's had been. Of course, Ted had admitted nothing about what he'd thought for a long while afterward and by that time, Tee Gee had made a one hundred percent improvement in appearance.

But that day Cynthia felt sick and she was scared. This ugly little thing was her baby? She was going to have to take care of it and live with it for the rest of its life? She just knew there was something the matter with it and everyone was being nice to make her think it was okay. When the nurse came back to collect him, she wanted to voice her questions but was afraid of what they might say.

When Mama came, she quizzed her. "Is he all right? Is he supposed to look the way he does?"

Mama seemed to think he was normal, but was she just trying to be nice?

She was kept flat on her back for ten days, not even allowed to dangle her feet over the edge of the bed. Bedpans were brought and taken away. Bed baths were given every day and the bed was made up with fresh heavy muslin sheets. Her stomach was bound with a wide piece of sheeting wrapped tightly around her torso.

The baby had a silver dollar, provided by Mama, wrapped in gauze over his navel under his belly band to ensure that he'd have a nice flat belly button.

On the tenth day, May was going to come with the car to take Cynthia and the now named baby to Coronado to put her in bed for another week while she took care of Tee Gee and made sure Cynthia would know how to do it when she finally took him home. May arrived, announced at the desk that she was there and came into the ward where Cynthia was the last one left of the four young women who'd all had their babies within a few days of each other. A nurse bustled in with Tee Gee and helped Cynthia out of bed. She stood feeling slightly dizzy with her feet and legs tingling like they were asleep while she watched the nurse get Tee Gee ready to go. She laid him on the bed, unwrapped him, took off his shirt, and, with practiced hands, whipped off his diaper and began dressing him again. Cynthia had seen male puppies, but never a baby boy. It must have shown on her face.

They were in the car when Mama asked her, "Haven't you ever seen a baby boy before?"

"No," Cynthia answered.

"Well, what did you expect?" May asked.

"Not as much as that," Cynthia said and Mama laughed.

In the beginning, when Cynthia and Ted went out on the street with Tee Gee, she made sure his face was covered with a blanket. She was still convinced that he wasn't normal and she was ashamed to have other people see him.

"Oh, may I see the baby?" perfect strangers asked.

"He's asleep right now."

That didn't stop them. They'd lift the blanket to look at him. "Oh, isn't he cute?"

"Are they blind?" she thought as she covered him back up.

Then one day, when he was three months old, he grinned a toothless grin at her. He'd filled out and there were dimples on his cheeks. She'd massaged his head while he was nursing, like Papa had told her to do, so the point was gone. He wasn't red anymore, the milk blister on his lip had disappeared and so had the white pimply things on his cheeks. He was adorable. She fell in love with him that very instant. He was adorable and he was hers. She was pleased with herself for having made such a nice baby.

Wood had come by the court one day to deliver something from Vera while Cynthia was still pregnant with Tee Gee. He stood around like he had something on his mind... and he did.

Wood was a nice man. He'd wanted to let Cynthia know he didn't care about her ancestry, but he had no finesse. His idea of letting her know this was to tell her nigger jokes. So she knew what he was doing and why... that he meant well and that if he'd had any idea, it was bothersome to her on some deep inner level, he'd have been upset.

Ted did the same thing, but she didn't let on to him that it bothered her either, and it did. Especially coming from him. He was her husband. Maybe he didn't care about what she was, but she did. Why didn't he know that? She'd laughed dutifully when Wood did it so's not to embarrass him or make them both uncomfortable. Why couldn't she have been that understanding with Ted? She'd expected more from him in sensitivity and understanding. Had it been too much to hope for? He'd never wanted to listen when she talked about her earlier life, so after a while she closed off a part of herself from him to avoid being hurt like she'd done all her life before she met him. This was a fault of hers, not his, she realized now. He was white; he'd lived on the white side of the fence. She'd lived on the other side. How could he understand anything about being colored? The fence separates everyone, even husbands and wives.

"Cynthia," Wood had finally asked that day. "Do you ever worry about the baby... that it might be... ?" and he trailed off, embarrassed.

"No, Wood," she answered. "I've never even given it a thought."

It was true; she hadn't. She never understood why either, because when she was pregnant with May-May she was worried. She asked the doctor about it and he assured her that the baby wouldn't be any darker than the darkest parent. She knew that wasn't true because Tee Gee was a little darker than she was so she worried. The doctor had also said, "You'll love it no matter what," but she wasn't sure about that either. Maybe she'd been more accurate when she'd told Mama that they were a lot alike than she'd realized.

The blockbuster novel, *Raintree County*, had been a Book-of-the-Month Club selection while she was expecting. It was written so ambiguously that one wasn't sure if the girl was part colored or not, or if she'd had twins and one of them had been colored and was taken away or if she'd only dreamed it. Cynthia read the book and she worried. She needn't have. May-May was born with her father's fair skin and reddish hair. All her worrying had been for nothing.

All that worry had been upsetting to Cynthia physically. She was sick the whole nine months with May-May, throwing up at least once a day. Their latest dog, Binks, part fox terrier, was concerned about her. He laid alongside her on the floor when she lay on the couch reading that darned book, followed her around the house, and went upstairs with her when she went to upchuck. He was so tuned in to her pregnancy, that every time she threw up, he did too... on the floor outside the bathroom door or at the foot of the stairs. It was bad enough cleaning up herself, but then she had to clean up after him as well. It was not funny at the time, but now, forty years later, she has to laugh when she thinks or tells about it. Bless his heart... he was a good dog.

CHAPTER SEVENTY

Cynthia and Ted were back home with the new baby; Cynthia from her stay at her mother's after the birth and Ted from his stay at Camp Elliot after the bombing of Pearl Harbor. They were a family now.

The new daddy came in one day soon afterward with a bundle and a folding canvas baby buggy.

"What's all this?"

"It's things for the baby from the Navy League."

Cynthia was highly insulted. "The Navy League? That's charity," she said. "Take it back and tell them thanks just the same, but we don't need it."

"I can't do that."

"Why not? I won't use it. I don't want it."

"It's a custom," said Ted. "Everyone in the first three pay grades gets a layette when they have a new baby. It's something they do. I can't take it back."

Cynthia had been eyeballing the buggy... they could use it. They didn't have a bassinet. The baby could sleep in it until he was big enough for the crib and they'd have a buggy for later.

"Well, if that's the custom. I guess I could use some of this stuff," she decided. She'd opened the bundle and had been looking at the contents while they were talking about it.

There was a brand-new crib blanket, still in its cellophane wrapper, six heavy flannel diapers she'd never use, two flannel sacques with decorative feather stitching, two undershirts, two gowns, two belly bands, two wrapping blankets, and a hand crocheted sweater with bonnet and booties to match.

While she was expecting, she'd filled the little chest of drawers with things bought piecemeal, a few each payday, at the dime store... rubber pants, quilted cotton lap pads, wrapping blankets, undershirts, gowns, sacques, regular sheets, and rubber sheets for the crib. Mama got her three dozen gauze diapers. Some of the girls from the vocational school chipped in for a nice crib blanket and came by to see the baby. Ted's dad sent a check; his mother sent a few dollars. Some of May's friends gave her gifts to give to Cynthia and a few people at Al's office did the same. The buggy had no pad so they bought one and Cynthia used the thick flannel diapers from the N.L. package to cover it. They came in handy, after all. She used the other things too after she'd swallowed her pride about accepting charity. She was like May in that respect, even though Mama had said, "I'm not anything like you." Cynthia had realized long before that even if Mama wasn't anything like her, she was a lot like Mama.

May had wanted to have the inside of the house painted, so she asked Ted if he would do it and she'd pay him what she would have paid someone else. The sixty dollars he got for that had paid the hospital in full, with ten dollars left over. Before Ted got orders to go overseas, he'd been made first Staff Sergeant, then Tech Sergeant. By the time he made Staff Sergeant, the doctor was paid, as was the wedding ring set and the refrigerator.

AFTER TED WAS MADE Staff Sergeant, with an increase in pay of twelve dollars a month, May stopped giving them the fifteen dollars a month. They'd lost the rations in kind too, but with all their debts paid, they did all right. Vera, who was not the money manager Cynthia was, was a little envious because Cynthia managed to buy materials and findings to make a new dress every other payday and she couldn't, even though they were still making more money. They spent a lot on food, preferring roast steaks while Cynthia and Ted lived on hamburger, chicken, canned tuna and salmon, baked beans and hot dogs, macaroni and cheese, and lots of vegetables. When the meat was gone, Vera ran up bills with the Helms Bakery truck driver and the milkman to tide them over until payday which started them off in the hole each time because those bills had to be paid first.

TED SHIPPED OVER IN 1942. He got about two hundred dollars for reenlisting but couldn't have gotten out if he'd wanted to, not with the country at war. Cynthia and Tee Gee got new clothes from the skin out, and shoes. Ted didn't need anything; he had to be in uniform at all times in public. They got a second-hand Horton washer with a mangle, a Taylor Tot stroller, and a Toidey seat. They also paid off a fifteen-dollar coupon book they'd bought for clothing and necessities at Whitney's. A budget was still necessary, but, by comparison, they were richer than they had been before.

CHAPTER SEVENTY-ONE

When the Japanese bombed Pearl Harbor, six weeks after the baby was born, Cynthia and Ted were in Los Angeles attending the funeral of his brother's wife. The news came over the radio just as they were sitting down to Sunday dinner at his older sister's. They couldn't believe what they were hearing.

They'd come in her parents' car. The Essex had been retired after thirteen years of service; now it was a blue 1937 Ford. Tee Gee had been left with May. Ted's younger sister and her husband, also a Marine, had come with them. All servicemen were ordered to report to their duty stations immediately. They took the time to eat dinner, but no one had much appetite.

On the way home, the highway was lined with service men thumbing rides back to San Diego. They picked up two other Marines; it was all they had room for. No one had much to say.

They took Ted's sister home first, dropped the other Marines off at a base, and returned the car. Ted left to report in at Camp Elliot. Later, her parents drove Cynthia and Tee Gee home. They heard nothing from Ted for over a week, had no idea where he was, and no way to reach him.

All Americans were in a state of shock. It was unreal... we were at war with Japan. What was going to happen next? Rumors flew like swallows returning to Capistrano.

There was concern that Japanese submarines were off the coast of California. There were practice blackouts. The radio was turned on first thing in the morning and wasn't turned off until bedtime. Newsboys shouted headlines about anything and everything that Washington knew and wanted Americans to know.

We'd been caught with our pants down by the Japanese at Pearl Harbor. They'd sneaked up on us like thieves in the night and we were angry. It was the Day of Infamy, never to be forgotten until now. In the nineties, the Japanese and peace lovers, ignorant of how it really was, are accusing us of unnecessary aggression because we dropped the bomb which ended the war, thereby saving many more thousands of American lives. There are those who would let the true facts be forgotten, just like there are those who believe there never was a Holocaust. America did *not* start the war; Japan did and let us not ever forget it.

Life resumed normalcy of a sort. Ted went back to work and came home for dinner except for every third night when he had duty. The Sunday dinners continued and the four friends still played games or went to the movies together on the weekends when neither of the men were on duty. The women in the court still *kaffeeklatched* in the mornings, but the rumors and the changes in their lives that were coming were very much on everyone's mind.

The aircraft industry swung into full gear and people from the Midwest started pouring into San Diego to build planes. The Navy men in the court were gone; the bay was empty. The streets were crowded with men in uniform en route to the South Pacific. All this didn't happen overnight, but it seemed so at the time.

Housing was built for war workers. Wives in military housing whose husbands were overseas were asked to vacate. Cynthia and her neighbors were lucky. They could stay where they were until their husbands came back and they did. Wives who had to leave housing went back home if they had families to go to. What did wives with no family do? Cynthia didn't know.

If she'd been in housing, and they'd been on a list for a place across the street from the Marine base, she could have gone to her parents' house. That wouldn't have been like running home to Mama if something were wrong with the marriage. Even so, she could have done it, but somehow, she never thought of it. 1715 Essex Street was her home now. She and Tee Gee would be there for thirty-three months before Ted came back and the world was at peace again.

A MONTH before Tee Gee's first birthday, Ted got his orders to go overseas. Tee Gee was just beginning to take his first faltering steps from one parent to the other or holding onto the furniture. He took his first steps alone a week later.

The morning of the day Ted left, Cynthia, in her robe, followed him out on their little front stoop. They kissed each other goodbye.

"Don't worry," Ted said. "I'll be back in eighteen months at the most. We'll get this war ended in a hurry."

The bomb did just that, but it took a lot longer than anyone expected.

There was no back-up for the military wife in 1941. No Chaplain or Commanding Officer's wife called. There were four wives with husbands overseas in the court. They were the only morale boosters they had. They were happy for each other when a V-mail letter came. Sometimes days went by with no mail, then two or three letters at once. It was a lift to the spirits, but always there was the underlying fear that the husband could have been killed after the letters were written.

The two Navy men were rotated home at eighteen months with orders for stateside duty. The other Marine wife and Cynthia, who had been friends for a short time, had a falling out and never spoke to each other again.

After Ted left, Tee Gee became fearful and insecure. If Cynthia walked from the living room around the dining area divider into the kitchen or went into another room out of his sight, he began screaming. If she stepped outside the door to check the mail or water the zinnias Ted had planted before he left, even though she was in plain sight, he screamed. The first time, some of the neighbors came running, thinking he was badly hurt. He was, but there was nothing anyone could do for it.

He saw his grandpa every week. May and Cynthia left him with Al on Sundays while they went to the movies. In time he grew less fearful of abandonment, stopped screaming and a bond grew between him and his grandpa.

Ted wrote little notes for Cynthia to read to Tee Gee at the end of his letters. He sent snapshots too, which they looked at together. Film was hard to come by for the people at home so Cynthia was unable to send many photos of Tee Gee as he grew.

They prayed to God every night, asking Him to take care of Daddy and bring him back home safe and sound. Then Tee Gee kissed a picture of Ted that she kept on a low table before he went to bed.

The weeknights they didn't go to Mama's or spend with Vera were very hard for Cynthia. Other husbands in the court came home for dinner, but not hers. Sometimes she and Tee Gee went for a walk at dusk; other times, after supper, they'd take the streetcar downtown to Lindbergh Field to watch a plane land and pretend that Ted was going to be on it. Another night, they'd go to the Santa Fe train station and watch the arriving passengers from the evening train stepping down and dispersing. Often, many were men in uniform.

"Wouldn't it be nice if Daddy was on that train? Look, there's a Marine. See?" she'd ask Tee Gee, half hoping that it would be true, but knowing, of course, that Ted was still somewhere far away and hoping he was still alive, wherever it was.

When Ted finally came home for a thirty-day leave... a stop from the Marine Corps after twenty-seven months... Tee Gee wasn't strange with his daddy like the other children in the court had been. When Ted came around the corner of the little street, Tee Gee ran to him. Ted put his sea bag down and picked up his little boy who had been eleven months old when he went away... now he was more than three years old.

At the end of the thirty days, Ted left to go back overseas for the Okinawa landing and this time Cynthia fell apart. She screamed sometimes too, like Tee Gee had the first time, but not out loud.

CHAPTER SEVENTY-TWO

Two of Cynthia's neighbors in the court separated from their husbands after Ted left. One stayed with her for a short while, then the other did too. It was nice to have the company. After they were settled, both got jobs in the aircraft industry. "No experience necessary. We pay you to learn." It sounded wonderful.

"Mama, could you take care of Tee Gee if I went to work at Consolidated?" Cynthia asked her mother.

"No," said May. "Your place is at home... taking care of your child."

Cynthia was surprised and thought, but didn't say, "You didn't stay home with me. You left me to live with Grandma."

Had May been sorry that she hadn't raised Cynthia herself? Cynthia could have worked and saved money to buy a house sooner than they did, but she stayed home and took care of Tee Gee. She wouldn't trust just anyone to do it and she didn't want Mama mad at her either.

Women working in the aircraft plant changed many things during the war years. Pants suits became popular. Most women would rather have been found dead than wear pants out in public before the war. Many men would have refused to be seen with a woman in pants too. But it wasn't suitable for a woman to be climbing around on an airplane under construction wearing a dress. Long hair might get caught in machinery, so snoods appeared to keep it under control for safety's sake and became fashionable for everyone.

Doing a man's job made women feel less feminine so dresses got fussier, with gathers, flounces, and fringe. Hair styles were fancier too, swept up in the back with curls on top or brushed back and pinned into rolls or chignons. They put silk flowers in their hair or, for glamorous evenings, flowers that glowed in the darkness of a movie theater or a night club.

The dime store sold fiber braids in basic hair colors. These, unbraided and fluffed, were used as rats for the pompadour-like rolls and chignons. Little clusters of imitation curls on a bobby pin were for supplementing one's own curls on a hairstyle. Hat forms, ribbons, flowers, feathers, and veiling to make sexy little hats for an evening on the town were sold in the dime store too.

Also sold were curlers, clippies, and lacquer... real lacquer... for keeping the back of an up-do up. At first, it was poured into the hands for smoothing the hair. Later, spray bottles were sold for it. This stuff wasn't water-soluble, and some women developed lung problems when they sprayed too liberally. It was also flammable. Women who smoked sometimes sprayed at the same time in spite of the warning listed on the container, though Cynthia never heard of anyone setting fire to herself.

There was no time for beauty shops. Women washed their hair at home, put it up on Hollywood curlers or in pincers and covered their heads with scarves if they had to go outside the home. At first, this was considered tacky by some, but soon became much more acceptable.

Occasionally, Mama wanted to keep Tee Gee for a week, taking him home with her, or Cynthia would go home without him. By the third day, she missed him so much, she'd go to get him. She needed him. He was the main reason she got up in the morning to face the day. Waiting for the mailman was another.

Rationing began as many things became scarce. Cynthia lined up with the others to get her stamp book at a nearby school building. The stamps were used like money, but not to replace it. Red and blue hard paper "coins" were used for making change. Red was for meat; blue for canned goods. Sugar was sold in limited amounts. Butter and bacon were in short supply... all needed ration stamps.

"They've got bacon," or "They've got butter." The word was passed along by the woman who'd already gotten hers and was heading for the cash register.

Cynthia stood in a store one day, looking at bottles of chili sauce and wondering if the stuff was hot. It didn't take a blue stamp and ketchup did. Then she thought, "It's only a dime. So what if it's hot? I can just throw it out." Saving the stamp was more important than saving the dime so she bought it and it was great, even better than ketchup. She told Mama about it. May was leery too; she and Al didn't like spicy hot food. Cynthia had to convince her.

"Try it, Mama. Really... it's not hot and besides, it only costs a dime and doesn't need a blue stamp. What've you got to lose?" After the war, neither of them ever went back to ketchup.

Butter was in such short supply that margarine finally came into its own. At the time, it was sold in a box like lard and looked like it too. With it was a capsule or packet of yellow color. Most people mixed in the color and put the mixture in a bowl. Some used it as is. To May, either way was tacky, so she never used it, even in the worst of the Depression, preferring the taste of butter anyway. During the war, she usually had to buy it, but hated mixing it, so Al mixed it for her, packing it back into the box, chilling it and then cutting it into quarters so it looked like butter. It didn't taste like butter, but May used it for the duration because she had to. After the war, many people never went back to the real thing and, in time, it was sold already colored and wrapped the same as butter.

Cynthia gave most of her sugar ration to Mama. Papa took so much sugar in his coffee and May did more baking than Cynthia did for herself and little Tee Gee. She used their red stamps to buy meat for their dinner when she went to Mama's on alternate Sundays and when her parents came to Sunday dinner in Sleepy Hollow. She and Tee Gee didn't eat a lot of meat... bacon when they were lucky, hamburger, and Spam, which many servicemen came home hating and refusing to eat because they got so much of it overseas. She used a lot of eggs and canned soups for just the two of them.

President Roosevelt had a little trick that made May dislike him more than ever. Once in a while, on a Sunday evening, he made the announcement that, as of midnight, all red stamps within a certain expiration date would be cancelled. For some who might be saving stamps for a special occasion, visitors, or a family get-together it was a dirty trick and it never failed to infuriate Cynthia's mother.

Other things besides foodstuffs were rationed too... tires, gasoline, and shoes. Soon, shoes appeared which were made of cloth with plastic soles. They didn't require a stamp so Cynthia gave her shoe stamps to Mama for Papa. She bought Tee Gee cloth sandals and the cloth shoes for herself. To tell the truth, some of the styles were very nice and the neoprene soles wore quite well.

A neighbor who had a car up on blocks in her garage gave May and Al her gasoline and tire ration. Al and May drove Cynthia and Tee Gee home when she came to Coronado and without the extra gas, they'd have to go on the streetcar. It was a thoughtful gesture on the part of the neighbor, which was not at all unusual for the times. People helped other people. It was the friendly thing to do... to help one another in time of need.

Silk stockings disappeared from hosiery counters; presumably, what silk was available was used for making parachutes. Nylons appeared, but not in large quantities. Like bacon, the women who had gotten her one or two pairs to a customer would whisper the word to the others. They were not as she as they are now, had little choice of color, but wore better than silk. Some women stopped runs with a dab of clear polish, but at the dime store, a lady, using as special needle, charged a penny an inch to mend a run, which was much nicer.

The dime store also sold leg makeup. Poured into the hand and smoothed on, it gave the appearance of wearing hose or having a tan. It didn't always go on as smoothly as it should and often rubbed off on clothes, but for some it was better than nothing at all. Bare legs with high heels and a dressy dress were considered tacky.

THERE WERE other things besides doing without that ordinary people were asked to do to help the war effort, like saving bacon grease and straining it into an empty coffee can. When the can was full, it was taken to a butcher for collection. It was said that the grease was used in the making of ammunition.

When a can of food was opened, it was washed out, the label soaked off, the bottom removed, the two lids placed inside and then stepped on to squash it flat. Probably to be melted down for further use. Everyone did it. Cynthia wasn't sure exactly why, but if it helped the war effort, nothing was too much trouble.

Empty toothpaste tubes, which were made of metal then, were supposed to be turned in at the drugstore before another could be purchased, but this was not a hard and fast rule. If you forgot and threw one out, it didn't necessarily mean that they wouldn't sell you another. And there was always baking soda and salt in a pinch.

One thing that Cynthia never knew the why of, as far as the war effort was concerned, was that vests for men's suits disappeared, as did cuffs on men's trousers. Some said it was to save the material for use in uniforms, but if material was already on... Glen plaids for instance... or unsuitable colors, how could it be used for uniforms?

One other thing... a twenty percent luxury tax was put on cosmetics during the war. A lipstick that cost a dollar was now a dollar and twenty cents. Twenty cents more wasn't all that bad and the money was needed for the war effort. The best thing about the luxury tax was that it was dispensed with after the war ended. Not right away, but since tax increases are usually forever, this was rare indeed.

Ted didn't talk about the war when he came home nor for years afterward. While she was writing this chapter, Cynthia read things to him and when she wrote the chapter on rationing in WWII, telling him what had been hard for people back home to get or to go without, he said "It must have gone to Europe. The Marines didn't get it. We didn't get anything, not even uniforms. That's why they called us the raggedy-ass Marines."

"How about meat, butter, and bacon?" she asked.

"We got canned bacon in one of the ration packs, but it was mostly fat. The Aussies sent canned beef, but apparently, they didn't know how to can meat because we could smell the ship before it landed and when they began unloading, our doctors rejected it. It was rotten, so they took it out past the reef and deep-sixed it. All we had was rations."

"I remember you had chickens. They're in one of the snapshots you sent home," Cynthia mentioned.

"I had only six, so we had eggs." (He had shared the tent with two other men). "We had bacon and eggs for breakfast. An Army medical team came ashore and killed four of my chickens and ate them. I went to the colonel and complained. He informed the Army CO that the Marines' area was off-limits to them, but that didn't bring my chickens back."

Cynthia had sent boxes to Ted with cans of bacon and cookies and other things she could no longer remember, but she thought she was only supplementing what the men were receiving from the military. She had no idea that Ted and the other Marines of the First Division were nearly starving.

"We thought we were doing without for our boys," she told him. Had the war in Europe taken precedence over the war in the South Pacific? That certainly hadn't been fair.

She'd always wondered why Ted would eat Spam when she'd

heard other service wives say their husbands had gotten so much of it they wouldn't touch it with a ten-foot pole.

"Didn't you get Spam?" she asked Ted.

"Never saw any of it," Ted told her.

Korea had been the same. The Marines had gone in first with no cold weather gear suitable for the extremes of the Korean winter. Ted came home with only a toe damaged from frostbite. He was lucky; others had fared much worse.

CHAPTER SEVENTY-THREE

Until WWII, many vacant blocks in Coronado were owned by the Spreckels company. Horses from the riding stables on Fourth and Alameda were tethered on them every day to graze on the wild oats and other vegetation that flourished there. Every block had two kitty-cornered paths across the length of it, which were short cuts for everyone... kids and adults alike... for going from here to there. Kids dug caves or tramped the oats down to make hidey-holes to duck into for games of tag or hide-and-seek. Cynthia went into the block across the street from her parents to fly kites, daydream, or watch clouds making pictures in the sky. Her golden sparkly feeling didn't come anymore; she'd lost it long ago.

After the war started, all the empty blocks which had been so much a part of the kids' lives were sold to a company that was going to build houses for the war workers flooding into the area from other cities and states. The houses weren't large; they were stucco and had two or three bedrooms. On Third Street, just a block away from May and Al on an alley corner, was one that had a small curved driveway in front... a good place for a little boy to play. Cynthia went through it, fell in love with it, and decided to buy it. It cost $6500. Ted was a

Marine Gunner now, the equivalent of the Navy's Warrant Officer, so they could afford to make the payments. Wouldn't he be surprised?

She took Mama through the house and she liked it too. She told Cynthia that the agent in charge of sales was someone they knew, a long-time Coronado resident. Cynthia had seen him around town ever since he was a young man and she was just a little girl. He'd grown up in Coronado the same as she had. He and Papa were well acquainted, although he was younger.

Cynthia asked Mama if she'd mind talking to him about her buying the house, which would be more convenient than making a trip back to see him herself. The following Sunday she asked Mama if she'd had a chance to talk to him.

"Yes," answered May. "But he said they won't sell it to you."

"They won't sell it to me? Why not?" Cynthia was disappointed.

"He told me the houses are only for war workers."

"Well, Ted's overseas fighting in the war. I should think that makes him more of a war worker than someone working in an aircraft factory, doesn't it?"

"I told him that," May answered. "But he said they still couldn't sell you one."

Suddenly the light dawned for Cynthia. "Oh," was all she said.

She'd been born and raised in Coronado. Her grandparents had owned their home there. A few other Blacks had owned their homes too. Her parents owned theirs, but now things were different. She'd heard stories about whites moving out of neighborhoods if Blacks moved in, but she wasn't Black and the agent knew it. Did he think Ted was Black? He'd never even seen him. Ted was Welsh and German and he was overseas risking his life to fight for his country. It wasn't fair... it just wasn't fair.

Cynthia and her mother looked at each other. Each of them knew the reason the house wouldn't be sold to her, but neither of them said anything and the subject was dropped. Every time Cynthia walked by the house on the way to her mother's, she felt a pang of regret. She still does when she thinks about it.

CHAPTER SEVENTY-FOUR

Ted's thirty-day leave ended just days before Christmas. He left to report in at San Francisco and wait for space available to return to the South Pacific so his family spent a third Christmas without him. Three of our days later he was still in S.F. Cynthia, taking a chance, went up on the bus with Tee Gee, not knowing if he'd still be there or not. He was, and they got to spend their anniversary together.

All the world, it seemed, was on Market Street that New Year's Eve. Confetti was curb deep. People scooped up handfuls to throw again. Serpentine was everywhere, draped over lamp posts and spiraling down from the windows onto the crowd. It was a night never to be forgotten. Servicemen with girlfriends and civilians too, were on the sidewalks and in the street, elbow to elbow, jostling, calling out greetings, everybody happy in spite of the fact that we were still at war. The tide was about to turn and, at some inner level, people must have known it.

The call came and Ted had to leave. After they got on the bus to the airport and it pulled away, she began to cry and couldn't stop.

The people on the bus who'd seen her kissing the Marine goodbye were giving her compassionate looks, which only made it worse.

Six months. Ted had said, only six months, but a lot can happen in six months. This time she didn't believe him. She was convinced she'd never see him alive again; his luck was being pushed too far. The Marine Corps had it in for them, and God didn't give a damn. Maybe Vera was right about Him after all.

She didn't handle the six months well. She became compulsive about house cleaning. If Vera called to suggest they take the kids to the park or something, she said she couldn't.

"I can't possibly. I'm going to wash the windows today."

If it wasn't windows, it was something else... washing, ironing, changing the paper in the kitchen cupboards, cleaning the house. She was driven and she couldn't sleep at night. Sometimes she went two days without going to bed. She was short-tempered and impatient with Tee Gee and she hated herself for it, but she was possessed; she couldn't control it. Vera was annoyed with her. May didn't know about it.

VE day. What did it mean to her? Nothing. Other men were coming home, sailors and soldiers, but not Ted. She was standing at a streetcar stop with Tee Gee one day, when a young soldier noticed the silver Marine Corps emblem she wore on the lapel of her coat.

"Husband overseas?" he asked.

"Yes."

"How long has he been gone?"

She told him the number of months.

"That's impossible," he said. "They rotate everybody home in eighteen months."

"Well, maybe they did you, but not my husband."

"I don't believe you," he told her. "Nobody stays overseas that long."

Suddenly she was furious. She wanted to hit him. "I don't care whether you believe me or not," she said. "My husband's been overseas that long and I ought to know."

It's a good thing that her car came then or they may have come to blows. She was angry that he seemed to think she was lying.

A SHORT TIME LATER, as she stepped off the streetcar at the Plaza in downtown San Diego, she heard newsboys calling that an atomic bomb had been dropped on Japan.

"Atomic bomb?" she thought. "That sounds like something from Buck Rogers."

When the six months were up, Ted really did come home again, with orders. They'd be going to Camp LeJeune, North Carolina.

They had less than a month to pack up and for him to report in. Two important days occurred while they were on the train. One was Cynthia's twenty-fourth birthday; Victoryover Japan Day (V-J Day) was the other. The war was over. The Japanese had surrendered. Peace at last.

Cynthia had long wanted to have a drink in a club car like she'd seen in the movies; it looked so glamorous. They were going to do it on her birthday, but because of the war's end, the club car was taken off the train. She never even got to see the inside of a club car. *Que sera sera.*

Ted left Cynthia and Tee Gee in New Bern in an antediluvian hotel called the Gaston which, in later years, they laughingly referred to as the Ghastly... enough said.

At the time, a month's stay was the limit, but because Ted was in the service, they were allowed an extra month while he looked for a place for them to live. An older Marine he met offered to let them stay with him and his wife, who were in military housing. They had orders and would be leaving soon. If Ted and his family were already in the house, they'd be allowed to stay.

Ted had come up every weekend while Cynthia and Tee Gee had spent nearly two months of the weekdays alone in New Bern.

Could this be any worse? They accepted the offer. Now the two of them were alone all day with an older woman who'd never had children, in a small two-bedroom house. Cynthia tried to keep out of the way as much as possible and Tee Gee was a very good little boy, but there was no place to go and nothing to do. The two women were polite, but it was strained. However, they survived, and soon the couple and their Irish Setter were packed up and gone.

Tee Gee had his fourth birthday in a house that was nearly empty... their furniture shipped four months before was still *en route*. They were living with what Ted could borrow from the quarter-master and the mess hall and what Cynthia could find to buy in the dime store of the little town not far away... Jacksonville... called J'ville by the Marines. Its main street was all of two blocks long and the sidewalks were rolled up for the night shortly after the sun went down.

THE FIRST TIME Cynthia and Tee Gee went to the commissary, she found herself waiting in line for meat alongside a girl she'd been in high school with for a short while. They recognized each other.

"Oh, God," Cynthia thought as fear grabbed her gut. "She'll blab about me and no one will want to be friends or let their kids play with Tee Gee." But she said, "Hi, Joyce."

"Cynthia Hudgins, isn't it? What are you doing here of all places?"

"My husband's stationed here."

"Oh, he is? Is he a Marine?"

"Yes." What did she think he was? "He's a Marine Gunner."

"A Marine Gunner?" She sounded surprised.

The butcher called her number and the conversation ended.

Cynthia felt sick. For weeks she fretted that Joyce would pass the word and it would be like Coronado all over again, but as time went on, they got acquainted with others and nothing happened except for an odd situation at an officer's wives luncheon, apparently caused by a similarity of names with a Colonel's wife.

Cynthia was seated at the high-ranking end of the long table and when it was discovered by her table mates that she wasn't who they thought she was, she was given an ice-cold shoulder. At the time, she'd thought it was because Joyce had been busy, but later she realized it had only been a mix up and, even later, she remembered that she hadn't told Joyce her married name. It had been snobbery, nothing more. Young wives wearing their husbands' bars, but Cynthia, jumping to conclusions as she always did, anticipating snubs as she always did, had taken it for something else. She didn't attend another wives' luncheon at Camp LeJeune or anyplace else for years afterward until the Commanding Officer's wife appointed her membership chairman for the wives' club at the Naval Mine Depot in Virginia. One did not say no to a C.O.'s wife then, and probably not now either. Incidentally, she never saw Joyce again at the commissary or anyplace else.

In San Diego, a Safeway store was half a block away from Sleepy Hollow and the commissary was downtown by the 11th Naval District building, a long streetcar ride away. Going to the commissary in LeJeune was Cynthia's first experience with military rules for wives since Ted had had to ask permission to get married.

Dresses only. No shorts, no trousers, no children! That last presented a problem since she knew no one to leave four-year-old Tee Gee with. Ted worked five days a week, the store was open the same, so she had to leave Tee Gee at home alone for the hour or so she'd be gone each week.

"Stay inside the house and don't open the door to anyone but me. Don't poke into anything that isn't yours. Play your records or look at your books or play with your cars and your tinker toys. Ok?" She took the bus to the store and shopped as quickly as she could.

Tee Gee would be sitting just inside the screen door waiting. He was such a good little boy, but she was always worried that something would happen while she was gone. Nothing ever did.

While at LeJeune, for in-depth shopping they took a bus to Wilmington once a month. The first time they sat in the bus station, Cynthia noticed there were two lines and two windows for tickets... one for whites and one for coloreds. She was sitting so she could see into the windows. There was a cigar box on the counter between them and all the monies taken in and given out in change went into the one box. This was her first introduction to Jim Crow... two lines... but all the money going to the same place. She poked Ted with her elbow.

"Look at that. The money is going in and out the same box. They let coloreds cook their food and they used to let them nurse their babies, but they can't stand in the same line to buy a bus ticket and they don't mind being handed money that someone colored has had in their pocket. That's just plain stupid."

The colored people went to the back of the bus although everyone stood in the same line to board it. It didn't make any sense.

She was in for a shock when they got to Wilmington. They looked for and found her old friend, the dime store. She needed to use the restroom so, leaving Ted and Tee Gee behind, she went looking for one. Two women's restrooms were side by side; one had a 'white only' sign. Two drinking fountains were on the wall between them. One said colored, the other said white. She stopped dead in her tracks, looking at them. She was stunned; she couldn't believe it. She didn't go into the restroom; she was afraid to. She still thought that some people could tell about her and she'd be ordered to leave and she couldn't bring herself to go into the other. She went back and got Ted to show it to him. They left the store to find a restroom in a restaurant where they decided to have lunch.

ONE AFTERNOON A KNOCK came at the door and she went to see who it was. A very large and very Black lady was on the porch.

"Can I help you?" Cynthia asked her.

The woman said something. It sounded like a question, but

Cynthia couldn't understand a word of it. "Is she using a foreign language?" she asked herself.

"I'm very sorry. Would you mind repeating that?"

The woman spoke again, but Cynthia still could not identify what she was asking.

"I'm so sorry, but I don't understand what it is you want."

On the third try, Cynthia grasped that the woman was asking if she needed housework. "Oh, are you looking for housework?"

The woman nodded. Her vernacular was virtually unrecognizable to Cynthia, who now felt like a fool.

"I'm sorry," she said, cheeks flaming... she could feel it. "I do my own housework. Thanks anyway."

The woman turned away. Cynthia closed the door, feeling sorry for her. The poor woman probably needed work, but why on earth would anyone need someone to help clean a tiny little two-bedroom house? She knew how poor Blacks in the South must be because she'd seen their dilapidated shacks of tar paper and metal roadside signs from the bus window on the way to Wilmington.

TED HAD COME SAFELY home from the war, but he was not unchanged. It took a while before Cynthia noticed it, but he didn't smile as often as he had before. When Tee Gee was a baby, he'd played with him and held him and loved him. Now he barely noticed him. She was in the kitchen one Saturday when Tee Gee came in from outside. Ted was in the living room, reading or listening to the radio.

"Mama," Tee Gee said. "You told me that when Daddy came home, he'd play with me."

Cynthia realized with a pang, "It's true. Ted doesn't play with Tee Gee."

She looked down at him. "I'm sorry, honey," she told him. "I thought he would." Mother and son looked at each other for a minute before Tee Gee went back outside to play by himself.

They were at Camp LeJeune for ten months when Ted was put

back to Master Sergeant and given orders back to San Diego. Their stuff was packed up while he was still Marine Gunner, but by the time it arrived four months later, he was a Master Sergeant, so they were charged overweight for their things. Somehow the papers that would have proved he was still an officer when it was shipped had gotten lost. They had no choice but to pay it.

They'd stayed with Al and May for a couple of months while Ted arranged for housing in Linda Vista. Vera and Wood lived there now too. The house she and Ted were allotted was on the fringe of the colored section, so Cynthia's paranoia surfaced again. Did someone know about her? Is that why they were put in that section? She was certain it was, imagining the colored neighbors were talking about her every time she walked to the bus stop for the whole time they lived there.

A contest on the radio during Cynthia's time in Linda Vista was held. You sent in a telephone number and if your number was called and you knew the answer, you won a lot of money. What the questions were or who put on the show is long forgotten. Since Cynthia had no phone, she sent in the number of the phone booth on their street. She left five-year-old Tee Gee for a few minutes and walked the half block to wait by the booth. Once, a tall, dark colored man approached. She thought he wanted to use the phone and was going to ask if he could wait a few minutes until the calling time for the contest was passed. He had something else in mind.

"Hello," he said. "Waiting for a call?"

"Yes, for that radio contest. You know about it?"

"Yeah," he said. Then, looking her straight in the eye added, "You know, I've had lots of women like you."

Cynthia's heart gave a flip-flop. "Be careful," she told herself, flushing, glad that it was darker now and the streetlight was not very bright.

"Oh?" she said, feeling sure she knew what was coming next. She looked at her watch. "It's past time for the call now. Guess they didn't pick my number. Good night."

She walked away, trying not to hurry too fast, hoping he wasn't following. She called to Tee Gee to unlock the screen door, hurried in, shut the inside door, and locked it. She was now convinced that everyone in the area knew what she was and she never went out without Tee Gee after dark again.

Now, in the nineties, Cynthia wondered if it could be that he thought she was a lady of the evening waiting for a call. Was it done like that in the forties? Possibly, but how could she know? When he'd said, "women like you," she'd thought something quite different, obviously.

Someone had once told her that colored people could tell a person of mixed blood, like she was, by the back of their neck. To her, the back of her neck didn't look any different than the rest of her, but she believed it. One afternoon, as she walked to the bus stop, there were two colored ladies behind her. She could hear them talking, but not what they were saying. She was sure they were looking at the back of her neck and one was telling the other, "Look at her. She's a high yellow, probably trying to pass. Maybe she thinks she can fool some people, but she can't fool me. What do you think?"

THEIR THINGS HAD JUST ARRIVED when Tee Gee had his fifth birthday so it was in a curtain-less house with boxes sitting around still unpacked, but not without furniture this time, but they had a nice Christmas with two trees in the large living room to make up for some of the Christmases they'd missed. May and Al came over for Christmas Eve and Vera and Wood, with Nancy and her little brother. May got a little swacked on eggnog and was enjoying herself. It was a really nice evening, marred only by the fact that Ted had received orders for China and would be leaving before their anniversary again. More months apart... would it ever end? It would also be the last Christmas that all of them would spend together. May would be gone before the year was out.

CHAPTER SEVENTY-FIVE

For once they'd had two Christmases in a row together... the one in North Carolina and the other a year later back in San Diego after Ted received orders to go back overseas between Christmas and New Year's. They'd been in North Carolina less than a year. Two months in a hotel in New Bern, one with the older couple, another in a house with no furniture, and finally, just as it was beginning to feel like home again... orders again.

Just before Christmas, at camp LeJeune, a truck came through the housing area with freshly cut trees from Canada. It was the most beautiful tree they'd ever had, before or since... so lush and green and fragrant, so fresh that there was still snow inside it when they cut the strings to release the branches.

Mama, ever the one to do the latest thing, had decided the year before to have a tree with nothing on it but blue balls and shine a spotlight on it. She had given Cynthia all their old ornaments, including some that had been on their first tree when Cynthia was a baby.

Things were still hard to come by with the war barely over. As they rode the bus around Midway Park, Cynthia looked at other trees in the windows and realized that they had the only tree that was completely decorated. Some had nothing, others had ornaments but no lights, and still others had lights, but no ornaments. She and Ted had been married longer than many of the younger officers, who were called 90-day wonders by the regulars because they'd been pushed so quickly through Officer Candidate Training as a result of the war. Cynthia and Ted had lights, ornaments, tinsel strings, and even a couple of boxes of saved tinsel icicles left over from other years.

Cynthia decided that it was a shame not to share their beautiful tree with others and told Ted to ask his "boys," most of whom had worked under him during their time overseas, young enlisted men and their wives, to come for an Open House.

"We can have it on Christmas Eve and all the ones who are staying on the base can come for eggnog," she told him.

"There's too many of 'em for this little house," he said.

"Well, you don't come and stay for an Open House," she said. "They'll come, have a drink and leave."

"Okay. I'll invite them."

SHE WAS TOTALLY unprepared for what happened. Since there was nothing to do at Camp LeJeune, they all came and they all stayed. The little living room was packed with more than half a dozen couples and several of the single men. They came in a swarm so she'd lost count. The kitchen chairs were brought in, the folding kitchen stool, and even the vanity bench. Some sat on the floor, wives sat on their husband's laps. Some stood, then played musical chairs when others went to the bathroom or to fill their punch cup. Someone took charge of the little record player, which played only one record at a time through a table radio, turning them and putting a new one on. The same Christmas songs and carols, mostly sung by Bing Crosby, kept playing over and over.

Cynthia kept taking the punch bowl to the kitchen to refill it, growing more desperate as the hours passed.

"What's taking so long?" Ted came out once to ask.

"Making more eggnog, but I'm running out of stuff. They weren't supposed to stay all evening. They were supposed to just have a drink or so and leave."

"They've got nothing else to do and no place else to go," he said.

"I know that, but I didn't plan on this."

She ran out of milk and began mixing powdered milk and diluted canned milk. She ran out of eggs, but she had whipped cream and vanilla ice cream, so she used them. The alcoholic content became almost nil, but no one seemed to care. They talked and laughed; the men reminisced about things that happened overseas, with the wives listening or talking amongst themselves. They'd come at seven. Finally, when it was nearing midnight, the bowl of what could no longer be called eggnog was down to dregs. All it had needed at the last was a tablespoon of Karo syrup to qualify as baby formula and the alcohol content wasn't enough to give even a tiny infant a buzz. They began saying their goodbyes and departed, calling "Merry Christmas" to each other as they separated.

"I think they had a good time," Cynthia said after they were gone.

"Sure they did," Ted answered. "They wouldn't have stayed so long if they didn't."

Afterward, Cynthia felt like she'd been the hostess with the mostest! It had certainly been an evening she'd never forget. She'd boldly done something she'd never done before... and it had been a success! Little by little, she was becoming surer of herself... even if it was only one step at a time.

CHAPTER SEVENTY-SIX

The time in Linda Vista a year later was a repeat of the years that Ted was away in the South Pacific. Cynthia and Tee Gee were alone. Vera was within walking distance and the ritual Sunday dinners had begun again, with drives in the backcountry or to take Tee Gee to a kiddy playground in Mission Valley. Cynthia didn't have a phone. Phones were still hard to get and there was no war this time for them to rate one, but there was one on the street half a block away. Cynthia could call Vera and Papa at work if need be. Tee Gee, now five, started kindergarten.

Mama and Cynthia could no longer meet in town to shop and go to a movie with Tee Gee in school, so, May began catching the bus on her day off to come see her daughter and adored grandson. It was always a nice surprise for Cynthia to see Mama standing on her doorstep. She'd fix a simple supper for the three of them and before it got too dark, May caught the bus back to town to go home. Luckily, Cynthia was nearly always at home on these days. Only once did a neighbor tell her that her mother had been there when she was away. She felt terrible that Mama had come and she hadn't been there for her.

Ted was in China only six months when Headquarters, First Marine Division was sent to Guam. The married men were assigned an empty lot in what would be the housing area. The next day, about twenty-five assorted lengths of piling were dumped on it. The following day, assorted Quonset hut parts appeared... floor beams, ribs, plywood, and fiberboard. The men who wanted their wives to join them had to build the Quonsets from scratch. They worked on them after hours on their own time with Ted, who was the handy helping the inept. When the huts were completed and the wives and families arrived and settled in, the Marine Corps docked them their quarter's allowance for the privilege of living in them. It was typical of the high-handed way the military treated married servicemen over fifty years ago when wives were considered excess baggage, more of a bother than anything else. Since husbands had to build the quarters, the wives felt they should have been allowed to live in them free and let the next ones give up their quarters allowance. Ha!

Ted sent Cynthia the papers she'd need to join him in Guam. She and Tee Gee needed shots, a passport, and their furniture would have to go into storage. The huts were furnished. She'd also need extra copies of the orders. She rented a typewriter for that. Six more copies had to be authorized and signed at the Administration Office on the base. This was all one huge pain in the neck... carting the typewriter home on the bus, making the extra copies, returning the typewriter, walking the whole length of the base from the bus stop to the Ad Building and back again on a hot summer day. After all this, only the copy for the furniture storage and one other was needed when she boarded the MATS plane in San Francisco to go to Guam the following October. Typical bureaucratic bushwah, as Papa would say.

Next, it was to the family doctor for shots. Tee Gee's made him sick and Cynthia's smallpox vaccination took with a vengeance. She got it in March and it was December before the scab finally dropped off. Good thing a smallpox bug had never gotten near her; she'd have died for sure since May hadn't allowed her to be vaccinated before.

Now for the passport. She found the office, got the form, and learned she had to have her birth certificate. From there, she went to Mama's to get it. When she was young, she'd seen it a time or two. It was hers, but Mama kept it in the black metal family bond box. She'd noticed nothing unusual about it then, but now, when Mama got it out and handed it to her, she'd seen something she hadn't caught before.

"This is the only one like this," May said as she'd handed it over. "Whatever you do, don't lose it."

Curious, Cynthia looked closely at it. She saw that her mother was listed as white and Papa was too, but now she saw the handwriting in the two spaces was quite different... so that was it.

"Look, Mama. Did you notice the handwriting on Papa's space is different? I wonder why that is."

"It is?" May asked as she leaned forward to take a closer look but made no comment.

From what Mama said about it being the only one like it, Cynthia knew it was something out of the ordinary, but she didn't say anything else. She could see that whatever it was, Mama didn't want to talk about it.

She went to three places that said, "passport photos.'" They were all around the courthouse, fleecing people because each time she took one of the photos to the passport office it was rejected. Finally, they told her where to get one that would be accepted and she returned with it the next day. The lady took the items, saying they'd have to keep the birth certificate. An alarm sounded in Cynthia's head.

"I'll get it back, won't I?"

"No. We have to keep it."

"I can't give it up," Cynthia told her.

"Why not?"

"I just can't. I won't be able to go to Guam to join my husband. I'll just have to stay here," and she started to cry. Tee Gee was only five. He was sitting next to Cynthia, hearing all that was being said. He leaned forward toward his mother with concern.

"It's alright, honey. I'm okay. It's alright. C'mon, we're going to go," and she stood up to leave.

The lady was still trying to understand why Cynthia refused to give up the birth certificate.

"You do want to join your husband, don't you?" she asked with concern.

"Yes, of course I do, but I can't give up my birth certificate."

"Are you adopted?"

Cynthia shook her head.

"Illegitimate?"

Cynthia, shocked at the thought, shook her head again.

"Then what? I can't help you unless you tell me. You have to tell me and I'll see what we can do."

Cynthia, ever the obedient law abider, swallowed hard, The voice of authority had spoken and what she'd said gave her a glimmer of hope. She wanted to join Ted, but she had to keep the certificate. Mama had said not to lose it... she had to obey Mama too. She told her problem, sobbing all the while. The woman had certainly heard tales of woe, but probably not like this one.

"So you see, I have to keep the certificate for my son's sake. I don't want him to be treated the way I've been most of my life."

The woman soothed her, trying to calm her down.

"I can give you a paper," she said. "You can have someone who knows the details of your birth fill it out. Then you have it notarized and bring it back to me."

Cynthia, still sniffling, thanked her, took the paper, and left. She had a headache; she was shaking. She'd told the family secret to a total stranger who might run and tell everyone. She looked at her watch. Papa was still at the office; she'd go to see him. Not telling him why she asked Papa if he could fill out the paper. It was no problem. He went to one of the secretaries and had her type in the information as he gave it to her, then he went to the office notary and it was done. She went back to the passport office and gave the paper to the woman. She looked at it, then at Cynthia.

"Algie Hudgins is your father?"

Cynthia nodded, thinking, "Oh God, she knows Papa."

She thought it was all okay and now she's pulled Papa into it. She had no idea how many people he knew and worked with knew about him. She hurried back to his office with her heart in her throat. He was just getting off work.

"All okay, Thum?" he asked.

"Yes, but I have to talk to you."

They rode the streetcar in silence. When they got on the ferry, she led the way to a quiet spot and poured out the whole story.

"I'm so sorry, Papa, but I didn't know what else to do and then, when I went back, the lady said she knew you."

"Yes, I know her. I've known her for a long time."

He didn't say any more than that about it except, "Let's just keep this between ourselves. There's no need for Mama to know."

After the passport was taken care of, before Cynthia gave the birth certificate back to Mama, she studied it. The 'white' for father was in Mama's handwriting. She asked Papa about it much later.

"When Mama registered your birth, she begged the clerk to put 'white' in both sections. He said he couldn't, but he left the one blank and she did," he told her.

"Oh," Cynthia said.

The rest of the summer passed uneventfully except Tee Gee got mumps and shared them with her. Then it was almost time to go to San Francisco on the train to board the shop that would take them to Guam. They'd stay with Grandma and Grandpa for a few days after their household effects were picked up. The moving van loaded with their gear was just preparing to leave, then a telegram came. If the dependent wanted to fly instead of going by ship, they should send a telegram immediately. They'd be allowed so many pounds of small household effects besides their luggage. Cynthia looked up from reading it just in time to see the back of the van with her household effects turning the corner. Too late now. She was dismayed, but nothing could be done about it. Some of it would go aboard the ship and arrive later. It took the usual four months and then her trunk sat on the dock for another week for some reason and was broken into. Ted lost parts of two tailored uniforms he'd had made in Australia. Cynthia lost dresses she'd made, single shoes from several pairs, other things, and worst of all, a braid of her mother's hair that she wore as a chignon. May had had her long hair bobbed in 1925 and Annie, who had been a hairdresser, made the braid for her.

They put in a claim which the military eventually paid, reimbursing them a mere fraction of the value. No amount of money could have made up for the loss of the uniforms... the material could never be matched, which made them unusable... or the braid, which was irreplaceable.

One last look around, and she and Tee Gee picked up their suitcases, left the keys with a neighbor, said their good-byes, and walked to the bus stop. Tee Gee would have his sixth birthday at his grandma's. It would have been aboard the ship, but they'd decided to have it early to be together one last time before they left.

CHAPTER SEVENTY-SEVEN

The year May died, the new Coronado Mortuary opened for business, and they had open house for a few days. May took Al with her to inspect it. He went along much against his will, just to please her. She went again with the neighbor across the street and when Cynthia came over one afternoon, she dragged her down there after dinner that evening, too.

May seemed to have a fascination with death. Was it because she'd helped her mother to lay out the dead in her youth? She always sensed when someone she knew didn't have long to live and she'd be right. Now she had chosen not to do anything about her cancer, maybe hoping what the doctor said wasn't true and telling only her sister she might have it. She must have known her time was getting short.

Cynthia knew Mama was having problems and not feeling well, but assumed it was the change. Menopause wasn't discussed in those days. A woman might talk about it with a friend or an older woman... her mother if she was still alive... probably not her husband, since female problems were hush-hush over forty years ago. Cynthia was only twenty-six; what did she know about menopause? May had let her think that was what it was.

Like Papa, Cynthia wasn't keen on going to an open house in a mortuary, but like him, she'd do anything to please Mama, so they went. After May's death, Cynthia learned that she had joked to everyone about being its first customer. She'd sold her piano too, shortly before she died, telling everyone she knew she was trading it in for a harp. Then she'd said, "Well, maybe I'll just get a new one." No one had taken it seriously, believing she was joking, but she wasn't, as time would tell.

Cynthia remembered the night they had gone together they'd first looked at the negligees hanging on a rack in the casket room. May had lovingly fingered a blue satin one. Then they'd started around the room looking at the caskets, which were lined around the walls of the room from the most expensive to the least, for the whole funeral package.

Mama had been dead and her ashes at Mt. Hope for weeks when Cynthia, alone in the house one day... Tee Gee was at school, Ted still in Guam and Papa at work... was struck with the memory. She and Mama had started with the most expensive caskets, working their way around the room with Cynthia looking at the prices and making comments about the costs and the quality of the satin linings. She stopped at one that cost three-hundred and fifty dollars.

"Good price," she remarked facetiously. "Nice satin, not top quality, but not too bad. I think I'd take this one."

She moved on before she realized Mama had stayed behind looking at that one.

"My God," she thought now. "That's the one Papa and I picked out for her the day we made arrangements. There wasn't much insurance and we were being practical."

May had sold her piano to a Chula Vista school just a couple of months before she died for that exact amount. The negligee wasn't included in the package so Cynthia went to Marston's and picked out a blue satin one. She was numb at the time, but a part of her must have remembered May looking at the blue one that night.

"Is that why Mama stood there so long that evening after I walked on? Did I unwittingly let Mama think that was the coffin she'd lie in on the day of her funeral? I had no idea then that she knew she was going to die. Did she sell her piano to pay for her funeral? Probably." But Cynthia would always wonder about it.

The morning of the day Cynthia and Tee Gee left for Guam, Papa went to work as usual, but would meet them at the train station later. May fixed breakfast for them and they sat at the table in the kitchen to eat. She was standing at the sink, when suddenly she gave a moan and burst into tears. Cynthia, alarmed, jumped up. She'd never seen Mama cry. She threw her arms around her mother.

"Mama, Mama, what's the matter?"

"Oh, you and Tee Gee are going to go so far away for so long and Tee Gee won't remember his grandma."

Cynthia looked into her mother's face.

"Oh, sure he will, Mama. We'll only be gone two years and you'll send him Toll House cookies and comic books."

May extricated herself and, reaching into her bra for the hanky she always kept tucked there, wiped away her tears and blew her nose. The moment was over. She was in control of herself again.

"I'm sure you're right," she said.

On the train a couple of hours later, Cynthia, looking back as it pulled out and started around the long curve before the station would go out of sight, saw her parents getting smaller and smaller as they stood side by side watching it leave. Just before they disappeared from her view, she saw Mama turn and start walking away with Papa following. It was at that moment the uneasiness she felt all the while she was in Guam inserted itself in her consciousness so when they were notified about the telegram at the message center, she knew exactly what it was going to say.

As it turned out, May was right. Cynthia asked young Tee Gee a few years later if he remembered anything about his grandma.

"Only that she sent me chocolate chip cookies and comic books," he said.

ON THE TRAIN to San Francisco, Cynthia met one of the other wives with a boy younger than Tee Gee and a girl of three or so. To Cynthia, who was twenty-six, their mother seemed younger than herself and not too experienced. The two boys played together with toys from a small bag Aunt Vera had packed with things to be opened one-a-day. Cynthia had packed some rubbery stuff that came in a tube that kids would blow bubbles with. They were very strong, almost like balloons... the latest thing. Even the adults around them were intrigued.

"Where are you and the kids going to stay when we reach 'Frisco?" asked Cynthia.

"I don't know," was the reply.

"You didn't call ahead and make a reservation?"

"No."

"Well, I have a reservation at the Marine Memorial Club. You can stay with me. We'll get extra cots brought in for the kids."

The other young woman appeared to be overwhelmed by traveling with two kids and a little lost, so Cynthia took charge, keeping the boys from being too unruly and when they reached the hotel, making the additional arrangements. After they were settled, Cynthia learned the other woman was a colonel's wife.

"Oh, my God," she thought. "Here I am taking over for a colonel's wife and Ted is only a warrant officer." After they reached Guam, they saw little of each other except in passing. Their quarters were at the upper end of the housing area with other colonels, captains, and the commanding officer. Ted and Cynthia were at the lower end with other warrants and lieutenants.

When the train pulled into San Francisco, the Negro porter opened the doors and pulled down the steps. As each woman stepped off, he took her hand to help her down. He lifted Tee Gee down and set him on the platform, then held out his hand to Cynthia. As she reached the last step, her hand was in his by her bosom, her face level with his. Looking boldly into her eyes with an arrogant expression, he flicked his forefinger on the tip of her right breast. She stared back, startled and shocked. Her eyes widened, but that was all. As she took the last step and he released her hand, she knew she had flushed and was thinking, "Was he letting me know he knows what I am or does he do that to all the large-busted women because he knows they'd be too embarrassed to make a scene? He'd just say it was an accident... but it was no accident. He did that on purpose." She was walking away with Tee Gee by then, but she wanted to turn back and slap his face. Of course she didn't and she would always wonder about it.

The colonel's wife had been impressed with the way Cynthia handled the kids. When it was decided there should be a nursery school for the younger children, she suggested and recommended Cynthia for supervisor.

Cynthia ran the school successfully for four months. The children learned nursery songs and circle games, had free play in the yard for which sand had been trucked in, played with clay provided by Ted, and drew on paper provided by Ted with giant crayons May sent at Cynthia's request. Most of Tee Gee's outside toys ended up on the playground too.

Cynthia rounded the morning with a juice break and a quiet time at the tables with heads on folded arms. Then it was time to go home. She ran her school like a benign concentration camp, the same way it had been done in her kindergarten twenty-one years before. The children were happy; the mothers were pleased and Cynthia earned $50 a month. Ted later told her the mothers had taken over when she left after May died, taking turns with the school, but it had folded shortly after.

"How come?" she asked.

"They couldn't handle the kids like you did," he told her.

"Really?" was all she said, but inside she was smiling.

CHAPTER SEVENTY-EIGHT

Cynthia was the first one of the first nine Marine Corps wives who went to Guam after WWII to step off the plane at Agana Airport. She and Tee Gee had their photograph taken for the Guam newspaper. Others had been on the plane, but when it landed in Hawaii after a rough overnight flight, some had gone off to sight-see and some had friends there.

That first night of the 33-hour flight to Guam, there was turbulence between San Francisco and Hawaii. Cynthia was scared. Tee Gee probably was too, looking into her face.

He asked, "Mama, are you scared?"

Cynthia, who always told the truth after she heard May tell Leroy's mother her daughter never lied, said, "Yes honey, I am."

"Don't worry, Mama. I will take care of you," said her brave little fellow who was just a few days away from six years old.

At the TOQ (Transient Officer's Quarters), Cynthia and Tee Gee showered and were lying down to take a nap when there was a knock at the door. Their pilot was anxious to get the trip over with; would she like to be on the plane? It would be leaving within the hour. She would and so would eight of the others, most of whom had children and were anxious to get the trip behind them, as well as see their husbands again after ten months.

After stops at Midway and Kwajalein, just before the landing at Guam, the plane was sprayed with DDT. The pilot was practicing instrument landing, which involved circling, circling, and more circling, each time coming down a little lower With all that circling, which had been making her dizzy, and the DDT, Cynthia was nauseous when she stepped off the plane.

"How about lunch?" asked Ted.

"Oh, no. I can't. I'm too sick."

She didn't know and he didn't say that the restaurant at the airport closed down after lunch and didn't reopen until dinner time.

"I want to see the Quonset anyway. Okay?"

They drove the narrow road from the airport to Camp Witek, the housing area. The drive made her feel better, but they had to wait until evening before getting anything to eat.

On the drive, she'd had the uneasy feeling that Japanese could still be in the jungle, which came right up to the sides of the road and was so dense you could see only a couple of feet into it at the most... kind of scary.

"Are there Japanese still in there?" she asked Ted.

"No. They're all off the island."

It wasn't true. She'd sensed it. After she left Guam eleven months later, two of the enemy were discovered living in a cave down a hill from the Officer's Club. They'd been surviving on its garbage.

May had a gift of this sort too. One night, when she and Al hadn't been married very long, she shook him awake.

"Al, Al, my aunt just died."

"Huh? What makes you think so?"

"I had a dream. She just died."

Sure enough. Shortly afterward, an envelope edged in black arrived. May's aunt had indeed died on the date that she'd had the dream.

When she first came to the States, Al took May on drives around the area in the Ford Bug he'd built himself. On one of the trips to the local Mission in the valley, May gave a shudder.

"There are Indians here," she said.

"Nah," Al answered. "There were, but they're all gone. There aren't any here now."

When they got to the mission, a priest met them and took them on a tour of the grounds.

"Are there any Indians here?" May asked them.

"As a matter of fact, there are," he told her. "Right over there, near where you just drove up, there's an old Indian cemetery."

"See?" said May. "I knew there were Indians around here."

THAT FIRST NIGHT IN GUAM, after they'd eaten at the Agana Airport restaurant and gone back to the barn-like Quonset hut, Ted asked "How about going to a movie?"

"Sure," Cynthia said, "Do they have a theater here?"

"Not exactly," he answered, "But they do show movies at the camp."

So off they went, with Cynthia expecting to go inside a building, but the screen and benches were in an outside amphitheater of sorts. It had no cover, like the outdoor theater in Tent City had had, but had benches in rows going up the side of a hill. When the film started, it started to rain.

"Let's get out of here," Cynthia said. "We're going to get all wet." So they left... but she noticed that no one else did.

A few nights with nothing to do after she was unpacked and was as settled as one can be when camping out, which was what the whole ten months in Guam amounted to as it turned out, she realized it rained every day in Guam and every night too.

"Do people go to the movies and sit in the rain all the time here?" she asked.

"Yep," said Ted.

"Well, do they just sit there and get wet or what?"

"Oh, they take ponchos and sit in the rain."

"They do? Well, do we have any ponchos?"

"I can get some," Ted said.

"So, why don't you? This sitting around every night with nothing to do is for the birds."

Ted brought home ponchos and after that, they sat in the rain at the movies several times a week. It sure beat doing nothing.

As the housing area filled up, Cynthia noticed many others had a lot of drop-in company.

"Is something wrong with us?" she wondered. "How come people drop in to see our neighbors and no one comes to see us unless we invite them?" she asked Ted.

"Because they serve liquor and we don't," he told her.

"Oh," was all she could say.

A commissary just completed and ready to open for business had burned down the night before the Marine wives arrived. There was an agricultural experimental garden somewhere on the island where some of the wives who had sent their cars on the ship went for vegetables, but for others, vegetables of any kind were at a premium. Women bought celery and heads of lettuce that would be considered garbage in the States and were glad to get them. Occasionally, Ted took a machete and went into the jungle to cut down a small palm tree for the core. The core, called heart of palm, was crunchy, sweet, and nutty. Cynthia made Millionaire Salad with it. She had no recipe, but they did have apples and salvaged stalks of celery. It was a lot like Waldorf salad and it was delicious.

Just-purchased flour, cereal, grains, and pasta of any kind were full of weevils. Cynthia threw much of it away until she learned to bring rice or noodles to a boil and skim off the dead bugs as they floated to the top. Bread that came from the mess bakery looked like it had been sprinkled with pepper. They got used to it, picked off the bugs they could see, buttered it, and ate it, ignoring the ones inside they couldn't see. Papa would have said, "Fresh meat. Can't hurt you. All they've been eating is flour."

One lived intimately with varmints in Guam. Rats, spiders as big as the palm of your hand, centipedes six or more inches long, bugs and lizards everywhere. Some women killed the lizards, but Cynthia couldn't bring herself to do it. They were cute and harmless. Reach into a cupboard for a pot and one might be in it. Dump it back into the cupboard and rinse the pot. It wasn't right to take a life just because it was in your way. The lizards were there first and besides, they ate bugs.

THE SPIDERS WERE ANOTHER MATTER. Ted had written to ask what color she wanted the bathroom. Green would be nice, she wrote back, envisioning a nice pastel. The bathroom was a small cubicle with two doors on springs that slammed them shut. Ted hadn't had time to put door pulls on the inside. The green was deck green, a green so dark it was like walking into a closet when you went into the bathroom and the door slammed behind you. Cynthia went in one day to sit for a while in the tiny room. She glanced in the shower and, in the darkness, not a foot from her was a Guam spider. She squawked and leaped to her feet to get out of the room as fast as she could. No handles on the doors. She tore her fingernails to the quick getting out.

Ted put the pulls on the doors and repainted the bathroom white. It took six coats.

One night as they sat in the cavernous living area of the hut, Ted looked toward Tee Gee's bedroom and, seeing two tiny points of light on the floor, he got up to see what they were. It was a Guam spider lurking just inside the doorway, the light reflecting off its eyes. Ted got the broom and swatted it, but not hard enough. It ran into the living area. He swatted it again and it turned and ran directly toward him. He couldn't move fast enough trying to get away from it. The only direction he could go to get both feet off the ground at the same time was up, so he tried to climb the broom to get away from it. Cynthia, watching, laughed so hard she cried. A grown man trying to do the impossible... shinny up a broom. It was the funniest thing she'd ever seen, like watching something from a Walt Disney cartoon.

THEIR PERSONAL RAT never found a way to get down into the hut. Every night at the same time, he climbed a coconut tree and, coming in one side, crossed the length of the hut on the main beam then went out the other. When the moon was out, they could see him clearly... he was only a dark shape otherwise, but they could hear him when there was no moon at all. Cynthia baked brownies one evening shortly before they turned in and left them to cool on the breakfast bar. There was enough light that night to see the rat. He wanted those brownies in the worst way, walking back and forth, leaning over into the aroma as far as he could to get closer, but it was too high for him. It must have been maddening for him. They fell asleep while he was still trying to figure out some way to get himself a brownie. In the morning, they were cool and untouched. Poor rat.

IT RAINED every day in Guam and because the Quonset had no windows to close, the wind blew rain straight through the hut so everything was always damp. Lights were kept on in the closets and the pantry to keep things from mildewing. Ted put slats in their screens on a single nail at each side, so when it rained, Cynthia could run through the house, turning them up like shutters to break the wind and keep out the worst of the rain. It didn't help the dampness, but it kept the floors and furniture from getting sopping wet.

After they returned stateside, Cynthia's cookbooks and the books she'd taken to read on the plane smelled musty for years afterward, like the cigar smell in Papa's books which is still faintly there twenty-plus years since his death.

. . .

THEY TOOK cold showers for weeks before the electricity was hooked up. Guam was hot and humid, but a warm shower would have been welcome. With only a kerosene stove to cook on, Cynthia made some of the best pies she ever made in her life, learning to judge the temperature with the back of her hand the way generations of women had done before her when there were no thermostats on stoves.

TED ARRANGED to have a kerosene refrigerator brought in from the engineers. A huge, towering rusty white monster and, because it had been the engineers', apparently it was used to men opening its door. From day one, it didn't like Cynthia. She wanted to get something out of it, but it refused to open. She shook and pulled, cursed it, and pulled some more, using all her strength. It rocked and began leaning over like it was going to fall on her, so she'd stop. She swore she could feel waves of hatred coming from it and the feeling was mutual. She couldn't fix a meal unless Ted was there to open it. A touch from him and the door fell open. He'd send one of the engineers over to look at it and the door opened like it was greased. The man would leave; the door wouldn't open. When they were finally issued an electric refrigerator, Cynthia was never happier in her life to see the last of anything as she was that damned kerosene refrigerator.

SOME OF THE men were still working on their Quonset huts for the next group of wives who'd be coming, and a friend asked if Ted would give him a lift back to camp in their borrowed Jeep when he was through for the evening. That night boredom set in the Quonset, so Ted and Tee Gee began playing a game of hide-and-seek. Ted ran into the pantry, which had a door with a latch on the outside because it kept coming open. Finger to her lips, Cynthia showed Tee Gee where Daddy was, tiptoed over and latched the door. They were giggling, waiting for Ted to beat on the door to be let out when there was a knock at the back screen door which was directly across from the pantry. A man she didn't know stood there.

"Ted said he'd give me a lift back to the base when I was through for the night," he said.

"Oh," Cynthia said, thinking *Oh, God, what do I do? What do I say?* And her mind went blank. She couldn't think of anything so she turned and unlatched the pantry door. It slowly swung open and there Ted was, sitting on the bottom shelf, calmly reading a news-paper from a stack on the floor. He jumped up.

"I'll be right with you," he said and went to get his keys.

When Ted returned, Cynthia was on pins and needles. "Did he say anything about you being in the pantry?"

"No."

"He didn't say anything. Did you say anything? Did you tell him what we were doing and why you were in there?"

"No."

"Oh, God. He's going to blab this all over the base and they're going to think we're screwballs," she thought.

Days passed. Cynthia kept asking if anyone at work had said anything. No one had, nor did any wives say anything to her. She kept wondering about what that man might have thought until she went back to the States and forgot all about it.

Time passed... a lot of time... over ten years. Ted was retiring from the Corps. There were trips to Camp Pendleton for papers to be signed, the usual military red tape. Cynthia, waiting in the car one day, saw Ted stop to greet a fellow Marine. Then he came back to the car.

"Did you see who that was?" Ted asked.

"No, you were too far away for me to tell."

He told her.

"Oh. Was that the guy in Guam that time, the one who never told anyone I had you locked in the pantry? He never said anything about it and I always wondered what he thought."

"Well," said Ted. "The first thing he said to me was, 'Where have they been keeping you locked up lately?'"

"Really?" she said, starting to laugh.

A KNOCK CAME at the front screen door of the Quonset hut late one afternoon in Guam. A young Marine stood there.

"There's a typhoon warning," he said. He had also said what number or color, but Cynthia could no longer remember.

"What do I do? What am I supposed to do?" she thought, then remembered that when they'd moved in they'd been given a mimeographed manual about an inch thick with the rules of the housing area and what to do in an emergency. She ran to get it.

Ted had told her that with the possibility of a typhoon, all the engineers would be on twenty-four-hour duty so their wives and families were to be taken to a cave at the camp for safe keeping because they wouldn't be available to help their own. Hastily, she thumbed through the manual until she found what she was supposed to do now that the possibility was here.

It said to move all the furniture to an inside corner of a room and cover it, then gather up all small items and put them into cupboards or drawers. With Tee Gee helping, they did that. Then her brain kicked in.

"We don't know how long this will be for," she told Tee Gee. "Get a change of clean underwear and take the pillow and blanket off your bed and bring them here to me."

Meanwhile, she got the laundry basket and did the same for herself and Ted. A box from Mama had come the day before with candy bars and comic books for Tee Gee so into the basket it went along with coloring books and crayons. They were going to have a roast for dinner, which was done and holding, so she wrapped it, pot and all, in newspapers and a blanket to keep it warm and added it to the pile.

"Get that little bag that Aunt Vera gave you with toys in it for our trip and put some little cars and things into it so you'll have something to play with," she told Tee Gee.

Just as she was finishing packing it all, Ted pulled up in their borrowed Jeep. "All ready?" he asked. "I can't wait long."

"I think so," she said.

When they reached the cave, there were cots set up and the other engineers' wives and children were already there. The men had to leave immediately so as they waited the women talked, wondering what would happen next. They knew they would be safe but were worried about their husbands. Tee Gee had gotten out his coloring books and crayons and little toys so the children were occupied and happy with something to do.

"Did you push all your furniture into a corner and cover it?" Cynthia asked, looking around.

They all shook their heads. None of them had.

"How about your little things? Did you put them in drawers or a closet like the manual said?"

They shook their heads again. She couldn't believe it. They were Marine wives, some of them older than she was. Didn't they know that regulations applied to them too?

It got very late and everyone was getting hungry when Ted came in. "They can't fix anything in the mess kitchen," he said. "Everyone is out on typhoon duty. You'll just have to wait until morning for something to eat."

"I've got our roast," Cynthia told him. "And I even brought a knife to slice it with. If we had bread we could make sandwiches."

"I can get bread," Ted said and left to get it.

Everyone got a warm roast beef sandwich from Cynthia's roast, the men, the wives and the kids, with Hershey bars divided up for dessert.

When Cynthia reviewed that night after the danger had passed and everything in the undamaged Quonset had been put back into place, she thought, "I was the only wife in that whole bunch who was prepared and what I took along took care of the rest of them. I guess I can do fairly well in a crisis." She felt pretty pleased with herself.

THE DEMON STIRRED and raised its head for a moment only once in Guam. Two of the other wives, one of whom had a car, invited Cynthia along on a shopping trip to the Army base. Cynthia and Tee Gee sat in the back seat as a conversation began about colored people. One of the ladies had been at a sale where a colored woman smoking a cigarette had used it to keep other women from getting too close so she could paw through a sale table and get first choice.

"Are you a nigger lover?" The question was directed toward Cynthia.

Cynthia's heart skipped a beat. "They know," she thought. "They've found out about me and they're trying to trap me." Her mind was in the old familiar turmoil, her heart pounding, her ears and cheeks flaming. Then reason took her.

"No. There's no way they could know, but please don't let her turn around and see me like this. Why do I always have to light up like a damned Christmas tree?"

It was only a second or two, but it seemed an eternity before she collected herself to reply as calmly as she could, "No." Then, consumed with shame for her cowardice and self-denial and feeling like a traitor to her family, she sent out a silent apology.

"I'm sorry, Grandma. Please forgive me."

JUST AFTER THEY'D moved into the Quonset, Tee Gee was nearly killed, or at the least badly hurt, by a falling coconut. Cynthia hadn't known before that coconuts came in a big husk and were very heavy. When one hit the metal roof it was like being barraged... a one-coconut war. They clattered down and fell off, hitting the ground with a heavy thud. Tee Gee was outside playing by himself, running around and around the hut. She saw him go past the front windows, then in a minute or so he dashed by again. Meanwhile, a coconut dropped off the tree that leaned over the hut and clattered down the rounded roof. She held her breath. It hit the ground behind him, barely missing him as he ran past the front again. She sucked in her breath. They had no phone. What would she have done if it had hit him? At the time, they were the only ones in the huts built at their end of the housing area. She called him in and kept him inside for the rest of the day.

Soon other wives arrived with children, so Tee Gee had playmates. One day, while he was playing with two other boys, she listened to them. She could hear every word... all they had was screens, no windows.

One of the boys said, "My daddy's a Colonel. What's yours?"

"Mine's a Captain," the other answered.

The first boy asked Tee Gee, "What's your daddy?"

Cynthia wondered what Tee Gee would say and laughed out loud when she heard it. "I dunno," Tee Gee said.

"And as it should be," she thought. "Kids have got no business wearing their father's bars. It's bad enough that so many military wives do."

After almost ten months, Ted came home with the news they were going to be transferred back to the States, so Cynthia wrote to Mama to tell her they'd be back sooner than expected. On Ted's next day off, with the borrowed Jeep, they went shopping for souvenirs. For some reason, Cynthia started talking about Mama. It seems, as she looks back, that she talked of little else that day as they drove to different places looking for things... a pair of lacquer vases, a strand of carved bone beads, hand embroidered linen hankies, which May loved, and a pure silk slip with gorgeous hand embroidery on the bodice. May would never see the slip, but she wore it at her funeral.

The next night Cynthia was alone. Ted had duty and Tee Gee was asleep. There is a Scottish superstition that a tapping is sometimes heard prior to a death. In the early part of the evening, a tapping sound started coming from the single drawer in a table desk that stood on long slender legs. Nothing was in the drawer but writing materials. There was no way for a lizard to get into the drawer and lizards don't tap, they slither.

Cynthia, thinking, "What in the world is that?" got up to open the drawer. Suddenly she was filled with terror. She wanted to open the drawer to see what it was, but she couldn't; she was frozen with fear. She got down on her hands and knees to look under the desk; she looked at it from all sides. There couldn't be anything alive in there. The tapping had no patter... just a steady sound like a dripping faucet. She walked around wringing her hands, wanting to open the drawer, telling herself she was being stupid, but she could not bring herself to do it. It went on for hours until finally she went to bed. In the morning it had stopped. She opened the drawer and nothing was disturbed, no sign of a lizard or anything else.

It was that evening that the knock came at the door and they were told a message was at the message center.

May never got the letter saying that her darling grandchild would be coming home soon. It came in the mail a few days after Cynthia was already back at Papa's. Later, a check on the time would reveal that the tapping in the desk drawer had been at the same time Tee Gee's grandma was dying halfway around the world.

THAT FIRST NIGHT back at Papa's, Cynthia put Tee Gee to bed in her old room, then sat up for a while with Papa while he gave her a moment-by-moment rundown on her mother's last three days on earth. Cynthia hadn't slept once the entire thirty-three hours of the flight so she fell asleep almost as soon as her head hit the pillow.

The second night May came back. Cynthia was lying on one half of her studio couch with Tee Gee asleep on the other, thinking about Mama when she noticed the faintest scent of May's perfume. It was

Friendship's Garden, a spicy carnation cologne. Cynthia had once given Mama some as a gift and she'd liked it so much, she'd worn it ever since.

"It's on the pillowcase," Cynthia thought, sniffing it. May often put scented soaps in the linen closet, but it wasn't. Nor was it on the sheets. As she sniffed about trying to locate it, it grew more noticeable. A faint breeze stirred the curtains and the scent became stronger, filling the room.

They'd never been a family who closed doors. Cynthia didn't approve of children closing the doors to their rooms, not under their parents' roof, nor of a parent expected to knock for permission to enter a kid's room in their home either. Papa was in his and Mama's room just across the landing; and both their doors were open.

"Papa," she called softly. "I smell Mama's perfume."

There was a silence, then, "I smell it too," he said.

The scent had drifted out of the room and across the landing. He got up to come and stand in the doorway. They were silent, both listening, both breathing the perfume, still growing in intensity, both wondering.

"Do you suppose it's Mama come back to see Tee Gee to tell him goodbye?" Cynthia whispered.

"Possibly," Al said.

As the words left his lips, the scent began to lessen. In a moment or two it had faded away completely. Al stood there another moment in silence and then went back to bed. Cynthia lay there for a while sniffing the air until she fell asleep.

TED CAME HOME a few months later. He'd packed up their things and sent them back piecemeal by mail. They got the rest of their stuff out of storage to begin weeding out the extras, selling some of theirs and some of Al and May's until finally it was settled to everyone's satisfaction. Cynthia and Ted moved into her parent's room; Papa and Tee Gee were sharing the other.

Not long after, Cynthia had a dream about Mama. She was coming out of their bedroom to cross the landing, looked down the stairs, and there was Mama standing in the entry looking up at her.

"Oh, Mama, I'm so glad you're back," she cried as she ran down to greet her mother.

May said nothing. Cynthia said, "Come upstairs with me Mama and I'll show you how we've arranged things." She led the way and May followed.

She pointed into the master bedroom telling her that she and Ted were in there now. Then they went into the other room. She took May to the closet first.

"See, Mama? Here are Papa's clothes. There's plenty of room for his things and Tee Gee's too."

Then she opened the drawers of the dresser just outside the closet door. "See Mama? Here's Papa's clean shirts and, in this drawer, his underwear and socks, just like you had them in the other room."

All the while, May had said not one word. Then she gave a shrug and said, "Well, I guess it'll work out all right."

Cynthia woke with a start. Mama had just damned her with faint praise, like she'd always done. It was too real to have been a dream.

"My God," she thought. "Was Mama really just here?"

Afterward, when she thought about the dream, she had to laugh. Her mother's words and the shrug were so characteristic, so like her, that ever since she's been sure her mother came back to check up on her.

May needn't have worried. Cynthia took great care of Papa... as best she could, anyway... for the rest of his life.

Once when she was in high school, she'd held her hands out in front of herself and said, "I have capable hands." May had given a snort and rolled her eyes. It was obvious she didn't think Cynthia was capable of anything.

"I wonder what you'd think about me now, Mama, if you were still around," Cynthia thought. "I'm seventy-four years old. I've been married to Ted for fifty-four years and I didn't come running back to you. I've lived through a typhoon in Guam and hurricane Hazel in Virginia and I was better prepared for both of them than any of the other Marine wives were. I've raised two nice kids and I took care of Papa, too."

CHAPTER SEVENTY-NINE

Al told Cynthia about May's last days after she put Tee Gee to bed on her first night back home from Guam. She hadn't slept for over 30 hours but was too keyed up to go right to bed. Al probably hadn't slept either and he looked exhausted. He needed to talk and she needed to listen. They sat in the living room, he in his 'Papa chair' and her in Mama's.

The Saturday before May hadn't gone grocery shopping as usual. Instead, she asked him to drive her to see her best friend. Millie had sent invitations to her son's wedding which would be the following Tuesday. Al sat in the car and waited for her. She was inside longer than usual and he was getting impatient. What she had been telling Millie was that she was very sorry, but she didn't think she would be able to attend the wedding. When she came back to the car, she said she wanted to take a drive around Coronado. When they got to First Street where there were no houses then, she asked him to stop. She sat looking at the bay and the San Diego skyline for a long time. Finally, she said, "Take me home, Papa." He told Cynthia he realized now that she was saying goodbye to Millie and to the town she had lived in for the past twenty-eight years. She cooked dinner that night, then went to bed earlier than usual.

The next day they didn't do much. Breakfast, reading the paper and they went out for dinner.

"I don't feel like cooking," she said. Afterward, they listened to the radio for a while and she went to bed early again.

The next morning, when he got up, she was already up. He shaved and dressed for work. As he started downstairs, he met her coming slowly back up.

"I'm sorry, Papa," she told him. "I can't fix your breakfast this morning."

"That's okay. I'll do it."

After he'd eaten, he went back up to say he was leaving and to see if she was all right.

"I'm going now," he said.

"Please don't leave me, Papa," she pleaded.

"Alright. I'll take the day off," and he went across the street to the neighbors to call and say he wasn't coming in.

This would be the first Monday in twenty-eight years that May didn't have a wash on the line by nine. The neighbor noticed it, he told Cynthia later. Al had known that things weren't right too.

She slept off and on most of the morning. At noon, he fixed her some soup, but she didn't keep it down. Later she complained she was hot so he went into the garage and found an old radiator fan. He rigged it to blow on her and it seemed to make her a little more comfortable.

Around five o'clock, she called him. She had started bleeding. She was too weak to get out of bed to go to the bathroom so he got a bucket and somehow managed to help her use it.

"Do you want me to call the doctor?" he kept asking, but she told him no.

For the next hour, he emptied blood at intervals into the toilet. He hadn't known at that time that he was flushing her life away, he told his daughter. She grew weaker but didn't want him to leave her.

A minute or two before six, the cat woke up, panicked and ran downstairs. May opened her eyes and, looking up at him, said "Bye." Then she closed her eyes again. He tried to rouse her, but there was no response.

He ran for the neighbors and called the doctor. The neighbor came over, held a mirror to May's face and said, "She's gone." The doctor came and told Al that she'd had a cancer which she didn't want him or Cynthia to know about. It had eaten into an artery and she had bled to death.

Al went back to the neighbors and sent the message to Cynthia, then sat all night with May until morning before he called the Coronado Mortuary.

Cynthia took over running her mother's house and caring for her father. He went back to work after the funeral and kept her scared half to death for months, telling her he thought he'd just step in front of a bus and end it all.

They spent a part of each evening during the time before Ted's orders brought him back to the States, talking about May, trying to fit what each had known about her into an incomplete picture that neither would ever really understand. Her friend, Millie, told Cynthia about May from her point of view and also things that May had told her, that she had never told her husband or daughter.

For years after May's death, Cynthia's faith in God was shaken to the core. She had asked Him to take care of her mother and He had let her die. She found herself siding with Vera's negative belief that He was responsible for bad things that happened. When had He ever answered a prayer for her? Not when she was a kid, when she had prayed to him for a friend or to let her die, and not during the war when she begged for Ted to come back home sooner than he had. He hadn't been listening. "Just like a man,' she thought as she wrote about it.

She decided that He didn't exist. There was no one out there. The people who believed in Him were just wishfully thinking. There was no Heaven, no afterlife, nothing. When you died, you just went 'poof,' snuffed out like a candle and that was that.

For a number of years she found solace in this, but no peace. These were the years that she began to fear she was losing her sanity. Then, one day, she realized that Mama had gotten exactly what she wanted... to die young and to die without pain It was a revelation to Cynthia. She'd just not gotten things the way she'd wanted them. He had made the decision and, for Mama, it had been the right one. She had accepted it without question. Slowly, Cynthia's belief in Him began to return. She hadn't really wanted to accept that, with death, came oblivion. She let Him back into her life and started praying again as she began to see that she had a lot to be thankful for and that sometimes bad things that happened are only so from one's own point of view. You learn and grow from experiences both good and bad, making it easier to manage the next challenge when it comes along.

CHAPTER EIGHTY

Cynthia and Ted and Tee Gee would live with Papa for six years after May's death. They were not good years for Cynthia. It wasn't easy living in Mama's house trying to fit into Mama's shoes, which she felt driven to do. Mama had lived by a strict schedule. Cynthia tried, but just couldn't do it. If it bothered Papa, he didn't say, but it bothered her.

Ted had first been stationed at Camp Pendleton and commuting every day in the Ford. They wouldn't own their first car until after Ted's father died, leaving them enough money to buy a second-hand Buick.

Then came Korea, the police action... the forgotten war. Ted went off again and Cynthia fell apart again. She began having severe migraines every weekend, would throw up, and pass out. Maybe Korea isn't considered a war, but to her it felt the same and it smelled and tasted the same. It isn't any different waiting for a police action to end so Ted could come home again than it had been waiting for WWII to end so Ted could come home again. People get killed in police actions just the same as they do in wars, so the waiting and the worrying and the fears are exactly the same.

. . .

THE MARINES WERE in Korea the first year with no cold weather gear but what they could beg, borrow, or "liberate" from the Navy. Ted just missed being caught at the battle of Chosen Reservoir, but he did come back safely, after a year and a day, with only one frost-bitten toe.

He came home just in time to miss his father's funeral. As Cynthia and Tee Gee came out of the chapel after the service, Ted's plane flew over the cemetery in Los Angeles on its way to San Diego. He'd looked down, then looked at his watch. She'd looked up, then looked at hers. It was a military plane.

"Daddy's probably on that plane," she told Tee Gee.

The Red Cross had mishandled the information concerning Ted's father's demise and not for the first time that Cynthia had asked for their help with something either. He was held up in Hawaii to await space available, instead of being allowed to fly straight through.

This time Ted was stationed at the Marine Base in San Diego and life fell back into its old patterns again. Visiting back and forth with Vera and Wood and their kids, playing games, going to the movies, to the beach and cook-outs in the back yards.

Cynthia had May-May and her demon took over her life again for the next six years. She became anxious and fearful about going to sleep, afraid something terrible would happen that she couldn't stop because she wouldn't know about it. She became compulsive again about keeping the house clean, making a list every morning... make bed, wash dishes, sweep stairs, dust, vacuum, clean baths, wash, iron, fix dinner, crossing everything off as she did it. Her neighbor across the street came over one morning for coffee and saw the list lying on the dining room table. She'd laughed.

"You need a list to remind you to do housework?" she asked.

The list helped keep Cynthia centered. She was afraid to stay in the house alone with the baby, afraid she might do something awful to her. Now they call it postpartum depression, but then it had no name, and she was afraid to tell the doctor about it. She was afraid to go out of the house because she thought everybody on the street was watching her. She had to keep it all inside, no one must know. If they knew or guessed, she'd be locked up. The thought terrified her. She lived in a constant state of fear that she couldn't talk about to anyone, not Vera, not Papa and certainly not Ted, who never wanted to listen to her talk about anything. Still, he did know something was wrong and asked Vera to try to help her.

One morning, just before Tee Gee left for school, she got angry with him about some small thing. From the kitchen window she watched him cross the street and start up the hill. She was washing the dishes when the thought popped into her mind that she'd strangled him and put the body under his bed.

"Don't be silly," she told herself. "You just watched him go off to school."

The thought persisted. She knew she hadn't, but it said she had. When she found herself going upstairs to look under the bed to see if she'd hidden his body there, she knew she was crazy. When she looked under the bed anyway, that cinched it.

She looked up a psychiatrist in the yellow pages, called and made an appointment. When Tee Gee came home, she left May-May with him and went to see the doctor. He asked a few questions, then took her into an examination room. He listened to her heart, took her blood pressure... the usual things, while asking her about herself. Of course, she held back about her ancestry. She couldn't face it yet herself. She held back about her fears of doing something to May-May and didn't tell him about the episode with Tee Gee.

He took out his little rubber hammer and began checking her reflexes. She got tickled. She'd seen cartoons and heard jokes about this. When he hit her on the right knee with the hammer, he was standing so close to her that she kicked him in the stomach on the reflex. He looked surprised and she was embarrassed. She wanted to laugh and was fighting to keep a straight face.

"If I think this is funny, maybe I'm not as crazy as I think I am," she told herself. She'd read somewhere that crazy people didn't have much of a sense of humor.

He suggested another appointment. She knew he knew she was holding back whatever it was she'd come to see him for. She made another appointment with his assistant before she left the office, but the next week, when she was supposed to go again, she called and canceled it. She never made another one.

THE HOUSE next door was vacated and an old woman moved into it. She was a long-time Coronado resident whom Papa knew. If she was in the yard, he tipped his hat and greeted her and she was pleasant enough so Cynthia assumed she was a friend. One day, when Vera and her family were getting out of the car in front of the house, the woman saw them and came outside.

"Did you know that those people you're going in to see are a bunch of niggers?" she asked.

Vera, who was loyal to the core, got very angry.

"I told the old bitch to mind her own damned business. What we do isn't any of hers," she told Cynthia after they'd come into the house. Cynthia knew Vera had a temper and may have said a lot more, but she didn't ask. The time she'd lived away from Coronado's nosiness made this even more upsetting to Cynthia. She hadn't had to face this sort of thing for eight years.

"That God damned old biddy. Why can't people like her just leave me alone? If I want people to know about me, I'll tell them myself. You know that."

She was deeply touched by Vera's loyalty, but for some reason, she didn't say so. She and Vera had always avoided sentimentality. "Too bad. Maybe the world needs a little bit more of it," she told herself when she thought about it.

There was more. The short time she lived there, the old gossip apparently made it her business to tell everyone else in the neighborhood too. Tee Gee had been playing with a Navy officer's son who lived down the block. He was a nice little boy and his mother liked Tee Gee, who was a nice little boy too. One day the phone rang and when Cynthia answered, it was the boy's mother.

"I'm sorry to have to tell you this," she began. "But I have to ask you not to let my son come and play in your yard anymore. I don't want your son playing with mine here either."

Cynthia was prepared to hear that Tee Gee had done something bad, but before she could ask what, the woman hung up. For just an instant, she found herself thinking, "I wonder what that was about. What could Tee Gee have done?" Then the light dawned.

Tee Gee had done nothing except have her for a mother and Papa for a grandpa. This was what she'd always dreaded... having her child hurt because of her. She told Tee Gee that the boy's mother didn't want him to play with her son anymore and he accepted it without question. She was glad about that. This happened before May-May was born when Tee Gee was only about eight years old. She wasn't ready to tell him yet. She hoped maybe she'd never have to. He didn't have her family name and once he was grown and away from Coronado, who would know?

The 'nice' little boy began throwing trash over the fence into the yard. When Cynthia went out one morning and found broken glass in the front yard from a bottle that had shattered when it hit, she was furious. She called the boy's mother.

"This is Tee Gee's mother. Your son has been throwing cans and bottles over the fence into our yard. If this doesn't stop, I'll call the police and if our dog gets hurt on a broken bottle, I'll see that you get the vet bill," and she hung up. It stopped.

Just before May-May's second birthday, Ted got orders for the Naval Mine Depot at Yorktown, Virginia. Papa had tears in his eyes the morning they left in the Buick to make the long drive across the country. Supposedly, they'd be gone for two years, but if the Marine Corps was anything, it was unpredictable. They'd been there less than two when Ted was sent back overseas again... this time to Okinawa.

CHAPTER EIGHTY-ONE

The drive across the country to Yorktown in late summer was hot and tiring. Cynthia called Papa collect every night as soon as they'd found a place to stop. She knew he'd be worrying. In Kansas, they didn't find a motel until midnight. The telephone was an old hand-cranked model. She cranked and the operator came on. She'd obviously been asleep.

"I won't be able to get through to California; it'll take too long," she said.

"I've been getting through quickly every night since we left home," Cynthia told her. "Please. My father will be worried if he doesn't hear that we're okay."

"Well, I can try," the woman said.

The call went right through. She told Papa where they were and how the day had gone. She knew the operator was listening in on the line, but what did it matter? Just before she hung up, she said, "Thank you," and the line clicked off.

The next afternoon the manifold gasket blew out on the Buick because of the extreme heat. They pulled into a garage on the side of the road in the middle of the plains of Kansas. Not much else was there; it was definitely what they call just a bump in the road. A man on a tractor was cultivating corn in a field across from them. Back and forth he went, with a cloud of dust billowing behind him. A group of farmers sitting around on a bench and chairs in the darkness of the garage were watching and criticizing how he was doing it.

They brightened up, watching with interest as the Buick pulled in and Ted got out to see about getting it fixed. Cynthia and the kids stayed in the car with all the windows open. The watchers stared at them and talked to each other, then stared and talked some more. Finally, one of them must have designated himself to find out more about these strangers. He got up, walked across to the car and, starting just in front of Cynthia's open window, walked slowly all around the Buick, stopping only to study the California license plates, front and back. Satisfied, he came to her window, leaned down and asked, "You folks from California?"

It was all Cynthia could do to keep from laughing. Where did he think they were from? Timbuktu?

"Yes," she said.

With his curiosity satisfied, he walked over to the group and sat back down. She imagined him telling the others, "Yup, them folks is from California alright. Look pretty normal, don't they?"

"I wonder if we're the most exciting thing that's happened for them so far today," she thought to herself.

Cynthia had thought people and places were pretty much the same in the U.S., but she was finding out it wasn't really so. She knew Californians were considered a little peculiar... fey... whatever... and maybe even nuttier than the rest of the populace, but she'd felt something like a specimen under a microscope with all those old men studying her and the kids while they'd sat waiting in the car in Kansas.

In Cincinnati they found a motel just off the highway, but there was no phone in the room. She went to the office, but they didn't have one either. The man took her outside to point out to where she could find one. It was in a booth down a hill by the side of the highway. It was very dark, but she didn't want to walk all the way back to their room so she took off alone, hoping that nothing would happen to her. She hated being on display in that lighted booth, but she put the call through, told Papa where they were and went back to safety as quickly as she could. The motel in Kansas had been in the middle of nowhere and the phone was an antique, but she didn't have to walk a quarter of a mile in the dark alongside a busy highway to use it.

In White Sulphur Springs they checked in fairly early in the evening. She used the phone in the office, thankful they at least had one. She was beginning to think California was the only civilized state in the Union. While she put the call through and was talking to Papa, the owner stood right there on the other side of the counter, leaning on his elbow and listening to every word. When she hung up, he asked brightly, "How's the weather in California? Sun still shining out there?"

"I'm sure it is," she said, looking at her watch, "It's still light there."

"Rain very much out there?" he asked.

"Well, it rains," she said. "But I've been places where it rains a lot more."

She walked away smiling, thinking that maybe if she'd stayed a little longer, he might have asked her if they were still having trouble with the Indians out there. Out there? Where did he think California was... hanging on a platform over the edge of the world?

At last they reached Yorktown and the Naval Mine Depot. Ted went to see where they would stay while Cynthia and the kids waited.

"We can't get into quarters on the depot until the fellow I'm replacing moves out. They have apartments we can stay in until he leaves and our stuff comes."

So they went to find the apartment area. It was nice with trees and a grassed area where children were playing. The buildings were large with several apartments in each. They found theirs and went inside. Unfurnished. She hadn't expected that.

"What are we going to do until our stuff comes? We can't stay here in an empty building with nothing." She was dismayed.

The quarters in Guam had been furnished. Ancient and unattractive stuff, but serviceable. Their furniture had taken four months to come to North Carolina, four months back to California, and four months for small stuff to come to Guam. She wondered how long this time.

It was four months again before she'd see any of her familiar things.

In North Carolina, they'd camped out in the house with nothing except borrowed cots, a table and chairs, and bedding. In California, they'd stayed with Mama and were still living out of boxes on Tee Gee's birthday in Linda Vista, but they had furniture. In Guam, they'd lived with borrowed silverware, bedding, dishes and pots and pans from the mess hall... giant sized for cooking tons of food... the coffee pot held half a gallon in it! Now they'd camp out in an apartment with borrowed cots and bedding, borrowed cookware, rounded out with stuff bought at the Lackey general store just outside the front gate of the depot which was every bit as good as a dime store... big, dark, and full of all sorts of things.

Their furniture would come and have to be put in storage until the house was vacated. It was maddening to live with this little dab of stuff, some of which wasn't even theirs, in an empty, echoing apartment with sheets draped over the windows for privacy, knowing their own things were so near and yet so far away.

May-May had her second birthday in the spartan apartment, not unlike some of the ones Tee Gee had had. This time they were more or less settled on Halloween when he turned thirteen.

In less than two years, Ted got orders to go back to Okinawa, so they'd return to San Diego and Papa, whose house was furnished, and put their furniture in storage for a while IF it ever arrived.

And wouldn't you know? The one and only time they wouldn't need it right away... They were back in Coronado, heading for Papa's with a moving van just ahead of them on Orange Avenue. It turned on Third and slowed. The driver was looking for an address.

"Oh, my God," Cynthia said. "You don't suppose..."

"I'll just bet it is," said Ted.

It was.

CHAPTER EIGHTY-TWO

Yorktown was very good for Cynthia. They made many acquaintances while they were there and had some wonderful times. She was invited to join a Canasta club which met weekly in the homes of the different members. She was appointed membership chairman of the Officer's Wives' Club too. Actually, she was told she must do it by the C.O.'s wife when she'd demurred. It helped her to get over the debilitating shyness she'd suffered from for so much of her life, so it turned out to be a good experience.

There were morning coffees for the wives whenever new people came aboard. Farewell potluck dinners when others got orders to leave and wetting down parties at the club when someone got an advancement. She and Ted were invited to Navy parties. The other Marines kept to themselves and didn't mingle with the Navy people except at club functions. Why? Cynthia didn't know.

On the cul de sac where they lived in the housing area, once a month or so there was a neighborhood fish fry. The fishing was good on the depot and the men fished as often as they could. A neighbor would call. "Have you got any fish in the freezer?"

Usually they all did, so the date and time were set. Half a dozen or more families showed up carrying salad makings and their fish. Some wives set to work making salad, some breaded and fried the fish while others made hush puppies. It was fun to be outside with compatible people on a hot and humid night in Virginia, drinking beer and soft drinks, talking and slapping mosquitoes while the kids ran around playing tag or hide-and-seek until it was very late and time to go inside and go to bed.

THE NAVAL MINE Depot was a very small station, only a hundred Navy Officers and their families lived aboard and only a handful of Marines. The Officer's Club had one major function a month with each department hosting one thing. For the Marines, it was the Marine Corps Birthday Ball in November. The wives dressed to the nines for these occasions. There was little else to dress up for.

Yorktown and Williamsburg rolled up their sidewalks, even on Saturday nights, at dusk. Newport News was kind of far and there wasn't anything to do there anyway. Virginia was a dry state. Sometimes after a club function at which no food was served, the Marines and their wives would pile into cars and drive to a fish place somewhere nearby in the woods. Or they might go to Newport News to a Chinese place where the food was excellent, one of those "with six you get egg roll" places, so the more the merrier. Sometimes a group would go into Yorktown for fish at Nick's World-Famous Seafood Restaurant. Cynthia and Ted agreed the seafood was great, but neither had ever heard of Nicks' before they went to Virginia, nor did they after they left.

Cynthia was one of four women who made their own clothes. It was fun to be admired for this ability and to be considered a fashion plate. When they showed up wearing their latest creations, the other women were waiting eagerly to see what they had on this time. The ultimate *faux pas* happened only twice. Cynthia sewed the same pattern for a dress as the Marine Colonel's wife did for hers. Fortunately, because they'd each used a different material, the only ones who noticed were themselves and they were both amused by it.

When it happened again, it wasn't so funny. A young wife showed up in a dress identical to the one the Navy C.O.'s wife was wearing. Each had gone to Richmond to one of the elite stores and was assured by a salesperson that it was one-of-a-kind. Obviously, it wasn't. That evening, the young wife and her husband made an early exit.

The movement toward desegregation was just beginning about this time. Of course, it was a major topic of conversation in Virginia. On an evening after a club function, when it was too hot and they weren't tired enough to call it a night, a small group met at one of the neighbor's, who was a born and bred Southerner. When the talk began, Cynthia sat saying nothing. Ted didn't say much of anything either. The room was dim and Cynthia hoped her flush would be credited to a little too much champagne as she sat, with her secret self cringing, listening to the group run down the race of which she was a part... like it or not.

The argument for and against waxed hot... mostly against. Her Southern acquaintance, a fellow seamstress, was vehemently against desegregation and was expounding angrily about it. Cynthia sat numb and dumb, thinking, "They don't know what they're talking about. All Blacks are not stupid, nor any of those other derogatory things they're saying. I should know," but she said nothing in defense of herself or the people in her life. How could she? If these people knew about her, what would they say? What would they do? What would they think of Ted for marrying her? Would they let their kids be friends with Tee Gee and play with May-May? Not likely... not in this Southern stronghold.

"Coward, coward, coward," she thought, despising herself for keeping quiet out of nothing but pure craven cowardice and selfish self-preservation.

That was the first of two times that her personal demon awoke and stirred while they were stationed in Virginia.

. . .

AFTER THEY'D BEEN in Yorktown for a while, Cynthia recovered a little from the insanity she'd been experiencing. Was it because she was out of Coronado? Was it because she was away from the pressures of trying to please her mother since she still had been living in Mama's house, even though Mama was no longer there?

She wasn't afraid to go out of the house anymore... or afraid to stay in it. She was still suffering from chronic insomnia with fears that she might be asleep if something terrible happened and not be able to prevent it. She'd go to bed some nights when Ted did, but she tossed and turned. She was afraid she was disturbing him, so she'd go into the living room and turn on the TV. Oftentimes she'd fall asleep watching it and, waking up to the darkened screen, would go to bed and, if she was lucky, fall asleep again for a few hours. Sometimes she'd sew into the wee hours until she got so sleepy she couldn't keep her eyes open, then go to bed and be wide awake. Other times she'd pace the floor, wringing her hands and crying out silently for God to please help her get some sleep and keep her sanity.

She was discovering that no matter how bad it was, every third night she'd fall asleep in spite of herself from sheer exhaustion.

She tried to talk to the doctor on the base. He wanted to help her, but since she was so reticent about what her problems were, he couldn't.

"Do you feel better in the daytime?" he asked.

She usually did. "Yes," she said.

"Then try to remember that," he said. "When whatever it is is really bad, just remind yourself that in the morning you'll feel better."

She began living her life one night and one day at a time. It did help.

Then she read somewhere that if everyone in the world could take all their troubles and throw them into one big pile and you could take out any one you wanted, you'd take back your own. It was yours and you were used to it; someone else's could be worse. It made sense and it helped too.

Ted got annoyed with her. He'd stand up and start for the bedroom to go to bed. "You coming?"

"No. I don't think I can get to sleep."

"Well, you can sit there and stay awake all night if you want to, but I've got to get up and go to work in the morning."

As if she didn't know that. As if she didn't get out of bed some nights so her flopping around wouldn't disturb him. Did he really think she couldn't sleep because she didn't want to? His insensitivity upset her, but as was her way, she said nothing, keeping her hurt feelings to herself. Ted couldn't or wouldn't try to understand what was happening to her. How could he? She didn't know herself and she couldn't talk about it.

THE WILLIAMSBURG insane asylum was alongside the Colonial Parkway, which they drove on the weekends to take Tee Gee to Richmond for orthodontia. Every time they drove past it and she saw the people inside, some sitting on benches under the trees staring into space, some wandering around like lost souls, others hanging onto the chain link fence watching the passing traffic, she was afraid she was going to end up there. She made a joke about it each time they went by.

"There's my home away from home," she'd say.

If Ted heard her, he ignored her, saying nothing.

She dreamed about being inside the grounds, sitting on one of the benches, staring into nothingness. Even after they left Virginia, from time to time she dreamed about the place and woke up thinking, "Well, I didn't end up there after all and I'm certainly not going to make the trip back there to do it now."

Many nights she got four hours of sleep at the most. Ted got up and fixed his breakfast. Tee Gee did the same and caught the bus to school. May-May would get up, turn on the TV and ride her spring horse while watching cowboy movies until she got hungry. Then she came in to find Cynthia who was dozing.

"I'm hungry, Mommy. Get up."

Another day would begin, with another night waiting for her at the end of it.

THE SECOND TIME her demon stirred was after their first Christmas in Yorktown when she went by herself to Richmond on the bus for the after-Christmas sales to spend the money Papa had sent her.

There were two very nice department stores in Richmond forty years ago. Perhaps they're still there. Cynthia spent the entire afternoon going happily back and forth between them, looking at everything on sale first, then going back to make a final decision about what she'd liked and buy it. It was like shopping with the money Mama had given her when she was a teenager. She got everything... undies, nighties, shoes, a classic navy-blue wool dress and an elegant gray wool suit with frog fasteners on the front. It was getting late, time to catch a bus and get back home.

She was standing on a corner, loaded with her packages, surrounded by a crowd of shoppers waiting for the light to change. She was just a little tired and thinking about nothing in particular when she looked across the street and suddenly became aware that she was looking at a sea of dark faces... what few whites, they were outnumbered three or more to one. She looked across to the opposite corner. It was the same, as was the corner facing it. She casually took a look at the people standing on each side of her... all dark. She was the only white face in the front of the waiting crowd around her.

"My God," she thought. "The whites down here are outnumbered. If I were white and my ancestors had done the things they've done to these people, I'd fear for my life every single day."

Suddenly the thought struck her. "My God. I look white. These people wouldn't know I'm not." She was frightened. To Black people, looking the way she did, she was the enemy. Her life would be at risk too if they decided to revolt or get even. Her heart started to pound and when the light changed, she hurried to the bus station, walking as fast as she could, anxious to put Richmond behind her and get back safely to Yorktown and her family as quickly as possible.

CHAPTER EIGHTY-THREE

Living in Coronado in the days when a flotilla of destroyers was tied up to tenders moored in the bay, one had to be prepared for the power to go out at any time. Coronado's power came across from San Diego through a cable laid on the bay bottom by the Gas and Electric company. On each side of the bay, just east of the ferry landing, was a huge sign, one side cautioning ships not to anchor east and the other not to anchor west. Even so, with the tidal movement, it sometimes happened that an anchor pulled the cable up and all of Coronado was without electricity until repairs could be made. May had always kept candles on hand and cans of Sterno because the stove in the new house was one of the first electrics. The automatic hot water heater was electric too, so it was back to the teakettle rushed upstairs to the bathroom if the power went out when Al had to shave and get ready for work. Cynthia didn't remember them ever having to resort to the Sterno, but sometimes they'd had to use candles.

This early training stood in good stead when Ted's orders took them back east to Virginia in 1954. They were in a little wood frame house on the Naval Mine Depot when hurricane Hazel hit the coast.

Warnings were on TV all day long as the sky darkened and the wind picked up. Around three in the afternoon, Cynthia got May-May in and then ran out to take her wash off the line. As she worked, the sky grew even darker, the wind got worse and the trees began whipping around. She became frightened, taking the last of the laundry down as quickly as she could, then ran for the little house and safety, as if that matchbox would have kept them safe if Hazel hit it full force.

She had read that windows should be opened a bit during a tornado so she cracked the windows. The school bus dropped Tee Gee off and Ted came in early. Just before dinner time, the power went off. Cynthia wasn't a Boy Scout and she hadn't been allowed into the Girl Scouts, but she was prepared. They broke out the candles and, using Sterno, she heated canned beans in her chafing dish for supper. By nightfall, all the other little houses on the cul de sac were in total darkness.

The wind was blowing fiercely, the pine trees furiously whipping back and forth when the knocks began at the kitchen door. The neighbors, seeing their light, began coming to see if they had extra candles. They did. A new mama from up the street came down. "I need to heat a bottle for the baby and I don't know how to do it. Can you help?"

"I can," Cynthia said. "I've got Sterno."

She gave her a can and passed out cans and candles to all who came to ask. On their little street that night, there was the comforting glow of candles and heated canned food for supper.

Fortunately, hitting the coast and the trees that surrounded them lessened some of Hazel's force in their area. None of the houses were damaged, although a few pine trees had gone down. They didn't realize just how bad it had been as Hazel rampaged up the coast until they went to Richmond the following week for Tee Gee's braces to be adjusted and saw all the blown-over road signs and trees on the way.

Cynthia couldn't believe that some of the others on the depot who were Southerners didn't keep candles or Sterno on hand for these emergencies, which happened so often on the east coast. Here she was, a California girl from the land of sunshine, mild climate and an occasional earthquake and theirs was the only one out of half a dozen families on the streets who was prepared for a hurricane. After it was all over, she was very pleased with herself, like she had been after the typhoon in Guam.

"If Mama was still alive, I could surprise her again." She smiled to herself at the thought.

CHAPTER EIGHTY-FOUR

They were back in California, this time to stay. Ted had orders to go to Okinawa again, but he was nearing retirement. This would be their last move. It was time to buy a home of their own. They were looking at model homes every Sunday, before finally putting a down payment on an empty lot in Clairemont, a sub-division of San Diego. The foundation for the model they'd bought was poured and the framing in place, when Ted was shipped off again for what would be another six months. It was to have been longer, but someone back in Washington had taken pity on them at last... or was it a clerical error?

Cynthia and the kids stayed with Al for three months. The house was completed sooner, but it was so close to Christmas that she wanted to wait to move in so that when Ted came home, they could spend their first Christmas in it together.

On New Year's Day, she and Papa moved her personal gear. The things in storage came the next day. Vera and Doris, another friend from high school, helped with some of the unpacking while Wood put up curtain rods. Tee Gee and Vera's son, now in their teens, helped to wax the floors and polish them.

One day, she ran out of shelf paper. She'd had to learn to drive before they moved in because, up on the Mesa, they weren't near a streetcar line. She hopped into the car and drove to the nearest dime store to get some and was driving back to the house, looking toward the ocean which could be seen then, not blocked by trees as it is now. It was a beautiful day... the sun was glinting off the water, the sky a cloudless blue. Suddenly, she was overcome with such a feeling of happiness it was overpowering.

"I'm happy! I'd forgotten what it felt like. I haven't been this happy since I was a kid in Coronado, before I started school."

As quickly as it had come, the feeling disappeared, but it was a turning point. After that day she began getting better.

Ted retired. He found a civilian job right away, working at night for a printing company that dealt with government contracts. On his first night, when he came home around midnight, she was waiting up for him and they had a bite to eat before going to bed. The second night it was the same. On the third night, Ted came home to find her sound asleep in bed. The awful insomnia began easing off. Not that she didn't still have nights when she got up to sleep on the couch, but at least she could get to sleep now most of the time.

On the nights when sleep just wouldn't come, close to her period or when the moon was full, she cleaned house or rearranged the living room furniture. The sound of the vacuum cleaner didn't bother her family, who were used to sleeping through the sound of the sewing machine. May-May was in school now, so Cynthia got up to get her off to school, then went back to bed until ten or eleven. Friends and neighbors made fun of her for being such a sleepy head. She never told them why it was, only saying that she'd been up late the night before. By the end of another two years, she was almost completely well.

One night, when Tee Gee was about fourteen and Ted was working, Tee Gee started a conversation that somehow began to get out of hand. There was something on TV that started it off; Cynthia couldn't remember what. He said, "I'll bet Aunt Vera wouldn't associate with Negroes."

Cynthia's heart gave a big thump. Calmly she said, "Oh, I think she might."

"I'll bet she wouldn't let Nancy marry a colored man."

"She might," said Cynthia, thinking, "What is this leading to? He acts like he knows something and is sounding me out." He pursued and kept insisting that Vera and Wood could be racists.

Finally Cynthia blurted out, "They are not prejudiced. I know."

"How do you know?" he came right back.

Cynthia paused... she had lain awake many nights wondering if she should tell him and how and why... an endless soul-searching that had gone on for hours with no answer.

"Well, he's asking for it; I guess this is just as good a time as any. Maybe he already suspects. He was five that time at the passport office and there was that boy's mother in Coronado." So, with a pounding heart and a dry mouth she said, "I just know, that's all."

"How can you be so sure?"

So... she told him.

Afterward he said, "I wish you hadn't told me." Cynthia didn't sleep that night, but the next day he seemed all right. They didn't discuss it again.

After Tee Gee left home, the Civil Rights issue began. Ted and Cynthia and May-May were in their favorite Italian place one evening when she first became aware of what was going on. Sure, it was in the papers and on the news, but she tried not to think about it too much. Her life had been going along serenely; there had been nothing untoward to upset her for a long time. May-May was fair with blonde hair and freckles; there was no reason for anyone to suspect anything. Tee Gee was olive-skinned with dark hair and eyes. She often wondered if people ever asked him about his nationality, but she never asked him.

She looked up from her dinner to see a crowd of colored people outside on the street. They were milling around and she got nervous. She drew Ted's attention to it.

He said, "Oh, those are those Civil Rights people testing this place to see if they'll let them in."

She was alarmed. "Let's get out of here," she said, but Ted was going to finish his dinner no matter what, so they stayed. A couple came in and were seated; the crowd dispersed. Cynthia breathed a sigh of relief. She started paying a little more attention to the news and found herself agreeing with the things she heard Martin Luther King saying. Later, when he was assassinated, she felt bad, but Ted seemed to think he had asked for it. She didn't argue the point.

May-May began coming home from school talking about Civil Rights and, when they went shopping downtown, Cynthia noticed there were more colored people about on Broadway than she'd ever seen before.

May-May was now about fourteen and Cynthia knew she should tell her. She had asked Tee Gee on the phone and he had said no, but she felt she had to, like she had with him, and was only waiting for a time that was right. He had forced the issue, but with May-May, it was Cynthia who would start the conversation that would lead to the disclosure. She talked to Ted about it but he made no comment... just the way he had done with Tee Gee. Afterward, when she told him it was done, he said nothing.

She told May-May, not knowing what to expect. May-May was highly dramatic, throwing tantrums, screaming and crying when things didn't go her way, but all she said was, "How neat!"

Cynthia was greatly relieved. Afterward, when they talked some more, she was able to laugh at May-May's reaction. Maybe her children's lives wouldn't be ruined by having her for their mother after all. They had friends; they'd been invited to parties. They'd never been persecuted as she had been or had felt left out of anything she knew about.

"Things *are* getting better. How about that?" she thought.

"Maybe they can be themselves and not have to hide all their lives like I have."

Still, she was very upset when May-May told her that she'd told her best friend, Kelly, about it. Cynthia talked to May-May about keeping it to herself, but May-May kept insisting it was all right. Kelly thought it was neat too. Cynthia, herself, had told one or two of the neighbors whom she had grown close to after many years of association, and it had been all right; they couldn't have cared less and it made no difference in their relationships.

"It's her life and her secret. She'll have to handle it in her own way, like I did," she told herself. She also told May-May a few of the things that had happened to her because of her ancestry, but not all.

Not too long ago, Tee Gee's wife called. "Mom," she said. "I told Charlene about our family secret." Charlene was their teenage daughter.

"You did? What did she say?"

"She said, 'Cool.'"

Afterward, Cynthia sat down and laughed. I guess the world really is changing after all," she thought. "All the grief I've put myself through all these years and my granddaughter thinks it's cool." But Cynthia had told her son's wife to advise Charlene to be careful who she told. We still have a long way to go. Hate, like still waters, runs deep.

About this time, Cynthia went next door one day to visit their neighbor. A sign was in the front window that hadn't been there before. It said, "My neighbor can be of any race, creed, or color." Cynthia rang the bell. As she waited, she was thinking, "A noble sentiment, but I wonder how they'd feel if they knew they already had a neighbor who was two out of three?"

The government cancelled its contracts with the printing firm Ted worked for. Ted was out of work for nearly a year, almost until their unemployment was about to expire. To keep the house, Cynthia was afraid they'd have to rent it and move in with Papa, but in the nick of time Ted found another job. This one lasted for a while, until they'd more or less recouped financially from the layoff. Then he was laid off again, but it wasn't quite as long this time before he found another job. The third job was the charm and Ted stayed with the company for twenty years, retiring with a small pension.

CHAPTER EIGHTY-FIVE

An unhoped-for long-time dream came true for Cynthia around 1959, shortly before Tee Gee graduated from high school, went to college for a short while, then joined the Air Force. He shook the dust of San Diego off his feet, returning with his family only for visits. She saw an ad in the paper for an electric organ at a price they could afford. Excitedly, she showed the ad to Ted and he was agreeable. She outgrew three smaller organs before ending up with the Thomas 3 manual organ she still has, but which she can no longer play because of failing eyesight. She never learned to play as well as she'd have liked to. Desire is not enough; one also needs talent. However, that first organ and the two that followed led to over twenty peaceful and happy years for her and a social life akin to that which they'd enjoyed in Yorktown. It appeared her demon had at last been laid to rest.

At first, she took private lessons because organ technique is different from the piano, needing a legato instead of a staccato touch. Then she took a beginning organ class at night school. The group of would-be organists of varying talents and experience had such a great time in the class that, at the end of the year, they decided to continue meeting at one another's houses throughout the summer on a weekly basis. When night school classes began again in the fall, they continued their weekly lessons. From simple refreshments of chips and dips, punch and dessert, the evenings grew to full-scale dinners with the hostess of the week going all out to impress the group with her culinary skills.

They had costume parties and Mexican parties... once a hippy party, sitting on the floor, eating spaghetti and drinking flavored coffees. They celebrated birthdays, anniversaries, had Christmas, and rang in the New Year, sharing their interest in music and becoming close friends over a period of more than twenty years. The last few, before it started coming to an end, as all good things must do, they went out to a restaurant for dinner then back to the home of the hostess for an evening of music followed by dessert. In the early days, the parties went on into the small hours of the morning, but as they grew older, they ended earlier. Time and age were taking their toll, but for Cynthia, especially, it was wonderful while it lasted. She never told any of them her secret.

As a rule, they never discussed politics, religion, or other controversial subjects, but during the desegregation and pre-civil rights year, she was in the same position she'd been in in Yorktown when desegregation was the issue of the day. She sat listening, contributing nothing, feeling the old traitorous, cowardly feelings that were so familiar. Once she spoke out, telling them, when they were discussing mixed marriages, that one day there will be one race. She was hooted down with "no way," and "never happen," but another twenty years or more have passed since that evening. Look around... it's been happening right under our noses.

Not too long ago, Cynthia watched one of the afternoon talk shows that feature off-beat subjects and controversial issues. The panel was made up of several young Southern girls who were white supremacists. They were making babies as fast as they could, they said, because Blacks would outnumber whites if they didn't do something about it. Cynthia was reminded of the day when she'd stood on a street corner in Richmond forty years before and seen it coming.

The girls were very young, very vehement about what they were doing and very hostile. One announced that her family was pure Caucasian for three generations back. The poor, ignorant innocent.... Didn't she know that in the South, where masters and their sons fathered children with their slaves, there were probably thousands of whites with Black blood they knew nothing about? Three generations were a drop in the bucket. Another said that her family was pure Irish for many generations back. Another ignorant child... didn't she know that the Moors, a Black race, had been in Ireland for centuries before, fathering the people called the Black Irish? Oh well, they were probably having fun making the babies, possibly unaware that raising kids is hard work and, often, not much fun.

Al came to dinner every Sunday with his dog, another Binks. Papa had his first stroke, a small one, and stayed with Cynthia and Ted while his house, which he'd been neglecting, was cleaned up before Cynthia would let him move back in.

In her mid-fifties, Cynthia went back to college, taking art classes and music. She had decided to get the art degree that she'd lost out on before, but it was not to be. She became a two-time college drop-out.

Al had a second stroke which left him partially paralyzed and incontinent... a semi-invalid, needing help with everything. He begged not to be taken to a hospital, so Cynthia cared for him for the last two and a half years of his life. His disposition remained unchanged; he didn't get mean, grouchy or hostile as oftentimes stroke patients do. He would look into her face while she was getting him up to sit in the wheelchair all day in the living room or putting him down for a nap or to bed at night.

"You are so good to me, Thum. I'm sorry it has to be this way."

"Don't worry about it, Papa. It's not your fault. We're in this together." She tweaked his big toe as she left the room.

His last words, spoken to the young man Cynthia had hired to help with him, while pushing him around the neighborhood in his wheelchair, were, "I guess I'm too good to go to Hell and not good enough to go to Heaven."

It had been a difficult two and a half years. Ted didn't give Cynthia a lot of moral support, finding things to do that took him out of the house. He left her alone a good deal of the time with her father, not wanting to hear her tell him how hard it was. His stock answer to that was, "Well, you know what you can do about it."

As if Cynthia would put Papa in a home. Never... only over her dead body! But she got tired. It wasn't so much physical as it was emotional. She felt so sorry for proud Papa reduced to having to be cared for like a small child. She'd been surprised and shocked at Ted's attitude because she thought he'd been fond of his father-in-law and that hurt her too. Al's brain hadn't been affected, only his motor skills. He knew Ted wasn't happy having him in his home.

AL CAME BACK the night of his death. Cynthia was devastated that she hadn't been with him when he had the heart attack to tell him good-bye. Tee Gee and his wife came down from Los Angeles that evening; everyone was exhausted and keyed up. Ted and Tee Gee both went to bed early, with Jan, Tee Gee's wife, following shortly.

May-May and Cynthia didn't want to go to bed. They decided to stay in the living room and lie on the couch for a while in the dark. It was very quiet, then "What's that noise?" May-May asked.

"What noise?"

"Can't you hear it? A humming sound..."

Cynthia listened. "Oh, it's probably a sympathetic vibration from a plane going over or the traffic down on the freeway."

It grew more pronounced, so she got up to try to find where it was coming from. She opened the front door to listen... nothing, no plane, no truck.

"I bet I know what it is," she told May-May. "It's that old clock we have out by the pool. It's been hanging outside so long it's probably gone berserk." She opened that door and listened, but it wasn't that either. Meanwhile, May-May was up walking around the room and listening.

"Here it is, Mom," she said.

It was coming from some ornamental metal shelves on which they keep knick-knacks. Here the vibrating hum was very strong. Cynthia touched each shelf with a finger to soften it, but it continued. She went to get Ted who stood and listened for a minute then went back to bed. Cynthia went to see if Jan was awake; she was. She got up to come out and listen too.

"Talk to it, Mom," she said.

"Papa, is that you?" Cynthia began. The vibration increased in intensity. "Papa, have you come to say goodbye?" It got faster and louder. "Oh, Papa. I'm so sorry I didn't get to say goodbye to you. Papa... I love you and I always will."

Immediately, the vibration began to lessen, dissipate and, in seconds, it was gone. Jan went back to bed.

"I should have gone and gotten your brother," Cynthia told May-May, but it was too late. He'd been so tired that she hadn't wanted to wake him. Now she wished she had. He and his grandpa had been so close when he was small, during the years that Ted was overseas.

May-May told Cynthia later that each time she'd walked away, the vibration had decreased, increasing as she came back up the hall. Still later, she told her mother that she'd reached down to touch the nested set of abalone shells that Amos had collected on the beach at Coronado years before and had gotten a shock from them. Well, Al had been an electrician, hadn't he?

THE NEXT MONTHS were pure hell for Cynthia. She'd loved Mama and grieved for her, but it was nothing compared to the grief she felt over losing Papa. Her heart felt as though something with taloned claws was tearing at it, trying to pull it out of her chest by the roots, leaving it bruised and bleeding like a chunk of raw meat.

She went to the cemetery with flowers every week for months. As she was placing a bouquet on the grave one day, a little voice inside her head asked, "What are you doing? Papa hated this place. He isn't here. If he's anywhere, he's at home with you."

It was true and she knew it. She'd often felt his presence and cried out to it in anguish when she was alone in the house. She knew it was wrong to keep his spirit tied to her with her grief, but she couldn't help it. Then one day, her little voice said, "Cynthia. If what happened to Papa happened to you and your kids took as good care of you as you took of him, for the same reason, you'd be lucky."

That was true too. She'd taken care of Papa because she loved him. What better reason is there than that? She'd been berating herself for things she should have done while he was still alive, keeping him tied to her with her agonizing. It was time to let him go. She spoke out loud, telling him she was sorry she was keeping him here and he could go if he wanted to and that she'd be okay. She felt him leave. He was there... then he was gone.

She would hear from him again a few years later.

CHAPTER EIGHTY-SIX

For the first twenty-two years of her life, Cynthia's emotional problems were a result of actions and words directed toward her by others. For the next thirty-nine, they were caused by her own paranoia and knee-jerk responses to conversations and situations that she perceived as threatening.

The twenty-five years between 1956 and 1981 were the most peaceful Cynthia had ever experienced. She relaxed and her night terrors faded away, except for her traitorous feelings when she sat close-mouthed, listening to the organ group arguing about Civil Rights and she told her closest neighbor, then waited to see if she'd be dropped.

Once the organ group attended a concert and one of the men made introductions all around to someone he worked with. When Cynthia was introduced with Ted, with a shock of recognition she realized the man had been a ferry hand when she'd lived in Coronado before her marriage. Keeping her face and emotions under control as best she could, she looked him right in the eye.

"How do you do?" she said.

Afterward, she wondered if he'd recognized her. She didn't know, but after weeks passed with no change in anyone's attitude toward her, she decided he hadn't. So much time had gone by, and she'd put on weight.

Her demon stayed quiet after that until 1981 when the Historical Society's phone call awakened him, tearing her apart for the last time.

CHAPTER EIGHTY-SEVEN

Many of Cynthia's memories centered around her school years from ages five to nineteen. Looking back at periods that she thought had lasted a long time, she was surprised to find they hadn't been as long as she'd thought, a year at the most, some less... only a summer or a semester. Did time pass more slowly then or did it only seem so? It appears to go so much faster now than even the young complain about it.

The book was progressing slowly. Sometimes other things she had to do took precedence, like going to the doctor, shopping for necessities, or cleaning the house. When she didn't feel well, the book languished with her as days passed and she worked crossword puzzles or watched daytime TV. Her preference was for shows that were entertaining or made her laugh, usually re-runs of old favorites. The shows she didn't care for, but sometimes saw parts of, were the ones with people telling the world the details of their off-beat and sometimes sordid lives and sexual peculiarities, to a host and an audience of different ages, sexes, and colors. She felt a surge of hope for society and the world when these listeners stood up to express their opinions by letting the people on the panel know that they did not condone their lifestyles or morals. Apparently, some people still have a modicum of good sense. Perhaps we're not all "going to hell in a hand basket," one of May's favorite expressions.

Cynthia wondered about the social changes that had come about in the last thirty years. It started with sex education in the schools, which was begun when Tee Gee was in the sixth grade. She had disapproved, but when he came home and said the other kids were returning their slips signed by parents who thought it was okay, she reluctantly signed his. Later came the "pill" and the promiscuity that followed because it removed the fear of pregnancy, promoted singles bars, living together, easy divorces, and broken homes.

Is this progress? She had once read that progress means change, but change does not always mean progress. She wished she knew who'd said it.

Whether to continue writing or not to write was not the question. The question was why? Why was she doing this at all? It had served its purpose for her. She'd discovered that she was her own worst enemy and a racist besides. She didn't hate anyone of color; how could she? She hated herself for being mixed and looking white.

"I could have lived with being dark," she thought. "It was looking like what I wasn't that I couldn't handle."

She had felt driven to write about her life. Many people had told her to do it, that she must do it because it was predestined and would help others. In what way, she couldn't imagine, nor did she have the faintest idea of what to do with it when it was finished... or even if she'd live long enough to finish it.

"Where's a fairy Godmother when you need one?" she wondered. "Or the little elves that come in when you're asleep at night and do the work for you I once read about? Well, this is part of another chapter done, with more than a few left to go. Save, spell check, and start thinking about the next one... this is thirty for now."

.   .   .

"Well, here I am," Cynthia told herself as she wrote on her yellow-lined tablet late one night. "Sitting up at nearly one in the morning after reading the latest *Writer's Digest* and scaring myself thinking about the editing that still had to be done. Not spelling... I'm still pretty good at that, although at seventy-three the old brains are getting a little mushy. The devil's instrument I'm using to write this on catches the typos, but my punctuation, besides some of its being outdated, has gotten a little rusty." It was true. Between failing eyesight and memory, sometimes Cynthia found herself thinking twice about a word as she did the daily x-word puzzle (Papa's joke) in the paper or asking herself, "Do I use a comma here or what?"

Ten years ago she started writing on her old beat-up typewriter. It was finished in about a hundred pages or so, but it had only a surface, no depth, no dialogue, no descriptions, no other people, only her own responses to others and things in her life.

Early on, a friend read part of it and said, "It needs dialogue." So Cynthia added some and it was finished as far as she was concerned. By that time, she was considering suicide for her wasted life, but she didn't do it. She put the manuscript away.

Ten years later, others told her it needed description, profiles of people, that it was very marketable and, since it covered such a long period of time, dating from 1887, it was possibly an epic. She'd walked away from that one, a former book agent, telling herself, "Sure, and epic. Ha! Another *Raintree County* or *Gone With the Wind*. Not likely." But like Topsy, it just grew, taking on a life of its own. She was creating a monster.

Three different friends offered to put it on their computers for her and all three had to stop for various reasons. Cynthia found herself back to square one. Ted said, "Let me do it for you," but by that time she knew it was meant for her to do. She agreed to let him teach her basic word processing on what she called "that evil entity," his computer.

It was not without just cause that she called it that, for as she was learning to use it, it ate four chapters, swallowing them whole without a trace. Sometimes it protected itself so she couldn't get into it and even Ted was hard-pressed to figure out how to defeat it and regain control. Was it afraid of her? She often threatened to beat it to death with a club and would have if she'd had one handy. At any rate, one of the prophecies that a man would help her had come true.

"So now what you are reading, if you are still with me, is a mish-mash of what was begone with all these other voices added which I, the obedient, eager to please, whatever I am... frustrated artist, dutiful daughter, obsessive/compulsive housekeeper, possible lunatic, mother, grandmother, great grandmother, or tired old lady, am slowly working my way through the pages that have been and are still to be written... the painful for me and probably boring for you story of my life."

CHAPTER EIGHTY-EIGHT

May-May worked for a while after Al died. Then she met and married Barry. They'd lived in Papa's house in Coronado for their first two years, so Cynthia saw her daughter often. Barry got orders to Long Beach when May-May was a few months pregnant. After the baby was born, May-May came down with him whenever the ship went out and they all came home for the holidays so, except for missing Papa, Cynthia didn't feel abandoned. Not until after orders took Barry and May-May to the East Coast. Surprisingly, they went back to the Yorktown area where May-May had lived for two years as a toddler and her twins were born there.

Cynthia went for a visit once and they took a drive around the Naval Mine Depot. The little house they'd lived in on the Wright Circle cul de sac and all the other houses had been torn down. Nothing was left to show they'd ever been there except the road.

Then came the phone call from the Historical Society, throwing Cynthia for a loop. Her old demon awoke again after twenty-seven years of a fool's paradise with her thinking maybe he'd gone away for good... and never wanting to see him again.

Then the exhibit and the first stilted draft of the book-to-be. Vera was in Oregon. Cynthia's neighbor and close friend, Jenny, had moved up to the desert. The organ group had faded away; time was taking its toll. May-May was on the East Coast. Papa was gone forever. Ted had retired for the second time and became so active in Masonic Lodges that he was always off going to this or that meeting. Alone again, lonely again, feeling abandoned again, Cynthia became despondent... then suicidal.

The writing that she had done so far had made her realize her own reactions to so many things in the past had been the cause of so much of her pain. Putting up the wall of pride she'd lived behind for so many years had kept other people out. She knew now she could have had more friends than she'd had in Coronado, even in high school, if she'd been more open and not gone behind her wall to lick her wounds and feel sorry for herself. Life or karma had given her a challenge. She hadn't wanted it, refused to accept it, face it, or try to learn to live with it. She'd been her own worst enemy.

Now here she was, feeling sorry for herself again. Like a sulky child, angry because she hadn't gotten all the things she'd wanted, stamping her foot in anger and frustration.

"Nobody loves me. Everybody hates me. I'm going out in the garden and eating worms."

She began thinking about killing herself like she had when she was just a kid and didn't know how. She still had a bottle of Papa's valium in the back of the medicine cabinet. Is this why she'd kept it?

"I'll take the whole bottle and get drunk," she decided but changed her mind after someone said that taking pills and drinking might not kill you and could leave you a brain-damaged vegetable, so she scratched that.

She couldn't drown herself by jumping into the bay because she knew how to swim and the idea of wading out into the ocean and swimming until she was too exhausted to turn around and swim back didn't appeal to her, nor did being eaten by sharks. She still remembered how nearly drowning had felt the day she'd tried to go out to the float in the ocean. It was scary, so that was out. She didn't want to jump off the Coronado Bridge either. That would do it, but suppose she changed her mind halfway down? Slitting her wrists in the bathtub had no appeal either, nor did getting out Ted's pistol and shooting herself in the head... supposed she didn't do it right? So... what else was there?

She'd heard the train go by down below their house every night for years. She found herself listening for it and noted the time. She watched it when it went past them as they drove to the Commissary or to the stated meetings at the Lodge. She thought about it a lot and the answer came.

"I know," she told herself. "I'll go down one night and stand on the track. When I see the train coming, I'll turn my back to it and put my hands over my ears. If I change my mind and jump off before it hits me, that'll be okay. And if I don't jump off in time, that'll be okay too."

She decided that this is what she was going to do. She made remarks to Ted about it, but he paid no attention. She told Nancy, who said, "Aunt Cynthia, please don't. What would I do without you?"

She wrote her plan to Vera, who wrote back that it was stupid... Vera, who'd always threatened to commit suicide herself whenever her life wasn't going according to her expectations.

She told her friend and former neighbor, Irene.

Irene said, "Oh, but that's so messy!"

"I don't care," Cynthia told her. "I won't be the one who has to clean it up," and she'd laughed.

"But think of the poor engineer. How will he feel?"

'I don't care about that either," Cynthia said. "That'd be his problem, not mine."

She worried it back and forth... to do or not to do was the question. To do began to take precedence in her thoughts and it frightened her. Did she really want to do this? It became an obsession. Yes. No. Yes was winning.

Where she'd heard the train go by at night only intermittently before, she now heard it every night whether she was listening for it or not.

"There goes my train," she'd tell herself.

She decided to do it on her sixty-third birthday. She'd wait until Ted went to bed and was asleep, then she'd slip out of the house quietly so as not to wake the sleeping dogs, walk down the hill and be there on the tracks when the train came. She was scared, but she was going to do it. She felt driven... was this her destiny?

On August 17th, Papa's birthday and the day before hers, she was home alone, thinking about the next night and her plan to shuffle off her mortal coil and see what was in store for her, hoping Papa would be waiting for her on the other side.

Around eleven that morning, the phone rang. It was Tee Gee's wife calling from Pennsylvania.

There were the usual pleasantries, then Jan said, "I had a dream about Papa this last week, Mom."

"You did?" This was odd because Jan and Tee Gee had been married only a short time before the stroke. They'd lived in L.A. at first and come down for holiday weekends. Because life had dealt Papa a blow, he no longer joked or laughed; he was changed. The Papa that Jan had known only from a few short visits was not the Papa he had been before. She barely knew him, so why had she dreamed about him?

"What was the dream about?" Cynthia asked.

"Well, in this dream, he came to me. I knew it was him and he said, 'The shells are in the wrong place.' I didn't have any idea what he was talking about, so I said, 'The shells?' and he said it again, 'The shells are in the wrong place.'"

Cynthia was thinking it was kind of a dumb conversation.

Jan continued. "I said, 'the shells?' again and he said, 'She'll know.'"

It struck a chord. Cynthia broke out in goose pimples.

"Oh, my God," she said. "I do know." And she told Jan about the nested set of abalone shells that had been in the family since Al was a boy, that Amos had collected on the beach in Coronado.

"We always kept them on the hearth, and I moved them to the buffet a few years ago."

"I wasn't going to tell you," Jan said. "And then this morning, I thought maybe I should."

"Good timing," Cynthia thought, but she said, "I'm so glad you did." She didn't tell Jan why.

Her head was in a whirl after they hung up. Who else would know that the shells had been moved but Papa? The message had to be from him. He'd returned to stop her from what she was going to do, and Jan had called just in the nick of time. If Jan hadn't decided to call, would Cynthia have done it? She still doesn't know.

It was after she told May-May about Jan's call that May-May remembered and told her she'd touched the shells while Cynthia was out of the room and gotten a shock from them the night Papa died. Al had used the shells as a focal point to come back. Cynthia put the shells back on the hearth, but Papa hasn't used them again. She feels comforted to know that wherever he was, he had still cared about her then and, hopefully, still does, even after twenty-two years.

Al came again to Jan in another dream a while later. They'd been going to take a trip to Paris from Belgium where they were living at the time. He was wearing a long robe and he told her that when they got to Paris, they should look up a little pastry shop on the Rue de la something... Cynthia couldn't remember now... because when he was in Paris, he'd been there and they had the best pastries. Jan asked him if he was a teacher, meaning a spiritual teacher. She said he'd smiled a little and answered, "Could be."

"So like Papa," Cynthia thought. "Not to commit himself. There are some things we aren't supposed to know, and he'd never say for certain, but he could hint."

Then Jan had asked him, "Why do you come to me, instead of someone else?" thinking, of course, Cynthia or May-May.

"Because you're a clearer channel," he told her.

"Probably so," Cynthia thought. "May-May and I have too many emotions where Papa is concerned. Jan doesn't have any feelings of that sort about him to mess up his ability to get through, so he's using her because she's a connection to us."

That was the last time anyone had a message from Al. Cynthia didn't make a mess for anyone to have to clean up, nor did she traumatize some poor railroad engineer. She put the original draft of the manuscript away and didn't think about it again for ten years. Then she got it out again and rewrote it.

This is it.

EPILOGUE

Two steps forward and one step back into the labyrinth of memory. This is the way this book has gone. It would have been easier, I think, to have written a novel with made-up characters and plot. I have been pulling up long-forgotten memories of the times, the people in my life, the places, and myself while trying to remember exactly when some of them happened. Is that the way it was and how old was I at the time? It moves along like a yo-yo, up and down, forward and back, retaining some sort of continuity, I hope, that, in the end, has resolved itself.

The original draft of my story ended with my suicide. I didn't do it, of course; I did other things... taking up the study of astrology for one, learning that the path of my life is in my natal chart. It's all in there... that there was something I could keep hidden and that keeping it hidden would be my undoing. That I am a writer is in there too and that writing about what I know, bringing it into the open and dispersing it, will hopefully, be of benefit to others who may learn something useful from it. I can't imagine what, but we'll see, won't we? Or will we?

Two people have written this book, which has taken twelve years from start to finish. The first person was the child in me who was still hurting, who hadn't reconciled the past with the present, who didn't want to be what she was. The other is the adult in me who has faced her demon and, I hope, laid it to rest for once and for all. The change in writing style which started showing up part way through the writing, bothered me until I realized it represents the change in me.

I have one home now and I look back on the other houses I lived in so many years ago as homes now too. The two worlds I've lived in are becoming one, as more and more people are accepting that we are all one, regardless of the color of our skin and other differences. This is a trend that I hope will continue.

The two selves I've been, the two lives I've lived, and the two worlds I've lived in have been blended into this memoir of one person, in one world, living one life and writing about it. I am no longer living two lives in two worlds divided by the fence of color. Instead, I am sitting on the fence looking at both sides, hoping, knowing, that prejudices will become a thing of the past when we move into the New Age. Differentiations will no longer be possible. Intermingling has already begun. One world—one race—Human.

I think my life would have been easier if I hadn't looked white and married a white man. I wouldn't have had the appearance of masquerading as someone I wasn't, nor been put into the situation of socializing with whites while having to keep quiet about my Black ancestry, which made me feel guilty and was so upsetting for me.

Now, all these years after that day on the street corner in Richmond and the fear I felt, knowing the Black people around me wouldn't know I was one of them, I realize having white skin had been a liability for me. Blacks who look black might consider it an asset, but not me. If I hadn't been born and lived to adulthood in a town where everyone knew about me, I could have passed. Would I have felt as guilty living the lie as I have? The years away from Coronado when I was accepted and kept my mouth shut did nothing for my sense of mortality... sailing along under false colors like a pirate ship and feeling disloyal to all the ancestors who'd preceded me.

I think my life might have been happier if I'd had dark skin. At least others, as well as myself, would have had no doubts as to who and what I am. Passing had its moments, certainly... and was enjoyable in many ways, but living a lie is eroding to the spirit. I liked being accepted as white, even when my conscience bothered me, and I felt guilty about it.

I'm not black to Blacks, nor was I to myself when I looked in a mirror at age six, trying to see what it was others could see that I couldn't. I'm not white to whites. What am I? I don't know. I only know that in our society I was unacceptable to either... to Blacks because I was too white, to whites because of the invisible drop. Not Black enough for one, too Black for the other. No wonder I've been a closet psychopath most of my life!

How do others like me identify with what they are? Do they have the same feelings? I assume they do, but I have no way of knowing. Do others who look white with Black ancestry (and who know it) have as difficult a time with their conscience? Is 'to tell or not to tell' a question for them? Is it better to tell and suffer the slings and arrows of the consequences than not to tell and undermine your own integrity? Aye, there's the rub. You're damned if you do and damned if you don't.

I suppose there will be those who will fault me for writing this book. Blacks will think, "What has she got to cry about? She could have passed if she'd wanted to." Whites will think whatever I got I deserved for being deceitful, for hiding my Negro ancestry behind a white facade (as if I could help it). I can relate to both points of view.

MY GRANDPARENTS DID NOT BECOME famous. They wrote no books, poetry, or music. They made no great discoveries in science or medicine. They were self-educated, but not without knowledge and that wonderful gift called common sense. What hardships or challenges they may have endured before and after the Civil War, before they came to California, I will never know. What I do know is that they were hard-working, lived decently and honestly, were devout Christians, respected and treated with respect, hated no one and had too much pride to ask for or accept charity. What they had, they earned, and they raised a fine son to carry on in their footsteps. I am proud to have sprung from the roots and to be my father's daughter.

If this book should be published, some people my age who read it may say, "That's not the way I remember those times," or "That wasn't the way I was taught in my school." This could very well be. I've written about my time and place. These are my memories of the way things were in Coronado, California, from 1924, when I was three years old until I moved away in 1940 when I was nineteen and of things that I experienced after that.

ACKNOWLEDGMENTS

This book was made possible through the support of the following individuals and organizations:

Kevin and Caroline Ashley
Claire L. Fishback
The Coronado Historical Society
Christine Stokes
Vickie Stone
Gail and Robert Bardin
Brian Trotier and Judith Bambace
Brad Willis and Laura Plumb
Jon Sinton and Laura Wilkinson
Allen Frances and Donna Manning
Susan and Mike Marrinan
Keith Prentiss and Marely Ramirez
Whitney Antrim and Kenan Guletkin
Josh Peters and Alexia Palacios-Peters
Ian and Christine Van Tuyl
Stephanie Kleewein Communications
Melissa Williams Design

ABOUT THE AUTHOR

Cynthia Hudgins is the author of The Other Side of The Fence. She was born in Coronado, California in 1921, and as a young student was recognized as a gifted poet and artist. She was the art editor of her high school paper and occasionally wrote poems and stories for the local papers while still in high school. She briefly attended college before getting married in 1940. As a military spouse, she and her family lived periodically in North Carolina, Virginia, Guam, and Coronado, and settled in San Diego. While in Guam, she created and ran a makeshift school for the children of service members.

She began writing *The Other Side of The Fence* in 1981 and completed the book in 1993. Cynthia Hudgins passed away in 2015 at the age of 94.

ABOUT THE CONTRIBUTORS

Claire L Fishback, Transcriptionist and Colorado Author

Claire L. Fishback writes horror (and more-er!) from the foothills of Colorado where she lives with her husband and pit bull mix, Kira. When she isn't penning the next spooky tale she coaches busy authors to create the writing life of their dreams.

Learn more about Claire and her work at clairelfishback.com

Kevin Ashley, Local Historian

Kevin Ashley is recently retired and now studies and writes about African American History as a lay historian. He writes a history blog called The Coronado Black History Project on Substack.

Learn more about Kevin and The Coronado Black History Project at kevinashley.substack.com

Made in the USA
Las Vegas, NV
03 February 2023

66769403R00330